DRINK UP AND BE A MAN

DRINK UP AND BE A MAN

Memoirs of a steward and engine-room hand

John J Mahon

SEAFARER BOOKS

First published in the UK by
Seafarer Books
102 Redwald Road
Rendlesham
Woodbridge
Suffolk IP12 2TE
www.seafarerbooks.com

ISBN   978-1-906266-19-6

A catalogue record for this book is available from the British Library

Some of the names – of people and ships – have been changed

Edited by Hugh Brazier
Typesetting by Julie Rainford
Cover design by Louis Mackay

Printed in Finland by Bookwell OY

Contents

Foreword

Ireland has changed a lot since John Mahon left its shores, experiencing seasickness for the first time aboard the form of transport used by many emigrants, a ferry. That set the course for a life on the ocean wave, where his experience of the hotel and catering industry was the resource upon which he built a life at sea.

John Mahon's story is, at times, a tough one, with some blunt descriptions of his life experiences. Those were dictated by his physical size, and by the doctor's conclusion after his medical examination:

> 'Four feet nine and a half inches, now for your weight.' I stood on the scales and the indicator pointed at seven stone exactly. 'Good,' he said, 'there is no reason why you should not go to sea.'

And so he did – and there, as for many other seafarers, alcohol became a support, a crutch, a relaxation and a problem, but one which he eventually overcame. As his book is published, John proudly records that he has been off alcohol for almost twenty-eight years.

He has spent many years away from the Celtic shores of his birthplace, and chronicles that he had no desire to return to a country of many changes but also, regrettably, one constant – governmental neglect of the maritime sector. Economic prosperity dominated in recent years as the Celtic Tiger prowled this westernmost nation of Europe. The Tiger was killed off in the explosion of a property bubble which destroyed Ireland's prosperity, returning it to recession and economic problems. The seas which surround this island, however, are potential pathways to recovery, providing the nation's trade routes. But governments and politicians have turned their backs on the sea, lacking foresight to realise that an island nation which has the fortune to possess one of the largest coastlines in Europe has enormous opportunity.

Among its many other elements, John Mahon's story tells how, in his own way, he did grasp the opportunity of earning a living from the sea.

Tom MacSweeney
Marine Correspondent, Cork Harbour, Ireland

***

This is a multi-layered book. It is not only an account of an eventful life, and one which most of us will not experience – or in some parts, would shudder to do so – but also an account of the dying days of a once great industry.

During the twenty years that John spent at sea he sailed on the last of the great classic liners of, amongst others, P&O, Royal Mail and the New Zealand Shipping Company. Not only are those ships now just a distant memory, so are two of the three companies, and the third is a tiny fragment of what it used to be. He then signed on ships of types which reflect his own decline, including a 'Hungry Hogarth' tramp and a pre-war bulk carrier belonging to Buries Markes, both among the companies that disappeared in the downturn of the merchant navy. Indeed, he says of one ship, foreign owned and British flagged – was this the beginning of the Red Duster becoming a flag of convenience?

From my own experience at sea, as an apprentice and then as a navigator, the people John describes are instantly recognisable. This is a wholly authentic tale of life at sea in that period, a way of life that has almost totally disappeared for the British rating. It is also a very rare document. There are few enough accounts by officers – to find one written by a rating is remarkable.

After coming ashore, John used the skills he learned at sea – being prepared to do any job, doing it until it was done, and realising, using a nautical analogy, that when you are on a lee shore and the rocks are close by, you do everything you can to get yourself clear and you keep doing it until you are in safe water.

John Johnson-Allen
Author of *Voices From the Bridge* (Seafarer Books, 2010)

I am delighted that at last a publisher has taken on this work, which John has been writing for many years – and it is fascinating reading. It will capture one's imagination with its story of what life was like at sea, living in a seafarers' hostel, realising you have a serious drinking problem and then giving up the drink.

It was in the 1960s that I went to live in the East End of London and worked at the Queen Victoria Seamen's Rest, Methodism's only seamen's mission. It was a completely new environment for me and I learnt a lot, because there were seafarers from all different parts of the world – and with 183 single rooms you can imagine there were many characters amongst them, all with their own personalities.

John Mahon was one of those who left a great impression upon my life and work there. He may be small in stature but he enthuses with energy and personality. He was always there for the underdog, sometimes the misfits of society, and usually he would find some good in them in spite of his own personal problems.

Christmas was always a special time at the mission, because the staff would be given their time off and we relied on voluntary staff and residents to help. On one particular Christmas day I knew that John had been a steward at sea so I asked him to lay the tables for the Christmas lunch. I left him to it and found that he had several other seamen working under his direction laying the tables. So he didn't do it – he had his fellow seafarers doing it! That's John.

Eventually, he left the mission and was able to find employment in the City of London, and he knew he had to give up the bottle because it was affecting his health and personality. He became extremely positive about his alcoholism and now has a good quality of life. Of all the seamen that I have met, John is a great inspiration to me and still is today, and I'm sure you will capture this as you read his book.

Terry Simco MBE
Former General Secretary of the Queen Victoria Seamen's Rest

Prologue

It was just after eleven o'clock on a warm sunny morning in May 1964 when I walked into the Brown Bear public house in London's East End. The contrast between the light outside and the darkness within blinded me momentarily.

'Good morning,' said the young barmaid in a chirpy west of Ireland accent.

'Morning,' I replied.

'What can I get you?' she asked.

'A Carlsberg, please,' I said.

She stood about five feet three, with natural copper-coloured curly hair, a pretty round face with freckles, smouldering dark brown eyes and a beautiful smile. She was dressed in a low-cut cream blouse revealing a good view of her ample bosom, and her short brown skirt showed off a pair of strong sturdy legs. She was what some folks in Ireland would describe as 'the class of a girl that would make a fine wife for a farmer'.

'Nice morning,' she said.

'Yes,' I said – and then the door opened and in walked a tall upright military type chap dressed in a pinstripe suit.

'A large pink gin, young lady,' he boomed.

'Certainly sur.' She turned to the shelves, ran her fingers over the gin bottles, shook her head, turned, looked at him, and said, 'I'm terrible sorry sur, but there's none in stock. I can't find it and the boss's out, is there annyting else that'd suit you?'

He looked at her and then at me in what seemed to be despair, proceeded to lecture her on the art of making a pink gin, and stomped out, ramrod straight.

'My God,' she said, 'some people are woeful peculiar, I'm only working here the last two weeks and trying to learn the job. I was never assed for a pink gin before. I thought it would be in a bottle like the rest of the spirits.'

I just nodded to please her.

'Well, I'll tell you now,' she said, 'I'm not used to that kind of a fella coming in here. The locals and the seamen are the best, they spend a rake of money, you can have a crack with them, and they never ask for all sorts of fancy drinks like him.'

Rarely would you see a City worker in the place. It was known as a seamen's pub, and for good reason. The Red Ensign Club was a merchant seamen's hostel just down the road in Dock Street, and the Shipping Federation – where registered seamen from all over the British Isles came to ship out from and many other young boys and men visited with the hope of getting away to sea – was situated in Prescot Street, a few yards further up the road. I was waiting to meet an old seaman friend who was on leave, and the Brown Bear was where we had arranged to meet.

I was on my second Carlsberg when three men came in, closely followed by Liam Doyle. He looked like he had been through a force ten gale with his dark curly hair begging for a comb to be run through it. His stockily built six-foot frame was bent over and he wore a crumpled old suit that he might have slept in.

'Ah, there y'ar John Joe,' he said, looking beyond me to the barmaid.

'What's your pleasure, Liam?' she asked, ignoring the other three who had come in before him.

'A large whisky, a bottle of Guinness, whatever me mate wants, and one for yourself Sheila.'

When we were served, we sat down at a table, and as we did so he gave a sigh and said, 'Jasus, John Joe, I don't know where I ended up last night, did you see me?' He took a sip of whisky and followed it down with a swallow of Guinness, but it didn't want to stay down so he rushed out to the toilet. When he came back, he said, 'I've been as sick as a dog, I musta had a bad drink somewhere last night.'

'Admit it, you just can't take your drink, you're getting on in years now,' I joked.

He came to life as though he had been woken out of a bad dream and roared, 'I'm only forty-two. I've a long road ahead of me, if the drink doesn't kill me. I must admit I'm getting worried about the blackouts and the times I wake up in a sweat, not knowing where I am, then the bloody shakes and dry retching come on. But the fuckin' depressions are the worst. It's hard to describe them. Ah, balls, I'll be as good as new after a few jars. I'm thinking of giving it up when I join the next ship.'

I told him about the City gent and Sheila's performance.

He grinned and said, 'Straight outta the bog, that one.'

Feeling livened up enough after he finally got a few drinks down, he suggested we take a walk up to the Black Horse – a cleaner and more comfortable pub where winos and all sorts of characters with hard-luck stories were barred. Quite a number of them, mostly ex-seamen, congregated in and around a lot of the pubs in the area. All with tall tales, 'I missed me ship and I'm skint, any chance of a quid mate?' That was one of the many approaches frequently used if you were a stranger to them. Or they would step up to anyone about to enter the bar and ask for what was commonly known as the 'entrance fee'. Others just walked into a pub and put the bite on anyone they thought might be an easy touch.

We settled down there and drank and talked until we were joined by an old friend and ex-shipmate of Liam's, Paddy Kelly, a Liverpudlian, who insisted on buying us a round of drinks. As Paddy was getting the drinks Liam said with a smirk, 'I think you'll like him. He was a deckhand with me on a Shell tanker. He's a very religious man, Catholic of course!'

'Balls,' I said, 'protect me from them characters.'

Paddy only had time to have the one drink with us, and as he was leaving he said, 'God bless you boys, we'll have a drink again sometime.'

Not with me, I thought. I had nothing against anyone who believed in whatever faith they were born into or chose just as long as they didn't try to preach to me.

We had another few drinks and Liam asked, 'Tell me now, are you still writing that book?'

'Trying to on occasions,' I replied, 'I've ripped up all I've written several times. I think I'll give it up as a bad job. I didn't have more than five years' schooling, and I get terribly frustrated when I can't quite express what I want to convey. When I'm in the mood I think I've got the makings of a good story, but then I lose confidence. I don't know a noun from a clown or a verb from a kerb.'

'Hush,' he said, raised an eyebrow, gave me a strange look, and carried on, 'That's a load of balls and no excuse for not doing what you want to do. Now listen to me, if you have a mind to do it, then get on with it. You don't have to come outta Trinity College to write a book. Get it down on paper, and if it's good enough the experts will put the stops and things in for you. Take my advice, write the book.'

We parted shortly after that, and the last I heard of him was that he had shipped out on a tanker bound for the Persian Gulf. That was forty-seven years ago, and I haven't seen or heard of him since. But I did eventually take his advice. Here is the book.

1

Setting out

I was born in the County Home in Rathdrum, County Wicklow, in the Republic of Ireland on 15 December 1942. My mother, Ellen Mahon, better known as Nellie, was forty years of age and single when she gave birth to me. She brought me home to our council house, which was one of nine situated in a place called the County Brook, surrounded by farmland and bogs, about two miles by road from the village of Enniskerry and roughly three miles from the seaside town of Bray. She told me that most of the neighbours welcomed her home and Mrs Woodcock gave her some baby clothes and offered to help her in any way she could. I can see now how much that must have meant to her, because in those days any unmarried woman or girl giving birth to a child was referred to as a fallen woman and a sinner, who was best left alone.

The priests raged about 'sins of the flesh' from the altar, but the word sex was never used openly. If anyone had suggested that sex education should be taught and a ban on the sale of condoms be lifted and do away with the stringent censorship, I'm sure they would have been banished from the so-called Land of Saints and Scholars. The men in frocks knew what was best for their flock!

Nellie Mahon stood five feet two inches tall and weighed about eight and a half stone. She enjoyed good health generally, but there were occasions when she wasn't too well. I once saw blood on the sheets that she had made out of white flour bags and I asked her if she was going to die.

'No, no, son,' she replied, 'I'll be all right tomorrow.'

She was as independent as she could possibly be under the

15

circumstances. I can remember from about the age of five how we were always traipsing down mucky country lanes, across farmers' stiles and through fields to all sorts of people's places. In fact, anywhere she could get a bit of work to supplement the few shillings she received from the national assistance. She would do any kind of work – washing clothes by hand, looking after children, house cleaning, gardening, plucking fowl. No job was too much for her. She seldom received more than a few shillings, but she was always assured of a meal for us and a bag of something to take home – vegetables, fruit and occasionally a bit of meat or butter. It all depended on who had what to spare on the day of our visit.

Our council house had two bedrooms and a front room, which served as a living room and kitchen where the cooking was done on the open grate, and that was our source of heat as well. It was bitterly cold in the winter and the only way to keep warm was to gather sticks, rotting wood and anything else that would burn from the bogs and glens. I remember cuddling up to my mother under a stack of old coats and a horse blanket and still feeling cold. A paraffin lamp and candles were our source of light.

Our fresh water came from a natural spring just down the road, and over fifty years on I can still remember the pure taste of that water and the sight of the beautiful silvery stream that ran alongside, in which you could occasionally see trout bobbing and weaving through the rocks in the bed. In spring and summer there was a profusion of wild flowers and sometimes we would pick some and put them in a jamjar at home. Then there was the wildlife – squirrels, rabbits, hares and many others, not forgetting the creepie crawlies and a plethora of birds. Of course, in the winter we made great haste to and from the well.

Our dry toilet was situated in a small outhouse adjacent to a little pigsty, a useful commodity to have if you wanted to breed pigs. The toilet seat was a long piece of wood attached to the wall on either side with a hole cut out of the centre and a bucket underneath. It was unhygienic, and using lime was such a messy job. It was much easier to carry out nature's functions behind the farmer's hedge using a piece of newspaper, or in its absence, a dock leaf or a good bunch of grass to wipe your arse. But there were odd occasions when one would reach round and grab a bunch of nettles. Oh, that sting!

***

I was a child prone to any illness going. If someone sneezed a mile away, I'd catch a cold. I had various chest ailments including bronchitis, and there were times when I was so ill that Nellie had to ask a neighbour to take a note to the doctor asking him to please come out to us, it was urgent. Then the waiting would begin. Sometimes the old doctor would arrive late in the evening, 'stinking like a brewery,' my mother said, and I recall that on a few occasions he never came at all. So she quite often applied generous amounts of Vick to my chest and back, put brown paper over that and then covered that with red flannel from neck to waist and dressed me up like a mummy. Then I'd be ordered to get in the pram, where I would be covered with an old horse blanket, topped off for good measure with an oilskin. Then she wheeled me the two miles to the dispensary, where she hoped to see Nurse Dunne, rather than the doctor.

When I did see the doctor, it was nearly always the same question. 'What seems to be the problem?'

She would explain what was wrong and he'd give a grunt, cough and say, 'Sounds like the old complaint. I suppose you've got far too many clothes on him as usual. Take them off, I want to examine him.'

By then I'd be opening the buttons on my coat and Nellie would do the rest, carefully removing my clothes and the flannel and Vick-soaked brown paper. The doctor would sound my chest and back, take my temperature and say, 'Just as I thought, the same old chest problem, there's nothing to worry about, he'll grow out of it. Continue with the embrocation and inhalations. I'll give you a prescription for some more and a cough mixture.'

Usually by this time she'd have me dressed, brown paper, flannel and all. On our last visit he put his hand on my shoulder and asked, 'Tell me boy, how old are you?'

I didn't know, so I looked up into my mother's eyes for the answer. She smiled and said, 'Six.'

He nodded and said, 'Small for his age.'

17

That was a revelation to me, because whenever I asked her how old I was or where my father was, her standard reply was, 'I'll tell you some day soon, son.' When we were outside I got into the pram, and as she was covering me I asked, 'How old is Christopher Woodcock?'

She stopped tucking me in and said, 'There's only a few weeks between you. That's enough now, snuggle down, we've got to be on our way.'

I wasn't satisfied. I said, 'He's going to school, why am I not going too?'

'Christopher doesn't have a weak chest like you have, that's why. Anyway, I don't think he's learning much more than what I'm teaching you. You can read the clock and you know the alphabet. Please be quiet now, we've got to get home.'

I shut up and fell asleep as she pushed me along.

I awoke to the sound of someone talking to my mother and recognised the voice of Mrs Tuite, a woman that put fear in me ever since the time she saw Nellie carrying me in her arms about a year previously. I stiffened and pretended to be asleep in case she looked in on me. I remembered what she had said – 'Nellie Mahon! Put that boy down, you'll kill yourself humping him around like that. And you, son, I want to see you walking like a good boy the next time I see you, you're far too big to be carried.'

Nellie's biggest fear was that the authorities might find some way of taking me away. She often said, 'I don't know what I'd do if they ever tried to take you away from me.'

My frequent illnesses played havoc with her work routine, because she would not ask anyone to look after me, not even for ten minutes. Being unable to go out to work meant there was a scarcity of food in the house and the storage of firewood would be running low.

She was a very independent woman, and the neighbours knew it too, so when they wanted to give her something, it was always on the basis that there was 'full and plenty' – 'The hens're goin' mad laying, so if it wouldn't offend you, here's a few eggs' ... 'Spuds are so plentiful, it'd be a woeful sin to waste them, here's a bag.' And once every two weeks, Old Sonny Rafferty called on us with a skinned rabbit and a sugar stick for me. He had been doing that for as long as I could remember, and we were always pleased to see him. Sonny and his young helper Michael Kelly set snares every evening to catch the rabbits and returned early the next morning to collect what he had caught. He sold the rabbits to butchers in Bray to help with his income from rearing pigs.

We had very good neighbours, except for a couple of peculiar old men in their seventies, living on either side of us. Johnny Lawless, the willowy old boy on our right, used to go prowling around in the dead of night shining his torch through people's windows and trying the doors. Bill Synott, on our left, was a craggy old man who always had something to shout about. Like the time he went to see Canon Kennedy in the village for some advice about his pension. He wasn't satisfied with whatever advice the canon had given him, so off he went to the Protestant minister, who wrote a letter for him, and within two weeks the problem was solved. After that, Bill told anyone that would listen how great the minister was. 'A bloody gentleman. He was the man to get things done, and he an Englishman too. I've a good mind to change my religion.'

I will never forget his beautiful garden, with its rows of vegetables growing so straight and the colours of the lovely flowers on the borders. Sadly though, unknown to us, Bill had put poison down, and when we came home one evening we found our adorable cat Murphy dead. I was inconsolable. Mother said she would have a word with Mr Synott. Bill was in his garden as she walked over to the fence and said, 'Excuse me, Mr Synott, I think our cat was poisoned. Have you put poison down?'

'Indeed I have, ma'am,' replied Bill. 'I was sick and tired of them bloody animals doing all the damage to the garden.'

A few weeks after Murphy's demise I became very ill, with a high temperature, a cold, sweating and a congested chest. I could tell Nellie was really frightened, and in her desperation she said, 'John, I'm going to wrap you up well and take you to see Dr Devlin in Bray.'

Someone had told her what a marvellous man Dr Devlin was, but she would have to pay him. He was a private doctor.

I remember the stone steps up to the doctor's front door, and my mother ringing the doorbell, then the door being opened by a young woman in a black dress, and the next thing I knew I was gazing up into a man's smiling face. 'I'm told you're not very well, John, let's see what we can do to get you better again.' He picked me up and carried me into another room and placed me on some sort of a bed, examined me and gave me an injection.

'John has pneumonia and should be in hospital,' said the doctor.

'Oh no, doctor,' said my mother, 'I would be petrified. I can't bear to think of my boy there in a big place like that without me.'

I fell asleep, and I remember nothing more until I woke up in bed at home with my mother lying beside me fully clothed on top of the bedclothes. I only had snatches of what was said and done that day, and it wasn't until I was fully recovered that she related the whole story. Dr Devlin had explained the reasons why I should be in hospital with such a serious illness, but he obviously saw how distressed Nellie was, so once she reassured him that our neighbours had a telephone and she would contact him if my condition worsened, he allowed me to go home. But he insisted that his driver should take us home in his car, and he said he would come to see me early the next morning.

'Thank God for Dr Devlin,' said my mother when we were home. 'You've had about three hours' restless sleep and I think your temperature has gone down a little. Now my little soldier, I've made you some soup and I'd like you to try to get a little of it down.' I managed about five or six spoonfuls and a small piece of bread and that seemed to satisfy her. I dozed off again thinking of how she had thanked God. That was rare. She had often said that if she wasn't afraid of 'Them' taking me away from her because she was neglecting to bring me up without a religious education she wouldn't go to mass at all. She believed a person didn't have to go to church to be a good person.

Dr Devlin arrived before eight o'clock the next morning and asked how I had been since he had seen us yesterday. Nellie gave him an up-to-the-minute report to which he said, 'Very good.' He took my temperature, examined me and then said my temperature was down a little and if that continued I would soon be on the road to recovery, but I must stay in bed and eat and drink as much as I could. He gave me another injection and praised me for being such a good boy, and for this I was presented with a brightly coloured box, which held a lovely little red truck. I couldn't believe my good fortune. I thanked him, and he ruffled my hair and said, 'John is over the worst, Miss Mahon, but we will have to be careful. I will be back tomorrow morning.'

She was relieved at this and asked him how much she owed him.

'Please don't worry about that now,' he said. 'I can arrange to be paid by the national assistance.'

'I would rather pay you myself, doctor. I have a little saved for emergencies. I don't trust some of them officials. They might try to take John away from me and put him in a home somewhere. The less I have to do with those people the better. But I'm worried that I might not have enough to pay you for all you have done for us already.'

'Please don't worry about payment or anyone taking your son away from you. I would never let that happen, so put those things out of your mind, you can rely on me. I want you to keep a clear head free of worry and just concentrate on nursing John back to health and strength.'

Dr Devlin returned the next morning and gave me another injection, and said that I had made such good progress there wasn't any need for him to return, but he would like to see us at his surgery in two weeks' time.

My health improved by the day, and in no time I was agitating to be allowed out to play. When the time for the appointment came, Dr Devlin was very pleased to see how well I was, and my mother asked him if it would be all right if she started me at school if my health stayed as good as it presently was. She explained that up to now she hadn't thought it sensible to do so because of my health, but I was nearly seven, so she thought I should start soon. The doctor agreed, and said that perhaps I could start after my next visit. We then said our goodbyes, and as we got to the door he said, 'John, here's two shillings to buy something for yourself.'

I looked at Mother, and she nodded, so I took it and thanked him. When we were outside, she said, 'He's a grand man, a walking saint.'

I nodded, gripping the two shillings tighter and thinking,

I'm nearly seven.

We walked up the town, both feeling jolly, me with more money than I'd ever had in my whole life, and Nellie looking carefree with a bounce in her step. It surely was a grand day!

The weeks rolled by, and I had never been in better health when the day came for our final visit to the doctor. He smiled broadly as we entered the consulting room, and asked Nellie how I had been since our last visit.

She beamed with pleasure as she told him how I had never been healthier in my entire life, and added, 'It's all thanks to you, doctor.'

He replied, 'Let's not forget your loving care.'

The examination followed. The doctor said he would like me to have some x-rays in a few weeks' time, but there was nothing to worry about – it was just routine – and he suggested that I should start school as soon as she could arrange it. That sounded exciting.

He assured her there was no need to worry about his bill and to rest assured that no one would ever take me away from her. I could see she was doing all she could to hold back the tears as she thanked him. We were on our way out of the door when he produced another two shillings and placed it in my hand. She started to speak, but he interrupted her by saying, 'It's just to celebrate John's recovery.'

I don't think the good doctor ever did anything about getting paid for his services through the assistance, but I firmly believe that if the authorities had made any attempt to take me away from my mother he would have fought vigorously in our defence. Out we stepped into the sunshine, another wonderful day!

Mother said that I should spend some of my money on a jotter and some pencils, because I would need them when I started school. We bought one jotter, two pencils (one with a rubber on the top) and a box of crayons, which left me with sixpence plus two pence which I had saved from our last visit to town. I was rich.

She needed to do a little shopping in both Liptons and the Home and Colonial. She bought goods in both shops because as she had told me some items were a little cheaper in one or the other of them, and if she wanted to buy a quarter of butter no oul busybody woman would be looking down her nose at her, as often happened in the village shops.

I can still remember the wonderful smells in those shops, but the thing that always fascinated me was when you paid your money to the assistants they would put it into a little metal container with a docket, screw a lid on, attach it to a carrier and pull a cord so that it travelled along overhead on a wire that made a sort of singing sound until it reached the office, where it would be attended to and returned with the receipt and any change there might be.

Having done our shopping we went to the teashop, and this time I chose a chocolate cake, which she allowed me to pay for. We sat at a table near the window, and it reminded me of how often we had to pass by because we couldn't afford to go in, and I could see people tucking in to their tea and cakes in the warmth. To this day I never take a window seat in a restaurant or café in case some poor unfortunate passes and sees me scoffing.

We took the bus to the village again, and then walked the two miles home, and on this occasion I was allowed to walk all the way.

***

I started school in the spring of 1950 aged seven years and three months. Mother told the teacher, Mrs Corcoran, that I could read quite a bit, tell the time, do small sums, write in a scrawl and I knew some of the catechism. Mrs Corcoran said that she would have to start me in the senior infants to see how I got on from there.

Most of the children of my age were a class or so ahead of me. Mother touched my hand and I followed the teacher into the classroom. I felt a sort of lightheadedness, having been parted from my mother for the first time in my life, and seeing such a huge collection of children, girls and boys, all in one place was frightening. I was only partly aware of the teacher introducing me as the new boy and her leading me to a desk, which I was to share with a red-headed boy called Jimmy O'Toole.

We started the morning with prayers and then Mrs Corcoran said, 'Hands up those who were at mass yesterday.'

I put my hand up like most of the class, but there were quite a few who kept theirs down. She looked around the room and although she didn't single anyone out for not going she cast her eyes in several directions and then said, 'Hands down.' Then she went into a long tirade about how important it was to keep the faith, and I lost interest.

Then it was the catechism, sums, reading, and lunchtime.

As I stepped out into the sunshine I saw my mother at the school gate waving me across. We found a cosy little place in the churchyard, where she poured some soup from a little flask into a cup and produced two slices of bread. I ate one slice and drank one cup of soup and that was all I could manage. From that day onwards and for the next three years the routine was set. She accompanied me to school every morning and came back with something for my lunch. She managed to get a few odd jobs in the village until it was time to accompany me home at 3 pm.

I adapted to school very well and progressed at a good pace, or so the teacher said, and that pleased Mother so much that she gave me the biggest hug I ever had from her. I really enjoyed reading and spelling but I found the catechism, sums and the Irish language hard going.

There was a great emphasis put on learning the Catholic faith, and if one could quickly answer questions from the catechism or any other questions on religion, they were looked upon with great favour, irrespective of whether you understood what it meant or not. It was necessary to memorise the catechism because you never knew when the priest might visit the school, and maybe pick you out at random to answer something from it, and what a shame it would be if you didn't get it right. And it was necessary for your first confession and first Holy Communion and, later on, your Confirmation.

Our old neighbour Johnny Lawless was becoming more of a nuisance, stumbling around at all hours, continuously trying our door and shining his torch through our windows. Mother decided we should go to see Canon Kennedy, with the hope that he might be able to help us.

We arrived and knocked on the door, which was opened by the housekeeper, a wrinkle-faced elderly woman dressed in black. With a scowl she asked, 'Can I help you?'

Mother replied, 'Yes please ma'am, I was hoping I could see the canon, if it's possible. There is something troubling me and my son and I would like to get his advice.'

'Well,' said the housekeeper, 'he's just had his lunch and usually he likes to rest for a while afterwards, but I'll ask him.' With that she was gone, leaving us standing on the doorstep. She returned within a few minutes and bid us to come in, he would see us in the parlour. She led the way into a sumptuous wallpapered and wood-panelled room with lots of pictures on the walls, a big brown desk with a chair, a polished table and a beautiful patterned settee on which she said we should sit.

The canon, it was said, was in his eighties. He occupied a matching armchair close up by a crackling fire of wood and coal and the room was baking. He half turned in his chair by way of acknowledging our presence and asked, 'What can I do for you, ma'am?' I could see he was very old with his white hair and wrinkled ruddy face. His hands were very thin and veined and he seemed very frail.

Mother thanked him for seeing us and explained how the ever-increasing strange behaviour of Mr Lawless was worrying her.

He was silent for a while and then he said, 'The poor man must be troubled in his mind, but there's no need for you to worry about him. He's harmless, you can rest assured of that.'

'That's all very well, Canon,' Mother replied, 'but it's very frightening.'

He responded, 'Now, there's no use in getting yourself upset, you'll see he'll soon get fed up with it and then you'll have peace of mind again. I'll pray for you and the boy.' He got out of his chair with a great deal of effort and stumbled over to a desk, took out a picture of the sacred heart and handed it to her with the instruction to pin it up inside the front door and told her that with that on the door no harm would ever come to either of us. Then he bid us good day with his blessing.

Mother said she was sorry she had gone to see him at all, and she went on about what a terrible shame it was for one old man to occupy a big place like that when there were so many people without a home at all, and in addition to that his church curate occupied a house just down the road with a housekeeper and a car under his arse too. Oh! How the world

25

was so badly divided.

My ears pricked up at the word 'arse' because I thought that to be a curse word.

We received the letter from St Vincent's Hospital with the appointment for the following Monday morning. We caught the bus from the village and travelled the twelve miles to Dublin. It was a great adventure for me, because I had never been to Dublin before. As we travelled along on the top deck, sitting in the front seat, I took in everything as we passed through places with names such as the Scalp, where I marvelled at how the big boulders strewn over the steeply sloping landscape did not fall down onto the road.

The closer we got to the city the more excited I became. I had never seen so much traffic or so many people in my whole life, nor had I seen so many brightly painted doors or so many monuments. We got off the bus at Stephen's Green, and as we had some time to spare we walked down Grafton Street, looking into the big glass-fronted windows of the stores. Passing Bewley's coffee house was an experience in itself, the aroma emanating from there is something I shall never forget.

After going to the hospital for my x-ray we walked over O'Connell Street Bridge, up O'Connell Street past the GPO and into Henry Street, and then into Moore Street, where the traders were shouting the virtues of their wares. I remember seeing women of all shapes and sizes, shouting, 'Get yor luv'lee herrin's here!' 'Juicy oranges, sweet 'n' juicy!.' 'Apples 'n' pears, gorgeous apples!' 'Fresh fish, straight off th' boat!' 'Flowers! Luvlee flowers!' The chorus of voices was deafening, but oh, so exciting!

Finally we caught the bus back to Enniskerry. I was amazed and thrilled at what I had experienced, and all the way home I daydreamed about the brand new world I had seen.

***

My grandmother, Annie Grimes, married Johnny Mahon and they had two daughters, my mother Ellen (Nellie) and Dolly my aunt, who married James (Jem) Hackett, and they had five children, four boys and a girl, before my grandparents died. Later Dolly caught the dreaded common disease of the time, tuberculosis, and died, leaving Jem behind with the young family.

Naturally, it was too much for him to cope with, especially in the times that were in it throughout the south of Ireland, not much of anything for most of the ordinary working class people except plenty of drudgery and poverty. James was not a well man so he had no alternative but to have the children taken into care and then he became a victim of the same TB.

My cousins Maureen and Peter went into convents. Maureen went to one in Booterstown, County Dublin, and Peter went to another because he was not old enough to go into the Artane industrial school with Tommy, Paschal and Jimmy. Peter would join them when he reached the age of eight. As it was, Jimmy just barely got in because he was not quite eight at the time. All five of them would be officially released on reaching the age of sixteen years. Sadly though, Tommy, the oldest of the five, died on the football field in Artane with a hole in the heart.

I had forgotten what my mother had told me about my relations until one day she said she had received a letter from Maureen, who had come out of the convent and had started working in a posh house in Blackrock, where she 'lived in'. The lady there arranged for her to have an interview in the dressmaking department in Arnott's store. She got the job and moved into digs in Dublin.

'Will she be coming to see us?' I asked.

'I don't know,' she said. 'I'll invite her when I reply to her letter.'

About six months later Maureen paid us a visit on a bright summer's day. Nellie hugged her and then our visitor turned and looked down at me with a smile and asked, 'Who have we here?'

'John,' said mother, 'my son.'

'Oh, I hope we will be good friends,' said Maureen. 'How about a hug, John?'

I loved her instantly and shyly moved towards her outstretched arms. She smelled different to anyone else I had ever been that close to and she was my cousin too, a real relation! She was a few inches taller than my mother, her hair was brown and her smiling eyes looked really nice to me. She wore a pink blouse with a brown skirt and brown sandals and I thought she looked *spiffing* – a word I had recently learned at school.

A few hours later, when I got used to her, I asked her about that nice smell she had. 'Oh, that!' she said. 'It's called perfume. Do you like it?' I nodded. 'Come on then, let's go to my room and I will show it to you.' As soon as we entered the room she picked up a little green bottle, carefully unscrewed the top, and held it out for me to smell. She stayed with us for three days and then she had to go back to work, and I was sad to see her go.

Her brother Paschal came out of Artane about a year later and came to live with us. He was five feet four inches tall with fair hair. I was thrilled when he arrived and although we had never met before I liked him, and to think that he was going to live with us was very exciting. When he had put his few things away, had some tea and they had chatted for a while he asked Nellie if I could take him for a walk to show him around a bit. She said, 'Yes, but don't go too far.'

I led the way through our back plot to Fisher's field and showed him where my best friend and neighbour Christopher Woodcock and I had found a place in the hedge where a hen had been 'laying out'. I told him about the ten eggs we had found in the nest and proudly explained how only three of them had been bad. He suggested that we should have a look to see if we could find some more, but we didn't. As we rambled around he asked me about school and how I was getting on there. I felt that I could tell him anything.

I told him about the lessons and the boys and girls I liked and disliked, the bullies, the name-callers and how I hated being called a bastard and a midget. How I hated Monday mornings when the teacher asked us to put our hands up if we had been to mass yesterday and how it upset me, especially if I hadn't been, and how I was often tempted to put my hand up just to avoid the shame of it. I stopped talking, expecting him to say something, but all he said was, 'Go on, tell me more.'

'Ah, fuckit,' I said.

He frowned so I hastily said, 'I got that word from Snotty Sleeve Burke, he's always dragging his sleeve across his nose and his sleeve looks like a team of snails has been crawling up it.'

Paschal nodded and remained silent so I blurted out how

angry I was about being so much shorter than almost all the children of my own age and some even younger. Some of them made fun of me and occasionally a boy would hit me just to get me to fight and I wasn't any good at it. But that sort of thing never happened if Snotty or his pal Hardy Arse was about. For some unknown reason they took a liking to me, took me under their wing and protected me. I was a fortunate boy because they were a formidable duo.

Snotty Sleeve was a big robust lad with a mop of unruly red hair over a round friendly face. His clothes had seen better days to say the least, and his canvas shoes were a poor excuse for footwear, with his big toe peeping out of the right one and the little toe always out of the left one as though they were looking out for him. I don't ever recall seeing him wearing any other kind of footwear.

Hardy Arse was slightly taller and thinner. He had black hair that seemed as though it had never been combed, his thin face was sallow and he always had a scowl on, as though he was ready to do battle with friend or foe.

'What age are those two boys?' Paschal asked.

'About two or three years older than me,' I replied.

He said that he had experienced similar things when he went to Artane and that he had been much smaller then than I was now. He continued, 'There will always be bullies, and not all of them will be children, you'll find them in all walks of life as you get older. I think the best way to cope with such people is try to ignore them, and never try to even your wit with them. We can talk more about all sorts of things another time, but now we'd better get home.'

I never told Mother any of this, but I felt much better after telling Paschal.

While we were out, Nellie had prepared a meal of bacon, potatoes and cabbage, which was almost ready.

Over the meal Paschal told us a bit about Artane, and how he had learned to be a tailor. He said that the school had arranged for him to have an interview with Delaneys, a tailoring outfitters in Bray, in a few days time, and if he was successful he would be starting off as an apprentice. The money wouldn't be much to start with, but he thought he'd be fairly good at the job and hoped to work his way up.

Nellie said she had a feeling that he would get the job, and then added, 'How could they turn you down, with that lovely haircut and you dressed up to the veins of nicety in that suit?'

Later Paschal read from the book he had bought for me, *Treasure Island*, and I went to bed a very happy boy with my book to read by candlelight. The candle burned late in the Mahon home that night, as Nellie and Paschal talked about many things. I read for a short while and then fell asleep.

A few days later there was more celebrating. Paschal had been given the job. He said that he was to start work the following Monday from 8.30 am to 6 pm. He was going to be paid ten shillings and sixpence per week and he would give Nellie six shillings a week for his keep. She said no, five shillings would be enough because he should have some for himself and she thought it would be wise if he could put a shilling or two in the post office every week. He agreed that was a sound idea.

The next morning Paschal and I went for a walk. It was a beautiful summer's day and we rambled all over the place until we got tired and lay down on the sweet-smelling grass. It was then I decided to unburden myself to him about my biggest worry and shame. 'I still wet the bed,' I blurted out, 'and I'm always annoyed at myself for doing it, but it still happens, what do you think I can do to stop it?'

He looked at me for a while and then said, 'Well, that's a big problem. I don't know. I think you should start by not having anything to drink at all for at least two hours before you go to bed.'

'I've tried that for longer than two hours and I tell myself before going to sleep, you're not going to wet the bed tonight, but it still happens.'

'I don't know what to say,' he said, 'but I'm sure you'll grow out of it.'

I hope that happens soon, I thought, but it was to go on until I was over twelve years of age.

The rest of the summer was a very happy time for me. Paschal, Christopher Woodcock and I had loads of fun playing games and wandering around wherever we pleased.

Although Paschal was working, he still made plenty of time for me, setting out sums and mis-spelling words for me to correct. And when I had completed those tasks, it was always a thrill to see the correct stroke and marks out of 10, which he always did with a red pencil, just like the teacher did at school.

***

I went back to school after the holidays with much more confidence, and I was going to be in the first class too. I was pleased to see my old friends Snotty Sleeve and Hardy Arse again and they hadn't changed at all. Snotty said, 'Fuck off,' and Hardy told him to 'Shut his fuckin' mouth.'

I shared a desk with Vincent Biranne. He was younger than me and much bigger too. We soon became best friends, and our collaboration was a very beneficial one. He was very good at sums and I was good at spelling, and the teacher never found us out. It was a busy time then because we were preparing for our first confession and Holy Communion.

We had to learn how to make our confession, and practise how to receive the Blessed Sacrament with small pieces of wafer. Mrs Corcoran warned that we must not gobble down the body of our Saviour, but let it melt on our tongues, and under no circumstances were we to move it around in our mouths, so we practised for perfection.

Then when you went into the confessional box you would have to say, 'Bless me father for I have sinned, this is my first confession,' and tell the priest all the sinful things you had done and the bad thoughts you had had and anything else you thought was a sin. The priest would then give you absolution and your penance.

Mrs Corcoran told us that it all depended on how good or bad we had been for the priest to decide on what penance to give us. We made our first confession the day before our first Holy Communion and my penance was two Hail Marys and two Our Fathers. I thought that I mustn't have been too bad.

When Nellie and I got home, she took my brand new bird's eye tweed suit from the box along with my white shirt and the traditional blue tie and white rosette. She had made a deposit on the clothes over eighteen months previously in preparation for the day with the agreement of the outfitter that she would pay as much as she could afford each week until the bill was paid and if any alterations had to be done he would do them free of charge. When the happy day came and she made the final payment I tried the suit on, no alterations were needed, and we both walked out of the shop with delight.

She kept it in the box wrapped up in brown paper and stashed away. Occasionally I'd ask to have a look at my new clothes and she'd say with a smile, 'You're a nuisance,' but I think it gave her as much pleasure as it did me. Now, here we were, just one day away from me wearing it for real.

When Paschal got home from work that evening, he admired the clothes and suggested that I should put them on. Nellie nodded and I dressed quickly. He fixed my tie and pinned the rosette on my lapel. Vanity was only a poor relation. They both commented on how nice I looked and how well the suit fitted. Next came the shoes, a black lace-up pair. Nellie told Paschal that the National Assistance Board allowed her one pair a year for me and she had saved the last pair to go with the suit, but she couldn't have saved them much longer because the ones I was wearing were nearly worn out. I put the shoes on, remembering how long it had taken her to choose them.

'A handsome young man,' said Paschal.

'Indeed,' said Nellie with a broad smile.

I went to bed shortly afterwards, but didn't sleep very well, and I was up at the crack of dawn, full of nervous excitement on my big day. Paschal had a day off work, and we set out early to walk the long way round to the church, taking the roads so that we wouldn't get too much muck on our shoes and clothes. We arrived a half-hour early and Nellie produced the magic little flask filled with tea, which she shared with Paschal, I couldn't have any because I had to fast from midnight until after I received the Blessed Sacrament. I wasn't hungry or thirsty anyway.

Soon it was time to go into church. Nellie wiped my shoes with a little rag and Paschal put his hand on my shoulder as we walked in with all the other parents and children. The rest is a bit hazy, my mind was in a whirl, but I remember receiving the Blessed Sacrament. It seemed to frizzle on my tongue so I eased it down my throat, being careful not to let it touch the roof of my mouth or my cheeks, and before I knew it the whole thing was over.

Later, I was allowed to do the customary thing of visiting

our Catholic neighbours, with the exception of Mr Bill Synott and Mr Lawless, to show off my new clothes and in reward for doing that I was given some money. When I got home I emptied out my pockets and counted nine shillings and sixpence. I was rich. Paschal suggested that we should all walk in to Bray and take a look at the sea, as it was such a lovely day.

I looked into Nellie's eyes by way of asking, can we?

'Yes,' she said, 'it's a special day. I think we should be off without delay.' I hugged her and then Paschal.

We went directly to the seafront. We walked along the promenade to the foot of Bray Head, where we sat on the warm grass, drank lemonade and watched the antics of others for a while and then headed back towards the town. When we reached the Sunshine Ice Cream Parlour Mother asked if I would like to have something nice in there. 'Yes please,' I replied. So in we went and sat down to study the big plastic menu with coloured pictures of delicious-looking fare.

I ordered a tall glass of vanilla ice cream with raspberry sauce, Paschal chose a banana split and Mother decided on a plain ice cream. I couldn't finish all my ice cream, but I certainly did enjoy what I had consumed. Paschal was about to pay and I said, 'Please let me pay.'

'No,' said Mother, 'I'm paying. You two go and have a look in the toy shops, you might see something you want to spend some of your money on, John. I have some shopping to do. We'll meet outside Lipton's in a half-hour or so.'

We visited all three shops that sold toys but I just could not make up my mind on what I liked the most. In the end I settled on a lovely black railway engine and a jigsaw puzzle of a farmyard scene, the first jigsaw I ever had. My bill came to four shillings and four pence so I still had loads of money left. We met Nellie at Lipton's and headed for the bus to Enniskerry. I asked her if I could pay the fares and she said yes. I was thrilled.

We walked home from the village. I was tired and thirsty but neither hungry nor sleepy. I played with my engine while Nellie and Paschal talked and I heard him saying that when he had saved up some money he would buy us a wireless. 'Boy oh boy,' I thought. The Woodcocks across the road had one, and occasionally when I visited their house Christopher's mother allowed us to listen to it, and sometimes she played a record or two for us on the gramophone. Christopher was never allowed to touch them, and that caused him a great deal of frustration, but for me it was exciting and mysterious to hear the talking and music coming out of those things.

***

I must have been nearly ten when Mrs Theresa Kenny approached Mother in Bray and asked her if she could look after her two-year-old son Peter and do a day's housework for her once a week. Mrs Kenny was a sturdily built woman, much taller than my mother, with short brown hair, high cheek bones and lips covered with a thick coating of lipstick, which made her look a bit like a circus clown I had seen in a magazine.

The Kennys lived in a place called Fassaroe, about two miles from our house if we took the short cuts through the fields. So that's how we went when my mother started working for Theresa the following week. Theresa told her what she wanted her to do and said she was welcome to help herself to tea and a sandwich if she wished and we would have a proper feed when her husband Pat came home around seven o'clock and then he'd walk us home. Then she was off on her bicycle, leaving us with Peter.

While my mother did the washing and the other jobs I played with Peter until he fell asleep, and then I helped her put the clothes out on the line to dry.

Pat Kenny, a tall thin grey-haired man, worked as a farm labourer for Mr O'Hooley, who owned hundreds of acres of farmland. They lived rent-free in what was called a gatehouse, in return for Pat checking and counting the livestock. He started that part of his job at 5.30 am each weekday, then he would report to the farmyard and be ready to start his labouring job from 8 am sharp. The task for the day could be ploughing or harrowing with the big horses, or any number of other jobs. Then whenever possible he would pack up at 5 pm and set out on his stock-taking check again, getting home around 7 pm.

For all of this he was paid four pounds and ten shillings per week with free milk and vegetables thrown in, and occasionally there would be free meat too, after the dogs or other animals had mauled the sheep and lambs during the lambing season.

Theresa was a strange woman. She could be very nice, but as quick as batting an eyelid her mood would change and she would become a totally different person, bossing my mother around or spontaneously breaking into song and ignoring us, and that used to frighten me. Then within a few minutes the singing would stop and she was back to being a nice person again.

That was one place I hated having to go to. By the time Pat got cleaned up and we ate it was nearly 9 o'clock before we set out for home, and trudging along country lanes and through fields in wintertime was no fun at all. Pat always accompanied us to the door and bid us goodnight.

He seemed very old to me in comparison to Theresa, who I knew was twenty-five. I asked Mother how old he was.

'Possibly in his mid-fifties,' she said. 'Why do you ask?'

'I think he looks like Mrs Kenny's father,' I replied.

'You must never say that to anyone else,' she told me.

'I won't,' I said. 'I think Mrs Kenny is mad by the way she behaves.'

She smiled and said, 'Ah no, that poor woman is very troubled, she's more to be pitied than laughed at.'

I didn't understand what she meant and I left it at that.

***

I was getting on fairly well at school, except there were several times when I couldn't go, because of colds and flu, and of course the bad weather. I was learning a bit about the history of Ireland, the Irish language, sums, and plenty about the Catholic faith. I was also learning more exciting things in the playground from Snotty and Hardy Arse.

Such as how to steal sweets and things from oul Mrs Ledwidge's shop in Bray. Hardy told me, 'Allya have to do is wait tillya see plenty a people in there an' den go in easylike an' whip what ya want, but don't scarper rightaway, just go out as you'd come in.' He said that sometimes he'd whipped things when she was in the shop by herself, because she was a 'quare oul wan', nearly blind and deafer than a river.

Then Maggie Molloy came over to us and Snotty told her to fuck off.

'No!' said Hardy. 'Maggie come overta the bushes an' show us yer knickers an' yer ghee, willya?'

'All right,' she said, and off they went.

Hardy shouted, 'Come on youse two.'

I waited to see what Snotty was doing. 'Aw fuckit,' he said, 'I don't want ta see her atall, she's just like me six sisters. Did you ever see a girl's ghee?' he asked.

I shook my head.

'Jasus! John,' he said, 'de'ya not know dey don't have mickeys like us, dey have akinda hole ting an it's called a ghee. Mary me big sister has tits on her chest an' lotsa hair on her ghee. I tellya dem girls is quare harps.'

Things started to change at home. Paschal was not coming home from work like he used to do. Sometimes he wouldn't be home until after I was asleep and on occasions I woke up to hear Nellie and him arguing. I didn't like that, it gave me a very uneasy feeling.

One morning I asked Nellie what the matter was, why was she arguing with Paschal last night?

'Well, John,' she said, 'he's been in that Artane so long he's just trying to spread his wings, but I don't like some of the company he's keeping.'

I didn't quite understand what she had said. I only knew that I missed seeing him as much as I used to.

Later on he didn't come home for days, and eventually he moved out to stay with friends.

Five months later, Maureen visited us and the talk got around to the possibility of her moving in with us. Nellie said that would be grand, but all that travelling to and from work in all kinds of weather wouldn't be very comfortable and the cost of the fares had to be taken into consideration.

Maureen said she had worked it all out and the money she was paying for her digs would be better spent if she paid that to Nellie for her keep, and besides, her boyfriend Dick Rafferty lived near us and he had a car. I just caught a glimpse of a frown on Nellie's face as Dick's name was mentioned.

Christopher Woodcock knocked on the door to ask if I could come out to play. Nellie said certainly, but not to wander off too far. When I returned, the good news was that Maureen would be moving in with us next month. Nellie said a new bed would have to be bought, but maybe they could come across a good second-hand one somewhere. Maureen suggested that probably it would be best to get a new one on hire purchase, to which Nellie said, 'I'm not in favour of getting into debt for anything.'

Maureen said there wouldn't be any problems because she would be able to pay it off by the week from her wages, and she had been saving a few shillings a week since she had started working, so if, God forbid, she was to lose her job she would still be able to keep up the payments for a good few weeks. Nellie said, taking that into consideration, she didn't mind and whenever she had a shilling or two to spare she would put that towards the payment. So it was settled at that.

A double bed was delivered from Cavendishes and shortly afterwards Maureen moved in. It was great having another relation living with us and getting to know each other was fun, but it wasn't the same as it had been with Paschal. She was a girl, and I couldn't talk to her about the things that were troubling me as I had so freely done with Paschal. He was now living with friends not far away and he visited us occasionally, but I never did confide in him again.

As the months went by, niggling little things were taking place between Nellie and Maureen. They did not always agree about things, and whenever Maureen said she was going out with Dick, Nellie found something unfavourable to say about him. Maureen tried to defend him, but it became impossible for her, and just like Paschal she moved out.

It was about this time that Nellie had her greatest setback. Mr Brophy the welfare officer dropped a bombshell when he said, 'I have a letter here stating that you have two relations staying with you now so it has been decided to cut your assistance money by five shillings per week from today.' He looked up from his desk and said, 'I am sorry.'

I was taking all this in and watching both of them as Nellie replied, 'I don't know where you got your information from, Mr Brophy, but it is wrong. My niece and nephew did contribute a few shillings, barely enough to feed them when they were staying with me, but they have gone now and I receive nothing from them. My circumstances have not changed at all except that the rent has gone up from two shillings to two shillings and threepence. What am I to do?'

He responded with a cold stare and said, 'I'll be in touch

with head office and we'll just have to wait and see. Unfortunately until then the present decision is the only one I can act on.'

He handed over the reduced weekly amount and we left. When we got outside I noticed how weak and drained she was as she leaned against the wall gasping for breath. I was frightened and didn't know what to say or do. I moved close to her and held her hand. She looked down at me, smiled and said, 'Well, I've still got you, Johnny boy! To hell with them anyway, let's go and get a cup of tea and a big cake for you.'

I don't know if she ever told anyone about the drastic drop in her money. If she did I never heard her, nor do I know if the original allowance was reinstated. I do know that she filled in several forms after that and never once complained. Probably because she thought they might take me away from her.

A couple of months after Maureen left, Mother received a letter from her saying that she was getting married to Dick in two weeks' time and she hoped we would come to the ceremony and a bit of a do afterwards. I had never been to a wedding, but my excitement was short-lived as she said we wouldn't be going.

Jimmy came out of Artane, but he only stayed with us for a few weeks and then went to England or some other place, and finally Peter came out of Artane. He went to work on a farm down the country and eventually went to England.

I reached my eleventh birthday on 15 December 1953. I was still doing well at school, and although I had not grown any, my health was much better and my wits were keen. I had learned that if I could distract the few bully boys that were intent on beating me up, I would save my skin, so I used talking tactics to distract them and it usually worked, but not always.

We always visited Mother's friend Mrs McLoughlin and her family in Bray on Christmas Day, that is, if my health was all right and the weather was reasonable. I enjoyed the party atmosphere there, and just after my eleventh birthday I had my first taste of whiskey. Someone held a glass out to me saying 'Have a little taste of this, son,' and before Nellie could protest I had taken a cautious sip of the golden liquid.

Nellie protested, 'Mick, you shouldn't have done that.'

Mick jokingly replied, 'Ah, sure there's no harm in it. In years to come he'll know the taste of it all right.'

***

Sunday 7 February 1954 was a dark and very cold day with showers of hailstones and a severe frost on the ground. Nellie and I made our way through Fisher's field and down to a boggy area, where there was always a good choice of rotting wood and other kinds of sticks that made good firewood. It was necessary for us to gather the wood because there was none at home and the house was freezing. We worked quickly, and soon were tying up our bundles with string. It was only a short walk back to the house, so I led the way in haste.

As I was trudging along I heard Nellie gasp. I looked around and there she was lying still on the ground. I ran back to her in shock and panic and asked her what was wrong. She just mumbled. I tried to lift her up but I couldn't. I just stood there looking down at her. Suddenly I remembered that Paschal was in a friend's house not far away. Blinded by my tears, I ran there faster than the wind, and managed to blurt out what had happened.

'John,' he said, 'I want you to go across to the Woodcocks and please stay there until I come to get you.' He was off and I ran across the road to the Woodcocks.

I explained in the best way I could to Mrs Woodcock what had happened.

She put her hand on my shoulder, saying, 'You stay here, son, and when everything's all right you can go home.'

By then Christopher had come downstairs and joined us. His mother told him to look after me, and maybe we could find some interesting games to play, then she said, 'I'll just go over to see what I can do to help.' Henry, her husband, asked her if she thought he would be any help. She shook her head, saying, 'I think it's best that I go alone, dear. Please get the girls to do the tea.'

Anne, May and Eileen, Christopher's sisters, were much older than us and we looked on them as adults. 'Christopher,' said May, 'maybe John would like to go up to your room or out to the shed for a while. We'll call you when the tea is ready.'

Christopher and I went out to the shed, which was filled with all sorts of interesting things from bicycles and tools to toys. I always loved going in there, but I couldn't concentrate on anything that day. My mind was completely occupied with the thought of my mother lying there on the cold hard ground. Was she all right? Would she die? Would she have to stay in bed? Who would look after us? I thought of Dr Devlin, and realised I hadn't told Paschal it was the good Dr Devlin that Nellie would have wanted to attend to her.

Christopher must have been reading my mind, for he asked me if Nellie was going to die. I simply shook my head, and the tears started. Christopher just stood still looking very uncomfortable.

Anne shouted from the back door that tea was ready, but I couldn't eat a thing.

Mrs Woodcock came back about an hour later and I caught the slight shake of her head to Henry. She took my hand and said, 'We'll go over now, John.'

When we entered the house I found a much different scene to the one we had left earlier in the day.

Some neighbours were in and Maureen came rushing to meet me with tears streaming down her cheeks. She led me outside and then Paschal joined us and he was crying too. Before either of them had a chance to speak, I said through my tears, 'She's gone.' They both nodded and I said, 'I'm going in to see her.'

I dried my tears, shook off Paschal's offered hand and went straight to the bedroom – and there lay Nellie in the bed with her hands clasped over a set of rosary beads. I made the sign of the cross and knelt down, but I didn't pray. All I could think of was the little streak of grey hair above her forehead in her red hair. She had always been so careful to tuck the grey bit in beneath her beret before we went out, and now everyone could see it.

I blessed myself again then stood up and walked slowly into the front room, where I was aware of people's eyes on me and I wished I could vanish.

I went over to Dick Rafferty, Maureen's husband, and he said how sorry he was about Nellie's death and asked if I would like some lemonade?

'Yes please,' I said. I took a few sips and suddenly had a

great urge to get out of that room. I told Maureen I needed to go out for some fresh air. She said all right but I must wrap up well and not to stray away from the front of the house. I nodded.

Once outside in the cold air looking up at the stars, I thought, if God's up there or wherever he is, how could he let my mother die like that? Then my mind took on another train of thought as I saw crates of alcohol, boxes of food, coal and wood being delivered for the traditional wake and I remembered that earlier in the day the place was freezing and all the food we had in the house was a half a loaf, a pot of mixed jam, some dripping and a few spuds.

Paschal came out and asked if I wanted to go back in or if I'd rather stay out for a while.

'I'd like to stay here a little longer,' I replied.

I asked him if he was going to live in the house with me. There was a silence and then he replied, 'Well, John, I don't really know what's going to happen. We've got to arrange the funeral first, and then we'll see what to do. You know what Nellie used to say, that if anything ever happened to her, she didn't want you going into a school like Artane, and I guarantee you won't.'

When we returned to the house there were a few more people there and Maureen said, 'Please have something to eat, John.' I told her I wasn't hungry and she said that I really should eat something. I ate two cream crackers just to please her and sat with Dick for a while before saying that I was going to bed.

I had a very strange feeling standing alone in the candlelit bedroom that Nellie and I had shared for all of my life, looking at the bed, then I noticed that there was a posh-looking quilt on it and new pillows. I pulled the clothes back to discover the sheets were new too. That frightened me, because I was still wetting the bed.

Maureen and Paschal came in and she gently asked why I wasn't in bed yet. 'I still wet the bed,' I said, 'I've tried lots of ways to stop but it still happens, so I was thinking of taking the new sheets off.'

'You'll do no such thing,' she said sternly. Then she smiled, pulled me close to her and said, 'John! You must not worry about that, I have no doubt it will stop in time. And besides, there's a rubber sheet beneath. In any case, if it does happen, I'll wash them out in the morning and no one will be any the wiser. You've had a dreadful day, and it's after eleven o'clock, so please try to get some sleep.' She kissed me and said, 'Goodnight, darling.'

I had never been called darling before. It gave me a good feeling.

Paschal stayed a little longer but didn't have much to say, except that he would probably be up all night with those who had stayed back for the wake and he would look in on me from time to time. As I lay there in the dark I heard the voices from the front room, but my mind was on Nellie and how we had got out of that very same bed that morning, and now here I was alone with the realisation that we would never share it again. She was gone forever.

Then my mind was racing with thoughts about the funeral. And would Paschal and I still live in this house? Or would I have to go into an orphanage? And would I ever stop pissing the bed?

I dropped off to sleep but then awoke with a start. I heard them talking in the front room and listened for a while before dropping off to sleep again I awoke at 8 am the next morning and, wonder of wonders, I had not wet the bed. Although there had been the occasional dry morning in the past, this one seemed extra special. I went into the front room where Maureen was sitting at the table drinking a cup of tea. She bid me good morning and told me that Dick and Paschal had gone to see the priest to make the funeral arrangements.

I went into the quiet room to see my mother, and stood there looking at her in the bed that had been bought when Maureen moved in with us, and thought of the only time she had ever attempted to hit me. It was a very cold morning, and as we walked along the lane I was whingeing about having to go to school in the cold. 'I'm fed up with your complaining,' she said, and made a swipe at me. I dodged out of the way, slipped and fell in the muck. 'That's it,' she said, 'we're going home.' And now I felt sorry for my behaviour.

I told Maureen I was going out for a while.

'What about your breakfast?' she asked.

'I'm not hungry,' I said. I walked out of the house and down to the spring where I stayed for a time, just looking at the water and the stream nearby, thinking of what it had been like there last summer. I don't know how long I stayed there, but when I went into the house, Paschal told me that Nellie's remains would be taken to the chapel at five o'clock that evening and the funeral would take place at ten the following morning and the burial would be in the Killegar graveyard. I moped around in a world of my own for the rest of the day and tried to stay out of everyone's way.

Finally it was five o'clock. Nellie had been placed in the coffin and carried to the hearse. Maureen, Paschal, Dick and I got into the big black car behind.

The trip to the chapel seemed to be over in no time, and soon the coffin was placed in the aisle near the altar. We knelt down to say prayers, but I didn't pray. I just kept my eyes shut until I heard movement around me, then I stood up and made my way back to the car with the others.

When we had left the house that short time earlier, I little realised that I would never return to it.

Maureen told me we were going to Mick and Carmel Rafferty's house, Dick's brother, where Maureen and Dick lived with them and their two children Michael and Mona, while they were waiting for a council place of their own. Carmel told me to make myself at home and Mick said it would be nice to have me staying with them.

That was news to me. I looked to Paschal and Maureen for some sort of explanation, but all I got was looks and smiles.

Later they took me up to the little bedroom that was to be mine for the rest of my stay there, and explained what they hoped would happen. As Nellie hadn't wanted me going into Artane neither did they, so they were going to get the necessary advice from the National Assistance Board and anyone else that could help to find me a good home.

I asked Paschal why he and I couldn't live in our house, and he said the authorities would never approve, and the county council probably wouldn't want to rent it to him anyway. Maureen said the old place held too many sad memories for her and she hoped to get a newer place and thought there was a good chance because she was expecting a baby. I looked at her and she smiled.

We were all up early the next morning and little was said until the big black car came for us at 9.30 am. More prayers

43

were said in the chapel and then the coffin was placed in the hearse and it moved very slowly out of the churchyard.

The service by the graveside went on for ages. The priest prattled on about the dearly departed soul of Ellen Mahon, but I had heard enough. He knew nothing about my mother. Neither he nor any of the rest of the dark-clad men of god had ever visited our home.

Finally, another prayer was said and as they were lowering the coffin down one of the straps broke and the coffin tilted precariously downwards. There were a few oohs and ahs, but good manhandling prevailed and the coffin was gently lowered to the bottom, then Maureen, Paschal and I dropped a little earth on top of it.

Maureen held my hand on one side and Paschal on the other as we made our way back to the cars, but before we reached them I had the urge to go back to the grave for one last goodbye.

'I want to go back for a couple of minutes,' I said.

'They will be filling in the grave now, John,' said Maureen.

'I don't care,' I said, 'I still want to go back by myself.'

They looked at each other and Paschal said, 'All right, but no longer than five minutes, promise?' I nodded and went back to the grave.

The diggers looked surprised and awkward as they saw me approaching. They had indeed started to fill in the grave, and there was only a small edge of the coffin still showing. I quietly said that I had needed to come back, to say my last goodbye.

The two men looked at me with what I took to be a look of sympathy as they moved back a short distance from the grave.

I stood there for a few minutes, then hurried back to where the cars were.

***

The next few weeks seemed hectic for both Maureen and Paschal. They were always going to see the authorities and all sorts of people, but they were optimistic that they would find me a good home.

In the meantime, I had settled in nicely in the family atmosphere. Carmel and Mick were very kind to me and Michael and Mona were great fun. Michael was about six years of age and Mona about four. Towards the end of the third week, Maureen came home full of excitement. She said the authorities had provisionally agreed that Mrs Theresa Kenny and her husband Patrick could become my legal guardians. She went on, but I wasn't listening.

She looked across the polished table at me and said, 'John, you haven't been listening, isn't it grand, Mrs Kenny's a lovely woman, and I know she'll take good care of you.'

'I don't want to live with the Kennys,' I said.

'Why?' she asked.

'Where is Paschal?' I asked.

'He has been held up,' she said. 'He will be here tomorrow morning.'

'I will tell you when he gets here,' I said.

I had a very restless night, and I was up before anyone in the house the next morning. I made myself a cup of tea and took it out to the shed, where I sat down in an old chair and tried to clear my muddled mind. I sat there for ages, and determined that I did not want to live with the Kennys, even if I had to go into a school, and I was going to tell Maureen and Paschal that.

I was in that frame of mind when I went back into the house and found Paschal there. He greeted me with a grin and asked if I felt like taking a walk down to the village.

Immediately we were out the door I said, 'Paschal, I do not want to go to the Kennys. He is a nice man, but she's mad, I don't like her.'

He stopped and said, 'Look, John, please try to understand. I would not be allowed to keep you because I'm single so we don't have much choice. I met Mrs Kenny twice and I think that she'll give you a very good home.'

That stirred something in me. I was very angry and said, 'You and Maureen keep saying how nice Kenny is, but I know her better than either of you and I don't want to live with her. I'd rather go into Artane.'

We were both silent with our thoughts as we walked to the village. He broke the silence by asking if I had ever been in a bar before. I shook my head, then he said, 'There's a first time for everything,' as he opened the door that led into the bar of the Powerscourt Arms Hotel. He asked the barman if he could take me into the snug.

45

The barman smiled at me and said, 'Sure, indeed you can, what'll you have?'

Paschal ordered a pint of stout for himself and a glass of lemonade for me and when the drinks were served we each took a sip and he said, 'We have to discuss where you want to go to. It's either to the Kennys or possibly Artane. You say you know Theresa Kenny better than Maureen and I do. Well, I know Artane better than you do, and it's a terrible place. Other boys beat you up and bully you. No, that's not the place for you. I wouldn't want you going to a place like that.'

'And I know I don't want to live with the Kennys,' I retorted. 'Is there anywhere else I can go?'

'No,' he said. 'Be reasonable, look at it this way. You're eleven years and three months old now. When you're sixteen you can leave the Kennys and do as you please. You could live with me or Maureen or even go to England if you liked, so you see, you'll only have to stay with them for four years and nine months, and listen to this, you can leave school at fourteen, and then you can get a job, although I would prefer that you continued going to school until you are sixteen.'

'If I can leave school at fourteen I will,' I said, 'and I will get a job too.'

I had hardly touched my lemonade, but he had finished his pint and ordered another one. He excused himself to go to the toilet and while he was away, I thought about what he had said and suddenly things seemed much clearer to me. Maybe living with the Kennys wouldn't be so bad after all.

When he returned he asked if I had thought about it at all.

'Yes,' I replied, 'I have and it doesn't seem as bad now, but I still don't like it. If there's any chance of going to live with someone else I would prefer it.'

'You're a hard man to please, Johnny Mahon,' he said, 'but look, here's another thing, Maureen and I will visit you from time to time to make sure you're all right. Mrs Kenny will be paid ten shillings per week by the Assistance Board for your keep and you'll still get one pair of shoes or boots from them every year, but I'll give her a pound or two now and again just to make sure you're not in need of anything.'

He finished his pint and said, 'We best be off now.'

Back at the Raffertys' not a word was said about our

46

discussion until I went up to bed and Maureen and Paschal accompanied me upstairs. All three of us sat on the small bed and he briefly told Maureen what he had explained to me and how I saw things more clearly now. She said that was very good and I would see that everything would work out for the best.

***

I moved in to my new home with the Kennys towards the end of March 1954. Theresa welcomed us with a smile and said, 'Folly me, youse can put John's tings in his room.'

We followed her and three-year old Peter into a clean little box room with whitewashed walls and a flagstoned floor, partly covered with a square of green linoleum. The furniture consisted of a single bed, under which was a chamber pot (better known as a poe), a chair and a small chest of drawers. Seeing the poe made me shudder with fear at the thought of wetting the bed that night.

'It's a bit cold in dis room,' said Theresa, 'but there's plenty of bedclothes and I'm hoping to get an oil heater in here next week.' Maureen and Paschal said the room was very nice, but yes, it could do with a heater.

They left about an hour later with the promise of coming to see me whenever they could. Theresa said they were always welcome and she would make sure and take good care of me and maybe fatten me up a bit.

As soon as they were out of sight, she said, 'You might as well put your tings away inta the drawers in your room and hang your coat on the nail on the back of the door.'

'Yes, thank you Mrs Kenny,' I said. I sorted out my things and was nearly finished when Peter came in and started rummaging through the holdall. He pulled out a favourite toy of mine, a little white car. I took the car out of his hand and he threw a tantrum, squealing and roaring and throwing himself on the floor.

Theresa, red-faced, came rushing into the room shouting, 'Didya hit Peter?'

'No, I didn't,' I said, holding up the car. 'I just took this back from him.'

'Yeh did didya? Give it to me this minute!' she said.

I handed the car over and she took Peter by the hand and

left the room. I took my time and carefully hid my favourite toys and comic books beneath my clothes. The only thing left to put away was my communion suit so I sheepishly returned to the front room carrying my suit. Theresa was sitting by the roaring fire with Peter asleep on her lap. Seeing this, I whispered, 'Where can I put this?'

'You don't have to whisper,' she said, 'he's jaded, but I don't want him to sleep too long. You can put it in the wardrobe in the spare room.' I did that and then re-entered the front room, which was cold despite the roaring fire in the grate. The floor was covered with linoleum and the walls were papered with a bright floral design. There was an oblong table by the wall covered with oilcloth and four wooden chairs around it and two easy chairs, one on either side of the fireplace. A Kosangas cooker was situated by another wall with its yellow supply bottle by the side, and high up on the wall there was a shelf with a Philips wireless set. I wondered if I would be allowed to play it. She smiled and said, 'You're all settled in now. Put the kettle on and make us a cuppa tea.'

I knew how to turn the gas on from my visits there. I checked to see if there was enough water in the kettle and then put a match to the gas, and when the kettle was boiling she guided me through the tea-making procedure and how much sugar and milk she wanted in her mug. She told me to do a half cup for Peter too.

Having done this, I sat down opposite her by the fire. Peter woke up and she held the cup to his mouth, but he pushed it away and she put it down on the floor next to my treasured car. I was tempted to pick up the car, but thought, better not.

She smiled at me and said, 'There's a good home for you here, but you'll have to do tings my way. Just remember that and yeh won't go wrong. I know you piss the bed and that'll have to stop, if you can't do it beyerself, I'll havta bate it outta yeh, an' another ting, don't yeh ever lay a finger on Peter, he's only a babby compared to you, so if he picks up anyting belonging to you, just let him have it, he'll soon tire of it, then you'll have it back, do you understand me?'

I nodded with a serious expression. I learned a lot more about her that afternoon, and I knew I must be very careful in everything I said or did.

Pat Kenny arrived home at 7.30 that evening, soaked to the skin.

'It's bucketing down,' he said, 'I'm glad to be in out of it.'

He turned to me and said, 'Well, you're here John, welcome.' Then he went to the bedroom and got out of his wet clothes and returned to wash himself in a tin bowl, while Theresa cooked sausages and bacon and buttered a pile of bread. I was hungry enough to demolish what was put before me, and I could see that none of them including Peter had any difficulty in putting their food away.

After tea, Theresa said to me, 'I'll show you how to do the washing up, it'll come in handy.'

She put a pinch of soap powder into a bowl, poured hot water in from the kettle, added a little cold water and washed the mugs first. 'Always do the tings widout grease first, and den you can do the rest of the tings. Do you understand?' I nodded and started drying up. She left me to it and sat down by the fire, taking Peter on her lap, and announced that Mrs Gormley and her daughter Betty would be coming over.

The Gormleys lived across the lane from us in a council house and their neighbours were the Laceys and further down the lane were the Husseys and the McDonalds, all of whom I knew vaguely from my previous visits to the Kennys, but I knew Mrs Gormley and her daughter Betty better, as they often came over to the Kennys when Nellie and I were visiting. Betty was thirteen years old and she knew lots about sums and all sorts of school lessons that I didn't. She used to show me easy ways to do the sums and sometimes we played noughts and crosses and other such games.

There was a knock on the door and in walked Margaret and Betty Gormley. Margaret came over to me straight away, gave me a tight hug and kissed me on the cheek. I was furnace-faced and wondered if there was any of her lipstick on my cheek.

She held me out in front of her, saying, 'John, you're a very brave young man, and it's very nice you're going to be just across the lane from us. You will always be welcome in our home, and you can play with my lot whenever you like. That'll be alright, won't it missis?' Theresa just nodded.

Margaret's lot, as she put it, were John, fifteen years of age, Brendan, fourteen, Betty, thirteen, Terry, eleven, and Eamonn the baby was five. She was bringing up the family by herself because her husband Joe was working in England, where he was doing two jobs, labouring on a building site through the day and working as a barman at night, in order to earn enough to pay for his digs and provide for his family. Sometimes he came home at Christmas, but he always came home in the summer and they enjoyed a happy family reunion.

The Gormleys were not unique in their family separation. There were countless other families in the same position throughout Ireland. It was often said, 'Ah sure, it's the best thing to do, go *over there*, where there's plenty of work and dacent wages, sure there's nothing here but poverty, hardship and drudgery for little money if you're lucky enough to have a job.'

My first night in my new home was a restless one, tossing and turning until I heard someone in the front room. It was Pat, who said, 'It's only five in the morning.'

'I know,' I said, 'but I couldn't sleep. I might as well stay up now.'

He proceeded to light the fire in the grate. The kettle was boiling on the gas stove, so he made a pot of tea and poured us both a mug, then we sat at the table and drank as he explained that before he left for work each morning he lit the fire and made sandwiches to take to work for dinnertime, then banked the fire so that by the time Theresa and Peter got up around eight o'clock the room would be warm, and the last thing he did before he left the house was to give them a cup of tea.

31 March 1954: the day Theresa Kenny started to train me in the way she wanted me to be.

At 7.30 am she shouted, 'Bring me a cup a tea, you know how I like it.'

A few minutes later I handed her the cup of tea and she settled on her elbow in the bed with Peter alongside her. There was no thanks, but another order, 'Get the poe from under here an' empty it in the ditch across the lane, then rinse it out an' bring it back here.'

I knelt down to get the chamber pot from under the bed and held my breath as I picked it up with its stinking contents and hurried out and across the lane to the ditch to get rid of it as quickly as I could, and in my haste some of the mess splashed over my hand. I flung the pot and its slop into the ditch in my fury and stood there thinking, 'You bloody eejit, now you've got to climb in amongst the briars to get the thing out.'

I retrieved the pot, washed it and myself at the water pump down the lane and was just about to put it under the bed when she said, 'That took you long enough, I thought you went to Bray to empty it, you'll need to hurry yerself boy.'

I never said a word. I was furious and disgusted, but consoled myself with the thought that when I left school at fourteen I was definitely going to get myself a job to get away from that sort of thing. But a lot of poes would have to be emptied before that opportunity came my way.

Theresa got up at 9 am. She cooked eggs and bacon and dished up two plates, one for each of us, and gave Peter something else.

'You've done fairly well dis mornin,' she said, 'you've kep the fire up an although you were slow emptying the poe, it's nice and clean, yer a quick learner!'

That made me feel a bit more at ease, but I couldn't relax.

'Deya like going to school?' she asked.

'I don't mind it,' I said.

'I'll keep you home for a while,' she said, 'I want to teach you things you won't learn at school.'

And that she certainly did. I think I must have become the only programmed domesticated robotic boy in the County of Wicklow, if not in the whole of Ireland. I quickly learned after countless beatings and arse kickings to do as Theresa said, and fast. Make the beds. Wash the floors. Get the water in. Gather the firewood. Saw the wood into blocks for the fire ...

I was still wetting the bed occasionally, so I used to wash the soiled section of the sheet, and sometimes the two sheets, hang them out on the line to dry and get them in and on the bed before she got up and she was none the wiser.

One morning she rose earlier than usual, and much to my annoyance it didn't take her long to spot the sheet on the line.

'What's that on the line?' she asked.

'It's the sheet from my bed. I'm sorry, I had an accident,' I said.

51

She reached out and grabbed me with such speed that I was dumbfounded. She pushed me up against the wall and demanded that I look at her. I looked up straight into her eyes with a hate I couldn't disguise.

'Now, you listen here, you little bastard, I told yeh I'd bate that dirty habit outta yeh! And bedad I will, an' no mistake.' She boxed my ears, and landed a few well-aimed kicks to my legs and arse. That hurt, but not half as much as it hurt my pride. I ran out of the house and down the field to a cosy place in the hedge where I sat to lick my physical and mental wounds.

I returned to the house after about a half-hour, and to my great relief Margaret Gormley was drinking a cup of tea with her.

They both greeted me simultaneously, with Theresa acting as though nothing had happened and telling me to pour myself a cup of tea and have a few of the biscuits Margaret had brought over.

'Me and Missis is going to Bray,' said Theresa, 'and Betty will be over to look after Peter. You make sure there's enough sticks cut up for the fire and enough water in the house, there's six spuds and a turnip to peel, do that an' lave them in a pot of clean water. That should keep you outa mischief.'

Betty, Peter and I had a nice afternoon, and Peter behaved himself much better than when his mother was around. Betty helped me to peel the spuds and turnip and asked if we should cut them up.

'No,' I said, 'we better not because Mrs Kenny hasn't told me to.

My education in domestication and subservience was nearly complete when she felt that she could rely on me to do the weekly shopping. I walked the mile and a half down to the main road and caught the bus from there in to Bray every Friday and went directly to the Kelly brothers' grocery shop with a list of what was needed for the week. That was the best part of the job, for once I had given one of the brothers the list and the bags they always gave me sixpence to spend and said the same thing every week until it became the norm: 'Off with you, mountain man, the goods will be ready in plenty of time for you to catch your bus.' That gave me nearly an hour to wander around town and buy whatever I liked with my sixpence, and to my great delight Theresa never knew those kind men gave me the money.

The hard work began when I got off the bus and had to struggle up the lanes with two heavy bags of shopping. Of course I stopped several times along the way for a rest before putting the bags on the table for her to check each item.

As time went on I took more rests along the way and she said, 'It's taking you a long time to get from Bray to here, what keeps you?'

'I know,' I said, 'most times the bus is late and sometimes the bags are so heavy I have to take an extra rest.' I thought I was in for a clout or a telling off, but she kept quiet and continued checking the goods.

That gave me the idea to gradually take longer returning from the glen after gathering the firewood and slow down by degrees when sawing the sticks into blocks to fit the fire. I also started to employ part of my old school tactic of distance and avoidance as much as I could without her getting suspicious. It had been reasonably successful for me at school. Of course, I had also talked my way out of tricky situations in the schoolyard, but that would not have worked with Theresa.

I didn't go back to school until about four months after my mother's death.

The distance from Fassaroe to Enniskerry was nearly three miles, along country lanes and through fields. I had to set out alone because Theresa said, 'I don't want you getting mixed up with any of the Laceys or Gormleys or any of dem others.' I couldn't work that out, because Margaret Gormley was supposed to be her friend and the Laceys were nice people.

But what she didn't know, or if she did she never mentioned it, was that once I was out of her sight I could walk the rest of the way with whom I liked. However, I couldn't do that on the way home – her strict instructions were that I should hurry home from school, have a sandwich and a cup of tea, and then get meself off to the glen to gather enough boughs and sticks and saw them into blocks for the fire. That was a routine that was strictly adhered to whenever I was allowed to go to school for more than a day or two at a time.

I grew to hate going to school because of my frequent spells of absence for no reason other than on her whim. I would just start to pick up on a lesson, and then I would be away again for another week or three, and I often wished I didn't have to go at all.

One bright autumn day I ran back from school as usual and found the house was empty. I had a sandwich and a cup of tea then went to the glen for the sticks. I hurried the job and was home in no time. I dropped my bundle and went into the house. Still no sign of anyone, so I decided to put the sticks in the shed and bring some of the reserve blocks that Pat and I had cut up into the house. That done, I went across to the Gormleys where there was a game of football going on and I joined in. I must have been there for about twenty minutes and was enjoying myself so much that I didn't hear Theresa calling me until Terry Gormley drew my attention to her. I crossed the lane and she shoved me in, closing the door behind her. And as she did so she pinned me to the wall with one hand and knee and I felt the wind being knocked out of me as she punched me in the stomach and ribs and I fell to the floor but she didn't let up – if anything, the assault got worse. She started kicking me with a vengeance that I believe to this day could have done me a serious injury or maybe even killed me if it had not been for Peter's frightened screaming. She stopped and I lay on the floor in agony. She pulled me to my feet and said, 'Let that be a lesson, I told you, I don't want you mixing with anyofdem and what deya do when me back's turned? I don't want you tellin' Pat or anyone else what's happened here today an if yeh do, it'll be the worse for yeh, do you hear?' I looked directly in to her wild eyes and remained silent. 'Straighten yerself up,' she said, 'there's nothing wrong witya.'

'I can't,' I said, 'I don't know where I hurt the most, I've got a splitting headache and I feel sick.'

'Go and lie down,' she said. 'I'll make you a nice cuppa tea and we'll forget all about it. I'll tell Pat you're not feeling too good after you fell and banged your head down the glen, you've got a headache and an upset stomach.'

I spent three days in bed after that assault. Although she seemed to have gone berserk there wasn't a mark on my face, but the rest of my body was like the colours of the rainbow.

I had plenty of time to think when I was in bed. I would report her to the guards, I would ask Mr Brophy from the National Assistance Board to put me in Artane, I would run away and tell Maureen and Paschal the whole story and ask them to get me into Artane. I was glad I had never begged for her to stop during her rage, and most of all I was glad I didn't cry. Somehow I felt that would have given her satisfaction.

But it was back to normal when she told me that Maureen and Paschal were coming to visit on the coming Sunday. 'You remember to keep your tongue in your head and tell them relations nothing,' she said.

They arrived and she made a big fuss of welcoming them before they had a chance to say anything to me and I was glad because I blamed them for putting me with that mad bitch. She went to make a pot of tea and then they were all over me,. Maureen kissed me and held my hand and Paschal clapped me on the shoulder, saying, 'It's fresh and well you're looking John.'

'Indeed he,' is said Maureen. 'How are you getting on, darling?'

'Good,' said I, thinking, if only I could tell you the truth.

'How about a bit of a walk, John?' asked Paschal.

'No,' said Theresa quickly, 'he's just over a heavy cold and I don't think it'd be wise for him to go out yet.'

They agreed with her and began talking about my health.

To change the subject, I asked Maureen if she had a picture of her baby. 'Oh, John, I'm sorry, she said, I meant to show it to you earlier. His name is John, what do you think of that?' She took an envelope out of her handbag and handed it to me. I looked at the first of the four pictures, which was obviously taken when he was a few weeks old. I handed it to Theresa and did the same with the others, which were taken at various stages of his nine months. She oohed and ahhed and was as sweet as honey in her praise of the child. 'You don't fool me, you evil old bitch,' I thought.

They left a couple of hours later.

I was twelve years old on 15 December 1954 and privately celebrated with the thought that I only had two years to go before leaving school and getting a job.

***

I had another long spell off school and went back in late February. My mother had been dead for over a year and I often wondered what she would think of me now. I hadn't

55

grown any, but I had changed a lot and I wished she were still alive so I could do all the chores for her instead of for Theresa.

I went out with Pat one spring Sunday afternoon to check the sheep and lambs and soon we came upon a little lamb lying on the ground all by itself. I thought it was dead and said so to Pat, but he shook his head and said, 'Just pick it up gently.'

I looked at him to see if he really meant it. He nodded go ahead.

I started to pick the little animal up, but was unprepared for the jelly-like substance that was all over it, and I nearly dropped it. Pat shouted, 'Hold on to her Johnny, she's just born.' He took the little animal from me, breathed into its mouth, shook it and gently smacked it and it came to life with a few bleats.

He grinned, wiped the lovely little thing in burlap, put it inside his coat and said, 'She'll be warm in there, I'll have to put her in the shed and feed her by the bottle if we can't find the mother.' We moved on down the field and before long we saw the reason why the lamb had been abandoned. Dogs or foxes had been worrying the sheep and had killed two lambs and badly mauled a sheep.

Pat said, 'This happens every year and it keeps me very busy, we best herd them closer to the outhouses, and we'll see if this little thing's mother claims her.' He put the little creature down on the ground and mother and baby found each other.

'Isn't that grand, he said, they're happy now. Look at that little thing, feeding to her heart's content.'

'It's a lovely sight to see,' I said 'and it makes me feel happy.'

'But I don't think you're happy living with us, are you?' he asked.

'No,' I replied.

'Theresa is not an easy person to get on with. I don't know what you think of me, John. I seldom say much to defend you when she tells you off. Well, I'm going to tell you why. You know by now she's a highly strung person and she suffers with her nerves. I think the less said the better mended with her. I have a suspicion she hits you when I'm not around, does she?'

I liked him, but not enough to trust him and tell him what had been going on. 'She gives me the odd clout when I wet the bed, but I haven't done that for nearly six weeks now,' I said.

'Good man yourself,' he said, 'maybe you're over it now. Listen, I'm going to get someone with a tractor to come and pick up the dead animals so you'd best go back to the house.'

On the way back I thought he surely must have known she was beating me, and then it dawned. She never kicked or beat me around the face or did enough damage to seriously injure me except for the time that Peter's screams brought her back to her senses – she might have done so then, but for the rest of the hammerings, they were concentrated around my body and arse.

I was barely in the door when she asked, 'Was any sheep kilt?'

'Yes,' I replied.

'Good,' said she, 'oul O'Hooley'll give us fresh mate soon.' I wasn't going to be eating any. That was for sure.

The next time Pat and I were out together he said, 'Johnny boy, I've got a tractor and trailer dropping off a load of blocks from a tree we cut up beyond in the yard last week. I told Theresa there was no need for you to go down to the glen for a good while to come, but she said no, she still wanted you to carry on with that job, she was in one of her moods and all I could get out of her was, "The devil finds work for idle hands." I'll tell you what to do,' he continued, 'don't kill yourself carrying big bundles, a small amount will do, but make the bundles look big in case she has an eye on you. Make a show of cutting up a few blocks, take your time and get the rest from what we have there.'

I confessed that I had used the reserve pile once before but omitted the story about the beating afterwards.

'That's all right son,' he said.

Maureen wrote to her in the summer and she said, 'Your relations want to come and see you. I'll write them a note to put them off, you can help me wit the spellin.' She sat down with my school jotter and a pencil and I sat at the opposite side of the table, far enough to be out of her grasp if she got wise to the game I was going to play. 'How deya spell Maureen's name?' she asked. I rattled it off and she said,

'You're too fuckin' quick, a letter at a time.' I did as I was told and watched her labouring over getting the letters down. She looked up and said, 'Disappoint, spell it.'

I became thicker than a block of granite and said, 'I can't spell out loud. The only way I can do it is to write it down first.'

'You war quick enough wit Maureen's name,' she said.

'That's different,' I said. 'I had her name in my head. Please give me a minute and I'll have it for you.'

I took another jotter and pencil from my schoolbag and printed *desapont*, scratched over it, shaking my head and said, 'No, that's not right.' I looked across at her and said, 'Sorry, I'll get it this time,' and quickly scribbled *deerserpont*, looked at it with the pencil in my mouth, stared at it with squinted eyes and declared, 'Still not right.'

It was too much for her to bear. She reached across the table to grab me but I was just out of reach and in her frustration said, 'A tick little bastard that's what you are and yeh'll never be good for anything. Just like that so-called family of yours, and that mudder of yours, bringing you into this wurld in her forties. Write that wurd again and do it right this time or I'll tump the lard outta you.'

'I'm sorry,' I said, with downcast eyes, 'the teacher says I'm a good speller.'

'Shut up and write the fuckin' wurd,' she said.

I knew I had gone far enough, but I couldn't resist printing *disappoynt*. I looked across at her and said, 'I've got it, that's it! That was a hard word.' She pulled the jotter across to her and told me to make a pot of tea. I gave her a few more mis-spelt words as the kettle was coming to the boil and by the time I handed her the mug of tea, she was finishing off.

It wasn't the first or last time she criticised my mother and relations. It hurt at first, but my consolation was that she never really knew my mother and she certainly did not know any of my relations, or me. She would never know my mind.

***

My second year with the Kennys started on a high. Theresa came home from Bray after a shopping spree and said, 'I've bought Peter a lovely tricycle and it will be delivered tomorrow. You can ride it to Bray for the shopping.'

She had arranged with Margaret to take care of Peter until after the trike had been delivered. The van arrived, she signed the delivery note and I helped her unpack it. It looked beautiful, red with silver mudguards and a bell on the handlebars. Oh! How I wished it belonged to me. She put it in the front room and told me to go over and bring Peter back with me. When he saw the tricycle he stood stock still staring at it.

Theresa said, 'That's yours, son, but listen to me now, John's going to use it every Friday morning to do the shopping an' there's to be no cryin' or cuttin' up about it. Deyeh understand?'

The rest of the afternoon was taken up with him getting used to his present, with a lot of encouragement from his mother and me looking on with envy. It was obvious the trike was a bit big for him, but determination was winning through. He fell off a few times but got right back on again.

Obviously she had not told Pat that she was going to buy it because he asked who owned it when he got home and Peter roared, 'I dooo!'

'I hope to God we can afford it,' he said.

Theresa responded, 'A course we can, it's only two shillings a week, an' besides, it'll save money on bus fares because young John's going to ride it for the shopping so there it is.'

'Is it big enough for that?' he asked, looking at me with that silent communication we had developed, and once he saw the glint in my eyes he said, 'I suppose it is at that.'

So began a pleasurable episode in my life, freewheeling down the lanes and pedalling along to town once a week. Being so small, I could ride the tricycle comfortably. There is no doubt about it. That was freedom.

The big drawback was that when I attached one of the shopping bags to the handlebars and put the other on the back the trike became very sluggish and difficult to ride. The trip to town was fun, but the return journey was hard work – but still much easier than having to carry the bags.

Nearing the end of my second year of misery with Theresa I thought I had the measure of her. There wasn't much I didn't know about her strange behaviour, the singing, the lip pursing, the nail biting and the agitated strutting around. I had learned to get out of the way when I saw the warning signs.

One morning she got up earlier than usual and caught me off guard. 'The fuckin' fire's nearly out,' she roared, grabbing me with one hand and punching my shoulder with the other. I managed to get out of her grasp and that seemed to drive her mad. She grabbed me again and punched me in the belly, which took the wind out of me and I dropped out of her grasp and fell to the floor but it didn't stop her. She proceeded to kick me anywhere she could until I lost consciousness. *Bastard* was the word that I shall never forget, because it was the word she used throughout the attack until I passed out.

I came to in the chair by the fire with a throbbing headache and feeling pain all over my body. She was standing over me, and when I looked up at her she said, 'Let that be a lesson to you to do as you're told.'

I stared her straight in the eyes and said, 'I've never told anyone about you beating and kicking me. You can go ahead and do it again if you like, but if you do I'll go to the guards and report you.'

'Shut your fuckin' mouth,' she said. 'That's the thanks I get for taking you in when nobody else would have you.'

'I'll have to go and lie down,' I said, 'I feel dizzy.'

She never said a word as I went to my room. I didn't care anyway. My mind was made up to run away just as soon as I felt strong enough and the opportunity showed itself.

I lay on the bed trying to get over the beating and thinking of where I was going to run to and then I fell asleep.

I don't know how long I slept but it had done me good. I woke up with aches and pains and could barely see through my right eye, but my mind was clear. I was going to get away from that mad woman, and with that in mind I felt better. I went into the front room and there she sat scorching herself by the fire. 'Willya have a sup of tea and a cheese sandwich?' she asked.

'Yes please, I'm hungry,' I said.

'Good,' she said, 'get that mirror out of our bedroom and take a look at yerself.'

I did so and wasn't surprised to see I had a black eye and a split lip. Ah, I thought, you weren't so careful this time. How will you explain this, you old bitch?

I knew she would come up with something, and she did.

She handed me the sandwich and put the cup of tea down by my side. 'Thank you,' I said. 'Where's Peter?'

'Out playing,' she said, 'and it's just as well, we have to have a chat.' I gave her an expressionless look and waited for what she had to say. 'Well,' she said, 'we don't want anyone knowing our business. I hit you because you let me down this morning. Remember when I told you I'd bate that bad habit of pissin' the bed outa yeh? I did, didn't I? You don't do it anymore.'

I remained silent and she went on, 'It's like that, the bating I gev you will remind you to keep the fire up. As I said, we don't want anyone knowin' our business, not even Pat, so we'll say you fell when you were down in the glen. Remember that and we'll get on better.'

'I will,' I said.

When Pat came home and saw the state of me he declared, 'My good God! What in heaven's name happened to you son?'

'I fell,' I said and then Theresa cut in, 'Cantya see the boy's in shock, he's had a terrible fall in the glen, no more questions now, give him a bit a peace.'

'Just a minute woman,' he said. 'How do you feel, John? That eye of yours looks terrible, is it hurting you?'

'Yes,' I replied, 'it's throbbing and my head feels like it's splitting.'

Before he had a chance to say a word Theresa said, 'It looks worse dan it did when yeh came home an if you're no better be dinnertime tamorrow, it'll be off to the doctor me boyo.' Pat nodded approval and said no more.

I never did go to the doctor, and four days later she said, 'It's about time you went down to the glen and get the sticks, you've had enough time lazin' about.'

'Right,' said I with a smile. I casually walked out of the house with my heart racing at the thought of what I was going to do.

When I got out of sight I took a short cut through the fields to the County Brook, where I hoped I would see Paschal, but when I got to the bog I was overcome with doubts and fear at what I had done already, so I sat down amongst some bushes to rest and think what my next move should be.

I decided to go straight to Kathleen O'Toole's house, where Paschal lived. I knocked on the door and she opened it, saying with surprise, 'John, it's yourself, my God, what's happened to you? Come in.'

As I stepped in I asked if Paschal was in. 'No,' she said, 'he's at work and he may be working late, if not, he should be home about six o'clock. Now, tell me what happened to you?'

'A fall,' I said. 'Can I please wait to see if he comes home at six?'

'Certainly,' she said.

About ten minutes later there was a knock on the door and there stood Pat Kenny. 'Ah, John, I'm glad I found you,' he said. 'Theresa is very worried about you and wants you to come home.' He turned to Kathleen and explained that his wife and I had had a little falling out earlier in the day, but she was worried sick about anything happening to me so the quicker we got home the better. She readily agreed.

We said our goodbyes and when we were outside he said, 'You're still limping and that face of yours doesn't look any better. We'll walk slowly. Tell me the truth now, you didn't have a fall in the glen, did you?'

'No,' I said, 'Theresa gave me a good hiding and I've had enough of her assaults so I decided to run away and see what Paschal could do for me, even if it meant going into Artane.'

He stopped and said, 'Tell me what's been going on from start to finish.'

I started telling him the whole story as we walked along at a snail's pace and still hadn't finished by the time we were nearing the house. He put his big hand on my shoulder and said, 'Theresa never listens to anything I say, so I say very little, but mark my words son, she'll bloody well listen to me this time.' I had never heard him speak like that before and it helped to bolden me up for whatever was to come when we got in.

As we entered the house Theresa leapt out of her chair yelling, 'Yabloodylittlebastard!'

Pat walked across the room to prevent her getting to me. He put his hand on her shoulder and said calmly, 'Theresa, John has told me all about what's been going on here. It's a good job he didn't tell Miss O'Toole about it or the guards would be here now to lock you up for cruelty. Maybe that would do you good. I'll tell you one thing and that's not two, you're to leave the boy alone from now on or you'll have me to answer to. I've a good mind to call the guards out to you now. That's to be the end of it! And now you can make John and me some cheese sandwiches.'

'I will in me arse!' she replied.

'To hell with you,' he said, 'I'll make them myself.'

I just could not believe how Pat had changed from the quiet person I thought I had known. Theresa was clearly shocked too. She kept quiet and fussed over Peter, who was howling on her lap. Silence, and then there was a knock on the door and in came Mrs Gormley.

She set her sights on me and exclaimed, 'Oh dear, what on earth has happened to you John?'

Before I had a chance to get a word out, Theresa said, 'Ah sure wouldn't you know it missis, he fell down the sandpit again an' frightened the life outta me when he dragged himself home. I kep him in bed for the last tree days an kep putting poultices over his bad eye an he's on the mend now.'

'How do you feel now John?' asked Margaret.

'Much better now, thank you Mrs Gormley,' I replied with a big smile.

'That's good to hear son,' she said with a serious look on her face.

'Indeed he's much better today,' said Pat. We played cards after that, but I guessed Margaret hadn't been fooled.

Theresa went to Bray the next day and returned a few hours later with several shopping bags and quickly said, as she put them down on the table, 'C'mere, I got you a few tings, look in that bag.' I opened the bag and oh! what a surprise, there were two pairs of long socks and a pair of jeans, long-legged! I felt like a man already. They were the first pair of long trousers I ever had. The clever oul hoor was sweetening me up.

'They're miles too long in the legs,' she said. 'We'll go over to Gormleys and see if she can do your trousers. If so, you can wear them rightaway. How's that?'

At the Gormleys a short while later, Margaret smiled and asked me, 'Do you like your new jeans, son?'

I was beaming brighter than an Irish lighthouse and said,

'Yes, Mrs Gormley.'

'Well then,' she said, 'you just take them into the Brendan's room, put them on and we'll see how much I'll have to turn them up.' I was in to the room and changed in record time. Margaret pinned up the legs and told us she would do the job there and then, it wouldn't take long. I could have kissed her, and I noticed that Theresa had a grin on her face.

Betty made us all a cup of tea while Margaret was working, and in no time at all I was wearing my brand new jeans and feeling ten feet tall. We left shortly afterwards, with Peter agitating, probably because of all the attention I had been getting. He quietened down when his mother presented him with a new teddy bear.

We were only in a short while when Maureen and Paschal arrived. When she saw me, Maureen pulled me to her and asked, 'What in the name of God has happened to your face?'

'I had a fall down the glen,' I replied.

Paschal said, 'I'm sorry I wasn't at home when you came to see me yesterday. Was there anything in particular you wanted to talk to me about?'

I shook my head, thinking, you're a bloody eejit if you can't work it out. 'No,' I said, 'I wanted to see my old home again and I was hoping I might see you too.'

Maureen wanted to know more about my accident, and that took both Theresa and me by surprise.

I gave Theresa a piercing look and said, 'I was standing on a high pile of sand and the next thing I knew I was lying on my back in the bottom of the sandpit with a terrible headache, and there was a lot of pain in my right leg, right side and shoulder. I still have a bit of pain in my side but I'm much better now.'

'Yes,' said Theresa, 'he's much better today. I'll give it another day or two and if there's no further improvement I'll take him to see the doctor.'

'Yes,' said Paschal, 'that's the best thing to do.'

***

The next morning I awoke expecting another dreary day. Theresa called for her tea as usual, but as I handed her the cup she said, 'I'll be getting up after I drink this, I'm going to Bray again this morning and I want to be off nice an early, you can mind Peter, I'll be back about four o'clock. You're standing straighter today an' you look well enough to me, so there'll be no need to see the doctor.'

Soon she was up, powdered and lipsticked with another nice flowered dress on. She cooked her own breakfast, fed Peter and was away. Peter was whingeing but I ignored him. I made the beds and tidied the house, so the rest of the day was my own until she got back. Peter went out to play with Eamonn Gormley in the lane, and a short while later Margaret came across to invite me over for a cup of tea and a piece of chocolate cake. I never had the opportunity of going over to the Gormleys' house for more than a few minutes when Theresa sent me with a message, and it was only because she was away that I could enjoy the luxury of having tea and cake with Margaret.

She filled two mugs with tea and placed a plate with a big chunk of cake in front of me and then sat down beside me.

'John,' she said, 'I have suspected for a long time that Theresa has been mistreating you by the way she never allows you out to play, and when she does send you to school you have to rush home and go down to the glen for sticks when all the other children are out enjoying themselves. I had a suspicion she was beating you, but I wasn't sure. I want to know if you really had an accident. Whatever you tell me will be strictly between the two of us.'

I opened up to Margaret that day and told her almost everything. She found it hard to believe that Pat didn't know what was going on even though I tried to convince her. I must have rambled on for at least a half-hour without looking at her, and when I did, I was shocked to see her crying.

I apologised with all my heart, and then became very scared in case I had upset her too much and she might be inclined to challenge Theresa.

'You poor boy,' she said. 'I'm glad I wrote to the NSPCC.'

'Did you really?' I asked.

'Yes I did,' she said. 'I thought about writing to them for a long time and put it off time and again because I wasn't sure how you would come out of it. I knew you were very unhappy, and after seeing you in the state you were in the other day I finally put pen to paper, so be prepared for a visit from an officer, but not a word to herself or anyone else.'

'Thank you,' I said. 'I hope when the officers come they will take me away from her and I don't care where they put me.'

She nodded, smiled and said, 'Well son, you've got your head screwed on right. I'll keep my eyes and ears open for you and I swear that not a word of what you have told me will pass these lips – but it's only for your sake that I'm not down the road for the guards to have that mad woman put behind bars. You are a very intelligent young man and you will do well for yourself. You are always welcome here, and if you ever need to talk about anything at all, I'll be here for you, don't you forget that.'

I was actually into my second week of continued attendance at school when I returned one afternoon to find a pot-bellied, balding old man sitting by the fire opposite Theresa. She made a big show of welcoming me home and said, 'It's himself, John Mahon.'

He turned to look at me through little pig eyes, lazily got out of the chair and said, 'C'mere bhoy.' I stood still, and he moved closer to me, saying, 'I won't ate you, stand still bhoy.'

He tousled my hair, looked down the back and front of my shirt and said, 'Sit down lad, I want to ask you a few questions.'

I sat and he asked, 'Do you like living with this nice woman and the family?'

I felt angry and then brave. I knew who he was, and from the way he asked me that question in front of Theresa I knew he wasn't going to be any good to me. I looked at the watch chain across his big belly and remained silent until he said, 'Look at me, are you deaf or what?' I looked him in the eye and noticed that his pudgy red cheeks were even redder, and he said, 'I asked you a question bhoy, answer me.'

'Yes,' I said.

'Good,' he said. 'Are you getting plenty to ate and drink?'

'Yes,' I said.

'Well, I'm Mister Heggarty from the NSPCC. We had a letter saying you were badly treated and that's why I'm here. Are you badly treated?'

I gave him a piercing look and answered, 'No.'

He nodded his head and said, 'I'm sorry for disturbing you, ma'am. Whenever the department receives such letters

66

we have to respond to them. Thank you for the tea, you won't be seeing me again.'

She walked out the door with him and they talked for a while before he waddled up the lane and got into his car.

'You took your fucking time answering him,' she said. 'Anyone'd tink you didn't have a good home here.'

'It wasn't that,' I said. 'I didn't know who he was and you're always telling me to keep my mouth shut.'

'I'll tellya what,' she said, 'I'll find out who wrote dem lies if it's the last ting I do. I'll tear them asunder, be it man, woman or baste!'

She raged on when Pat came home. He never said a word, and I went to bed for the first time without asking her permission, my first act of open rebellion.

A month or so later, on a bright August Sunday morning, she was up before the cocks crowed or the lark had a chance to get a warble out and declared, 'It's such a grand day, we'll all go to Enniskerry an' have a great time.'

'Doing what, may I ask?' said Pat. 'Annytingatall,' she replied and then broke into 'The yellow rose of Texas'. Pat gave me a worried look. I just raised my eyebrows and gave him a nod. Peter was in a gleeful mood, obviously getting the vibes from his mother. She had her way. We set out on foot after Pat had checked the livestock. We walked around the village for a while and then she gave me a pound note to get us four ice creams from Windsor's shop.

The shop was crowded and there was a long queue outside so a fair bit of time passed before I joined them on a seat underneath the town clock. 'What the fuck kep yeh?' she snarled.

'A big queue,' I replied, handing her the change.

We ate our ice creams and all of a sudden she jumped up and shouted, 'I fuckinwell want to go home,' and started ripping her blouse off. Pat put his arms around her and she violently shook him off. He grabbed her again and it seemed like all the fight had gone out of her. She leaned against him and he managed to steer her out of the village and up a lane which led to some fields and a short cut to Fassaroe. As we made our way she was becoming more erratic, trying to rip her clothes off, squealing and roaring incoherent nonsense. It was taking him all his of time and strength to hold her, half carry and half drag her along. Peter was bawling and I was scared. I held onto his hand tightly as we walked along behind them. He got her home eventually and by that time she had become zombie-like.

Pat asked me to run over to the Gormleys and ask Margaret to please come across. The doctor arrived about an hour later and diagnosed a nervous breakdown. He sedated her and some time later the ambulance arrived to take her to a hospital and Pat had to accompany her. 'Don't you worry about a thing Pat,' said Margaret, 'everything will be fine here.'

He returned four hours later looking worn out. Margaret had gone home and Peter was asleep in bed. I put the kettle on as he flopped into Theresa's chair, which was out of bounds to the both of us, but she was out of sight now.

I thought it strange that he chose to sit in her chair. Was he rebelling in some way? As we drank our tea he said, 'The doctor told me that Theresa is likely to be in hospital for about a month, so I would like you to look after Peter and run the house as best as you can. I know it's a lot to ask, but I've no one else to turn to.'

Everything changed for the better for me from then on. I could play the wireless when I liked and there were no more poes to empty, but it took a long time to make Peter understand that things had changed and it was not in his best interest to try to bully me. I worked out a routine for doing the housework. The floors were washed or scrubbed on Monday and Wednesday. Clothes and one sheet and one pillowcase from each bed were washed on Tuesday, and Friday was shopping day. On Thursday evenings, Pat and I made out a list of what groceries and things we needed from Bray. I left Peter with Margaret Gormley and enjoyed cycling to town. Instead of Peter's trike I was now riding Theresa's bicycle, which she had recently decided to let me use. The trike had served me well, but the bike was much better.

She would have thrown a fit if she could have seen the changes in the shopping list since she went away. There was no longer the need to buy white bread and margarine for him and me and brown bread and butter for Theresa and Peter. All three of us ate the same. Butter for all! A few of the other luxuries were twenty Players for him along with his regular weekly ounce of plug tobacco, a Swiss roll, sixpence-worth of broken biscuits and the *Wicklow People* newspaper. We were living on the high side!

I was happier than I had ever been since moving to the Kennys.

Pat continued to visit the hospital every Sunday for several weeks and each time when he came home it was always the same, 'Not much change for the better.'

Good, I used to think. I won't lose any sleep over her.

Pat, Peter and I were getting on very well, apart from Peter asking for his mother occasionally. The weeks became months, and then after about three months Pat came home from a visit and told us that Theresa was coming home the following week. I asked him if she was well now.

'Musha, John, I don't know what to think,' he said. 'She doesn't seem any better to me.'

She arrived in an ambulance the following Wednesday when Pat was at work, but thankfully Margaret Gormley saw the arrival and came right over, which saved me some of the embarrassment of the reunion. Peter was all over her and I was apprehensive. While they were talking over a cup of tea, I slipped into the bedroom and put clean sheets on the bed and checked to make sure the poe was in place, and then silently slipped into the front room again. Margaret and Betty left us, and there we sat opposite each other without a word exchanged. She seemed morose for quite a while and then she surprised me by asking would I like a cup of tea. 'Yes please,' was all I could say.

The rest of the afternoon seemed to drag on forever until Pat got home. There were no hugs or kisses. He just said, 'Ah! You're home, I hope you're feeling better.'

Theresa was very silent at first, and this lasted for about a month. Then she gradually started getting back to some of her old hateful ways, picking arguments with Pat, continually calling me a 'little bastard', usually accompanied by half-hearted attempts at a punch or a kick, most of which I dodged, and strange for her, she never pursued me. That was a change for the better.

***

Peter started school in September 1956, when I was thirteen

years and nine months old. Theresa accompanied us on his first day and I was dreading going back after yet another long absence, but I secretly hoped the next few months would be my last of having to put up with the embarrassment of feeling so lost amongst my contemporaries because there was no chance of me catching up on the lessons. Peter was missing his mother for the first few days but then he started to get used to the other children and was settling in nicely. I started to pick up a bit too. I became more relaxed both at school and in the Kennys' home. I didn't have to run back from school any more because of Peter, and I enjoyed strolling home at a leisurely pace. I didn't have to go to the glen either. Life was becoming a bit of a luxury.

This went on for about a month until one evening Theresa told me that she wanted me to stay home from school for a few days to help her prepare the spare room because two of her cousins, Seamus and Michael, were coming up from Wexford to do some plastering work for a few weeks in Dublin and she was going to put them up.

'Who is going to take Peter to school?' I asked.

'He can go with Eamonn Gormley and the Laceys,' she replied. I didn't know it then but that was the end of my school days.

The cousins arrived in a battered old van one morning. They told Theresa they expected to get the job done within a few weeks and that would be that. Theresa decided they should have a single room each, so I had to share the large bedroom with her, Peter and Pat. Oh, how I hated that. I felt totally trapped, no longer able to enjoy the solitude of my little room, but the worst thing was when she got up to move her bowels in the dead of night. That really made me furious, but there wasn't a thing I could do about it.

I didn't see much of her cousins during their four-week stay. They were up at dawn and back after dark, and the little I did see of them didn't impress me. When they left I went into Michael's room out of curiosity and had a look around. I saw a balled-up newspaper under the bed. I picked it up to find it was full of human excrement and the stink was overpowering.

I decided to leave it there until Theresa came back from the Gormleys' and anxiously waited to see her reaction. What an experience that was. She put on a performance, ranting, raving, swearing, strutting around and kicking anything in sight. I cautiously moved out of range and was gleeful at the sight of how mad it had made her.

I was hopeful she might suggest that I could move back to my own room, but not a word was said and I wasn't brave enough to ask. She calmed down after a while and said, 'Get rid of that fucker's dirt, saw up the sticks and don't be back here for two hours.'

I was off with the offending package, which I chucked as far as I could into the hedge, cut up a few blocks and then went out into the sunlight of a blustery day. How good it was to be out by myself. I rambled through the green fields down past the disused sandpits and on to my favourite spot by the river, which flowed down from the Wicklow mountains, past my old home, on to where I was sitting and then down to the sea.

I sat and thought about getting a job. It was just two months to my fourteenth birthday and I was optimistic – hadn't John Gormley got a job in the Royal Hotel in Bray, and Brendan his brother was a messenger boy in Liptons. He rode a big bicycle, which he was allowed to take home every evening. I once asked him if I could have a go on it and he said sure, but he thought it would be too big for me. He lowered the saddle as far as it would go but it was no use. I couldn't get my leg over the crossbar, let alone reach the pedals. All the messenger bikes were the same size as far as I could see, so that job was out. Still, it wasn't the only job. I was sure to get something.

***

My long-awaited fourteenth birthday came on 15 December 1956, and I was full of hope for the future. Margaret and Betty Gormley came over to play cards that evening and the talk got around to my birthday.

Theresa said, 'John wants to leave school and get a job. I think it would do him a lot of good. What do you tink, missis?'

'I can't see it doing him any harm at all,' replied Margaret.

Buoyed by Margaret's reply, I suggested that I should go to Bray and look at the job advertisements in the shop windows.

'That's very enterprising,' said Margaret, 'and don't forget the newspaper ads.'

Then it hit me, I would surely be in for it when the Gormleys had gone, for saying so much in front of them. But it wasn't as bad as I had thought it was going to be.

Theresa roared, 'So now you're going to tell me what you'll do and won't do. As long as you're in this house, you'll fuckinwell do as I say and dontyaforgetit!'

But after Peter had gone to school the next morning, Theresa said, 'You might as well ride my bicycle in to Bray an' have a look in them windows, you might find yourself a job.' That was sweet music to my ears. I was elated. It was a cold morning so I wrapped up well and was soon on my way.

I went to the two shops that had adverts in the windows, but there was nothing for me on either of the boards except a messenger boy's job in the Home and Colonial. I knew that wouldn't suit me unless their bicycles were smaller than the ones Liptons used. I strolled past the shop and there were two bikes outside. They were the same size as the one Brendan rode. There was no point asking about the job.

Four months of fruitless searching for jobs passed until one afternoon Margaret Gormley came over highly excited and said, 'Missis, John! My son John has just told me there's a job going in the International Hotel in Bray. They're looking for a pageboy and I think that you would have a good chance of getting it, John. What do you think?'

Theresa cut in, 'Indeed, that's grand altogether but do you tink he's got a chance atall, wit him bein' so small?'

Margaret said, 'Of course he's got every chance. Height or size doesn't come into it. They prefer smaller young men for that job. He's smart and intelligent and when he smiles at them with those dimples he'll capture their hearts.'

I was embarrassed, but I was taking it all in, especially about the smile. If Margaret thought it would be in my favour then that's what I would do. I would smile until my jaws ached if necessary.

Theresa interrupted my thoughts by asking about the wages.

'Oh, I don't know,' replied Margaret, 'it won't be more than a pound or so, that's what my John started on, but it's a

72

great opportunity. He said that if John gets down there between half past eight and nine tomorrow morning and asks for Miss Ryan, the manageress, he should stand a good chance.'

Sleep didn't come easy that night. I tossed and turned and heard every little sound including Theresa's bowel movements, which infuriated me more than ever. I dozed off for a while and then lay awake for about an hour before I decided to get up.

I heard Pat getting up, so I put the kettle on and presented him with a mug of tea as he came into the room. He whispered, 'Thanks John, good morning. I don't suppose you got much sleep last night. It's not an easy thing to do when you go to bed with something on your mind.'

I nodded and told him I was very nervous, but I was going to do my best.

'Well,' he said, 'that's all any of us can do. I'd be frightened too if I had to go into one of them big places, but the way to look at it is, they can't eat you alive and all they can say is no, we don't need you. And if they do, there'll be plenty more opportunities in the future. You'll get on well in life, son.'

By eight o'clock I was at the bus stop, dressed in my smartest clothes. My mind was racing with thoughts of what questions I would be asked and how I should answer them. I decided I would try not to think about it any more, and instead I started thinking of Nellie and what she would make of it all.

I got off the bus in the Quinsboro Road and walked slowly towards the big hotel in the distance. It was only 8.30 so I decided to hold on for fifteen minutes. It seemed like hours before I walked up the steps and approached the front door, which was opened by an old man dressed in a purple frock coat with gold braid around the collar and four rings on each sleeve.

He stood erect and looked very tall as he looked down at me and asked, 'What do want boy?'

'I've come to see Miss Ryan about the pageboy's job, sir,' I replied.

'Indeed, follow me,' he said. He led me through the foyer with its columns, beautifully papered walls, mirrors and paintings to the reception desk, dodging all the people milling about in the area. All Ireland's here, I thought.

He said to the smiling blonde receptionist, 'Miss O'Connor, this lad is here to see Miss Ryan about the pageboy's job.'

'Thank you, Andy,' she said, smiled at me and said, 'Excuse me for a minute, I must attend to this lady.'

I looked behind me and saw a grey-haired lady dressed in a brown suit with an orange scarf draped around her neck fastened with a big golden brooch. I stepped aside and stood a few feet away in order to allow her to transact her business in private.

A very attractive tall blonde lady came out of the reception and introduced herself. 'I am Miss Ryan, the manageress, please come with me.' She led the way into a room full of small polished tables with four upholstered chairs around each. She closed the door and pulled out two chairs from a table saying, 'Miss O'Connor has told me that you have come about the pageboy's job.'

'Yes miss,' I said.

'Well,' she said, 'tell me a bit about yourself.'

I began, 'My name is John Joseph Mahon, I am nearly fourteen and a half years old, I can read and write fairly good, I know how to be polite and I did have a job before but only for a short time thinning turnips.'

She smiled and said, 'John, look at this table. Imagine it's all sticky with beer and coffee stains. How would you go about cleaning it?'

I thought, that's easy, and quickly said, 'I would get a bucket of warm soapy water with two clean cloths, one to wash it with and the other to polish it.'

'Good,' she said, smiling broadly. 'I saw how you moved away from reception when Mrs MacNamara needed to do some business. That was the right thing to do.'

A point for me, I thought. 'Thank you, miss,' I said with a smile, remembering what Margaret had said.

'I can offer you the job,' she said, 'but the hours are very long, from 7.30 am to 7 pm with a break from 1 pm to 3 pm every afternoon except for when we get busy, then you would be expected to work through to 8 pm. The pay is one pound per week, we cannot pay overtime, but we will arrange time off in lieu when it is convenient to do so. You can live in or out, your meals and accommodation are free, and you will have one day off every week.'

'Thank you,' I said. 'I live in Fassaroe, which is roughly three miles from here and the bus only covers half of the way. I think it would be better to live in.'

'Yes,' she said, 'if your parents agree.'

'I live with foster parents,' I said. 'I will have to ask them, but I don't think they will mind.'

'What religion are you, John?' she asked.

'Catholic,' I said.

'You can tell them you will be given time off every Sunday morning and holy days of obligation to go to mass and you will have one full day off every week. You will get tips from some of the guests and visitors, but you must never appear to be looking for them. If you did you would be dismissed instantly.'

'I understand,' I said.

'Good,' she said. 'Now, uniform, I think we have some small monkey jackets that will fit you. Do you know how tall you are?'

'No miss,' I replied.

'I think you are about four feet five, nice and compact,' she said with a smile. I felt my face burning as she said, 'You will need a pair of black trousers, white shirts, a black clip-on bow tie and a pair of black shoes or boots. You will have to supply them yourself.'

'Yes miss,' I said.

'Do you think you could start work a week from today at 9 am? That is the 30th of May.'

'Yes miss,' I replied as calmly as I could. I could hardly remember leaving the place, but I think I would have been capable of doing somersaults or any other kind of saults that might have been asked of me. I felt so good. Five minutes later I found myself sitting down on a wooden bench looking out over the grey choppy Irish Sea and thinking I'm free from that hoor at last.

I got back at 1 pm and found Peter and Eamonn Gormley playing marbles in the lane. I gave each of them a sugar stick and then went inside to find Theresa and Margaret drinking tea. They both looked at me, but before either of them had a chance to say anything I declared, 'I got it! I got the job!'

Margaret couldn't conceal her delight. She jumped up,

grabbed me, hugged me tightly, kissed me and exclaimed, 'Oh, thank God!'

Theresa gave her a strange look and said, 'I wouldn't take it that far, missis.'

Questions were being fired at me in rapid succession so I waited until they had quietened down and then explained the whole thing in detail, but with emphasis on the need for the black trousers, bow tie, shoes and shirts. Then I made the point again about having to live in and watched Theresa closely to see what reaction that would get.

Margaret came to my aid, telling us how little she had seen of her son John since he had started work in the Royal Hotel, over a year ago. 'You know, missis,' she said, 'it's woeful to think of the long hours the hotel staff have to put in for the miserable pay they get in this country. Sure if it wasn't for the few tips they get the job wouldn't be worth doing at all. Still though, my John has learned a great deal since he started working there. They pick up a lot you know, from all the posh people and all them foreigners too.'

Theresa looked at me and said, 'Well, we'll have to get you the tings you need but it'll cost a lot an' you only going to be earning a pound a week, it'll take an awful long time to pay it off. Acourse we won't be able to get a pair a trousers to fitya.'

'There's an old pair of John's that I can cut down to fit,' said Margaret.

'That's very good of you,' said Theresa.

Margaret gave me a sly wink as she left. Everything seemed to be going my way. How could I lose?

'There's a few tings we have to get straight,' said Theresa. 'Don't you tink that because you're starting work and livin' in dat place you'll be outa my control. I'm responsible for you until you're sixteen an dat's a year an a half away. So listen to me. If you havta live in dat's all right but you'll havta come home on your day off an' bring any tips you get witya.'

I wondered if she would let me keep any money from my pay and speculated that if she allowed me five shillings a week I would be well off and so would she. She was already getting ten shillings a week or maybe more for me, and with a further fifteen shillings from my pay she should be very happy.

I was one happy boy that evening. I sat down to a plate of

spuds, cabbage and lamb. I ate the spuds and cabbage and left the lamb.

'What's wrong wit the mate?' Theresa asked.

'Nothing,' I replied, 'I'm off meat.' Remembering the sight of the dead sheep and lambs had put me off, and it would play a big part in my decision to become a vegetarian later on.

Pat was delighted for me. He asked me a few questions about the hotel and I responded gladly – the grandeur of the place, the uniforms I had seen and all the rich people that were going around in there dressed in nice clothes, even the children.

We had just finished eating when there was a knock on the door and in walked Margaret with her daughter Betty, saying, 'God bless all here.'

'Him again!' I thought, and then I felt terribly guilty. Maybe there was a God and it was him who had convinced Miss Ryan that I was the man for the job.

I smiled, making sure Margaret would see my dimples.

'I have brought the trousers over to see what alterations we'll have to do to get this young man togged out,' she said, 'and as they say, we'll do it "be hook or be crook".'

She handed them to Theresa, who ordered me to try them on. I took them into the bedroom, put them on, and they were much too big, so it was with a sinking feeling that I stepped back into the front room.

Theresa commanded, 'Over here.'

She rolled the legs up, pulled the waist tight, shook her head and shoved me over to Margaret, who took a box of pins from her bag and said, 'Once we pin them to the size we need, I think we'll make a swanky job of them and it won't take any time at all to run them up on the machine.'

With that, she set about measuring me, pinning everywhere and marking with a special sort of chalk which I had seen the like of before when Paschal took a piece of it home from work. When she was finished, Margaret helped me get out of the carefully pinned-up garment and promised that she would have it ready the next day.

Sleep came easy for me that night, so easy in fact that I never heard Theresa's bowel-moving ritual or Pat getting up the next morning. Fortunately I was up before the Quare Wan shouted for her tea.

I got on with my daily routine, and things were back to normal. Betty came over later to ask Theresa if I could go over to her mother to get a final fitting on the trousers. Theresa looked at me and said, 'You heard the girl, get yourself over there.'

I ran across the road and Margaret came out to meet me with outstretched arms. She hugged me so tightly that I thought she'd squeeze the living daylights out of me, but it felt so good.

She released me and said, looking into my eyes, 'You've done it, young man, I'm proud of you – and now try these on.' She handed me the trousers and I looked at her. 'You can go into the boys' room,' she said. I whipped my short trousers off and was into the long ones in a flash. I just could not believe that they were the same as the baggy ones I had tried on the night before.

I was overjoyed when I returned to the living room and Margaret was all smiles as she saw how they looked on me and said, 'I could have taken them over, but I wanted to see you by yourself. Remember when I told you that things would change for the better. Well this is just the beginning of a new and better way of life for you. Just watch your p's and q's and don't get downhearted by what anyone says, especially Theresa. You've put up with enough from her.'

'I know she told you we had a visit from that old clown Heggarty,' I said.

'Yes,' she said, winking, 'if she ever gets her hands on whoever wrote that letter, she'll kill them. What was he like?'

'Useless,' I said.

**

The morning of 30 May 1957 dawned and the day got a little older before it was time for me to report for work. My emotions were a cocktail of nerves, apprehension, excitement, and fear as I walked up to the door of the International Hotel.

Andy opened it for me, saying, 'You're the new young fella starting today aren't you?'

'Yes sir,' I said.

He responded with a smile on his florid and wrinkled old face and said, 'Now son, there's no need to call me sir, I just work here, just as you'll be doing as soon as I tell Miss Ryan you're here. Remind me to tell you about the time I walked all the way from Quebec to Montreal.'

I didn't have a clue what he was talking about and was very confused as Miss Ryan joined us and said, 'Good morning Andy, Good morning John.'

He saluted her and uttered one word, 'Ma'am.'

'Good morning Miss Ryan,' I said.

'So here you are John. Are you nervous?' she asked.

'Yes, very,' I said.

'It's quite natural, but you will find that we have a very good staff here and they will help you to get settled in. You will meet Declan, the other boy, soon. He has been working with us for four weeks now and he's doing a good job. I hope you will get on well together. I will take you to the linen room and get a nice jacket for you.'

She introduced me to Maisie the linen keeper, a plump red-haired young woman with a serious look on her face who looked me up and down and said, 'I doubt we have anything small enough to fit him, but leave him with me and I'll see what I can find. I might have to put a few stitches in one of the small ones.'

'You're a gem, Maisie,' said Miss Ryan. 'I don't know what I would do without you. Will you please arrange for John to have a cup of tea in the staff room and then please ask Declan to show him to my office at 10.30.'

When she had gone, Maisie got as close to a smile as I would ever see from her and asked, 'How old are you, John?'

'Fourteen and a half,' I replied.

'My God boy, you're very small but you're very good looking,' she said.

I felt sure I wasn't going to like Maisie, but I remembered what Margaret had told me about not minding what some people would say and watching my p's and q's. So when she produced a bundle of white jackets and told me to try them on I obediently tried on several before I found one that was a better fit than all the others. 'Ah, that's better,' she said. 'I'll put a few tucks in the sides and turn up the sleeves an' Fanny's yer aunt!'

A very pretty girl in a light blue uniform dress came in to collect clean sheets and pillowcases. She had brown hair over a pale olive face and beautiful brown eyes. Maisie said, 'Angela, this is John, he's starting work today. Would you ever take him down to the staff room for me, and if you see young Declan tell him I want to see him.'

Angela led the way along a corridor, down a flight of stairs and along a poorly lit winding corridor with a number of doors on either side, 'The living quarters,' she explained. She told me that we were in the heart of the building now, where as well as the accommodation there was the boiler room and workshops. She ushered me into a brightly lit room where a number of men and women of varying ages were seated at long tables, some eating breakfast, others just chatting. Almost all of them looked towards us as Angela said, 'This is John, and he's starting work today.' I was acknowledged with hellos, the nodding of heads and smiles, but there were a couple of young men far too busy studying the racing pages to be disturbed. Angela asked me if I would like tea or coffee.

I felt adventurous and decided on coffee, as I had never tasted it before. It tasted good. 'I've got to get back to cleaning the rooms,' she said. 'See you later.'

I felt very self-conscious and uncomfortable sitting there with several eyes on me, but fortunately Declan bounced in and introduced himself.

'I'm going to get something to drink,' he said.

I watched him as he walked away and thought he looked very smart in his uniform. The jacket had brass buttons down the front and a white glove hung from a shoulder lapel, and there was gold braid on each sleeve and down the sides of his trousers.

I guessed he was about six or seven inches taller than me and probably a bit older. His hair was dark and curly. He came back and sat beside me with a cup of something. 'We have to report to Miss Ryan's office in twenty minutes. Would you like a smoke?'

'No thanks,' I said, 'I don't smoke.'

We reported to Miss Ryan on the dot. She was typing at her desk and looked up as we knocked and entered.

'Please sit down,' she said. 'I have invited you both because John is not experienced in this business, so I will be expecting you to help him out in any way you can, Declan. Have you finished polishing the tables in the lounge yet?'

'Half of them, miss,' he replied.

'That's good,' she said. 'John will help you a little later. Now, be off with you and make those tables shine.'

She turned to me and said, 'I need to get your date of birth, address and next of kin and then we'll be finished.'

I gave her the details and she presented me with my white jacket and asked me to try it on. It fitted much better than before and she praised Maisie's handiwork and said she would get her to alter another couple.

In the lounge I found Declan looking out of the window. I glanced at the tables and saw that he had not done half, as he had told Miss Ryan, but only four of the sixteen.

He picked up his cloths and the Min furniture cream, poured some onto a tabletop and started to rub vigorously.

'I know an easier way,' I said. 'Can you please show me where I can get some hot soapy water and clean cloths?'

He led me to a cupboard with all sorts of cleaning materials and equipment. I found what I needed, poured a little liquid soap into the bucket and half-filled it with hot water. I washed four tables, dried them off and then put a small amount of Min cream on a cloth and polished them. He continued to do the job the hard way and I didn't care.

A tall fair-haired man came in and introduced himself as Jim Cox, the head porter.

Declan said, 'Jim, can I work between 1 and 3 pm today? I have to take my sister to the dentist at four o'clock.'

'I could have done with you this afternoon, but I'm sure we'll manage, go ahead. Please finish off here, I'm taking John away.'

I followed him out and he said, 'I'll show you where we change first, it's only a cubby hole under the stairs by the reception, but it's handy.' The first thing that caught my eye was a notice pinned to the wall – 'Activity, Efficiency, Co-operation and Fun, but Curly Headed Dividends are sure to come.'

Then he showed me around from the top to the bottom of the building and told me about my duties as we went. He introduced me to Mervyn, the hall porter on duty. A stocky grey-haired man who shook my hand and wished me good luck. I followed Jim down to the staff room and he asked if I would like a hot drink. 'Coffee, please sir,' I said.

'My name's Jim,' he said. 'You can call the owner of the hotel and his three sons, sir, and the guests of course, but it's first names for the rest of us.'

We sat down with our drinks and he asked me where I came from. I told him Fassaroe.

'I suppose you'll be living in,' he said. 'I'll see what room they're putting you in and show you later on. You'll be off from 1 to 3 pm this afternoon to do as you please and then it'll be you and me on afternoon teas. Nothing to worry about, I'll show you the ropes and you'll make a few bob.'

I spent my two hours off drinking lemonade and reading a newspaper down on the seafront and was ready for anything when I returned to work. Jim Cox was standing by the reception as I entered. I went straight to the closet for my jacket and he followed me.

'It's a bit quiet now,' he said, 'but we may be busy with the afternoon teas, which start in thirty minutes. We tend to get a lot of outsiders coming in. Sometimes it gets desperately busy. There's only you and me today so I'm going to show you how to write out the order chits. One copy goes to reception for billing and the other goes to Mrs Sand in the stillroom – she is the woman in charge there and her assistant is Rosie Reid. Make sure you always hand the orders to either one of them so they can't accuse you of not handing one in. When the guests have finished get their bill from reception and collect the money. I'll introduce you to the stillroom women.'.

When we entered the stillroom the first thing I noticed was how high the counter was. I could just rest my chin on it.

'Ladies,' Jim said, 'this is John Mahon our new boy, he'll be working with me this afternoon.'

'If he can reach the top of the counter to get the trays off,' said the bluey/grey-haired, chubby-faced, portly woman.

Jim ignored her comment and said, 'Mrs Sand, she's in charge here, and of course we musn't forget her able assistant Rosie.' She was a young girl with straight fair hair and a round face, a bit older than me, I thought. She wore glasses with thick lenses and I could tell she was shy because she blushed when Jim mentioned her name. Nevertheless, she reached across the counter, grabbed my hand and shook it with the strength of a ploughman. She was a strong country girl from the County Clare.

There was an announcement over the public address system, calling for 'Mr James Cox to report to reception please.'

I followed him along the hall and discovered that some new guests were booking in. While he took them up to their room I stayed at reception, where the short dark-haired woman on duty said, 'Your name is John, isn't it?'

'Yes miss,' I replied.

'I'm Miss Colgan, the assistant manageress. I hope you are settling in all right.'

As Jim had predicted, we were very busy with the afternoon teas. I only encountered one obstacle and that was the height of the stillroom counter, but I managed to improvise. I found that if I stood on my toes and stretched my arms as far as I could along the counter, I was able to pull the tray towards my chest for balancing as I picked it up and it worked perfectly.

In a lull, I said, 'Jim, I have been putting the bill face down on the table in front of the person that has given me the order, is that right?'

'Proper order,' he said. 'Of course, there will be times when you'll get a loudmouth in a group who will do the ordering and tell the others what they should and shouldn't have, but when it's paying-up time, most of them bastards sink into their chairs with not a peep out of them. Always make sure you stick the bill under their noses. But remember, do it as politely as you would to the more decent people.'

The rest of my working day went in a whirl, and before I knew it I was crossing the road to the railway station, where my bus left from. I had twenty-five minutes to wait before the next one left so I decided to go to the café with the jukebox in the Albert Walk and bought myself a Pepsi Cola with some of the tips I had made. I counted how much was left after paying for my drink and I still had five shillings. I couldn't believe how generous the customers had been and it certainly didn't seem like hard work to me. A song came on the jukebox. It was 'St Theresa of the roses', and the irony of that song wasn't lost on me. I boarded the bus for Fassaroe and for what I hoped was going to be my last night of having to sleep in the same room as the Kennys.

When I got off the bus I went into the bushes to put a sixpenny piece in my sock. That was one coin Theresa would never see.

I walked up the lanes feeling happier than I could ever remember and it obviously showed when I walked into the house because I got a warm smile from Pat and Theresa was inspired to say, 'You look like the cat dat swallyed the canary!'

I replied with a good deal of confidence that I'd had a great day. I looked directly at her and said, 'I made four shillings and sixpence in tips too.'

I think I was looking for some sort of approval from her, but there was none coming. She stayed as cold as she had always been towards me, and all she said was, 'Give it to me.'

I did, but it was money well wasted, because from then on she would get what I decided to give her. I thought of the sixpence that was in my sock and was sorry I hadn't kept more.

We discussed my travelling to and from work, and for the first time Theresa allowed me to speak without telling me to shut up. I explained that I had been told I might be expected to do overtime at very short notice and when the summer season started we would be very busy.

Pat asked what time I had to start tomorrow morning.

'Seven o'clock,' I lied, 'but there isn't a bus that early, so I'll have to leave here no later than six o'clock and I might have to run part of the way.'

'It'll be a very long day for you John,' he said.

This wasn't lost on her. 'They want a lot for a pound a week,' she said. 'Still an' all, there's mannies a young fella lookin' for work, you're lucky to have a job, you mind ya keepit! We'll havta tink of gettin' you a secondhand bike. Until then, you get home here as often as ya can and make sure you save the tips an' bring them home with a packet a twenty Sweet Afton when you come.'

I was braver now. So I chanced it further and suggested that I would ask the staff in the hotel if they knew of anyone with a bike for sale. I was expecting her opposition to that but to the contrary, she said, 'That's not a bad ting to do, but if yeh find one, tell me about it first.'

I was off at an ass's gallop as they say and there was no stopping me. 'I nearly forgot to tell you the most important thing,' I said. 'The manageress said it would be better if I lived in because she couldn't guarantee what hours of duty I might be expected to work, but she said I would definitely get one day off every week unless I was absolutely needed on that day.'

'Get home as often asya can,' was all she said.

'Home!' I thought. It might be yours missis, but it never has been mine.

***

The next morning I walked up to the door of the hotel with a confidence I had never known before. Andy opened it, smiling and standing straighter than a telegraph pole. 'So you're back for more today, young fella?'

'Yes Andy,' I said, 'I had a great day yesterday.'

'And long may it last, boy,' he said.

I excused myself and made my way to the staff room, where I saw Jim Cox sitting at a table by himself. I got a cup of coffee and a bowl of corn flakes and sat down beside him.

'Do you know where I might be able to buy a second-hand woman's bicycle?' I asked.

'Is it a woman's bike because they're without a crossbar?' he asked, smiling.

I nodded.

'Indeed, I know a man in this very room that's bound to fix you up.' With that, he addressed a dirty-looking man sitting at the next table. 'Bob, you wouldn't have a woman's bike for sale, would you?'

'Jim, it's you're lucky day,' said Bob. 'I have the very thing, it's a grand machine, a Raleigh, the best make. I done her up last week and the only thing she needs now is a lick of paint. I wouldn't take a copper less than two pounds ten shillings for her.'

'Jesus, Bob, you're a hard man,' said Jim. 'It's for young John here, he just started yesterday, he comes from out in the sticks and badly needs it.'

Bob responded, 'Well, two pounds is as low as I'd go.'

'We'll have a look at it later,' said Jim. 'Don't you be selling it before we do.'

As we headed for the reception area, Jim explained that Bob looked after the boiler and was also the general handyman and could turn his hand to anything. 'I'll bet you anything you like that the bike'll be in proper order,' he said, 'and he'll even ask you what colour you want it painted. I have to deliver the papers. Declan will do the brass and you can make a start on the tables in the lounge, and when he finishes he'll be in to help you.'

My head was spinning with excitement as I set about my task, and there were only three tables left to finish off when Declan languidly dragged himself in and flopped into a chair without a word. I carried on, ignoring him. He eventually stirred himself and made an attempt at cleaning the last table. I left him to it and walked out and down to the toilet.

I was on my way back to reception when Miss Ryan came around the corner, 'Good morning John,' she said, 'please see me in the office at 11 am.'

Jim and Mervyn were standing by the reception when I got there. Jim asked if I would like to have a look at Bob's bike, and led the way to the basement, where he stuck his head in to the boiler room and shouted for Bob.

Bob appeared from somewhere within, even dirtier than before, and said, wiping his brow with a black rag, 'I suppose you boys want to see the bike.' He took us to his workshop, which was very tidy and clean with all sorts of tools hanging on the walls, and over in the corner stood the object of my desire.

Bob said, 'Have a look at it, take it out here in the middle of the room, lad.'

I wheeled the bike over to the big bench, rested it there and stood back to get a good look at it.

'Well, what do you think of it?' asked Jim.

'It's just right for me but I haven't got any money yet.'

'There you are Bob,' said Jim, 'you've got a customer.'

'I'll tell you what we'll do,' said Bob. 'If you can pay me five shillings a week starting a week from today you can have it and I'll even paint it whatever colour you like. Two pounds, take it or leave it.'

'Of course, said Jim, if John was to pay up a bit quicker than the eight weeks, I suppose you'd knock a few shillings off?'

'No,' said Bob, 'but I'll throw in a light with a battery this very day.'

'I'll buy her,' I said.

'A sensible lad,' said Bob. 'What colour would you like her painted?'

'Red,' I replied instantly.

'Red it is then. I'll paint her today and you'll be riding around in style the day after tomorrow.'

I reported to Miss Ryan at eleven o'clock. I felt relaxed, despite being very excited at having made the first major decision in my life.

'I have arranged for a bed and a locker for you in a room with three other men,' she told me. 'Danny is a comis waiter, Michael is a waiter and "Buzz", Mr Dixon, is a lounge waiter. You are not obliged to live in, but you will have a place to wash and change.'

'I would like to live in, miss,' I said.

'Good.' she said. 'I hope you get on with the other three men and you will be comfortable. If you have any problems at all, please don't hesitate in coming to see me. You will be responsible for your own property and therefore you must be careful to lock away any valuables you have. Please ask Jim to show you to your room now.'

'Thank you miss,' I said.

I followed Jim down to my room in the basement, and as we stepped in I was disgusted to see the how untidy and dirty the room was. Clothes strewn all over the place, plates with dried-up food, cups and mugs with mould in them, rubbish bins full to overflowing. The smell of sweat and stinking socks permeated the air. None of the beds were made except one by the barred window. Thankfully it was mine. I immediately tried to prise the window open but it wouldn't budge. Jim then tried, but it was no use.

'I'll ask Bob to loosen it up a bit,' he said. 'Look at the state of this place! It's a bloody disgrace how some people choose to live.'

I agreed with him but decided to keep quiet and thought at least it's better than having to hear and smell Theresa on the poe.

I learned a lot more about the job that day, and made eight shillings and three pence in tips. I tried to remember the people who had given me the biggest tips. The big American who had patted my head and asked my age, which I told him grudgingly. The way I saw it, I was a working man now and therefore should not be patted on the head like a child, but the anger diminished as he placed a half-crown on my silver salver.

I didn't know it then, but I would have to get used to the way some people treated me like a child – not cruelly, but being affectionate towards me because of my diminutive size. But such well-meaning words and gestures would only help to build up my inferiority complex and a bitterness within me for being so small. I was in that frame of mind when I went to the café in the Albert Walk for a plate of chips and a Pepsi Cola.

I realised for the first time in my life that I was alone and free to do as I pleased. Back at the hotel, I went to my room, where I found the other three occupants.

Buzz greeted me with, 'You're John, are you? Well, we thought there was only going to be three of us in here this season, but I suppose it can't be helped, we'll have to put up with it. You're not a big fella so you won't take up too much room.'

No, I thought, you'll make up for it, you fat pig! Buzz seemed very old to me, probably about sixty, a barrel of a man with sleeked-back dark hair and little pig eyes in a fat face.

Michael Doran, a good-looking man of about five foot ten with brown hair, got off his bed and came over to me, stuck his hand out and said, 'Johnny Mahon. Well, well.'

We shook hands and I said, 'Michael, I didn't know you worked here.'

'Indeed I do,' he said, 'and have done so for nearly two years at that. Let me introduce you to God's gift to women, Danny.'

'Ah, go an' take a flying jump,' said Danny, rubbing Brylcreem into his dark hair. He stood about six feet tall and looked like an athlete. I later found out that the only athletics he ever participated in was with the females and it didn't matter where the venue might be ... in the bedroom ... up against a wall ... or ... anywhere at all. He asked me if this was my first job.

I nodded yes.

'You'll like it here,' he said, 'and if you don't mind the long hours you'll make a good few bob.'

'I bet you'll make a lot of tips because you're only a kid and they'll have pity on you for your size,' said Buzz.

Michael and Danny both turned on him with sour looks and Danny said, 'You oul miser, you never think of anything but money.'

'And,' said Michael, 'if he gets up to sing a song or two in the lounge you'll be put in the shade, Buzz.'

Buzz just chuckled and left the room dressed in a tuxedo suit – and like his face, it too had seen better years.

'What's this about you being a singer?' Danny asked.

'He's a good one too,' said Michael. 'He used to come to our house on Hallowe'en and sing a song – remember that, John?'

'You'll have to give us a few numbers sometime,' said Danny. 'Now listen, just to put you on your guard, it's rumoured that Buzz is a relation of the family that own this place. He never gets paid any wages. He just works for the tips every season from May to September then goes home to Kilcock in the County of Kildare.'

'Where he gets up to some other wheelin' an' dealin', no doubt,' Michael added. 'We don't know if he has any influence with the family or not, but it's best to be on the safe side. If you want to learn how to be a miser, just take a leaf out of his book, but pay no heed to what that old balls said about your size.'

'I'm off to the dance,' said Danny. 'See you later.'

When he left, Michael said, 'I'm sorry about the loss of your mother, John.'

'Thank you,' I said.

'Well, I'm off to the pictures now,' he said. 'If you ever want anything or there's something you need to know, you just see me or Angela. I'm not saying we have all the answers, but we'll help you anyway we can. Good luck to you.'

'Thank you Michael,' I said. 'Is Angela the housemaid I met yesterday?'

'The very same,' he said.

I was left alone with my thoughts. I remembered how much I had enjoyed going around the neighbourhood on Hallowe'en nights as most of the children from miles around did, all dressed up as clowns, tramps, and all sorts of funny characters, with painted faces or wearing cardboard masks to do a little party piece like singing a song, reciting poetry or doing a bit of comedy in return for fruit, nuts and usually a few coppers, as was the custom. My mother used to wait for me in the shadows with a bag to put the 'goodies' in. I was delighted with the praise I got for my singing. Oh, how I treasured those happy memories.

I knew Michael from those days, though I had known some of his brothers and sisters better than I knew him, because he left school shortly after I had started.

I looked over my present surroundings and thought, it's a dump, but at least I'm away from that bitch Theresa. I went to the bathroom and found that, just like the rest of the staff accommodation, it was filthy. I set about cleaning the bath with the scourer and a packet of Vim which was on the sink, and once I had done the job to my satisfaction I filled it up and took a bath. When I pulled the bedclothes back to get into bed I saw a brown envelope peeping out from under the pillow. I pulled it out to find a message from Jim.

It read, 'John, a good lock for you, and you can open the window if you wish, it's eased now. Jim.'

I put the lock on my steel locker, feeling very moved by the way Jim had thought of me, and it was with a happy heart that I went to bed.

***

I awoke at six o'clock the next morning full of enthusiasm and leapt out of bed while the others were sleeping. I washed in the bathroom, and as I was cleaning my teeth I realised that I would definitely have to see Theresa in the afternoon break, otherwise she might turn up at the hotel and make a show of me.

I went to the staff room for coffee, a drink I was getting to like more and more, and there to my delight sat Jim and Bob, who told me the bike was ready for me – a day earlier than I'd expected.

'You can have her now, and I suppose you'll need a lock and chain for her too, that'll cost you an extra three shillings. I'll show you a place in the boiler room where you can keep her and that's where I'll leave her for you, so when you're off duty today you can ride around like Lord Muck.'

My first job was to clean the brass, which Mervyn showed me how to do after introducing me to the other hall porter, Max. Then he told me that when I had finished I was to help Declan finish off cleaning the tables in the lounge. There was a lot of brass to do and it took me nearly an hour to finish, but when I went into the lounge I found just four tables done and Declan asleep in a chair. That angered me, so I shook him and asked if he was going to help me with the job.? He stretched, raised his arms, yawned and said, 'Yeah.'

'Let's get on with it,' I said.

He got up slowly and went at it in his usual way, and I did the job my way.

When we had finished, he said, 'I'm going to the staff room for a few minutes and that's where I'll be if anyone wants me. Will you come down and get me if they do?'

I went back to the reception and found the entire area packed with luggage and a big crowd of people around the desk. Jim took me aside and asked where Declan was.

'He's just gone down to the staff room,' I said.

'Please go down and get him for me, John' he said.

I found Declan lying on an old settee in the staff room and told him how busy it was upstairs and Jim wanted him up there immediately. He rubbed his hands and said, 'We'll make a few bob out of them.'

'How?' I asked.

'When you take guests up to their rooms they always give you a tip. Well, mostly they do, but sometimes you get a skinflint that wouldn't give you the steam off his piss,' he said.

Jim frowned at Declan as we approached and then said, 'You boys will do just as Mervyn, Max and I will be doing, taking the guests up to their rooms, just as soon as we get the wink from Miss Doyle at reception. This crowd is the first of the bus tourists this season. Most of them will be here for the week and they'll be out on the bus touring around most days.'

The guests were settled in without a hitch, and that's when I learned how important it was to be *one step ahead* in the hotel business. Between normal duties, Jim had shown me around the corridors and the layout of the rooms, and when things were slack I went around by myself and made some notes, so

I was fairly confident when I started showing people to their rooms. Soon it was all over and I went to the toilet to count my tips. I had made six shillings.

Mervyn came into the toilet as I was combing my hair. He checked to see if there was anyone else there before he asked, 'How did you do for tips, John?'

'Six shillings,' I answered.

'Listen son,' he said, 'if you're ever asked that question again just say not bad and no more.'

We met Jim and Declan at reception, and each of us was happy in our own way with the added earnings of the morning.

Jim said, 'John, you'll be off between one and three this afternoon, I suppose you'll want to take the bike out for a spin?'

The words were barely out of his mouth when I replied, 'Yes, I have to see my guardian.'

He looked at his watch and said, 'It's twenty to one so you be off with yourself and do your very best to be back on time, but be careful.'

I went to the staff room where I made a corned beef sandwich and gobbled it down on the way to the boiler room to take out my prized possession. I arrived near the Kenny's home about thirty minutes later, but before I could be seen from the house I went through a hole in the hedge to separate the money I was going to give to Theresa from what I would keep for myself. I decided on four shillings and sixpence for her and reasoned that with the twenty Sweet Afton cigarettes she should be pleased. I took my boots off and secreted a half-crown in each sock and kept a shilling in my pocket and thought, if I don't make any more tips for the rest of the week, I've got the first payment for Bob and a shilling to spare. As I rode along the lane I saw Mrs Gormley in the garden, and I stopped to bid her good afternoon.

'Well, I do declare John, wherever did you get that bike? The colour of it!'

'I bought it,' I whispered, 'for two pounds and three shillings, and I asked the man to paint it this colour.'

She tittered and said, 'I don't suppose you've told Herself yet?'

'No, I've got to break it to her gently, and it would be

much easier if you were there,' I said.

'Go on,' she said, 'I'll be over in a few minutes.'

I had just handed over the money and cigarettes to Theresa when there was a knock on the door and in walked Margaret saying, 'Good afternoon, is that your bike out there, John?'

'No, well, it might be,' I said.

'What's dis?' asked Theresa.

I explained that the head hall porter had got a bike for sale at a cheap price and I had said that I would like to buy it – but only if I was allowed to, I lied.

'We'll take a look at it,' she said, and with that she led the way outside, followed by Margaret, Peter and myself. 'Jeezus missis,' she declared, 'would yeh take a look at that colour, Holy Christ, it'd put a body to shame. Can you imagine you or me riding in to town on that, missis?'

Margaret laughed and said, 'We're a bit too old, but it's a good make, a Raleigh, and it's sturdy. It all depends on how much he's asking for it.'

'How much does he want for it?' asked Theresa.

'Two pounds, and three shillings for the lights,' I replied, 'and that includes the lock and chain.'

'It's a bargain,' said Margaret.

'You're right, missis,' said Theresa. 'I'll get it for him.'

Margaret stayed for a cup of tea and then went home so I was left with the Quare Wan.

'How are you to pay for it?' she asked.

I told her that Bob wanted five shilling a week and I thought that I could make enough in tips to pay it off.

She nodded and said, 'In that case you mightaswell get it, but you make sure you don't lose that job – and you're ta come home as often as yeh can an keep dem tips for me until yeh do.'

I was in a euphoric state as I went freewheeling down the lanes and pedalled along the main road and all the way back to the hotel, arriving shortly before the afternoon teas were due to be served, which I would do with Jim.

The afternoon went very well, and soon it was knocking-off time. Jim asked if I was going out, and I said I was thinking of going out for a spin around the town.

'Good for you,' he said, 'but I'd like to sit down with you and put you in the picture about a few things first.' I followed him to the staff room, where he asked me if there was anything I wished to talk to him about regarding the job.

I said that I really liked the work and I intended to learn as much as I could about it and as fast as I could, but I was unhappy about the untidiness of the accommodation.

'It's nearly the same in all staff quarters in hotels,' he told me, 'and I've worked in many over in England and several in this country. All the team want to do when they get off is get out of the hotel as quick as they can to enjoy themselves and unwind – mind you, once someone takes the initiative the others usually muck in. Another thing, I don't want to offend you about your height but there's no getting away from it, you are tiny, and the guests will take to you because of it. So you take advantage of it and you'll make money. I noticed you pulling a face when our regular guest Mr Coyle patted you on the head. You'll have to prepare yourself for a lot more of that, because you'll be treated as a novelty, but don't let it upset you. Just carry on doing a good job and let any comments and head-patting fall off of you like water off a duck's back.'

'I hate being so small,' I said, 'but I'll do my best to keep a cool head.'

'I know it's easy for me to say don't let it bother you,' said Jim, 'but it'd be a strange old world if we were all the same. Remember, you are short in height, but you are built in proportion. Think of the poor unfortunate cripples and all the other poor people with mental illnesses and things. Look on your height as an advantage, especially in this business – and milk it for what it's worth.'

***

The weeks went by and the season became much busier. I was enjoying my new-found lifestyle, and was picking up something new about the job and life in general every day. But I hated having to visit Theresa at least once a week.

On one of my visits, I told her the hotel was very busy now and the manageress had told all the staff that we would be expected to work overtime at very short notice and although time off in lieu was still the policy, overtime would be paid in certain circumstances. Miss Ryan had never said a word of it. It was my fabrication and I felt very pleased with myself.

I suggested that if I couldn't get up very often maybe I

could get Brendan Gormley to bring her the cigarettes, my pay and the tips I had made. I could see by the look on her face that she was thinking about it as she went to put the kettle on. I stayed quiet, thinking she has never given me a few shillings back for spending money nor even mentioned it, so it pleased me to think that I had one over on her by holding back more and putting it in the post office. She put a cup of tea on the table in front of me and said, 'I tink that'd be all right but you'd havta lap the money in newspaper to stop it rattlin' an den put it inta an envelope wit the cigarettes.'

I got Brendan to do a delivery for me and enclosed a note with the tips saying 'six shillings overtime for working three afternoon duties'. There were no complaints so I did that a couple of times and then I went for the big one. Five shillings for working my day off. That worked too. So off to Dublin I would go on my day off. I was flying high, but I still felt the need to visit her once a week for a couple of hours just in case she caught on to my game.

One evening in late July I was about to go off duty at 7 pm when Miss Colgan called me to reception and asked, 'How would you like to help out in the lounge tonight, John, serving drinks and keeping the ashtrays and tables clean?'

'Yes miss,' I said, 'I would like to try it, but I might be a bit nervous at first.'

'You'll do fine,' she said. 'Just take one order at a time. It's all cash in the lounge. Get five pounds float from John, the dispense barman. Just remember some people can be very strange when they have drink taken so be on your guard. Just keep an eye on Buzz to see how he goes about things. You can work from 9 until 10.30 and we'll see how you go.'

I was excited as I stepped into the lounge. The man at the piano was playing and nearly all the people were singing 'She'll be coming round the mountain,' and then a man got up and sang 'My wild Irish rose,' and after him a woman sang 'The Mountains of Mourne', and so it went.

I took my first order from a foursome of young English people for two pints of Guinness, a Babycham and a crème de menthe.

I went to the dispense bar and queued up behind Buzz and the other lounge waiter Jack, and when they had been served I gave John my order. He started pouring the pints and said,

'It'll take a few minutes to do these. What's your name son?'

'John,' I said. 'Miss Colgan said you would give me five pounds float.'

'I was coming to that,' he said, as he topped up the pints. 'Your order is twelve shillings and sixpence, so how much change have I to give you out of five pounds?'

'Four pounds seven shillings and sixpence,' I said.

'Good man yourself,' he said. 'You can give me the float back when you finish work.'

Buzz stopped me in the corridor and said, 'I didn't know you were going to be working with me tonight, but now that you're here, keep an eye on me – and if I point to a table you're to serve them people.'

I served countless drinks after that and it didn't take me long to learn why Buzz directed me to serve certain tables. The people at those tables were either drinking draught Guinness, which took longer to pour, or they didn't tip him. So that's how it works, I thought.

Too soon my first evening of cleaning and serving drinks was over. I repaid the float to John and went to my room to count my tips. I couldn't believe that I had made five shillings and eleven pence in such a short time. I had made fourteen shillings that day. At this rate I would have the bike paid for in no time.

The lounge work became a regular part of my duty, and because of this I was given an extra hour off in the afternoons.

I hadn't been much good with sums at school, but I found it very easy making up the cost of the orders from the price list that had been written up for me. Soon I had memorised the prices, and to my surprise I found that I could take three and sometimes four orders at once without writing them down. I was also able to calculate the total cost of my orders while I waited my turn in the queue. This surprised not only me but John, Jack and Buzz too.

I was into my fifth week of working in the lounge from 8 pm to midnight when one night I was beckoned over to a table where four well-dressed people sat, two men and two women. One of the men asked me would I get them a drink.

'Certainly sir,' I said.

He ordered two large gin and tonics and two large whiskeys with soda and said, 'Buzz has been looking after us for the last week but he's a bit slow tonight. What is your name?'

'John,' I replied.

'Well John, please keep an eye on our table as you go about your business and when you see us signal it will mean that we need replenishing. Don't bother coming over, just get the same order again and we'll look after you!' He winked and I was off for the order. They were delighted. When I served the drinks the man introduced me to his brother-in-law Jack and his wife Christina – 'and Mary, my wife, and I'm Derek,' he said. Both women were blondes and they had the most make-up on their faces that I had ever seen on any woman – it reminded me of some of the Red Indians I had seen in the pictures. He paid for the drinks and gave me a half-crown tip, which was a big tip to me, and incentive enough for me to keep a close eye in their direction. I knew nothing about sex except what I had heard from Snotty and Hardy at school, but there was something that stirred within me as I stood close to those women getting a quick sly peep down their low-cut blouses.

'I see you've served my customers. There's nothing can be done about it now, but we'll have to have a talk about things later,' said Buzz.

Later that night, when we were in our room and he was counting his money, he said, 'Now, young fella, there's a thing or two you've got to learn about this business, and firstly, whenever you see me serving tables more than once, you're to leave them tables alone.'

'Why?' I asked, as if I didn't know.

'Because they're my customers. You poached one of my tables tonight.'

I got a wink from Danny and a nod from Michael. 'Excuse me,' I said, 'those people called me over and told me they were parched and that you didn't seem to be yourself tonight, that's the reason I served them. Besides, I didn't know there were any rules about who serves which table.'

'There is,' he said. 'They're not written down or spoken of, let's say, it's a gentleman's agreement and I'd like to see you keeping to it – and another thing, when I indicate a table to be served, you get yourself over there and attend to them pronto, do you understand?'

'Yes,' I said, 'I understand perfectly. The reason you want me to serve the people on those tables is because they're draught Guinness drinkers or they don't tip enough.'

'That's enough, you cheeky pup, you're getting too big for your britches,' he said.

'Right,' I said. 'If Miss Ryan or Miss Colgan tells me you're in charge I will obey your instructions, but not until then. I will serve anyone who wants a drink and I don't care if they give me a tip or not.'

The silent duo clapped and Michael said, 'John's right.'

'Bloody sure he is,' said Danny. 'Waiting for a pint of Guinness to be poured takes up precious time and slows down your earning power. Am I right Buzz?'

He never said a word. But I learned that I could stand up for myself. Out of respect for his age, I tried to keep away from the customers I took to be his best tippers. In years to come I would thank Buzz in my mind for that very sensitive and important lesson on tipping in the catering world.

I was enjoying all aspects of my job but my favourite was working in the lounge, where I found the happy atmosphere just marvellous and of course my ability to memorise the orders and calculate the cash was an added bonus. This in turn made me even more diligent in ensuring that the tables were sparkling, but because I was so keen on doing a good job and getting on with it I tended to ignore Declan's lazy attitude in sharing the workload until one morning I had just finished polishing the brass and I found him sleeping behind a big window curtain. In anger I hit him in the face with the end of the curtain. He awoke with a burbling start as though he didn't know where he was.

'You should have done at least half of the job by now,' I said. 'Instead, you've done feck all!'

He started to argue, and in my fury I picked up the tin of Min cream and threw it at him, hitting him on the side of the head.

'You little bollix. You've cut me,' he said.

I stood my ground until I could see he wasn't going to retaliate, and I was relieved because I felt sure he could have done me some serious damage. I left him standing there and went to the staff room for a cup of coffee. I took my time, and when I returned there were only two tables left to do. He went out without a word and I finished the job.

Just before my break that afternoon Jim told me that Miss Ryan wanted to see me in her office. I went through the reception to her office and found her door open. I knocked, she beckoned me in and said, 'Please sit down John. How are you?'

'Very well, thank you miss,' I replied.

'That's good,' she said. 'Usually, halfway through the season rumours start up amongst the staff about who will be kept on the permanent staff and who will be let go, it's silly really, but it always happens. I have asked you in to offer you a permanent job. What do you think about that?'

She obviously hadn't heard of my performances with Buzz and Declan, and I was grateful, but I wondered if she would be offering me the job if she had known that.

I smiled at her across the desk and said, 'Yes miss, I would love to work here, thank you very much.'

'That's good,' she said. 'I want you to go to Diffney and Fenlons the tailors in Henry Street Dublin tomorrow where they will measure you and make a nice uniform for you.' She showed me a picture of a boy in a blue uniform with a high collar and brass buttons down the front, similar to Declan's. 'I want you to work until 11 am tomorrow, have something to eat and then catch a train to Dublin. Go straight to the shop in Henry Street and they will attend to you. Do you know where that is?'

'Yes miss, I do,' I replied.

'That's good,' she said. 'There's no need to come back to work when you've finished with the tailors. Enjoy yourself in town.'

I nodded, stood up in a daze and was about to step out of the office when she said, 'John, I have not finished yet. How were you going to pay your fares?'

'I have some money,' I said.

'This is hotel business and your expenses must be paid,' she said. 'Here is two pounds, and I don't want any change.'

I don't know how I got through the rest of the day, with my mind racing in several directions at once.

***

I caught the train from Bray to Dublin the next day and

enjoyed the journey as I had done so often on my days off. The scenery was beautiful along the coast and the Irish Sea was especially lovely when the sun shone, and nearly always there were boats and ships to be seen, which always got me thinking about where the big ships had come from and where they were bound.

I had learned no geography at school. However, I had started to learn and I knew a little about places in Europe, Africa, Australia, America and Canada, mostly from what I had read in newspapers and magazines and of course from the pictures in the cinema, and last but not least by keenly listening to people's conversations about foreign countries, standing within earshot but not giving the slightest indication that I was remotely interested. From what I had seen in the cinema, my perception of America was that everyone was rich, with big cars and nice houses, and I admired the paper boys speeding down the road on their lovely bicycles and dressed up in grand clothes, hurling their deliveries across the manicured lawns towards the front doors.

I also thought I knew a bit about England because of the stories I had heard from people who came back for holidays, and I picked up a lot from the television too, which was in the lounge of the hotel adjacent to the foyer where the hall staff stood on duty. It was frowned upon if you were found to be watching it.

My two favourite places in Dublin were the Theatre Royal and the Royalette café. I always enjoyed the stage show and then the big picture on the wide screen, and after that I would go to the café and gorge myself with sausage, egg and chips followed by trifle or whatever else took my fancy. Then I would go around the city taking in the sights and sounds, and it was on one of my earlier visits that I found Guiney's clothing shop in North Earl Street, where they sold drip-dry shirts to fit me and I bought two. I also found Kingston's men and boys shop in O'Connell Street, where they sold the most wonderful but expensive clothes for boys in the same style as the men's. I started buying an item of clothing nearly every fortnight in there, a shirt and tie, a pair of trousers and a jacket which took four weeks to save up for. I never could wear any of my nice clothes when I visited Theresa, and I couldn't wear them in Bray either, just in case I should bump into her in the town.

I found the tailor's shop without difficulty. A short, corpulent, balding, elderly man with a tape measure draped around his shoulders came out from behind the counter and asked, 'What can I do for you boy?'

I told him my name and the reason I was there. He looked in a book and said, 'Yes, you're down here.' Then he proceeded to measure me with very little to say except for a few instructions – 'bend your arm', 'stand up straight', and so on – and soon it was over. He said, 'Tell Miss Ryan I will be in touch when I require you to return for the fitting.'

I stepped out onto the street and retraced some of the steps that Nellie and I had trod on my very first visit to Dublin. It seemed such a long time ago and so much had happened since then, but the memory of that visit was strong and I wished she were still alive to see how I was doing.

I only stayed in Dublin about an hour and then caught a train home.

I paid Theresa a visit the next day and told her about the uniform and Miss Ryan's offer to keep me on the permanent staff. I explained that there wouldn't be many tips throughout the off season and I might not get enough to buy her cigarettes.

I had to make another brief visit to the tailors for my fitting, and three weeks later my beautiful uniform was delivered. Talk about cock of the walk. I was he!

***

The busy time came to an end, and except for a few guests the place was almost empty. There was a staff dance at the end of the season, and the build-up to this caused me some anxiety. I could not get a dinner jacket to fit me, but once again Angela came to the rescue. She suggested that I should wear 'that nice navy blue jacket that suits you so well', and she would buy me a really nice bow tie to go with it. True to her word, she came back a few days later with a light blue bow tie and said, 'That will go perfectly with your jacket and dark trousers, and you've got to promise me the first dance.'

I blushed and she tousled my hair.

The party was a great success, but after dancing with Angela I felt very uncomfortable for quite some time. It was the very first time that I had attempted to dance and I became acutely aware of how short in stature I really was. I was conscious of my head barely reaching up to her breasts, and it seemed like forever before the music stopped and I was saved from any further embarrassment. I firmly resolved that I would never dance again.

Michael asked me if I would like to sing a song, and before I knew it he was introducing me.

'Ladies and gentlemen,' he said, 'we have a young man to sing for your pleasure. I give you our own Johnny Mahon.'

Hearing my name like that made my head spin, and as he ushered me up to the stage it felt as though I was not in my own body. However, I pulled myself together with as much control as I could muster. I told the piano player that I had never sung with any sort of musical accompaniment before, but I would try with the song 'MacNamara's band.'

'Okay young fella,' he said. 'Have you got another for an encore?'

I suggested 'Come back Paddy Reilly'.

'That's fine,' he said. 'We're getting near the end of the evening so there'll only be room for the two songs. You just start off and we'll follow you.'

I went into the first song feeling very nervous but enjoying it, and it seemed that my colleagues liked what I was doing too, because at the end of it the response was uproarious. It was the same for the next one except that they wanted more, but the piano player thanked me and announced that there was just time for a final dance. I felt both elated and exhausted.

Shortly afterwards it was the time for goodbyes to most of the staff, some of whom I had become very fond of, and all of whom I had learned something from. Buzz trundled off, and that marked the end of the money making in the lounge. I was deeply sorry to see Angela go, and Michael was due to leave a week later after he had done a duty as head waiter for a big wedding reception.

That day came and it was a big do. After the meal there were the usual toasts and speeches and then the band struck up, and about twenty minutes later Michael suggested I should get over to the microphone and sing a song, reassuring me that he'd taken the liberty of asking Miss Ryan if she would allow it. 'I'll announce you and surprise my friends, what do you say?'

I sang 'The Rose of Tralee'. It went down well, so I followed it with the 'Red River valley' and that brought on even more applause, hoots, foot stomping, and roaring for more.

I was overwhelmed by it all. I don't think my performance was worthy of the response I received, and as at the staff dance a lot of the credit had to go to the band. Jack the piano player deserved a medal for his expertise in keeping up with me. Michael came up on stage and quietened them down by saying that he was sure I had another song for them but it would definitely have to be my last because I had my duties to attend to. He handed me a glass of lemonade, saying, 'Kill 'em.'

I turned to Jack and said,' I'll finish off with "Sixteen tons" if that's all right.'

'Go ahead son, I'll follow you.'

As I stepped back to the mike I noticed some of the staff were standing by the door, including Miss Ryan. I pretended not to see them. I went into the song and all too soon it was over. Miss Ryan complimented me. Michael handed me an envelope containing twenty-five shillings, with thanks from the best man.

That's how I became known as the Singing Pageboy.

***

I had paid for the bicycle within four weeks, and by the end of the season had bought some nice clothes and had nineteen pounds ten shillings in a post office account. Except for the bicycle, Theresa knew nothing about any of this.

Jim and I were the permanent daytime hall staff, with a temporary man by the name of Seamus O'Donoghue who came in for our days off and special functions, dinner parties, weddings etc.

It was a comfortable experience working with those fine men. They never spoke down to me and they always treated me as their equal. By this time I had become so confident that I felt capable of tactfully transacting with anyone, from the awkward and ignorant folk to the nice *gentle people*, who were in the majority anyway.

I was on duty at lunchtime one day when I noticed a very elderly lady struggling with the main entrance door so I rushed to open it for her – and it was then I noticed she was blind.

'Good afternoon, madam.' I said.

'Good afternoon to you too,' she replied. 'You sound like a young man. Now, tell me, is lunch being served?'

'Yes madam,' I replied.

'Good,' she said. 'I need you to guide me to the dining room.'

I led her to the dining room door and thankfully Danny spotted us. He opened the door and bid her good afternoon and asked if she would be having lunch.

'That depends on what's on the menu,' she said.

He read the menu to her and she said, 'That's splendid, yes I shall have lunch.'

She was the first blind person that I had ever met, and it made me very emotional. I thought she was probably about sixty years of age and I wondered if she had always been blind. I tried to imagine how it would be to have a permanent blindfold on. Never being able to read or see the flowers and birds and all the other things I took for granted. Somehow, my short stature seemed far less problematic than the predicament that unfortunate lady was in, and Jim's words came to mind.

Danny came out of the dining room to tell me that the old lady had declined his offer to guide her out and had asked for me to do so. I escorted her along the hall, through the door and down the steps to the street.

'Thank you,' she said. 'I enjoyed my lunch and I shall come again next week. Please take this shilling in appreciation for your kind attention.' I took the shiny new coin and felt very uncomfortable taking it from her because she was blind, but consoled myself with the fact that she was well-dressed, well spoken and probably could afford it.

The old lady returned once a week for lunch, and each time I got a bright one-shilling piece and Danny got his one shilling and sixpence. Then a few weeks before Christmas she did not appear and we never saw her again. She never told either of us anything about herself, and we were in no position to ask. There have been several times through the years that she has gently crept into my memory, and I can't help but feel that in some way she played a part in shaping my future.

***

I celebrated my fifteenth birthday with one thought in mind. Only one more year to go before I would be free of 'that hoor' Theresa. The hotel was very quiet apart for the occasional functions, so tips were scarce. It took Theresa quite a time to get used to the fact that she couldn't expect the twenty Sweet Aftons and at least four or five shillings a day. However, this worked in my favour because she was always pleased when Brendan delivered the envelope with the note and money for working overtime on my day off or for extended afternoon duty. Sometimes it was necessary to draw the money from my post office account but it was well worth it.

One afternoon Jim asked me if I would like to help out at a function being held in the Woodbrook Golf Club that evening. He said he had suggested me to go along with him to Miss Ryan, and she had agreed, but only if I wanted to.

'I'd love to go,' I said.

'Good,' he said, 'we can go together when we finish duty. Aren't you going to ask about the readies?'

'I didn't think of that,' I replied.

'Well,' he said, 'there's two pounds in it for me and as much as I can eat and maybe I'll get a few jars as well, there's always plenty of free gargle at those sort of affairs. And for you, me young bucko, it's one pound and your chances.'

We arrived at the club just after 7 pm with the help of a lift from Tony, the cocktail barman. The party was due to begin at eight, and dinner was to be served at nine. There was still a lot of work to be done with laying up the tables, polishing hundreds of glasses, and generally getting everything into place. There were a number of casual waiters and waitresses from an agency in town, along with us two and the permanent staff at the club. We got stuck in together and had everything ready with time to spare for a drink and a smoke. I had only been smoking for a week.

Tommy Morgan introduced himself to me. He said that he came from County Sligo, he was sixteen and he had been working in the club for over six months. He said he really liked his job, and then asked me about mine and finished up by asking my age.

I told him I was fifteen and enough about the job to satisfy his curiosity.

'I'm going to the toilet, see you later,' he said.

I went over to join Jim and a couple of the casual waiters, who jokingly referred to us as 'culchies', in other words country yokels, which was a bit of a joke really because Bray is only twelve miles from Dublin City.

A tall distinguished-looking man in evening dress approached us and introduced himself as Mr Flynn the manager. He asked us if we knew where Tommy was. I said that he had gone to the toilet, and Mr Flynn asked me to see if I could fetch him.

I searched all over inside the club but Tommy was nowhere to be found. So I went outside in case he was having a sly smoke and called his name a few times, but there was no answer. I was about to go back inside when I spotted someone over by a clump of bushes. As I got a little closer I could make him out with the help of a light on the gable end of the building.

I saw that he was furiously trying to stuff his big mickey back in his trousers and I said, 'That's a quare place to be pissin.'

'Whaat?' he said, in a voice labouring for breath.

'Mr Flynn is looking for you,' I said.

He gulped in some air before he replied, 'Fuck him, he'll have to wait till I can get me breath back. And you thought I was pissin'. I wasn't, I was pullin' meself off.'

'What do you mean?' I asked.

'Are you trying to tell me you've never had a wank?' he responded.

I was blushing from head to toe and was glad we were still in the semi-darkness. I didn't know how to answer him so I kept quiet. 'When the people go in to dinner it will be our job to clear the glasses and tidy up the bar and we'll have a chat,' he said.

When the crowd were seated for dinner and we started cleaning up, he asked, 'Have you ever had a wank?'

'No,' I replied.

'Wet dreams, what about them?'

I felt slightly more comfortable with that question because I had often experienced the most wonderful sensations and woken up with a sticky substance between my legs, on my belly and on the sheets, but I always kept it to myself – and now here was my chance to learn something from him. 'I think so,' I said.

'Well, a wank is like that 'cept you have to play with your prick, rub it and stroke it until it gets really hard and keep at it until you shoot the spunk. That's what I was doing out there, pulling meself because I saw right up a smashing bit of stuff's dress, she was wearing small white knickers and her hairs was sticking out of the sides. Jasus! It gave me a massive hard-on an' there was nothing for it but to have a wank, an' when you found me I had just shot me load.'

I was thinking of what he had told me and he said, 'I can't believe you don't know about such things at your age. Anyway, your spunk can make babies if you stick your prick up a girl's thing, it's called a varginer. That's the best thing of all if you can get a girl to do it with, but the next best thing is wanking.'

'How do you get a girl to do it with you?' I asked.

'That's the hard part,' he said. 'I've only done it with one waitress and it was grand altogether.'

'Did you make a baby?' I asked.

He stopped polishing the glass, gave me a serious look with raised eyebrows and said, 'Ah, sweet Jesus, John, are you joking or are you really that thick?'

'Thick about them things,' I replied.

'In answer to your question, no, we didn't make a baby. She made me promise to pull me prick out before I shot me load and I did. But wanking will have to do until I find another girl. I'll tell you what, I'll show you the one I had to pull meself off over when they come out again, and you keep an eye on her when she sits down. She'll probably be showing herself off again and you can get a good eyeful. Then you can pull yourself off over her.'

Dinner was over and the dancing started. Tommy and I were kept busy picking up glasses, emptying ashtrays and helping out in general, and I kept a keen lookout for open legs and the sight of knickers. The big disappointment was that so many of the girls and women were wearing long evening gowns. I had a few glimpses before Tommy came over to me and said, 'Bejasus, she's doing it again, even wider this time. Now, here's what we'll do, I'll walk down the hall and stand opposite her, not looking at her, but in the other direction, she'll be directly across from my left-hand side and when I walk away you'll know exactly where to look. Once I walk away it'll be outside for me to have another pull at meself. I just can't help it. A bloke told me that if you wank too often you could go blind or even go mad, and probably you'll get hair on the palms of your hands, but I don't give a fuck. It's too good a feeling not to do it.' With that, he walked down the hall and stopped about two-thirds of the way down. I pinpointed his position and a few minutes after he disappeared I went to take a peep.

Yes, there she was, with long blond hair, a low-cut frilly blouse and her legs open. I got a full view and could feel a stirring in my loins. I wanted to run out to join Tommy and put his instructions to the test, but instead I decided to leave it until I got back to the hotel and promised myself that I would return for further viewing later on. I got two more eyefuls and then she was gone.

It was two o'clock in the morning when Jim and I were driven home by one of the golf club staff. He dropped me off at the hotel and then took Jim to his home.

I was fortunate, because it was my day off so I could have a good lie-in if I wished, and besides I didn't feel like going straight to bed anyway. Tommy had given me a big brown envelope with the instructions, 'Put it under your coat and only take it out when you're by yourself, you'll love the pictures.'

I was delighted to see that Danny, my only companion in the room, was fast asleep. I opened the envelope to find pictures of girls and women in varying poses. Mostly they were adverts for underwear, but there were a few of women without any clothes on at all. I couldn't see what Tommy called their pussies but I didn't care. I had never seen the like before and they gave me my first real hard-on.

I went to the bathroom with my pictures and the memories of the girl in the club and proceeded to follow Tommy's instructions. What a wonderful thing this wanking is, I thought, but I must find out some way about the going mad or blind and the hair on the palm of the hands. I would ask Danny about it the very next time he started talking about girls.

The opportunity came that evening when he was telling me about a smashing girl he'd met at a dance and how he thought he was in love with her. I asked him, 'How do you know when you love someone? Do you get a hard-on all the time when you're in love?'

He looked at me for a while before answering, 'No, not really, and you don't have to love someone to get a hard-on, but I know that since I first clapped eyes on Brigid I nearly always have a root on whenever we're near each other, and I think that's a part of love.'

He was quiet for a time, and then he asked, 'Do you masturbate?'

'What's that?' I asked.

'That's a fancy word for playing with yourself, wanking!'

I reddened to the gills and he said, 'It's no crime or any harm either. But you know it's a mortal sin and you have to tell the priest about it in confession. I haven't been back to confession for over three months now, because when I confessed fucking two girls three times and wanking nearly every day the penance that priest gave me was far too hard. He ordered me to do three decades of the rosary twice. I said to myself, 'bollocks' and walked out of the chapel and I don't think I'll bother me arse going back. I think it's all bullshit.'

'Does fucking a girl mean you stick your mickey in her?' I asked.

'Has nobody told you anything about sex at all?' he asked. 'Yes, that's how to do it, but it takes lots of practice and you get better at it the more you do it. I try to get as many rides as I can, sometimes me an' Brigid do it four or five times a night. Now, I best be off for another ride on Brigid. That's your lesson over for today.'

I pleaded, 'Oh, please, there's just two more things I want to know.

'Fire away then, but be quick!' he said.

'Can you go mad or blind by wanking and will hair grow on the palms of your hands if you do it too often?' I asked.

He jumped out of his chair and I thought he was going to hit the ceiling as he roared with laughter, then he sat down again and became serious as he said, 'I heard that too, but I read in a posh English doctor's book that masturbation doesn't harm you at all. So there you are, you can pull your wire to your heart's content. What was the other question, be quick now.'

'No, that's all, thanks Danny.'

I couldn't wait to see the back of him because I wanted to look at my pictures again. Such was my sex education. I viewed girls and good-looking women in a more interesting way now, but it would be several years before I would get the opportunity to enjoy the real thing.

***

The spring was just around the corner and it was wonderful when it came. It was a delight to see the buds on the trees, the wild flowers, lambs skipping about, all sorts of birds flying around and the farmers ploughing the fields.

I knew we were about to enter into the busy season again when one evening Buzz appeared in the doorway of our room, puffing, panting and dragging a battered old suitcase behind him. Danny spotted him first and shouted, 'John, willya look at what the cat dragged in? There goes the peace in our happy humble home.'

'Still here boys?' said Buzz. 'I hope youse haven't been up to any divilment since I've been away.'

'You oul hoor,' replied Danny, 'back for more money grabbin', eh?'

Michael returned about a week later and our room was fully occupied again, much to my delight. I felt that we were a family again and although I had no love for Buzz, he seemed to show me more respect as a colleague after I had stood up to him. I asked Michael if Angela was coming back.

'No,' he said, 'she's working in a hotel in London.'

The season got into full swing and it was money-making time again. It was also the time for renewing old acquaintances, as some of the guests from the previous year returned. Among them were a mother and daughter named Flowers and their friend Mr Watson, and I was pleased to see them again. Mrs Flowers and Mr Watson seemed old to me, probably in their late fifties. Her daughter Denise was about thirty-five years old. She always seemed very solemn, but

110

when she smiled her face lit up and her blue eyes sparkled. She was never too far from her mother's side. They were from Preston in Lancashire, and I was thrilled to have a surprise up my sleeve for them. I asked if they would be in the lounge that evening. 'But of course,' was the answer.

Since their last visit I had begun my career as the Singing Pageboy. I was encouraged to do a few songs each evening – without any extra pay, of course, but who needed money with the glory that was in it? And besides, the tips were always more generous after the performance. This used to annoy Buzz, especially when he asked how much I had made in tips for the evening. My lips would be clamped tighter than a duck's bum. And that got him all hot and bothered.

When my three favourite guests came into the lounge that evening I ushered them to a table near the piano, and later on as Bill introduced me I watched their faces, seeing looks of surprise and broad smiles on all three.

I dedicated my first song to them, and at the end of it they led the applause with so much enthusiasm that I thought their behaviour was bordering on rowdyism – and from such gentle people too! When I finished my third and last song I stepped over to their table to be greeted with hugs and kisses and a handshake from Mr Watson.

I had afternoon tea with them in a couple of the nearby hotels during their stay and they made me promise I would go over and stay with them for a holiday in their home, which they explained was just down the road from the Preston North End football ground. I couldn't explain to them that I would have to work hard at coming up with some real good lies to convince Theresa to let me go in the first place. But I was determined to go and I would. We said our goodbyes, and I told them I hoped to get over to see them around the end of September.

About a week later I told Theresa that two of the guests had invited me to spend a week or two with them in England when I got my holidays.

'What will yeh use for money for the fare?' she asked.

'They said that if I let them know in good time they will send me the return fare,' I lied. I rushed on, 'I told them that if I was allowed to go, it wouldn't be until the end of the season.'

I think that's what swung her thinking pendulum in my favour. 'Well, she said, 'more money nor sense I'd say, if they've got that kind of money, I don't see any harm in it atall, yeh mightaswell write to them and say yeh can go.'

In reality, of course, I was going to have to pay my own fare, and I would need some spending money too. I didn't see that as a problem because the season had been good so far and there was still the month of August before things started to slow down. I already had thirty-four pounds in the post office, and I had managed to save that without giving her any reason to suspect that I'd been holding back anything at all. In fact I was giving her more money than I had done the previous season, by paying for my so-called overtime for my day off and four out of five afternoons. I begrudged her every penny, but I reasoned that it was worth it for my freedom. But what annoyed me most as the time went on was that she never once offered me a few shillings for myself or even showed any appreciation for the money, she just took it for granted. Well, she'd get a big shock in a few months when her little money-making robot toddled off.

Earlier in the summer I had started singing occasionally in the Arcadia dance hall, which was under the same ownership as the hotel, and I also made a few guest appearances with the George Daniels Road Show, which was situated in a tent across the road from the hotel, and I loved it. It was after one of the shows that I met Anne Moore. I was in the queue behind her at the ice cream stand. She smiled and said, 'You were very good and I was screaming for more when you finished.'

I thanked her through my blushes and felt very shy. She was about three inches taller than me, and my ever-present complex was heightened, but I thought she was the most beautiful girl I had ever seen. She had brown hair to match her dark brown eyes. She wore a flowery dress down to her knees and when she reached up to the counter for her ice cream I had a good look at her shapely legs, and I loved her white flat shoes. Then it was my turn. I bought a cone with a chocolate flake in it. I had the feeling that she had gone, but as I stepped out of the throng there she was standing a few feet away looking directly at me and my heart skipped a few beats.

'I thought you had gone home,' I said.

'Oh, no,' she replied. 'I wanted to ask you something about the Arcadia dance hall. My brother told me you often sing in there with the big bands. What's it like? He told me that when you sing there the crowd stop dancing and gather around the stage just to listen and look at you. Is it true?'

'Well,' I said, 'I stand on a very high chair so lots of people can get a look at me. It's a gimmick really.'

'Is it very frightening with all those eyes on you?' she asked.

'No,' I said, 'when I'm up on stage it's a bit like not being there at all, like being in a different world. But sometimes I'm not very good at keeping in tune. It's really the band that makes me seem better than I am.'

We had finished our ice creams and it was time to be moving. I asked her if she lived in the town.

'Yes, just up the road, I've always lived here. What about you, where do you live?'

'In the hotel,' I said.

'I thought you did,' she said. 'I see you nearly every day on your way up town and you look very handsome in your uniform. I work in the tobacconist and sweet shop about a hundred yards from the hotel. But I have to be going now.'

'Can I walk a bit of the way with you?' I asked.

'Yes please,' she said, 'I would like that.'

So off we set. She showed me the shop she worked in and suggested that I should call in to see her whenever I was passing. And it wasn't long before we were in the centre of town and close to her house. We said goodnight and I was fit to leap out of my skin.

I pondered how it was that I had become quite capable of dealing with both the guests and my colleagues, and able to get up to sing without a blush, and yet I felt shy and self-conscious with that beautiful girl. Aw, feck it! I said to myself as I bounced along the street back to the hotel.

The very next morning, as I made my way up to town to collect the English newspapers for the guests, I couldn't resist going into the shop where she worked, and my heart took a jump when I saw her behind the counter in her yellow shop coat.

We laughed, and she said, 'I didn't expect to see you so

soon, John, but it's grand.'

'Yes,' I said, 'it's nice to see you again, Anne. I need to buy some cigarettes and I see you sell the brand I like.'

'And what would they be?' she giggled.

'Craven A,' I said. 'I like them because they have the brown paper around the top and I like the black cat on the box too.'

'Do you like cats?' she asked.

'I love them,' I said. 'We haven't got one in the hotel. I wish we did though.

'I love them too,' she said, 'but we can't have one at home because of my sister's weak chest.'

So began my morning visits to the shop, but it took over a week until I could pluck up enough courage to ask her if she would like to go to the pictures to see a Victor Mature Biblical thing. She said she would love to go, and that's when that heart of mine started its antics again. I told her I would be off duty on Monday evening and if it suited her we could go then.

'Yes,' she said, 'I'll be able to go all right. I'm allowed to go to the pictures once a week, but I'm not allowed to go dancing yet, I'm only fifteen and I wouldn't be allowed in anyway. My brother Christy tells me all about it when he goes and that's how I knew about you.'

We arranged to meet in the foyer of the Roxy at seven o'clock.

I was pleased I had become friendly with Harry, an usher from the cinema. He used to drink in the public bar of the hotel and I told him about the cashier refusing to let me in to the evening shows because she said I was too young. He had a word or two with her and she let me in from then on. I counted the days and at last the time came.

When I got to the cinema I could see her through the glass door in a red dress with a white collar, standing talking to another girl. At first I didn't know what to do but I decided to brazen it out and go over to them. She saw me coming and raised her hand to beckon me over. She introduced me to her friend Carmel, a tall pretty girl with long blonde hair, roughly the same age as Anne.

'I'm pleased to meet you, John,' she said. 'My boyfriend William and I saw you singing in the Arcadia a few weeks ago, you were very good.'

My face was burning and I felt awkward and uncomfortable. She looked right into my eyes and said, 'I can see I'm embarrassing you.'

'I'm waiting for William,' she continued. 'He must have been held up, you two go on, I'll just wait a bit longer. And if he doesn't come I'll just go home, maybe he's working late.'

As we were about to go in I realised I hadn't bought the tickets. Anne chortled and said, 'It's a good job it's a Monday night and not the weekend, you'd stand no chance of getting one at all at this time.'

'Don't I know it,' I replied. 'Where would you like to sit, the stalls or the balcony?'

'I've already got my ticket for the stalls,' she said. I got mine and we entered the dimly lit interior. I whispered, 'Please lead the way to where you would like to sit,' and she responded by taking my hand and leading me to two outside seats about midway in the rows. She let go of my hand as we settled down, but then I took her hand in mine when the lights went down and was as happy as could be. I don't remember anything about the trailers or the picture, but I do remember how proud I was to be sitting next to that beautiful girl.

August was a great month. Anne and I went out on walks as well as our regular visits to the cinemas. We even went on a picnic with Carmel and William, and that was fun although I felt very uncomfortable at the way they were behaving, hugging and kissing and rolling around in the grass. We were lying on a blanket about ten feet away from them but I stole a few glances in their direction, one of which proved to be very fruitful. I caught the sight of Carmel's black knickers when her dress had ridden up. I looked away quickly, but couldn't resist another quick look, then I turned my attention to Anne. I kissed her on the cheek and suggested we should go for a walk along the riverbank. So off we wandered holding hands with not a care in the world except for the feeling in my loins and that was a very pleasant one. We walked and talked about all sorts of things from the pictures we had seen to our present surroundings, the birds, the flowers, the river and our own ambitions.

She told me that she would like to go into fashion and design.

I told her how one of the guests in the hotel had told me all about his job on the big passenger liners, and how he had given me the address of the shipping company that he worked for, P&O in London. I said that I had written to them and sent some photographs. I hadn't received a reply yet, but I was hopeful, and in addition to that I was going to visit the Mercantile Marine office on Eden Quay to see if I could get a job on a ship through them.

After all that we sat down in the grass and she said, 'John, it would be great if you could get work on the ships, but I'd miss you.'

'Well,' I said, 'I'm sure I'd get home from time to time and then we could have that time for ourselves.'

She smiled and we hugged and kissed for a long time. I gently touched her breast and she firmly shoved my hand away.

We continued to kiss for a while and then went back to join Carmel and William for our picnic. They were both fast asleep, so I picked two blades of grass and handed one to Anne, silently indicating how we should wake them by tickling their nostrils. They awoke with a start. We laughed and tucked into our food. Shortly afterwards we made our way back to our respective homes.

I was very happy and felt that I was really in love, but I wished I could do the things with Anne that Tommy and Danny had explained to me.

The season was coming to an end but I didn't feel so sad about it this time round, partly because of my impending trip to England, but even more because in a few months' time I would be sixteen years old and free from Theresa.

Towards the end of September I asked Miss Ryan when it would be possible to have my holidays, explaining that I had been invited to spend a holiday in England and needed to let my friends know when I could go.

'You write to your friends and arrange your trip,' she said, 'then let me know the date and you can go whenever it suits you.'

***

Three weeks later I boarded the *Leinster* in Dublin for the overnight trip to Liverpool, my head swirling with excitement. My friends met me when I disembarked the next morning, and we boarded a train for Preston, where I stayed with the Flowers for a week. There was much talk about anything and everything. I even told them how unhappy I had been living with the Kennys, about my plans to leave them as soon as possible, and that it was my ambition to work on passenger liners and see the world.

I explored Preston, taking in the market where my hosts had a fruit and vegetable stall, and the Preston North End football ground, which was at least ten times the size of Bray Wanderers. I noticed the different names of the products in the shops, and the greater variety of everything. I ate Bird's Eye frozen peas and drank my first cup of Ovaltine. For the first time in my life I slept in a bed with an electric blanket. I listened to the strange accents of the people.

Of course, some of it was familiar. I spotted an advertisement for the Royal Liver Insurance Company and immediately recognised the logo that had been on the book that my mother had had at home. She used to pay the insurance man a penny a week, and he always wrote in that little book. This brought back a flood of memories of a time that seemed so long ago and far away.

Finally the day came for me to board the boat for Dublin. Denise accompanied me to Liverpool and there we said goodbye. I never saw them again. We corresponded for a time, but that dried up, mainly because of the changes that started to take place in my life.

Nothing much had changed at the hotel except that most of the staff had gone. Danny my old roommate was still there, and he asked about my holiday and wanted to be told all about England. I told him as much as I could.

He asked, 'Did you get a ride?'

'Yes,' I answered, 'many' – and waited for it to sink in before adding, 'but only on buses.'

I still had three days of my holiday left, and much as I dreaded it I had to visit Theresa, so I decided to get it over with the next day. I walked through the door with the thought that I wouldn't be doing this for much longer. She stopped me in my tracks and shouted, 'What's that rag doing around your neck? Get it off.'

I tried to explain that it was a cravat. But before I knew it she was ripping it from my neck and punching me at the same time. I stepped away from her, and to my surprise she stayed where she was and said, 'I won't have you goin' around dressed like a tinker. You might be working, but you're still under my care.'

I stared straight at her and thought, not for much longer, that's the last time you'll ever hit me, you oul bitch. I calmly walked to the door and said, 'I'm off.'

I turned sixteen on 15 December 1958. I started to think of when it would be a good time to see the welfare people about going my own way, and after much pondering I decided to leave it until the spring. I was almost certain I would get permission to leave the Kennys, and that being the case I intended to write to Theresa. My biggest fear was that when she received the letter she might come down to the hotel, make a scene and quite possibly get me sacked. Midwinter was not the time of year to be out of work and without a roof over the head. May was the best time to do it – the hotels would be taking on staff then, and if I lost my job I could easily get another one.

***

Mary the receptionist handed me my first pay packet for 1959, and it was different this time – money was rattling around in it where in the past it had been a flat packet containing a pound note. I opened it to find that there was two shillings and nine pence short.

'Excuse me, miss,' I said, 'I'm short in my wages.'

'I know nothing about it,' she said. 'I put in the exact amount that I'm told to and that's that.'

I went to see the assistant manageress, Miss Colgan, and asked if there had been some kind of mistake.

Scowlingly she replied, 'There's no mistake, you're sixteen now, and you have to pay for part of your insurance stamp. It's all part of the price of getting older.'

I protested, 'That's not fair at all, it means that my wages has gone down, just when I was hoping for a rise.'

'That's how it is,' she said.

The warning bells were clanging in my head, I knew it would not be wise to pursue it any further, because she had full control since Miss Ryan had gone away without a word to anyone. She had already sacked a chambermaid and a waitress and I didn't want to be the next one to go.

As I was about to leave I asked, 'When will Miss Ryan be coming back?'

'She won't!' was her reply.

I suspected the mention of Miss Ryan would get her hot under her collar, but I didn't wait to find out. I went straight to the staff room and made myself a cup of tea, and to my good fortune Jim the head porter was sitting there smoking.

'What ails you, John? You look like a fella fit to kill.'

I told him what had happened and then explained how I intended to deal with it. I said, 'I'll be leaving my guardians in May and I don't want to be out on my arse before then, so I've decided to hold my horses until I can get another job and be off from here.'

'It's all part of the exploitation!' he said. 'They know they've got you by the balls and that's when they put the squeeze on. Still, you've got your head screwed on the right way and I hope it all works out for the best. I'd best go back to do my last hour. If I was you, I'd be off for a jar.'

I knew he didn't mean that suggestion unkindly, he was just trying to let me see that he treated me as an equal. But there would have been more chance of me winning the Irish Sweepstake than getting served alcohol by any barman, because I looked about twelve years old – so I had been told by far too many and far too often. However, Jim had ignited the thought of a drink so I bathed and put on clean clothes to go to the licensed victualler's, which was situated between the Albert Walk and the seafront.

I had plucked up the courage a few months earlier to go in there and ask for a miniature cherry brandy and a crème de menthe and had my story prepared in case the assistant asked any questions. I would say, 'It's for a guest at the hotel who doesn't like anyone to know she drinks, that's why she asks me to get these messages for her,' and for good measure if it seemed I was going to be refused I would add, 'I can go back and get a note from her if you like.' It wasn't necessary, though. The man served me without question. Maybe my uniform had done the trick or dazzled him.

I had tasted a lot of alcohol since I started in the job and I couldn't understand how people enjoyed it so much. Most of it was far too bitter for me, but the liqueurs were different, I liked them. It became my ambition to try the whole collection available. Besides, I saw how jolly and friendly most people got during and after drinking. Of course, I had witnessed drunkenness and bad behaviour too, and I listened to the stories and comments.

'Ah, sure, it's not his fault, it's the drink!'

'He's a grand man, but an awful bollocks with drink taken.'

'He'd drink it off of a sore leg.'

'She'd drop her drawers for anyone after a few jars.'

I purchased three miniature bottles that evening without any bother, a Tia Maria, a cherry brandy and a crème de menthe, and walked down the Esplanade on the cold winter's evening and sat in a shelter to take a swig of the crème de menthe. It tasted good so I had another swig and soon the bottle was empty. I finished off the cherry brandy next, and not long after that I had a wonderful feeling of well-being. It was a manly thing to drink! Will I drink the Tia Maria? What if I get drunk? Ah, feck it, I thought, putting the bottle to my mouth, and it wasn't long before that little bottle followed the other two into the Irish Sea.

I felt a dizziness coming over me and found that I was unsteady when I got to my feet, but oh, so happy. I wobbled my way back to the hotel and was barely in the door to my room when I felt my stomach churning over and just made it to the sink in time to spew out the green and red liquid.

***

On my next visit to Dublin I went to the Mercantile Marine office on Eden Quay to see if I could get a job on a ship.

The place was dimly lit and there was only a tall thin balding man with strands of hair pulled across his pate to hide his baldness.

'What do you want sonny?' he asked.

'Good morning sir,' I replied, 'I have come to ask if there is any possibility of getting a job on a ship? I am presently employed in the International Hotel in Bray.'

'No, you're far too small, sure you'd stand a good chance of fallin' down a scupper!' he said.

I had nothing to lose so I said, 'I don't know what a scupper is, sir, but I can assure you I have no intention of falling down anything, I can look after myself. Thank you for your time.'

I made for the door and he said, 'Hold on! You can speak up for yourself. Let me see your height and your chest size.'

He came out from behind the desk and said, 'Come over here by the wall and stand under this measure.'

I did as I was told and he pulled the level down on my head. 'Step away from the wall,' he ordered. I did so and we both looked at where the level was. I was just a fraction over four feet nine inches. He shook his head and said, 'No need to measure your waist or chest. Just as I thought, you're far too small. Sorry, boy!'

I nodded and walked out of that office with my ego shattered. It took me weeks to get over the shock of that experience and the realisation that my size could hold me back.

***

My visits to Fassaroe became very infrequent. I was convinced that Theresa didn't care if I ever went there at all, just as long as she got her money. I kept Brendan busy with the wages and the so-called overtime money. I was dipping in to my savings but it was worth it.

Theresa had started to buy a lot of stuff on hire purchase a few months after I got my job. Furniture and such like, solely on the strength of the money she was getting from me. It had never occurred to her that my contributions would come to an end, or if it did she wasn't worried. I think she believed she had such a hold on me that I was too weak to do anything about it.

When spring came I went to the National Assistance Board office to enquire about what I had to do to leave the Kennys' care.

'Excuse me sir,' I said to a mountain of a man who ambled over to the counter, 'my name is John Joseph Mahon and I live with Mr and Mrs Kenny in Fassaroe. I would like to know if I can leave their care now and go my own way?'

He looked down at me with what I took to be a scowl of distaste. I got the impression that he resented me taking up his time. He cleared his throat and said, 'I'll see what's on the files. M-A-H-O-N, you said?'

I could see him over in the corner of the office opening and closing the doors of a big brown cabinet until eventually he found what he was looking for and returned to the counter saying, 'I've got you here,' indicating a green cardboard folder. I was tempted to say, no you haven't, I'm standing right in front of you, you bog-trotting old balls, but thought better of it, so instead I said, 'Thank you sir,' and stayed quiet while he was reading the contents.

Finally he looked up and said, 'It's all in here bhoy. You can leave your guardians any time you like. But be warned, if you get up to any mischief you'll be put away for a long time.'

There was a turmoil raging around in my cranium as I thanked him and was out the door, down the stairs and onto the pavement as though I was floating on air.

As I was bouncing down the street, caution came over me. I had to write my goodbye letter to Theresa. What would she do when she received it? Ah balls. If she did come down to the hotel and kick up a fuss, I didn't care. I was thinking of leaving the hotel anyway. I had learned a lot and I loved the old place, but I was worth more than seventeen shillings and three pence per week. The season was just around the corner and I could easily get another job. I would do the letter that very night.

I went in to see Anne and there she was, all by herself, looking pretty in a pink dress. We kissed and she pushed me away, saying, 'You look like you've just won the sweepstakes.'

'Better than that,' I declared, 'I'm free!'

At seven that evening I met Anne again, and I asked her if she would like to go to the pictures, but she said she'd rather have a walk down to the front and hear all about my plans. I wasn't feeling as confident as I had been earlier on, mainly because I had sat down and given a lot more serious consideration to what I had to do. Nevertheless, my determination was strong to get on with whatever was necessary, and it was in that frame of mind that I started to outline my plans to Anne as we walked down towards the sea front.

'I'm going to write a letter to my guardian tonight,' I said. 'After that I will have to wait and see if she makes a fuss. I want to do the season to earn as much as I can, but not in the

International, they take two shillings and nine pence out of my one-pound wages and that's not good enough. It won't be hard to get another job. Anyway, whatever hotel I'm working in, I will leave and go to England at the end the season.'

'Will you be going to your friends in England?' she asked.

'No,' I said, 'I'm going to London.'

We sat in a shelter near the bandstand and she said, holding my hand, 'I think you're very brave, but it all sounds very tricky to me. Of course, you've been to England once. Would it not be a good idea to write to your friends over there to see if they could put you up until you can get a job?'

I held her hands and kissed her and then explained, yes, I had been thinking of that, but it really was my intention to do things alone. I admitted that I was a bit scared of the whole thing. However, I could always write to my friends in Lancashire if I needed to.

Later that night I sat on my bed in the quiet of the room to compose the most important note of my life, and after several attempts I finally managed something like this:

John J Mahon
International Hotel
Bray, County Wicklow
20 May 1959

> *Dear Mrs Kenny,*
> *I visited the welfare officer yesterday and he told me that I am now free to go my own way in life, just as long as I don't get into any trouble.*
> *Thank you for looking after me, and goodbye.*

> *John*

I enclosed my pay for the very last time.

I went around in trepidation for the next three days, and then on the evening of the third day I was having a cup of tea in the staff room when Hughie the night porter came in to tell me that there was a man at reception asking for me. I thanked him and went straight up to see Pat standing by the desk and looking very ill at ease. I hurried up to him and said, 'Hello Pat.'

He looked down at me with a smile and said, 'Ah, son, I'm sorry, but Theresa sent me with this letter for you and I'm to get a reply from you.'

I showed him to a seat in the lounge and asked him to please wait until I got my coat so that we could get out of the hotel and talk in private.

I opened the envelope on the way down, and the note read:

Theresa Kenny
Fassaroe

> *I new you wor up too sumtin and I did knot noe what but i will forget the hole ting if you send me 10/6 a weak thats all.*

> *Theresa*

The cheek of her, I thought. I went in to the public bar to get Pat two bottles of stout and 20 Players and asked Ned the barman to put them in a brown paper bag for me. I handed the bag to Pat as we stepped out of the front door. He looked into it and said, 'Sure there was no need for you to do that son.'

I took him down to the café in the Albert walk, where he had a cup of tea and I had a Pepsi Cola. I asked him to please tell Theresa that I was intending to go to England very soon and I would need every penny I could earn so I wouldn't be sending her any money.

'Good man yourself,' he said, 'I'm pleased to hear you saying that. Now's the time for you to begin your future, and God bless you. I'm sorry for coming down, but you know what she's like, I had to come to get a bit of peace. I'll be off home to her roaring and bawling.'

'I want to thank you for all your kindness to me,' I said, 'I'll never forget you.'

'I only wish I could have done more for you,' he said. 'Goodbye and good luck, son.'

We shook hands and I felt easier, but I had the feeling that wouldn't be the last time he would be forced to come to see me, or worse still, the *Quare Wan* herself might come. So it was time to be moving on.

***

A couple of weeks later I heard they were looking for a lounge waiter in the Esplanade Hotel down on the sea front. I phoned and asked to speak to the manager or manageress, and the very next day I attended for an interview with the proprietor, Mr Lavelle.

He asked if I had a reference. No, I replied, but I could get one from the International Hotel if he wanted me to do so.

'That won't be necessary,' he said. 'I have seen you at work, and heard you singing in the lounge too. Would you sing a few songs in the lounge here each evening? We have a wonderful pianist, her name is Rita Hart, and I'm sure the two of you together could liven up the evenings.'

I said that I would love to sing.

'Good,' he said. 'I will pay you three pounds a week, live in. You will have one day off each week and your hours of duty will be from 9 am to midnight with time off for meals and three hours off each afternoon. Of course, you would be expected to do extra duties for special functions and covering for absenteeism through sickness. Your duties will also include vacuuming, glass cleaning, dusting, polishing and generally helping to keep your area of work clean and tidy.' He asked when would I be able to start.

'In one week's time, after I have given my notice in,' I said. 'But I want to have a day off before starting my new job. Could I please stay on the premises the night before I start?'

'Haven't you got a home?' he asked.

'No sir,' I said, 'I have just left my guardians with the permission of the welfare officer and I'm starting out on my own.'

'In that case,' he said, 'when you leave the International, come here directly, settle yourself in and then you can have three days off before you start.'

I started my new job in June 1959. In many ways I was sad to leave the old friends, and indeed the old hotel itself. I had grown so fond of the place that I knew almost every nook and cranny of it. It had not only been a job for me there, but a launching pad to my future. I had learned so much about people. Their behaviour and how to tactfully react to the most difficult of them, even though I often felt like kicking their shins or jumping up to give them a rap in the mouth. I also learned a lot about the world in general. And last, but certainly not least, Danny's sex education. I still hadn't put the major part of his advice into practice, but I was living in hope.

The Esplanade was a much smaller hotel, but the hours were shorter and the majority of my work was in the lounge. The room I shared with Noel, a 35-year-old, religious, gentle barrel of a man, was much nicer than the one in the International.

I enjoyed my work, and getting up to sing my three songs each evening with Rita Hart on the piano was fun. She was a marvel at being able to keep me in some form of order as I warbled my way through, and it didn't take too long for her to work out a way for me to stay in tune. Well, some of the time anyway!

Mr Lavelle handed me a paper one morning and pointed to an advert which read

Dark nights are bright in the lounge of the Hotel Esplanade
With Rita Hart at the piano and our own inimitable
Johnny Mahon

Seeing my name in print brought on the turkey-cock effect. Red face, chest stuck out, and feeling six feet tall, just as it had done when the Manchester United team had stayed in the International Hotel and my picture had been taken standing between Bill Foulkes and Duncan Edwards. The picture was printed in the *News Chronicle*. It wasn't very good, but it didn't stop me buying six copies of the paper. Sadly, that was just a short time before the Munich air disaster.

During my time in the Esplanade I went out to Enniskerry to visit my cousin Maureen and Dick her husband and their children, John and Noel and the baby Dermot. And for the first time I was able to tell them everything about what went on from the time I moved in with the Kennys to the time Pat came to see me in the hotel.

Maureen said, 'John, I wish to God you had told us. We were under the impression she was looking after you all right. I know she was a strange sort of a person, but I never suspected her of being any way cruel, she always seemed so caring whenever we visited, and of course Pat was such a nice person too.'

'Yes,' I said, 'he was always very kind to me, but she bullied him too.'

I told them I was going to England at the end of the season, and Maureen asked if I had anyone to go to.

I explained that I planned to go it alone. They both suggested that maybe it would do me good to stay with them for a while before I went. Maureen also said she would write to Jimmy and his wife Eileen. They lived in London, and she was sure if they couldn't put me up they would be able to get me digs somewhere.

I thought about that prospect before answering, because I wanted to be independent. My plan was to go over by the mailboat from Dun Laoghaire to Holyhead and get the train to London, booking in to a B&B and then going to the Alfred Marks Catering Agency to see about a job. However, the thought of spending some time with my relations before going seemed very appealing. 'Yes,' I said, 'I would like to spend a few weeks here before I go, thanks.'

'Now now,' said Maureen, 'there's no need for thanks, John, you're one of the family. I'll just drop Jimmy and Eileen a line anyway, it's ages since I've written to them. Did I tell you they've got a son?'

'No,' I replied.

'Well indeed they do and his name is Jimmy. He must be about six months old now.'

The season was in full swing in Bray and all the businesses were doing well, as indeed was I. The larynx was in good order and that was pulling in an extra few coins.

One evening, after doing my act, I was back to serving drinks when I caught a signal from a table with four elderly people sitting at it. I went across to take the order and the baldy man wearing horn-rimmed glasses reached out his big paw to tousle my hair. I stepped back and glared at him. He looked surprised then smiled at the other three and said to me, 'No offence Scobie. I wos jus tryin' to be friendly like. Your singin' wos bleedin' 'ansome son. Do ya know ooh Scobie is?'

'No sir,' I replied frostily, 'I haven't a clue.'

In fact the names of Scobie Breasley and Gordon Richards and several other jockeys had been thrown at me since I had started working by those whom I had come to refer to as smart arses. There wasn't much variation in what they thought were their very own clever observations ... 'If I had been your size, I would have been a jockey, you could be another Scobie or Sir Gordon.'

Baldy said, 'He's one of the finest jockeys the world's ever seen, an' with your size, son, you could be just like 'im.'

That was enough for me, 'Oh a jockey, yes sir,' I said, 'I know what you mean, but I have heard of small men that have shovelled horse shit for years and never got anywhere at all, and besides, I'm scared of horses.'

This brought on laughter from his wife and the other couple.

'Yeah, lad,' he said, 'please get us a drink, two pints of Guinness, a sweet sherry and a port.'

'Certainly sir,' I said. His friend tipped me a wink as I left the table.

When I returned with the drinks, Baldy paid and attempted to give me two shillings tip, but not before he made sure that everyone around would see him doing so. He held the coin out to me with a flourish and loudly said, 'This is for you, lad.'

'That's not necessary sir,' I said.

'Go on boy, take it.'

'Thank you sir, no,' I said. I excused myself, saying, 'There are lots of people needing drinks and if I don't attend to them I'll get the sack.'

His friend said, 'When you have taken care of the others, will you please get us another order in?'

I was kept quite busy throughout the rest of the evening, and that's how I liked it. The time always seemed to fly when we were busy, plus the coins built up faster in the tips pocket. I made countless replenishing trips to Baldy's table, and during these I learned that his name was Murphy and the other couple, who had just met the Murphys that evening, were Minnie and Doug Thomson. They came from Tilbury in Essex, which they told me was about an hour's run on the train from the centre of London.

Doug said, 'If you're ever in London, John, you must come to see us. Tilbury is a quiet place except for the docks. They are always very busy. All the big P&O passenger ships sail in and out of them, and lots of other ships. I'm sure you'd enjoy seeing them.'

'I wrote to the P&O Company in London a few months ago,' I said, 'to ask about getting a job on one of their ships. I sent them a photograph of me singing on the stage.' I had to leave it at that, because thirsty people with empty glasses needed to be served.

When I served the Thomsons and Murphys their last drinks that evening, Doug asked me if there was anywhere we could have a quiet word. 'Yes,' I said, 'I'll have to do a circuit of the lounge to see if anyone needs anything and then I'll be able to tell my colleague Noel that I'm slipping out for a quick cigarette.'

'Right,' said Doug, 'when I see you heading for the door I'll follow you out.'

It was nearing closing time and quiet enough for me to take a break, so I caught Noel's eye and gave him the prearranged signal that I was off for a smoke.

Doug wasted no time in following me out. I held out my packet of Craven A to him and he showed me the cheroot he was holding in his hand saying, 'I prefer these. I liked your quick response to old Jack this evening, John. How old are you?'

'Sixteen years and seven months exactly,' I said.

'I suppose you get fed up with people like Jack coming out with what they think are funny remarks about your youth and height,' he said.

'Yes,' I said, 'sometimes I wish I was six feet tall and could kick them around like a football.'

He laughed and said, 'You didn't need to kick Jack around to get through to him. Are you on duty tomorrow evening?'

'Yes, from 6 pm,' I said.

'Good,' he said. 'I think I might be able to arrange for you to have an interview with a shipping company in London, but it would be subject to you having a satisfactory medical examination and being found suitable for the job.'

Had I heard him right or was I dreaming? All I could say was, 'Thank you sir.'

We returned to the lounge, where non-residents were starting to leave. Rita was finishing off with 'Goodnight sweetheart', and finally the national anthem.

I said goodnight to the Thomsons and the Murphys as they were leaving. Mrs Murphy held back and said, 'I hope Jack didn't upset you, he don't mean no harm, he's always joking, he just opens his big mouth and sometimes he offends people. You're a lovely boy.'

'Thank you ma'am,' I said, 'I'm used to people joking with me. I hope you both enjoy the rest of your holiday.'

I told Noel about what Doug had said as we cleaned up the lounge, and when we finished we took two beers each to our room and talked into the night about the possibilities of me getting away to sea. I hardly slept at all that night, thinking of what Doug had said. Not only would it be a chance of seeing foreign countries, it would prove that old fecker in the marine office in Dublin wrong. But more important, it would prove to myself that I could do a job as well and maybe sometimes better than any of those fellows much bigger and taller than myself.

Minnie and Doug Thomson came into the lounge just after seven o'clock the following evening. There were only a few customers scattered around the lounge, and Noel told me he would hold the fort while I spent a bit of time with them.

I served the Thomsons drinks and Minnie asked if I was allowed to sit down with them. 'No,' I said.

Doug said, 'You mentioned that you had written to P&O. Did you get a reply?'

'Yes, they said they did not recruit by mail, but if I was in London I could phone their personnel department.'

'Well,' said Doug, 'a close friend of mine has a friend in the personnel department of the company. Through him you could get an interview. That will be the easy part but, of course – it will be up to you at the interview.'

'My size might be a problem,' I said with a flaming red face. 'The man in the marine office in Dublin said I was too small.'

Doug responded, 'That is something I will have to go into. I think the minimum height to get in to the merchant navy is five feet two inches, but to the best of my knowledge that minimum is at the discretion of the shipping company. What height are you John?'

'Four feet nine inches,' I replied.

I had to excuse myself to attend to a group of new arrivals, and then I gave Noel an update on what Doug had said.

'Sounds promising to me, John,' he said.

My new friends came in every evening for the remainder of their stay and I sang a different song for them each night until we had to say goodbye. They gave me their address and telephone number with the instruction to make sure to phone them when I got to London. Doug promised that he would write and let me know what he found out about any height restrictions in shipping companies. I gave them Maureen and Dick's address. Doug and I shook hands and Minnie kissed me goodbye.

Pat Kenny paid me two more visits before the end of the season. Theresa had found out where I was working and sent him down to the hotel. Her message was the same on both occasions. Please send her ten shillings a week. My answer was a flat no. Naturally I was deeply sorry for what poor old Pat would have to put up with when he got home, but there was nothing I could do about that.

The season came to an end and I was off. During my period of work in the Esplanade Hotel I had saved forty-five pounds, and that was after I had kitted myself out with a suit, a topcoat, shirts, underwear and shoes for my trip to England.

***

It was the end of September 1959 when I moved in to stay with the family in Kilgarron Park, Enniskerry. My intention was to stay for about three weeks and then skedaddle off across the water to the 'Land of Plenty'.

I felt self-conscious and uncomfortable at first. Visiting was one thing, but actually staying with them was another thing altogether. However, the happy family atmosphere was a wonderful experience and the three boys John, nearly six, Noel, four, and Dermot, three, were a delight and a tonic for me. Money was tight, as it was for most working-class people, but there were always substantial and healthy meals put on the table. Maureen was not only good at producing the food. She was also a wizard with the needle and the sewing machine. I have seen her whipping up a pair of trousers or a jacket for one of the boys in no time at all from an old jacket or any piece of material.

Dick was not in the best of health, with a weak chest, but he had done his best. He was a self-taught motor mechanic and a good one. He would spend hours working on an old car or lorry until he was satisfied that he had achieved as much as he could to get the often clapped-out old vehicle back on the road, and he never had any complaints. Often the person for whom he had done the job would promise to pay him later, and most of them did, although sometimes it would be in kind – a sack of spuds, vegetables and on the odd occasion a bag of coal. His main income came from selling firewood.

Jimmy replied to Maureen's letter, and he also wrote to me with the invitation to feel free to come over any time that suited me, and to rest assured that there would always be a roof over my head with him and Eileen.

Doug Thomson also wrote to me, and the news had me leppin' out of me skin. Yes, there was a minimum height for joining the merchant navy, but it did not apply if a company chose to employ a person below that height. He went on to say that his friend would arrange an interview with P&O when I came to England.

So the future was looking bright, but I was reluctant to leave my new-found comforts and the pleasure of the new friendships I had built up among some of my old schoolfriends and others of my age in the neighbourhood. Travelling on the bus to the cinema in Bray with friends on Saturday evenings was a thrill, and after the show eating fish and chips in a café before catching the last bus home to Enniskerry. I enjoyed myself so much in my new environment that the months just seemed to whizz by.

Christmas came round and I was swept along on the tide of goodwill. I was still living with the Raffertys in late March when I saw an advertisement in the evening paper for staff wanted in a Wimpy Bar in Dun Laoghaire. I applied, and soon I was bashing out the burgers and was as happy as the proverbial pig until the novelty wore off.

After a few weeks of this I went to Bray on my day off and got a job in the Grand Hotel on the seafront. The duties were very similar to those in the Esplanade and the pay was the same, three pounds a week, 'live in'. I worked for eight weeks in the Grand, and what I remember most of that time was the amount of Dubliners that came out mainly on weekends for the singsongs and how they enjoyed themselves. A lot of them liked mixers in their drinks – whiskey&pep, ginanorange, Macardle's ale with a sup a raspberry or a sup a blackcurrant, lagger an' lime. Those sort of orders always aggravated Tom the barman, who was from Galway and had little time for anyone from Dublin. There was no charge for a drop of mixer except if you wanted an individual small bottle – then there was a charge, but not for 'a sup' in a glass of any drink. Tom complained so much about their taste that he was like a never-ending recording and it was always the same. 'Dem feckin' Dubliners! Always lookin' for somethin' for nottin. A fella'd have to be up woeful early in the mornin' teh be up teh dhim.'

I never did any singing in the Grand, nor did I care to. On reflection, I think I had lost interest in it and had recognised that I wasn't much good and it was unlikely that I could ever earn a living at it. My big ambition now was to go to England, and above all to get work on the ships going to foreign parts and as far away from Ireland as possible.

2

Keep your wits about you

I left the Grand Hotel towards the end of August 1960 and went to stay with Maureen, Dick and their three boys for a couple of weeks before boarding the *Princess Maud* for London via Holyhead. I stood on the deck with tears streaming down my face as I waved goodbye to my family. The vessel slowly edged away from the quay and eventually out of sight of land. I was on my way.

I walked around the deck until the cold air drove me below. I found the tea bar, bought a cup of tea and managed to squeeze myself into a corner in the packed lounge amidst the chattering, laughter and singing. I didn't want to talk to anyone and hoped that I would be left alone, but that was not to be.

I had been sitting in my corner for about five minutes when I spotted a pudgy, friendly-looking lady coming straight towards me. She smiled as she asked in a soft Dublin voice, 'Are you travelling by yerself son? Is it your first time?'

'Yes ma'am, I mean, it is my first time going over to look for work. I travelled over to Liverpool by the *Leinster* a year or so ago, but that was just to visit friends in Preston,' I said, thinking, I wish you'd leave me alone lady.

'I was no older than you when I first came this very same way, and that's a long time ago now,' she said. 'Is there anyone to meet you at the other end?'

'Yes,' I replied, 'my cousin will be meeting me at Euston.'

'So you're going to London,' she said. 'There's plenty of work there, but you mind yerself and keep your wits about you. I'm with me son and daughter-in-law. We live in Cheshire and we've just had a fortnight's holidays in Dublin.

It's always grand to go back home no matter how poor you were or what sad memories you left behind you in days gone by. It'll always be home – and you'll find that too, son, you mark my words.'

Just as she left someone near me started retching, and that was enough to send me scurrying to the toilet to puke. I found the place crowded with men and boys of all ages in various forms of disarray. The smell of body odour mingled with vomit and the sight of it all over the sinks and on the floor caused me to be violently sick, and when the ordeal was over I gingerly stepped out of that stinking place and found it hard to keep my balance with the movement of the ship. One moment I was walking up a steep hill and the next I was holding onto the rail with all my strength to prevent myself from being thrown forward.

An elderly steward came along the alleyway and saw my plight. 'Give me your arm, lad, I'll help you. There's an empty cabin just around the corner where you can get your head down. You look all in.'

He led me to the dimly lit twin-berth cabin. 'You lie down now and I'll be back with something to settle your stomach.' I could hardly believe my good fortune, and was contemplating giving him five shillings tip when he returned with a packet of cream crackers. 'You probably don't want to eat anything,' he said, 'and you're thinking you'll never want to eat ever again, but believe me, if you can just get a couple of these biscuits down, you'll feel much better. They'll help to dry up the acid in your stomach. I'll be back to see you later, try to get a bit of sleep.'

I ate two biscuits and lay as still as I could, and the next thing I knew the steward was back and the movement of the ship was less erratic. 'We're out of the worst of it now,' he said. 'How do you feel?'

'Much better thank you,' I replied. 'What's your name please?'

'Larry,' he said.

'Thank you Larry,' I said. 'I would like you to please take this five shillings for all you've done for me.'

'I will not!' he said. 'This cabin was booked and paid for, but the passengers never showed up. I could have made a few quid out of renting it out again, but there were no takers and that's the reason you're here free of charge.'

After much persuasion he reluctantly took the five bob and I was pleased. 'Where are you heading for?' he asked.

'London,' I said. 'There's a possibility I might get an interview for a job on the big passenger liners. But I have three years' hotel experience and I think I'll stick to that because the way I've been feeling on this trip suggests I'd be no good at it.'

He held up his hands and said, 'That's pure rubbish you're talking. You're giving up before you start. You take my word for it, if you get a chance of going off to sea on one of the passenger jobs, jump at it, there's no better life. I had twenty years of it before I got married and settled down. I sailed in all the big liners, cargo ships and tankers too. My problem was that I could never hold onto any of my money. I pissed it right up the wall. I got far too fond of the booze and it wasn't until I met my wife ten years ago that I started to get sense, and now I never touch a drop. We're as happy as the day we first met and I don't miss the drink at all. Don't worry about the way you're feeling now, this can be one of the roughest sea passages in the world. You'd be wrong to compare this trip and this old rust bucket to the big vessels that sail the oceans of the world.' He looked at his watch and said, 'Once I get to talking about the old days I lose all track of time. I'd better be off to check on the occupants of my other cabins if I don't want the push.'

When he came back later he told me of his first trip to sea on the SS *Strathnaver*. He had been employed as a scullion and every time he looked at a plate with even a bit of food on it he was sick, and it was worse when he had nothing to bring up at all, and that's when he was introduced to dry toast and cream crackers. He was sick on and off for about a week and then he never looked back.

Feeling much better, and very hopeful about a seagoing career, I said goodbye to him at the gangway and headed off to catch the train. I boarded the train to London, found a seat, curled myself into a ball and slept for most of the journey to Euston. As the train approached the station I was excited and a little apprehensive too. Would I recognise Jimmy, or would he recognise me?

There had been no need for me to worry. I spotted him

coming along the platform just about the same time as he saw me. We both waved to each other and soon he was hugging me and welcoming me to the 'Big Smoke'.

He took my small reinforced-cardboard suitcase and led the way down to the underground station, which he told me was called the Tube. I had never seen anything like it. The crowds, the big glossy advertisements on the walls and the big red, white and blue logo really impressed me, but not half as much as when I witnessed the first train coming through the tunnel. Jimmy gently pulled me back, explaining that the crowds could be very unruly in their haste and it was always safer to stand well back from the edge of the platform. 'Just watch them,' he said. I did, closely. The train came to a stop, the doors opened automatically and out stepped hundreds of people who scurried hither and thither. A large percentage of those who had been standing on the platform boarded, and the train was on its way again.

We boarded the next train that came along and were on our way to Paddington, where we changed to catch a connection to Earls Court. We then walked a short distance into West Cromwell Road and an even shorter distance to number 56, where Jimmy, Eileen and their one-year-old son Jimmy lived in a large room, in which they cooked, ate, relaxed and slept. The bathroom and toilet was a few steps down the stairs.

Jimmy tapped on the door and entered. I followed, and there stood his lovely wife Eileen, with brown hair and eyes to match. She came across the room smiling and embraced me.

'Welcome to London, John,' she said. 'We're a bit cramped here, but please make yourself at home.'

Junior, who was happily playing with a teddy bear on the floor, quickly abandoned it and crawled over to satisfy his curiosity by checking me over and using me as a means of pulling himself up to a staggering position. 'You're in, John,' said, Jimmy.

After a breakfast of rashers, sausages, eggs and tomatoes we settled down for a long chat about our families, friends, neighbours and *quare hawks* in Donegal, Eileen's part of the country, and ours in County Wicklow, and finally about the jobs I had done.

Jimmy told me there was a job going in the hotel he worked in, the Onslow Court in Queen's Gate, and he had put in a good word for me with the manageress. He explained that the job was serving the senior staff in their dining room. I wouldn't be making any tips, but at least it would give me a start. I could live in, and if I wished he would arrange for an interview in a couple of days time when I was rested.

I said I'd like to get a start as soon as possible. I told them about Mr Thomson and the possibility of getting an interview with the P&O shipping company, and I felt that if I was working when I went for the interview it might be in my favour.

Jimmy junior was asleep now, and Jimmy had to go to work at 1 pm. Eileen said that after Junior had his sleep she would take me out and show me around if I wasn't too tired.

'No,' I said, 'I'm not tired at all, and I'd love to see a bit of London.'

Junior must have sensed that I was anxious to be out and about because he started gurgling and then stood up in his cot with his little arms outstretched to his mother. She lifted him out, dressed him, and then we were off down the stairs to the hall, where she took what she called a pushchair from beneath the stairs. I carried it down the five steps to the pavement and she unfolded it and placed the happy little fellow inside.

'We'll take a walk up to Kensington High Street and I'll show you where I work,' she said.

That's strange, I thought. 'How do you manage to go to work when you've got a baby to look after?'

She smiled and looked even lovelier in the sunlight as she replied, 'A lot of married women go out to work over here, John. I leave Jimmy with a childminder and then either Jimmy or I pick him up in the evenings, it depends on what duty he's on and whether I have to work late.'

As we walked along in the warm September sunshine, I was taking in everything, the big red buses, the street signs and all the well-dressed people. We reached the High Street, where Eileen was pointing out the shops and buildings of interest until we came to Barkers of Kensington.

'This is where I work,' she said. 'I drive one of the lifts. It's a good job, and as you see it's not far from home. Would you like to have a look inside?'

We walked around the ground floor, but I didn't see much difference to Clerys store in Dublin. Later, in a nice little café, she asked was I going to have tea or coffee. I said that I couldn't resist the coffee because of the delirious smell of it. She gave me a quizzical look and said she would like a pot of tea for one and a wedge of chocolate cake – and laughingly suggested that I should give it a try because it was 'delirious'.

Back at the flat that evening, Eileen pulled out and made up a camp bed, pointed out the curtain that Jimmy had rigged for the benefit of my privacy, and said, 'There you are sir. It's not the Ritz, but it's yours for as long as it suits you. I have a nice bit of steak for our tea with egg, chips and onions, how's that?'

I asked her many questions about London and played with little Jimmy until his bedtime. She told me more about her home in Donegal and how she sometimes missed her family. She asked how I had felt about coming to England, and added, 'Ah, maybe it's far too soon to be asking you such a question, sure you've only just got here.'

'No,' I said, 'it's not too soon at all. I've wanted to come over here for a long time, and never more so since I thought of going to sea – and if I can get a job on the ships I will be delighted, providing I can do the job.'

Jimmy arrived home just after 10 pm looking tired, but he was smiling as he declared that he was off duty for the next three days, so he would show me around some more. Then he told me that Miss Smith, the manageress of the hotel, would like to see me in a couple of days' time for an interview.

I was thrilled and a bit nervous, but this would be my first step nearer to going to sea. The memories of the interviews I had experienced in Ireland were not good. I was nervous at each one of them and had a feeling of being stripped naked for the world to see. Nevertheless, it had to be done.

The next morning I awoke at ten o'clock to the sound of the door opening, and I said good morning from behind my curtain. Eileen said she hoped she hadn't disturbed me. 'No,' I lied, 'I was thinking of getting up.'

'Jimmy's gone out for the paper,' she said. 'He'll be back soon and then we'll have breakfast.'

By this time I had slipped my trousers and vest on and was in the process of pulling the curtain back when Jimmy came in and said, 'The dead arose and appeared to many! My god, it's a gorgeous day out there, the sun's splittin' the trees and it's far too good to be missed. Just the day for showing John around Hammersmith and Shepherd's Bush.'

Shortly afterwards, we boarded a bus for Hammersmith, went upstairs and occupied the two front seats. It was a big red bus just like the ones I had seen in the picture house and in photographs. As we chugged along, sometimes at a snail's pace because of the traffic, I noticed a couple of public houses with a sign on the board outside stating 'free house'. I was naive but not so much so that I believed they actually gave away the drink for nothing. I asked Jimmy what it meant, and he explained that those pubs were free to sell any brand of alcohol and were not subject to the rules of the breweries that owned a large percentage of the pubs in London.

We walked around Hammersmith, which I didn't think much of. I found the atmosphere very different to that in Dublin or Preston. Most people seemed to be in a hurry, scurrying to and fro as though their very lives depended upon it. We walked and talked our way to Shepherds Bush and the market. It was different there, with the traders extolling the virtues of their wares, a jolly place. I was fascinated with all the stalls and shops, the goods on display and the crowds just strolling around.

I spotted a shoe shop selling boys' shoes and remembered how I had lusted after a pair of suede boots I had seen on a little old man who had been on holiday in the Esplanade Hotel. He was about my height, and I reasoned that his shoes would have fitted me. So began a long hunt for a pair just like them, but alas, my searching was in vain. I could not find a pair of boy's size three and a half in any of the stores in Dublin or Bray.

I asked Jimmy if we could go in to have a look, and we were barely in the door when a short thin man with a hooked nose that would put any self-respecting parrot to shame came rushing over to us, saying, 'Good afternoon gentlemen, can I be of any assistance?'

'Yes please,' I said. 'Do you have any suede boots to fit me, size three and a half, four?'

'I'll see what we've got. Please take a seat,' he said and was off at a gallop.

Nosy came back with two boxes. 'It must be your lucky day, young man,' he said. 'I have a pair of shoes and a pair of boots with elasticated sides, try them on.'

Both pairs fitted. I was delighted, and wanted to buy both of them. While Nosy attended to another customer Jimmy asked me how much I was prepared to pay.

'Between five and eight pounds a pair,' I said.

'Right,' he said, 'leave that to me.'

Nosy came back with a broad grin and asked, 'How did you get on, do they fit?'

'Just right,' I said.

'Yes,' said Jimmy, 'we'll take the boots if the price is to our liking.'

'Well,' responded Nosy, lightly running his hand through his hair and looking as though he was having to make the biggest decision of his whole life, 'they're on sale now for just five pounds a pair and that's a giveaway price.'

Jimmy stood up as though we were about to leave and so did I. 'We'll give you seven pounds for the two pairs,' said Jimmy.

Nosy responded, 'That's robbery, that's what it is. Make it nine pounds. How do you expect a family man with many mouths to feed to make a living at such a price?'

Jimmy took a few more steps towards the door and I thought damn it, there go my lovely boots – then to my surprise Nosy said, 'Oh, all right, you can have them for eight pounds. What do you care if my children starve?'

The deal was done and out we walked, Jimmy gleeful, and me equally so. 'I know that old Jew man,' he said. 'He wouldn't sell anything at a loss. Possibly I could have got him down further, but I think we got a bargain.'

It was time for something to eat. 'There's a nice clean little café around the corner where we can have a sandwich and a drink,' said Jimmy, 'but first I want to show you something. A large number of Irish live in this area and a fair amount of coloureds too, so there's lots of house owners offering digs, some better than others. It's the ads in the windows I want to show you, because I think they'll soon be a thing of the past.'

He led me to a dirty littered street where most of the

141

buildings looked grim and in need of a coat of paint to say the least. The window coverings ranged from dirty old lace and rags to newspapers, with the odd good pair of curtains in between. I thought, if they look so bad from the outside what must they be like inside? He steered me towards several windows with notes stuck in them advertising rooms to let, all with a similar theme:

SINGLE ROOM TO LET
NO CHILDREN OR PETS
NO IREISH OR CULOUREDS NEED APPLY

'You'd think some of them would check their spelling,' I said. 'Why the bar on the Irish and coloureds?'

'I'll explain when we get to the café,' he said.

***

The day came for my interview with the manageress of the Onslow Court Hotel, which turned out to be a formality and I was given the job at four pounds per week 'live in' for staggered hours, which I was used to. I started work towards the end of September 1960. The accommodation was a cubicle with a curtain for privacy, nothing to feel at home in, but still it was a roof over the head. The work was much easier than what I had been used to and the hours were less too, but I missed the tips and the contact with the paying guests.

I phoned Doug Thomson a few days later. He said he was very happy to hear from me and quickly told me that he was going to have to hand the phone over to his wife, otherwise she would strangle him with the cable in her attempts to get it out of his hands to talk to me. She came on the line asking me a stream of questions at the speed of a machine gun's rat-a-tat-tat. How long had I been in England? Where was I living? Was I working? How was my health? When I had answered all her questions, Doug came back on the line.

'I'm pleased to tell you it only remains for a suitable time to be arranged for the interview with the P&O shipping company,' he said. I could hardly believe my ears.

A visit to the Thomsons was arranged for the Friday of the following week, when I had a day off, and a few days later I received a letter with a train timetable from Fenchurch Street to Tilbury Riverside and instructions on how to get to their house by bus from the station.

I arrived at the Thomsons around noon on a cold day in October, and despite the cold outside the warmth of the welcome within was akin to being wrapped up in a package of sunshine, with hugs and kisses from Minnie and a manly embrace from himself. I liked their house. It was clean and everything was tidily in order. The bookcases were full with a large variety of interesting titles by some of the world's famous authors, but the large collection of record albums from classical to the latest releases of the time really caught my eye.

We sat drinking tea, and they were both full of questions. How was the trip across? Good, apart from the seasickness. Did I miss Ireland? No, I intended to start a new life in England.

They asked me about my family in Ireland, and I told them that I was just getting to know them properly when I came to England. I told them about life with my mother before her death when I was eleven years old, a bit about my time with the Kennys and my visit to the welfare officer who gave me permission to leave the Kennys officially. I could see Minnie had tears in her eyes. She excused herself and left the room.

Doug told me to phone the P&O personnel office to set up a suitable date and time for an interview. Once again my mind was in a spin and all I could think of was how sick I had been on the *Princess Maud*. I told him of my reservations.

'John,' he said, 'don't let that worry you. They make allowances for all "first trippers". Do you remember I told you about our son Vic, and him being a seaman. He was sick on his first trip, that's over twenty-five years ago and he's still going to sea, he's chief cook on a tanker up the Persian Gulf at the moment. You might not know it, but the Irish Sea can be one of the roughest in the world. If you pass the interview and the medical I have every confidence you will make a fine young steward.'

Minnie came into the room and announced, 'Lunch, gentlemen!' We enjoyed a hearty meal, and I barely had room for the gooseberry tart and custard 'afters', but I managed to clean my plate, and I could see that pleased Minnie. I enjoyed their company for a few more hours and then it was time to go.

I phoned the P&O offices at ten o'clock on the Monday

morning and gave my name to the man who answered. He asked me to please hold on, and when he came back on the line he asked, 'Mr Mahon, are you working at the moment?'

'Yes sir,' I replied.

'What day would be suitable for you to come here for an interview?'

'Friday,' I said. 'That is my day off.'

'Good,' he said. 'Next Friday, 11 am. You will find the personnel entrance in St Mary Axe. Don't forget your references, and when you get here please ask for Mr James.'

That was it, another step towards my dream.

***

The big day came and I was up at dawn. My only problem was deciding on what tie to wear with my white shirt and blue suit. I decided on a blue one. That decision made, I was ready to present myself. I left the hotel at 8.30 am and had over an hour to kill after familiarising myself with where I had to go. I had a coffee in a café and walked around until ten minutes to eleven. Then I walked down the narrow street of St Mary Axe and through the doors of the personnel department. I nervously introduced myself to the man in the small reception office. He looked at some papers, then asked for my references and said, 'Please take a seat, Mr Mahon.' I sat next to two other young fellows and a very pretty girl. All three of them nodded and smiled at me. I reciprocated, but not a word was exchanged between us and that gave me more heart. I thought they must be as nervous as I was.

I was the first to be called. The receptionist led me to a room adjacent, knocked on the door and ushered me in, saying, 'Mr John Mahon.'

'Thank you Mr James,' said the big grey-haired, red-faced man behind the desk. He smiled and said, 'Good morning young man. I have read your references and you have the experience necessary for a steward's position. However, you are not yet eighteen and you can't become an assistant steward, which is an adult rating, until you reach that age. We have vacancies for bellboys. The pay is twelve pounds and ten shillings per month for a voyage of approximately three to four months. Why do you want a job at sea?'

'I think it would be a great opportunity to see and learn

about other countries, the people and their customs,' I said.

'Yes, there's that,' he said, 'but there's a lot of hard work and it would not be a case of you going ashore as soon as the vessel docked. You might be needed to do any number of duties when you get into port, and quite possibly you might find you couldn't go ashore at all. How would you feel about that?'

'Not being able to go ashore would be a disappointment, but I would consider it a big bonus whenever it was possible to do so,' I said.

'Have you ever been on a ship or a boat,' he asked.

'Yes sir,' I replied, 'three times. An overnight trip to Liverpool and a return trip to Dublin and a trip to Holyhead on the mailboat. I was seasick on all three occasions, but I think I've found a remedy for that, dry cream crackers.'

He nodded and smiled. Then, after a few more questions, he said, 'I am prepared to employ you subject to a satisfactory medical examination, and possibly you may have to undergo another in the Shipping Federation. Can you take our medical today?'

'Yes sir,' I replied. 'Today is my day off.'

He picked up the phone and asked someone what time he could make an appointment for me, repeated 3 pm, hung up and said, 'You have lunch, Mr Mahon, and report back to Mr James at 2.45 pm. He will give you the necessary paperwork for your examination, and when you have completed your medical please report back to him.'

He stood up, indicating that the interview was over. I left the office on a high – but not so high that I forgot I still had to have the medical. I slowly walked along the pavements, dodging my fellow pedestrians and feeling as light as a leaf, neither knowing nor caring where I was going until I found myself outside a greasy spoon café in Leadenhall Market. I went in and ordered a cheese sandwich and a cup of tea, both of which were handed to me within minutes. An eat it 'n' beat it place, I thought as I sat at a small table in the corner and went over what had happened so far that morning.

I studied the sailing schedule of the P&O vessels over another cup of tea, the names of the ships and the arrival and departure times for the various ports around the world. I recognised a lot of the names, and they seemed to jump off the page at me: Hong Kong, San Francisco, Los Angeles,

Vancouver, Melbourne – I remembered that one because of the Olympic Games in 1956 – and several more. There were many that I had never heard of: Kobe, Yokohama, Manila, Fremantle, Adelaide, Sydney. I ordered another cup of tea and went over the list again. It was even more interesting the second time around, so I decided to buy myself a world atlas.

I left the café and strolled around at ease, popping in and out of bookshops. Although I read a lot, I had never been in a bookshop until that day. I looked at the collections of atlases and compared the prices, but decided to put the purchase off until after my medical because I didn't want to be carrying anything into the doctor's office.

I reported to Mr James at 2.40 pm and he directed me to the doctor's office a couple of floors above.

'Please sit down, Mr Mahon,' said the doctor.

I did so, and was glad to because I now felt that my legs had turned to rubber. I was thinking that this was one of the two biggest hurdles I had to get over in order to secure a future at sea. He seemed to squint and asked, 'When was the last time you needed to see your doctor?'

'Roughly about seven years ago,' I replied, 'but I have been to a dentist about three years ago to have eight bad teeth pulled and a number of fillings done.'

He ummed and said, 'So, you have enjoyed good health except for your teeth for a long time.'

'Yes sir,' I said.

He stood up, and that's when the examination really began.

He stethoscoped me, banged my knees with little things that reminded me of drumsticks, foraged around in my mouth and ears, and then asked me to drop my trousers and underpants. He put rubber gloves on and told me to bend over. I did so, feeling very embarrassed as he spread my cheeks. 'Stand up straight,' he commanded and when I did so he weighed my balls in his hand and said, 'Cough.' That I did and all I could think of was how small my mickey looked ...

'Get dressed,' he said. 'You are in very good health, now let's see how tall you are.'

I could see the measuring stick by the wall and went straight to it, thinking, 'This is it!'

He guided me to the centre and brought the movable piece

down on my head and said, 'Four feet nine and a half inches, now for your weight.' I stood on the scales and the indicator pointed at seven stone exactly. 'Good,' he said, 'there is no reason why you should not go to sea.'

I thanked him with a grin as wide as the River Thames, and where I was bouncing earlier in the day I was now positively leppin' with delight, so much so that I passed Mr James's office and was out on the pavement before I remembered.

I took the stairs two at a time back to his office with a new-found energy. I had to wait for about thirty minutes before Mr James handed me a letter for the Mercantile Marine Office in Dock Street and explained that I was to go there and present the letter. I would then be photographed for an identity card and seaman's discharge book, and when this had been done I was to await further instructions by letter from him.

He suggested I should go to the Mercantile Marine office straight away, so he gave me directions and presented me with a little map with the MMO clearly marked.

I thanked him and was on my way in the direction he had explained. I looked the map over but it meant nothing to me. Back in Ireland in those days I would have been classed as an *eejit*, but today they would probably say I was 'disalectric' with maps.

I found the office after asking several people along the way and handed my papers to a lantern-jawed young man who introduced himself as Mr Osborne. He read the letter and stepped away from the counter, consulted with an older colleague and then returned. He said, 'I will take you to have your photographs taken and then we shall get the necessary particulars down.'

The photos were taken and the forms were nearly completed when he said, 'We have to measure your height.'

Alarm bells were ringing in my head at that. Could this be the place that all my ambitions would be shattered?

'I've just had a thorough medical,' I said, 'and I was measured too. I'm four feet nine and a half inches tall.'

He smiled and said, 'It's necessary to have such particulars printed on both your ID card and your discharge book.'

So we got that over with, and the paperwork was soon finished.

Before I left I asked where the nearest telephone box was, and I was directed to the Red Ensign Club just around the corner. As I entered a vicious-looking brute of a man dressed in a dark uniform came over to me and asked, 'What d'ya want here sonny?'

I moved back a few paces so that I could look him in the eye and said, 'I have been advised to come in here by an officer from the MM Office to ask if I can use the telephone.'

He looked down at me distastefully and snorted, 'Ask the receptionist.'

I went over to the desk and found a much friendlier countenance, that of an elderly man with grey hair and smiling eyes set in a red, red face. I asked him if I could please use the phone and would it be possible to make the kind of call where at the end of it I could be told how much it cost.

'Yes, son,' he said, 'come into the office and I will arrange that small thing for you.'

I gave him the Thomsons' number, and in moments I was spluttering out all the events of my day, not once stopping to take a breath until I had unloaded the lot to Doug, and as I rattled on he was relaying my story to Mrs T. When I finally had to stop to suck in some air it was his turn to speak and he said, 'John, I have to hand this phone to you know who, she is as excited as you sound.'

After I had talked with Minnie for a while I hung up and paid the man for the call. I left the club and found the Tower Hill underground station without much difficulty. At the rate I was getting around London I would soon know it better than Dublin.

Eileen and Jimmy were at home to hear my happy tale, and once again I gave it to them in rapid fire. Eileen placed a cup of tea and a plate of mixed sandwiches down in front of me. I demolished the lot and held up my cup for a refill, and she smiled approvingly as she poured the tea. 'It seems like hungry work, preparing for going off on those posh liners,' she said.

Jimmy studied the sailing schedule, scratched his ear a few times, and asked me what I knew of the places listed. He was a well-read man, and I guessed that he would tell me something about most of the countries, if not all of them.

He stood up from the table and went over to the bookcase,

returning with a world atlas, a jotter and pen – and he proceeded to educate me in the geography of the world.

***

I received a letter from P&O on Thursday confirming that my medical had been satisfactory and when I had received my discharge book and identity card I was to telephone the personnel department. If I was leppin' with excitement before I was positively gallopin' now.

Friday, my day off, I was up and rarin' to go. I left the hotel at 8 am, and before long I was standing outside the Mercantile Marine office waiting for it to open. The old doors finally creaked open, and in I stepped to collect my books, which would be my passport to a career at sea. If that wasn't proof enough that I was as good as any other man despite my height, I didn't know what was.

Mr Osborne came over to the counter with a brown envelope in his hand and said with a smile, 'Good morning, Mr Mahon. I bet you've had some restless nights thinking of getting these.' He slid the envelope across to me.

I whipped the contents out, and there before my eyes was the blue seaman's discharge book with my name on it and the same on my red identity book.

Mr Osborne picked up both books and said, 'Your photos have come out very well. Please sign them and take great care of them, and if you should lose either of them you must report it to this office without delay. The numbers on both of these books are exclusively yours.'

I phoned Mr James at P&O. There was no need for me to go to the office, he would write to me with instructions for joining my first ship, and he would give me plenty of time to give my notice in to the hotel. Next I phoned the Thomsons and gave them the good news and promised that I would phone again within a few days.

Then it was off to explore some of London and the bookshops to buy my atlas. I was a happy lad until some doubts entered my mind. What if I couldn't do the job because of seasickness? How much different would it be from the work in hotels? What about the uniforms? Would there be some to fit me?

I doubted it, and cursed myself for not having asked Mr

James about such an important thing. I tried to put the doubts and fears out of my mind but it wasn't easy so I buried myself in several bookshops and eventually bought the atlas, after which I just wandered around until I came upon a Lyons Corner House. I looked inside and realised I was very hungry, so I went in, sat down, studied the menu and decided on a gammon steak with chips and tomatoes.

I handed in my notice the next day, and that gave me the freedom to talk to my colleagues about going to sea. My last week in the Onslow Court Hotel went by in a flash. On my last day, Jimmy came on the late duty and presented me with an official-looking envelope. I went to the staff quarters, opened it carefully and read the instructions to join the *Himalaya* in Tilbury Docks on 3 November 1960.

A footnote said that if I had any queries not to hesitate in phoning Mr James. That I did, to ask about the uniforms, and he assured me there was no need to worry, the naval outfitters had a shop in the docks and they would supply me with all that was necessary. I would need a cap, a pair of blue trousers, three pairs of white trousers for the tropics, three white jackets, a mess jacket, several pairs of white and blue socks, and two pairs of shoes, black laced for normal wear, and a white laced pair for the tropics. I asked him if I would have to pay for all that lot.

'Yes, Mr Mahon,' he said. 'You can pay cash or you can sign for it and it will be deducted from your pay at the end of the voyage.'

I had twenty-five pounds saved, but I might need that for travelling and other expenses. I remembered my mother telling me to do my best never to get into debt.

I phoned the Thomsons and we talked for ages, and it was agreed that when I had started 'working by', storing and generally preparing the vessel for her next voyage, I would stay with them in my very own room. I was both happy and humbled by all their kindness. My mind went back to when I had first met them, and how fortunate I had been to do so.

***

I left the hotel and stayed with Eileen, Jimmy and Junior for about eight days before taking the train to Tilbury and my new career. I caught a taxi from the station to the docks, where a policeman stopped us at the gate and the driver said, 'A crew member for the *Himalaya*.' The bobby glanced in at me and waved us on.

We pulled up at the crew gangway, and the driver handed me my two little suitcases. I stood there on the dock looking up at the massive white ship and wondered, where do I go from here? A crane was swinging a big crate onto the deck with directions from a man dressed in a battered peaked cap and a long dark overcoat tied around the middle with a rope. He was standing by the ship's rail giving hand signals and letting out the occasional curse that I'm sure would not have been approved of if there had been any passengers on board. There was a line of men dressed in grey and white striped jackets and denims passing brown boxes from the back of a big blue van along the quay and right up the gangway into the ship. Ants, I thought. I saw the naval outfitters just across the way – it was a bonus to know they were so close. I carried my cases to the foot of the gangway and decided to wait for a lull in the storing before attempting to set foot on it.

Suddenly a tall fair-haired man came over to me and asked, 'Are you joining, mate?'

'Yes,' I replied, 'I'm a bellboy. Can you please tell me where I have to go?'

'I'll do better than that,' he said, 'I'll take you there.'

He introduced himself as Pete, and explained that this was his first trip too. We were inside the ship now, and I couldn't put a name to the smell. It seemed to be a combination of must, stale air, body odour and paraffin oil and I didn't like it. Pete led the way along what he called the working alleyway, then up two flights of stairs, which he told me were called companionways. He stopped outside a small office and said, 'This is the second steward's office. See you later.'

I knocked on the open door and was greeted by a heavy-set man with three silver rings on his sleeve. I placed my books and joining papers on the desk and said, 'John Mahon, sir.'

He looked me up and down and said, 'You are the smallest young man to join my team – still, being a bellboy your height may well be to your advantage.' I didn't know exactly what he meant but I took it to be a good sign.

He explained about the duties in preparation for the sailing on 11 November, and how I would be expected to 'muck in' whenever and wherever required. Then he directed me to my cabin, no. 43, and asked, 'Have you any valuables in your gear?'

'Not really,' I answered.

'Nevertheless,' he said, 'leave it here for now and pop over to Miller and Rayners. Buy yourself a combination lock and while you're there you can get kitted out with your uniform – and when you have done that and locked your gear away, you are to report to Mr Morris. You will find him in the tourist restaurant or down on the quay with the storing gang.'

I retraced my steps down to the working alleyway, dodging all sorts of people coming and going, and went in pursuit of my cabin. After much doubling back on myself and going around in circles I found it. The door was shut. I knocked and turned the handle. It was open so I stepped inside.

There were eight metal bunks in sets of two, one up, one down, and at the foot of each couple of bunks were two wooden drawers and two metal lockers, five of which I noticed were locked. Situated beneath a porthole was a tea chest covered with a floral cloth, and on top of that was a collection of drinking glasses, mugs and two clean ashtrays. I was not impressed by what I saw – somehow it didn't fit in with my image of what the crew accommodation on a luxury liner would be like – but I was used to the crummy conditions of staff rooms in hotels. My biggest worry was, would I be able to secure a bottom bunk? I just couldn't see myself getting up to the top bunk without a ladder and I couldn't see one in the cabin.

I crossed the dock to the outfitters, where a tall thin man picked out the smallest sizes of the items of uniform that I needed, but the only thing that really fitted was the cap.

'Not to worry,' he said, 'I will sort it out for you. Let me take your measurements to have the alterations done. When do you sail?'

'On the eleventh of this month,' I said.

He set about measuring me, and when he had finished he said, 'I shall mark your order urgent so they can hurry it up. Are you working today?'

'Yes,' I said.

'You will need to have a mess jacket, then. Let's see how it looks on you again.'

It hadn't shrunk any, but he convinced me that with the sleeves tucked up it wouldn't look too bad. He took a card full of shiny silver buttons with clips from a drawer and placed them on the counter and they looked beautiful, with little anchors and a rising sun hammered into the metal. 'Here we go,' he said, and proceeded to put the rings of the buttons into the holes specially made to fit them, then he secured each button with a little clip, and when he had finished he said, 'There you are young man, job done. Come back in four days and hopefully I will have the rest of your things.'

I was about to leave with my meagre bundle when I remembered the lock. He produced a combination lock and handed it to me, then carefully added it to my bill. I lined up the numbers that were on a tag attached and bop, it opened. I locked it and tested it again with the same result. I put it in my pocket, thanked the man and left.

When I got to my cabin the door was open and inside was a big dark-haired, dark-skinned man. I looked up at him and said, 'My name is John Mahon, I have just joined and I was told that I'm in this cabin. Can you please tell me which locker I can use, and will I be able to get a bottom bunk?'

'I'm Cyril,' he said. 'This is an assistant stewards' cabin. You'll have to go to the bellboys' cabin when they finish doing whatever they're doing in there. In the meantime, you can use that bottom bunk near the porthole, and that locker with the open door is where you can put your gear. Have you got a lock?'

I proudly showed him my recent purchase and told him I was off to collect my suitcases from the second steward's office.

'It's good to get it done before lunch,' he said. 'You've got twenty minutes. We have a break between one and two o'clock. You get on with that and I'll arrange for the peak steward to make up your bunk.'

Back at the office I found a man with one and a half silver rings on his sleeve.

'Excuse me sir,' I said, 'I have just returned from the

outfitters and I have come to take my suitcases to my cabin and then I have to report to Mr Morris.'

'I am Mr Morris,' he said, 'You carry on, and report to me at muster in the tourist saloon at 2 pm. Sharp.'

I picked up my suitcases, and when I got down to the working alleyway I was approached by a shortish brown-skinned young man, dressed in the now familiar mess jacket and dungarees, 'I help you, I help you,' he said. With that he reached out and took one of my suitcases, indicating that I should follow him. I gave him a look with raised eyebrows. He smiled and said, 'OK, you no worry, I help you, you nice boy, I help.' He led the way to the cabin and I wondered how he knew which one I was in.

It was all cleared up for me when we entered. Cyril was there, drinking beer with three other men of varying ages. 'Fernandes!' he said. 'Thank you for helping our new man.'

Fernandes bowed out, and when he was gone Cyril explained, 'He is our peak steward. In other words, he makes our bunks, keeps the cabin tidy, wakes us up in the mornings with a cup of tea and again in the afternoons with tabnabs or biscuits. He takes our dirty uniforms to the laundry and returns them a few days later, all clean and crisp. You can have suits cleaned and anything you care to mention and they do a very good job.'

One of the others said, 'John, my name is Richard.' Then he introduced me to a feminine type of man with brown hair and what I took to be a light coating of makeup on his face, who he said was his best friend Francis, and he pointed to a tall blond man and said, 'that's Justin.'

'What are tabnabs?' I asked.

'Tabnabs are cakes. Fernandes is not paid to look after us. He signs on as a topas' – I gave him a quizzical glance – 'a general dogsbody. He cleans up whenever passengers are sick or when we spill food on the decks and things like that. He does all sorts of other cleaning jobs too, but he has other mates with him and I think they do all right for money with their side jobs, like cleaning our cabins.'

'Come on dear,' said Francis, 'we're late for a bevvy – the place will be crowded.'

Richard looked at his watch and exclaimed, 'Jesus! It's ten past one. Why didn't you stop me rabbitin'?'

'Are you coming with us?' asked Francis.

'No thank you,' I said, 'I have to change and make a phone call.'

'Come over later if you have the time,' said Richard. 'You just ask anyone where the canteen is.' And they were off.

I changed quickly, made my way onto the dock, found a phone box, phoned the Thomsons, and then looked for a likely candidate to direct me to the PLA (Port of London Authority) canteen. I spotted a tall red-haired fellow wobbling unsteadily towards me, dressed in a mess jacket and jeans. I smiled at him and asked, 'Can you please tell me where the canteen is?'

'Och, fuck ye pal.'

That stopped me in my tracks. 'The same to you,' I said as I watched his slow progress past me.

He stopped and I thought, I'm in for it now! Instead he bawled with laughter and said, 'Yer're a spunky wee bastard.' Then he pointed to a shed-like building and said, 'O'er there ya wee shite.'

'Thanks,' I said, and soon I was in one the strangest places I had ever seen. It was crowded with dockers and seamen eating, drinking, playing cards and darts, in what looked like the inside of a large barn with a high ceiling and a floor covered in a combination of spilled drinks and mud. There were long tables with benches around them, and the only contribution to decoration was a jukebox and the optics behind the bar. The counter was surrounded by a large group of men. I excused myself to get through the throng, and when I had made my goal I found that my head barely reached the top of the counter. One of the dockers, a big-bellied unkempt character, said, 'Ere mate I'll liftya up.'

I scowled at him and replied, 'I'll make it without you.'

This seemed to take him aback, and even more so when one of his companions said, 'Ay 'Arry you've met your match.' That brought forth a hail of laughter and guffaws, and a heavy-set man in the group said, 'Ignore them stupid bastards.' I gave him a smile and ordered a sandwich and a mug of tea. When the barmaid served me I went to find a seat and spotted Pete, waving me over from the back of the hall. He made space for me on the bench and I sat next to him, with few words until I had wolfed down my sandwich.

'I forgot to tell you about this place earlier,' said Pete. 'How have you been doing?'

I told him about my activities and asked him if he would show me where we had to muster. 'Yes,' he said with a laugh, 'I'm an old hand now. I've been here three days. We've got ten minutes to spare before then, you come back with us.'

He introduced me to the four fellows with him. Two of them were 'first trippers', and that boosted my now flagging confidence. The other two were about to make their second trips and were trying to outdo each other with their tales. I could have listened to them for hours, but it was almost time to muster.

All six of us went back to the ship. There must have been at least sixty men and boys in the saloon, mostly wearing mess jackets and jeans. Mr Morris came in and sat down at a table, opening a big ledger which I later learned was referred to as the 'tick on' book. He started by saying, 'Good afternoon gentlemen, there is a van on the dock with dry goods stores and those of you whose names I call first are to report to Mr Black on the dock.' He started rattling off names and I was listening intently for mine. Eventually it came and I answered, 'Here,' and hurried out. Pete caught up with me and said, 'Slow down John, there's an army of men to do the job. I was just like you on my first day. I don't mind working but there's a bunch of skivers amongst them and I'm damn sure I'm not going to carry them.'

We reported to Mr Black, a leading hand with one silver ring on his sleeves. A pale-faced sourpuss with a brylcreemed head of hair, he grunted and ticked us off his list. I wondered why he seemed so miserable. But my wondering was soon forgotten when I noticed that a number of the gang were giggling and far too many of them were looking at me. Balls to the lot of them, I thought, I'll show the whole fecking crowd what I'm capable of.

Pete told me, 'You stand behind me and I'll pass the boxes to you,' and it soon became apparent why. He was much taller than me, and he was prepared to stoop down to place each box in my arms without making it obvious to the others. Unknown to me, he had also arranged for his friend Peter, another 'first tripper', to take the boxes from me.

We worked at a steady pace for the rest of the afternoon

and finished twenty minutes before knocking-off time at 4.30. I thanked Pete and he asked, 'What for? You pulled your weight, and more than some of them other blokes. Did you enjoy it?'

'I certainly did,' I said. 'It's so different to the work I've been used to.'

We went to our respective cabins and a much-needed shower. The water was off, so a 'bird bath' had to do. I donned my favourite shirt and suit and was almost out the door when I realised that I didn't have any shoes on.

Richard and Cyril were the only two in the cabin. They laughed, and Cyril said, 'John boy, slow down, the birds will wait.'

'I'm going to stay with my friends,' I said. 'Good night.'

It wasn't long before I was ringing the doorbell of the Thomsons' house. Over a cup of tea I told them everything that had happened since the last time I saw them, including what I had experienced on my first day on board the *Himalaya*. As ever, I was made to feel very welcome.

'I think it's going to take me a while to get used to the different words they have for things on board ship, such as companionways for stairs,' I said to Doug.

He smiled and said, 'There, you see, you've started with the stairs, soon you'll be talking like an old salt. You are on the threshold of a new way of life and a good career. But there can be pitfalls too, and alcohol is one of the biggest of all. You can fall into the trap of becoming too fond of it – and that is where some people, mostly young men, get into all kinds of trouble.'

I told him what Larry the steward on the *Princess Maud* had told me about the very same subject.

Later, after the evening meal, Minnie showed me to my room and produced a pair of blue pyjamas, telling me she had bought two pairs as a gift and that she had guessed my size, omitting to say that in fact they were boys'. I wanted to hold her close and give her a big hug in my gratitude, but instead I took her hand and held it gently, thanked her and turned away because I felt the waterworks welling up.

***

The next morning I was given a lift back to the ship by the

Thomsons' son-in-law, Jock, an electrician who was working on a ship further down the docks, and this arrangement continued for the rest of our time in port. When I got to my cabin I was surprised by the number of men there drinking beer and chattering away. The beer drinking at that time of the morning didn't bother me at all – I had often seen men doing the same in the hotels I had worked in. What surprised me was the sheer number of men in such a small place. There must have been ten at least. I had to worm my way around them to get to my locker.

Cyril told me that most of them had been out on the booze the night before and they were just having a few 'liveners'. I asked him what that meant.

He looked at me closely and answered, 'It means that they need to have a few to get themselves right for the day, some people say the hair of the dog, a sort of pick-me-up after a heavy session. I don't believe in it myself. As far as I'm concerned, it only starts you on the same old merry-go-round, it's not for me.'

We mustered and 'ticked on' at 9 am. I was on the storing gang and so was Pete, who said, 'The same routine as yesterday, is that all right with you?'

We worked steadily for an hour and a half, and then the leading hand shouted 'smoko lads, be back here at eleven sharp.' There was a cheer and we scattered. Pete and I went to the canteen, where I noticed that I was still getting strange looks from seamen and dockers alike and observed the sly nudges and smirks. It hurt, but I pretended not to notice.

The rest of the day went very quickly for me. I knew I had worked as hard as any of my shipmates and that gave me great satisfaction. I felt a sense of belonging. I was starting to remember the names of some of the men, and that made me feel good too.

When I went to my cabin there were only three men there, Cyril, Richard and a new face to me, Nobby.

Cyril said, 'John, the second steward has told me you'll have to move out of here and into the bellboys' cabin in two days' time.'

'Right,' I said.

The water was on so I had a shower. All clean and tingling, I dressed and was off to the Thomsons, just like the previous evening. We sat and chatted, and I told them about having to change cabins. Doug said, 'If they have any sense, they will promote you to a steward's job, with your experience.'

My third day of working on the big white ship got off to a fine start. I met Pete and Peter at the gangway and we had time for a cup of tea before 'tick on'. When we reported to the saloon, we found there were more men than usual there, most wearing mess jackets but quite a number without. This indicated either that they were first trippers or that they were disobeying orders by not wearing them.

My first assumption proved to be right when I heard someone hiss in lowered tones, 'More fucking first trippers.' I looked at him and made a mental note to keep an eye on him.

We did many and varying jobs that day, but the one I enjoyed the most was laying up tables for a special luncheon the following day. I stood back to check if the cruets were dead centre, the cutlery was exactly in line and the side plates were correctly placed. I sensed someone behind me and turned around to see a good-looking blond-haired man with two and a half silver rings on his sleeves smiling down at me. I smiled back, full of confidence in knowing that I had done the job right.

'What's your name, young man?' he asked.

'John J Mahon, sir,' I answered.

'Where did you get your training?' he asked.

'In hotels in Ireland sir,' I replied.

'You have done a very nice job, thank you. We shall leave the wine and water glasses off until tomorrow.'

I asked him if I should cover the settings over with a tablecloth.

He smiled and said, 'Yes please do that, but before you do, what is your rating?'

'I'm signing on as a bellboy,' I said.

'What age are you now?' he asked.

I told him that I would be eighteen on 15 December.

He rubbed his face and said, 'Right. Well, John, I shall know where to find a good man when I need one. Thank you.'

As he strode off to inspect the other tables I went over to Pete and Peter, who were standing by their tables just across from mine. Peter said, 'You'll get an assistant steward's job before we sail. I've heard there's some dispute up north,

Liverpool I think, and it seems that's causing a shortage of stewards – so you could be in there.'

Pete said, 'I liked your touch about covering over the lay-up. He's a senior head waiter, his name is Whitfield and he's taken a shine to you.'

'I'm not raising my hopes,' I said. 'I know I can do the job, but it doesn't matter either way. What matters is, I'm here.'

Pete responded, 'The difference is, your wages would be greatly enhanced. What are you on now?'

'Twelve pounds ten shillings a month,' I replied.

'You see,' he said, 'I'm on thirty-four pounds ten shillings a month, it's a big difference.'

I agreed that the improvement to my income would be welcome and left it at that. I didn't tell them I wasn't too interested in the money, it was more a case of proving that I could do either of the jobs and therefore I would be on par with any of my colleagues and I could call myself a seaman.

At 'tick on' the next morning, ten of us were told to report to Mr Whitfield in the first class saloon. I was pleased to see that both Pete and Peter had been included in the team. We reported to Mr Whitfield, who was as immaculate in his uniform as he had been when I had first clapped eyes on him the day before.

He smiled and said, 'Right men, we have eighty guests for lunch today and I want everything to be perfect. I will assign your tables to you now, but I want some cleaning, dusting and polishing done first.'

It hit me as he gave me table 10. 'Jumpin' Jasus,' I said under my breath, 'I haven't got my uniform yet.' I remembered the white monkey jacket in my locker. I had carried it over from Ireland just in case any future employer would give me a job and then not have a uniform jacket to fit me. Shortly after I had started in my first job I became acutely aware of how difficult it was to get anything to fit me, especially uniforms.

I told Mr Whitfield I expected to collect my uniforms the following day.

'That is a problem,' he said.

'I've got a monkey jacket I carry with me. It's very smart with a starched white shirt and a black bow tie,' I said.

He gave a little chuckle and said, 'Very resourceful, young

man, but it wouldn't be in keeping with the uniform policy. Go over to the outfitters now and tell them that I sent you because you need a jacket to serve a special lunch today.'

I went over to the shop, now crowded with about six catering crew in there. The man who had attended to me before saw me, and disappeared briefly to return with a large brown paper parcel, saying, 'Your order came through this morning. Let's hope they fit better this time.' He handed me a jacket and stood back to observe the fit from a short distance. I didn't feel comfortable in it at all. The sleeves were still too long. I didn't mind that so much, I could turn them up, but the rest of it was nearly down to my knees. I thought, this thing makes my legs look even shorter, I'd be ashamed to wear it. I was too furious to pay attention to what he was saying as he took the jacket off me, and it wasn't until I had calmed down that I noticed he was diligently turning up the offending article with some sort of sticky tape.

'This is only a temporary job,' he said, 'but it will be all right if you go careful with it. I'll get on to head office this afternoon to make sure that the alterations are done properly this time. You sail on the 11th, so it will have to be a rush job.'

Back on board, Pete introduced me to John, a seasoned old hand in his late twenties. This was going to be his third trip. We shook hands and I showed them the jacket.

'You've had a taste of Miller and Robbers efficiency,' he said. 'I think I have the solution to your problem, though. There's at least three of the Goanese crew that I know of who do alterations, and they're damn good at it too. I'll see if I can find the chap who made a great job on a pair of trousers for me.'

Mr Whitfield came over to us. I showed him the jacket and told him that I was disgusted with it, as indeed I was with the rest of the stuff. He nodded his head as if he understood my predicament and frustration. I put the jacket on for his inspection and he said, 'It's not too bad, you know, it is good enough for you to wear today. Have you got dark trousers?'

'Yes sir,' I replied.

Mr Whitfield called us together at 11.15 and told us to break for lunch and to be back no later than 12.30.

My new acquaintance John said, 'Let's go down to see that tailor.' He led the way along the working alleyway and knocked at an open cabin door. A wizened-looking old brown man came out to us. 'Ah, Pereira!' said John, 'my young friend needs to have some alterations done to a jacket. How soon can you do it and how much do you want for the job?'

Pereira moved his head from side to side in a rhythmic sort of way and said, 'You give jacket to me early this evening and pick up breakfast time tomorrow, you pay seven shillings and sixpence. Okay?'

As we walked the short distance to the canteen, where we had agreed to meet Pete, I said, 'I think I'll go back to the outfitters, get my gear and ask Pereira to do the lot.'

**

The special lunch was a success as far as I was concerned. It was a set menu, leek soup, rainbow trout, fillet steak with all the trimmings and fresh fruit cocktail for dessert followed by cheese and biscuits and coffee. I expected it was going to be an all silver service do, and was disappointed to find that the fish and steak were on plates with garnish, so the only chance I had of showing off my skills with the fork and spoon was to serve the carrots, peas, and chips or boiled potatoes from the silver dishes.

The six guests on my table were of middle age. Of the four men, two were going grey, one was bald, and one had a mop of dark hair. He was thin and his spectacles were more off the end of his nose than on – he reminded me of the absent-minded professor. The other three were corpulent and sour in their demeanour. The two women both had hawk-like faces and it was obvious their dark hair was dyed. I think they were all business people.

Between courses I kept a respectable distance from the table, far enough away so as not to give the impression of eavesdropping and near enough, if needed. They ate their fill and soon it was over. There were no speeches or toasts. People were starting to leave, and my lot stood up *en masse*. They thanked me and were gone. No tip, but I didn't care.

We were responsible for our own cutlery, and there were containers of hot soapy water in the plate house adjacent to the galley where we washed it. I did mine at the end of each course and already had it in the wooden box ready to return to the 'silver man'.

Mr Whitfield came over to me and said, 'Well done, young man. Return your cutlery to Smith in the silver locker, have a break and be back here at 3.30.'

I returned the cutlery, and as I was doing so Pete and John came along with theirs. John said, 'I hope you're hungry, John, I've had three steak meals put away for us and we've got plenty of time to enjoy them.'

John explained that very few of the European catering staff ate the crew meals. They weren't much good, too bland. The trick was to have one of the galley staff put something from the menu away for you each meal. For that little service you had to pay the bloke when you reached Australia, and how much you paid would depend on how good he was at getting the things you liked. The other payouts in that area were to the Goanese pantryman – he was the boss of all the Goanese crew. The reason for giving him a bung was because he had everything in the way of fruits, juices, and anything you'd care to mention in that line. And another thing to bear in mind was that sometimes you might have a nice passenger who liked, say, a glass of tomato juice every day – and even if it was off the menu you could still get it. Not to mention what you wanted for yourself.

When we reported back to Mr Whitfield he told me to report right away to the second steward, Mr Littlewood. I knocked on his open office door.

'Come in,' he said, looking up from his paperwork. 'Mahon,' he said, 'there is a possibility we may be able to promote you to an assistant steward's job before we sail. You are one of three boys who will be eighteen years old during the voyage. However, it will be subject to the approval of head office.'

'Thank you sir,' I said. 'If I am successful, what will my duties be?'

'Mainly your job will be to serve eight or ten passengers with their meals in one hour and then a further sitting of the same number of people. The other duties are serving afternoon teas or serving children's meals, washing decks, replenishing bar stocks, polishing silverware and whatever else needs to be done for the efficient running of our department.'

163

I thanked him and rolled out of there dizzy in anticipation.

I returned to the saloon after a quick smoke and found Mr Whitfield and the team sitting around a large table to accommodate ten diners, which I learned later was referred to as an 'aircraft carrier' by the old hands. He waved me over and indicated for me to sit down and join them.

'How many of you gentlemen are first trippers?' he asked.

Six of us raised our hands.

'Right,' he said, 'I have some important advice for you.' Then he told us some of the rules we had to abide by on board.

It was strictly forbidden to fraternise with the passengers, and their accommodation was out of bounds to all crew members except those whose duties it was to be in the area. Anyone contravening those rules would be in serious trouble. They could be logged, and that meant going before a senior officer, usually the staff captain. He would enter the offence in the logbook and then decide on the penalty, which could be a 'first warning', the loss of a day's pay or something like that. The log entry was serious and could lead to the person being dismissed from the merchant navy. The rules and regulations were in the articles of agreement, which we would be signing in a few days' time.

***

Two days before sailing Mr Littlewood sent for me and told me that as from that moment I was an adult rating, an assistant steward. I thanked him and asked if I had to change cabins. 'No,' he replied, 'stay where you are.'

I went back to the saloon and made straight for Pete, who was polishing a porthole.

'I've got it!' I said. 'I'm an assistant steward now and it feels great.'

He got down off the chair he had been standing on and grabbed my hand, shaking it with his metal-polish-stained paw. 'Congratulations mate,' he said.

Then I went to Mr Whitfield and told him the good news, which I suspected he knew already – and quite possibly he had played a big part in my promotion.

'That is very good news,' he said with a broad smile. 'Have you sorted out your uniform problems?'

I told him that Mr Pereira was doing the alterations, but I still needed a pair of white shoes.

'The ship's company are signing on articles this morning,' he said. 'I want you to go up to the ballroom now and sign on as soon as possible, then you can go ashore to buy your shoes. I think you could find a pair in Gravesend. You might have problems getting the regulation style, but try to get a pair as plain as you can – you'll probably have to shop around. If you're not back by tick-off I will do it for you. Off you pop.'

I found the ballroom and waited for what seemed an eternity before I signed on. I was a crew member!

I caught the ferry from Tilbury Riverside across to Gravesend, and soon I was browsing the shoe-shop windows. I then started systematically entering shop after shop, but all to no avail. Eventually I ended up buying two pairs of plain white ladies' slip-ons.

I was back on board an hour before tick-off. I showed the shoes to Mr Whitfield, who shook his head and said, 'They're certainly not regulation, but they look good. We are finished here for the day, so go and join the other chaps, they will tell you about the emergency drill tomorrow.'

I joined Pete, Peter and John, who explained the routine for the exercise and showed me how to put the cork lifejacket on. Then Pete said, 'I'm going to have a drink in Gravesend tomorrow evening with John, Peter and Joe, another Irishman in our cabin – you haven't met him yet, he's had to go up to London but he'll be back tonight – and I'm hoping you'll come too. It's a goodbye to Blighty drink, as we're going to be away for nearly four months.'

'I'll be with you,' I said. He told me the name of the pub, which I soon forgot. I think it was the Queen's Elbow or the King's Knees. It really didn't matter because at least two of us would be leaving the ship together.

I told the Thomsons about the promotion as soon as I stepped through the door, and they seemed even happier than I was. 'That calls for a little glass of my special home-made rhubarb wine with our dinner,' said Doug.

As usual, the meal was perfect, and the wine added to it. After the washing up, we returned to the living room and chatted about my promotion and the forthcoming voyage.

Doug gave me some advice on the things to look out for and things to avoid both on board and ashore. I thanked him and promised to keep my wits about me. He asked Minnie if she would like another glass of wine. 'No thanks dear,' she replied, 'but maybe John would like another glass.'

The next morning Doug woke me with a cup of tea at 6.30 am. I went down to the kitchen with mixed emotions, sad at leaving my friends but glad that sailing day was near. We sat at the kitchen table, each with our own thoughts, and I said, 'I will miss you both and all your kindness, your delicious meals, and the goodies for lunch, Minnie. Oh, I forgot, the electric blanket too.'

They laughed at that and the atmosphere was lighter.

Jock arrived and it was time to go. We said our goodbyes with tears and I was gone.

I boarded the ship and dodged my way to my cabin through all the men scurrying hither and thither, changed into my working clothes, took my lifejacket out of my locker and left it on my bunk, and then went in search of my friends. I spotted Pete and John heading towards the gangway. John was suffering with a hangover and Pete wasn't his usual self, he was quiet and appeared to be depressed.

Later on when we got a chance to talk he told me that the main reason he was going to sea was to save enough money for his wedding and his honeymoon, and hopefully enough to make a deposit on a home. He intended to stay at sea for two years to achieve that, but he planned to get married in a year's time.

Fortunately we were kept busy that day and that helped him to get back to his old self. Pete, Peter and I were assigned to the tourist saloon along with the rest of the men required to work there for the voyage. Mr Whitfield put some of us to work on getting out the linen, glass and silverware and others on the general cleaning of the saloon. Most of us worked like beavers to get the jobs done, and by lunch break the tables were ready to be laid up.

After tick-on we put the finishing touches to the job and then we had to be familiarised with our duties on the emergency drill. My duty was to direct the passengers up to the boat deck. I walked away from my station several times to ensure that I would know where to go in a hurry, and when I was satisfied that I could find it from various parts of the ship I went up on deck to find the lifeboat that I had been assigned to. Once I was sure I knew exactly how to find my way there as well, I collected my lifejacket and then went back to the saloon.

The place was crowded with men just killing time before the drill. One of them came over to me. He was in his late twenties, with sleek dark hair, an angular face and very white, almost chalk-like skin. With a twisted grin, he said, 'You're John?'

'Yes,' I said.

'I'm Joe. Where do you come from back home?'

'Enniskerry,' I replied. 'Do you know it?'

'Do I know it? I used to go out there camping every summer. There's not much of that place I don't know, I've hiked all over the place, it's grand. Pete and John sez you're coming out for a gargle with us this evening.'

'Yes,' I said, 'I'm looking forward to it, but I'm not used to drinking.'

'Ah, don't worry a thing about that,' he said. 'A few brown ales won't hurt ya. I plan to be off here no later than six o'clock, an' if you'd like to come with me that'll be fine. I'd best be off an' get my cap and lifejacket.'

Damn! I had forgotten my cap. So down to the cabin I went to find six fellows drinking beer. I got my cap and darted back to the saloon with just minutes to spare before the alarm bells rang their deafening sounds. We stood by our emergency stations until the officers came around on inspection and then awaited the alarm for boat stations. It duly came, and I had no difficulty in finding my boat. I noticed some chaps looking for theirs. I didn't get any pleasure out of seeing their confusion, but rather a sense of being pleased with myself for doing my bit of homework. Seeing all the officers and crew mustered on both sides of the boat deck made me realise just how big a ship's company it was, including nurses, stewardesses and other women in varying uniforms and insignia. Everyone wore a hat, which fitted my romantic image of being a seaman – and to be a member of such a large body of people was very gratifying.

Drill over, lifejackets and hats stowed away, we reported to our respective leaders. I reported back to the saloon, and on my heels were Pete and Peter. Mr Whitfield told us to knock off for the day, but to be ready for the final preparations tomorrow and to report to him at 8 am.

I accompanied them to their cabin and we sat down to talk. I said that Joe had told me he wanted to be off the ship no later than 6 pm.

Peter jokingly said, 'That Mick, it's a wonder he can read the clock!' He smiled and continued, 'Of course you're a Mick too – tell me, is it true that you still sleep with the pigs in the house?'

'Not only that,' I replied, 'we had the chickens, a goat and a donkey too. I didn't mind it at all except for when the goat ate me straw bed.'

Joe came in amidst the laughter, and said, 'I hope youse buckos are in the same 'umour when we get down to some serious drinking.'

All five of us went in to the King's Neck in Gravesend at 6.30. They ordered pints of their favourite beers and I didn't know what to order. I was dithering when Joe came to my rescue and suggested a bottle of brown ale and ordered one for me.

The barmaid asked half-heartedly if I was old enough to drink.

'Indeed he is,' said Joe, 'he's nearly nineteen. Show her your ID, John.'

I caught on quick and pretended to go through my pockets. Coming up with nothing, of course, I frowned and put on a disappointed look and said, 'I must have left it on the ship.' She said nothing but nipped the cap off the bottle, poured half of the contents into the glass and slid them across the counter at me. Joe paid for the order and we all sat down at a table.

I felt ill at ease, but it didn't last for long, as the chatter and joking along with the sweetish beer all helped to relax me. The conversation got around to shipboard life, the good and bad things about it. Pete, Peter and I were all ears and bursting with questions for the old hands.

Joe was embarking on his fourth trip and John on his third. Pete asked how many people behind the scenes had to be paid off by us.

Joe said, 'Firstly there's the peak steward, his dropsy is

twenty-five to thirty shillings, depending on how good he is – that's from England to Australia, then the same again roughly every four weeks. It costs sixpence an article for laundry and a shilling for an express job, that's very handy if you haven't got many jackets or white trousers. Mostly it's tropical "rig of the day", and you can go through some gear. It only takes an accident, a spilled bowl of soup or somebody bumping into you – and of course you can't get away with serving any more than two meals in the same clothes, you'll find that out for yourselves.

'Then there's the platehouse men – they're nearly always first trippers except for the odd one or two who prefer to work there permanently. It's a hot and dirty job, and they deserve a bung. It'll be up to you to drop them what you consider they deserve. I can't remember when there wasn't a shortage of side plates, so the best thing to do is get one of them to hold on to the amount you need. You know about the pantryman and the cooks that will put some good food away for you, of course you can always get yourself something on the second sitting and put it in your dumb waiter. Then there's the bellboys, they will lay your tables and burnish your cutlery for you at an agreed price.

'I can't think of anything else at the moment. Are we having another one here or moving on?' It was unanimously decided to have another there.

Pete stood up to get another round in, saying, 'Same again, boys?'

There were no refusals except from me. I still had a half bottle left and asked Pete to leave me out this time.

He grinned and went to the counter, and when he returned with a tray of pints there was also a bottle for me –

'John boy, I couldn't leave you out this time. You can pass on the next round if you want.'

I got the next round in, including another brown ale for myself, thinking it was safer to get them in where I had been served than to attempt it in another pub where I might be refused service. I felt great after my two bottles of ale and was as happy as any fellow of my age had the right to be. John and Joe told us tales of their experiences around the world and the girls in places with strange-sounding names. We finished the beer and Joe led the way to another pub, which I think was called the Queen's Knuckles.

The beers I had consumed had given me an air of confidence that I had never known before and I walked in with the others without reservation. My feeling of wellbeing was boosted even more when I spotted a dwarf sitting on a high stool at the bar. I looked him over quickly from the side, in a way that he wouldn't be aware I was doing so. He was a dapper little fellow, dressed in a dark suit, pink shirt and a polka dot tie to match. He wore a pork pie hat perched at an angle and his black boots were gleaming. Very smart, and it was apparent he had his clothes made to measure.

John ordered the drinks and the young barman asked politely if I was old enough to drink. Joe came to the rescue again, we went through the same palaver as in the other pub and it worked. This was a much busier house. In fact, the place was packed with groups and couples, individual men and women and a few soldiers thrown in for good measure. The jukebox was blaring out and the chattering left little room for conversation, but the atmosphere was good.

I enjoyed my company and all that was going on around me. John drew our attention to three young women seated on a couch along the wall and said, 'I've been watching them brassers. What a better way to spend the last night in England than to be buried in one of them for the night? I bet you could do with one of them, John, couldn't you?'

'I don't know,' I said. 'What's a brasser?'

That brought on gales of laughter from my gang, so much so that people were staring at our table.

Joe said, 'It means they're on the game – do you know what that means?'

'I think so,' I said.

'They're prostitutes – surely you know what that means,' he said.

'How do you know they're prostitutes, Joe?' I asked.

'John and I have been in here before,' he replied. 'You just watch them.'

At that point I knew I was going to be sick. I excused myself and dashed off to the men's toilet. The cubicle was empty and I threw up. It reminded me of my trip across on the mailboat and what Larry the steward had said about drink.

I gargled with the tap water and was ready for more brown ale. On my way back to my friends, I spotted the dwarf being helped off his stool by another man of average height. I slowed down, hoping that he was coming my way so I could compare our heights, and he was. As he was about to pass me he looked up at me and said, 'Right mate!'

'Yes, thank you,' I said.

The boys made fun of that and I laughed along as though it was hilarious, but I went into my own world for a spell, oblivious of what my friends were saying. My thoughts were on a different track altogether. I knew how difficult it was at my height and looking so young. I had been referred to as a midget and a dwarf, and even as a little oul' man cut short, in Ireland. So I wondered how that little bandy-legged man fared. My ears pricked up as John was saying, 'I heard that little bloke is known as the poison dwarf, and he's a pimp.'

I couldn't resist asking, 'What's that?'

More side-splitting laughter at my ignorance. Joe spluttered into his beer and Peter, the quietest one of us, explained what it meant. Would my street-level education never end? We had another round of drinks.

We had about an hour before catching our ferry back to the Riverside, so Pete suggested we could finish with a few in the Prince's Ankles, which was just by the ferry, and we could get a carry-out there too. The barman's questioning my age was no different to what I had experienced in the other pubs, but Joe and I had our convincing act together and I was served my brown ale. We ordered our carry-outs when we were on our second drink, and they were ready for us when we left for the ferry.

Joe was about to order the last round and I said, 'Please leave me out this time, Joe.'

'Ah go on witcha Johnny, another one won't killya. Drink up and be a man.'

***

The short trip across on the ferry was a variety show for many reasons. There was singing, dancing, arguments, puking and even some jolly jack playing 'Life on the ocean waves' on a mouth organ. We piled into two taxis and were on board in no time at all.

The brown ale had taken its toll on me. I was tired and unsteady but very happy. I said goodnight to my friends and made it to my cabin, it was darkened and some men were asleep.

The young fellow occupying the bunk above mine was reading a comic by his bunk light. He gave me a glance and asked, 'Who are you?'

'I live here. I'm John.'

'I'm Keith,' he said. 'Just got here a couple of hours ago. You're very small, aren't you?'

That deserved a sharp reply, and I would have given him one except for the sleeping men. I was furious and thought, wouldn't you be surprised if I gave you a dig in the kisser, you prick. And then had a good laugh to myself at the thought of me trying to reach up to rap him in the top bunk. I undressed and got into my bunk and it wasn't long before I fell asleep.

Fernandes, the peak steward, woke me the next morning with a mug of tea, which I didn't feel like drinking, but I held onto it so as not to offend him. I felt awful, my head was pounding and my stomach was sick. I didn't know if I wanted to puke or go to the toilet. I went for a shower and felt much better after it. Then I had a go at the mug of tea, and it revived me even more.

I tried on one of the two jackets that Pereira had altered for me and it felt just right.

All seven of my cabin mates were getting ready for work, and Cyril introduced me to those I had not yet met, saying, 'Richard, Francis, Harry, Nobby and myself are the regulars in this cabin. Mark, yourself and Keith are the three new additions.'

'We haven't met properly yet dear,' said Francis, 'you're a bona 'omie!' And then he kissed me on the cheek.

I reared back in shock and reddened to the roots. Keith laughed, but I noticed that Cyril and Nobby were not even smiling.

Nobby said, 'Pay no attention to her, she's harmless.'

Francis retorted, 'That's right dear, I like my men B. I. G.'

Had I heard right? Her/she? Francis was a man. Was it because he spoke girlish? I would ask Joe or John later.

I left in confusion and made for my friends' cabin. They

were all there nursing their sore heads and weakened bodies.

Joe was the first to speak. 'Jasus John, I'm dying. Fuck the gargle, I'm giving it up after I get a few liveners.' He opened a large bottle of beer and drank from it.

A few minutes later we joined the assembly waiting in the saloon to report to Mr Whitfield. 'Good morning men,' he said. 'When I call your name, I will give you the numbers of your tables.' When the roll call was over, there were three absentees. 'I have nearly broken the record,' he said, 'only three adrift.'

I was given tables 14 and 15, to accommodate four people on each. They were near the revolving door from the galley. Very convenient, I thought. Pete got 18, a long eight table.

Mr Whitfield announced, 'When you are satisfied your tables are ready, you can have a one-hour break.'

Pete and I took a casual walk to the canteen, and once we had our mugs of tea I led him to a corner, saying that I had something to tell him in private. We sat down and I told him about Francis and his strange behaviour.

He laughed and said, 'Do you mean to tell me you don't know anything about those people? I'd have thought with you working in hotels you'd know all about them. You're not having me on are you?'

'No,' I said, 'but come to think of it I have worked with a few men who were a bit girlish – not quite like Francis, but not a kick in the arse away either.' He burst out laughing and then the penny dropped. 'Sissies,' I said, 'more woman than man – but none of them ever kissed me like Francis did.'

'John,' he said, 'those people are known as homosexuals. Sometimes they're referred to as queers, pufters, brown hatters, shirt lifters and any other number of names, all of which I have no doubt you will hear on this trip. Their sexual preference is to go with other men. Let's have another cup of tea before we go back.'

We polished brass and mirrors until Mr Whitfield called out, 'Lunch, men, but hold on a minute. Gather round please.'

He advised that those of us who could go ashore should pay strict attention to the notice board on the gangway, stating what time we had to be on board before sailing, and he went on to explain how much trouble we could be in if we did not adhere to that order. 'And finally,' he warned, 'I do not want anyone in my saloon stinking of alcohol. Drunkenness will not be tolerated.'

I linked up with Peter and Pete and headed towards the canteen. I stopped off at the phone box to say goodbye to my dear friends the Thomsons, and when I joined my two shipmates Peter said, 'I've taken the liberty of ordering a brown ale for you.'

'But what about what the head waiter said about the smell of alcohol on our breaths?' I said. 'I know I can clean my teeth and gargle, but I don't want to do anything that might get me booted off the ship.'

'Listen son,' he said, 'I've worked in some of the best hotels in the country. The Dorchester, the Strand Palace, the Savoy and the Regent Palace, to name a few, and I've looked after arseholes, all sorts of famous people, and some of the richest people in the world. I know what it's all about. You just watch me on this trip.' He threw a packet of strong mints on the table and said, 'If you're worried about the alcohol fumes, there's no need, these mints will do the trick. Get yourself a packet at the bar.'

I wanted to be adventurous and drink a couple of bottles at least, to get the same nice feeling I had experienced the night before. Ah, feck it. I'd have one or maybe two. Caution was the word – but one or two bottles wouldn't hurt me.

Pete also decided to be cagey. 'I'll have one more and that's it. A brown ale for you, John?'

'Yes please,' I said. The first one gave me a bit of a lift and by the time I had finished the second bottle I felt just right. Pete and I had a couple of mints each and all was well.

The afternoon went quickly, and soon the passengers were starting to embark, in dribs and drabs at first and then in droves. We were all dressed in our high-necked uniform jackets with blue epaulettes and silver buttons with the company's logo of a rising sun and anchor on them.

Mr Whitfield called us together and said, 'As you men are not required to assist in the passengers' embarkation and you have everything ready here, you can knock off when I have finished. I want you back at not a minute past 6.30 pm. The first sitting will be served at seven and the second sitting at eight. It will be up to you to get the first sitting out in time for you to prepare for the second. I will not insult your intelligence by telling you how to go about that, but suffice to say diplomacy is the key word. That's it, thank you all.'

Pete and I went up on deck and were amazed to see the big crowd of people on the dock and all the activity. Balloons floating in the air, streamers from ship to shore and vice versa, and a band was playing all the old sea shanties. Two ambulances were on standby and some sturdy-looking policemen and women were on the prowl. Porters humping trunks and cases, chauffeurs accompanying people along the dock and up the gangways. And all manner of people were coming aboard. Elderly couples, individuals, young couples with children, and so it went.

Once the bulk of the passengers were on board the band stopped playing and a crackling sound came through the public address speakers, then a voice – 'The SS *Himalaya* will be sailing in one hour. All visitors ashore, please. I repeat, all visitors ashore. Thank you.'

By this time John and Joe had joined us. They had just finished a passenger direction duty. We stayed there watching the disembarking visitors, many with tearful faces, and I felt sorry for them.

'Aw, fuckit,' said Joe as the ship moved slowly away from the quay, 'let's go down to the cabin for a gargle. We've bought another carry-out and there's a few brown ales in it for you, John.' I thanked him for being so thoughtful and gave Pete a nod and we both followed the others down to the cabin. I promised myself that I would only have the one and I stuck to it.

Some of the passengers on the first sitting started queuing outside the saloon door at least ten minutes before dinner for what was commonly referred to as a running sitting (no reserved seating). We got our jugs of water, butter and rolls from the pantry and waited for the onslaught of the hungry.

The dinner bell was rung and in they rushed like a flock of sheep with the dogs nipping at their arses. I was nervous at first, but determined to do my best.

Two young couples sat at one of my tables and a family of four sat at the other one, a couple in their forties, with a boy and girl in their early teens.

There was plenty to choose from on the menu, written in

the French style. It soon became apparent that I would have to explain to the occupants of both tables what some of the dishes were. I went about it in the most tactful way, and I knew how to put them at their ease. In the few exchanges we had I recognised that these people were ordinary working class, going out to Australia on the 'assisted passage' for what they hoped would be a better way of life. Towards the end of the meal, the lady of the family asked me if I was going to be their steward for the voyage.

I told her I didn't know who was going to be on my table, but they would know what table they were on when they got back to their cabins, as their seating arrangements and other information would have been left for them by the cabin steward.

'We would really like to be on this table, John. You have been very good to us.' she said.

I blushed – and thought, I'm going to have to do something about this bloody blushing.

'Is there someone I can see about getting on your table?' she asked.

'The dining room head steward, madam,' I replied. 'You will find him by the mirror in the centre of the room. Please excuse me, I have to get my tables ready for the next sitting.'

I was ready for the next sitting with eight minutes to spare and went over to Pete, who was polishing his water glasses. I helped him put the finishing touches to the job and then we went out to the silver locker for a quick smoke and a brief comparison of our experiences with our first 'bloods'. That was what the long-serving stewards called the passengers. I didn't like the expression and promised myself not to use it.

I had four young couples on the second sitting, and it went much the same as the first – no hard work, but I was glad when it was over. I was tired and irritable. Irritable, because some of my colleagues had been making fun of me with what they thought to be very clever jibes. I have to admit I must have looked very funny holding my tray close to my chest with eight plates stacked on it. Each plate was covered with a 'chop-cover', a lid to keep the food warm, and on top of that I had to balance two vegetable dishes, which meant that I could barely see over the top. However, by midway through the first sitting I had almost perfected the level at which to carry the tray, and by the end of the second I had it down to a fine art. I had even mastered the entry/exit through the revolving doors.

The highlight of the evening for me was when a Cockney who thought of himself as the life and soul of the party dropped his tray full of dishes in the exit revolving door. He was the big mouth who had earlier said, 'Look, there's a bleedin' tray carrying itself – no, no, there's a dwarf be'ind it.' I couldn't resist going over to where he stood in a mess with a look of confusion on his face. I stood there in front of him, looked him straight in the eyes and then walked away.

After stowing the cutlery and glassware we were finished. I went to my cabin, stripped off the uniform, and went for a shower. I was just putting my shirt on when Pete came in to ask if I would like to pop around to his cabin for a drink.

Yes, I was all for it. The ship was making its way down the English Channel and apart from the slight movement and the sound of the engine I might just as well have been on a train.

John and Joe were in the cabin drinking beer and talking about football. Pete opened a bottle of brown ale for me, and a bottle of pale India ale for himself. We talked about what we had learned over the two sittings and the passengers. I told them about the fat cockney and his remarks and how I had the perverse pleasure of seeing him in distress when he had dropped his tray. Joe said in his best Dublin, 'Aw, fuckim, you'll always get pricks like that, no matter where you go. Ignore the bastards.'

The next morning the movements of the ship were not as steady as they had been the night before, and when I headed out to the toilet I nearly fell when she gave a heavy roll. I steadied myself and went on my way, only to find that I couldn't walk a straight line. We turned to at 6 am, and my morning jobs were sweeping up a section of the saloon, dusting and laying up my tables – and then it was our breakfast and time to ready myself for the first sitting at 8.15 am.

The Roberts family, whom I had served the previous evening, sat down at table 14. Mrs Roberts was smiling broadly as she said, 'Good morning John, we're with you for the trip to Fremantle. That Mr Whatsisname is a very nice man. I asked him if we could sit at your table and he said certainly. We don't know anything about the fancy names on the menu, we're used to plain cooking and that's all. Will you please look after us?'

I said it would be my pleasure. We briefly discussed the menu and how the movement of the vessel was affecting all the family. None of them could face a cooked breakfast, but they felt that they should eat something. I suggested cereals with just a small amount of milk, or better still without milk, and maybe some fresh dry toast. They settled for tea and toast only. Easy for me, and thankfully so, as I was feeling queasy myself.

Table 15 was occupied by two elderly couples, Mr and Mrs Shine and Mr and Mrs Bright. The Brights were going to Perth to see their five grandchildren for the first time and the Shines were accompanying them. These are hardened old crows, I thought, and to prove me right they scoffed full and plenty, and damn it, they were among the last to leave, which made me put a spurt on to be ready for the second sitting. I need not have worried, though, for my friends Pete and Peter came over and helped me lay up. It was done in a flash and we had time for a smoke before the next 'round up'.

I had four young couples on the second sitting – Mr and Mrs Chalk and Mr and Mrs Cheese on table 14 were bound for Melbourne, while Mr and Mrs Salt and Mr and Mrs Vinegar on table 15 were all bound for Sydney, and all were travelling on the assisted passage, as were the Roberts family. The eight of them were not unlike the Roberts when it came to the menu and not knowing what cutlery to use. I put them at their ease and was glad that they were not a domineering bunch. It would make my job easier, I hoped.

They were all going out to a better way of life, they hoped. I had no views on that because I was ignorant of the facts, but I couldn't help thinking of the irony of it. Here I was starting a new life on an English ship, and these people were leaving a country full of work. It was beyond my understanding.

After breakfast, Mr Whitfield gave us more morning jobs. Pete's job was the same as mine, polishing three brass portholes each, and Peter's was polishing mirrors.

Lunch was an easy job for most of us. A lot of the passengers stayed away because the lady that had looked so beautiful and gracious alongside the dock had now taken on a rocking and rolling motion with the occasional dip. The only member of the Roberts family to show face was David, and he was looking green around the gills. He attempted a go at a buck rarebit and scarpered within minutes. But my old crows, the Shines and Brights, made up for it. They ate their way through the card, down to the cheese, biscuits and coffee.

It was while I was carting in their groceries that I was sick for the first time. Just looking at the food started me off, and looking at the way they were scoffing everything didn't help at all. When they ordered more coffee, I had to tell them politely they could enjoy it at their leisure in the lounge or the library. It was nearly time for the next sitting.

I had no sooner got the words out than Pete, Peter and another chap appeared and started fussing around the table with comments like 'John, your second sitting passengers are queuing outside the door,' and 'Excuse us please, thank you sir, thank you madam.' My crows got the message and stirred themselves into leaving. That was my first real experience of solidarity. I didn't know the meaning of it then, but I would in time, as I would the meaning of camaraderie.

There were fewer passengers on the second sitting. I was sick twice between sittings, but managed to get two cream crackers down and keep going. Nothing was going to interfere with my determination to succeed in my seagoing career. Trying to keep my balance was another problem I would have to overcome, and it didn't hurt at all when I saw some of the longer-serving crew taking the odd 'flip, flop, fly'.

I had just three of my eight passengers in and they didn't stay long. The Big Beautiful White Lady that I had stood looking up at in amazement from the dockside in Tilbury had turned into a Bitch. She was pitching, bouncing and damned well doing as she pleased.

Pete and I were about on a par with the sickness. To our surprise, Peter hadn't been sick at all, but credit to him, he took no pleasure in seeing us struggling through it. He said that someone had told him we were in the Bay or about to enter it and it was said that it could be very rough. I hadn't a clue what he was talking about and I didn't want to show my ignorance by asking questions.

When I went to my cabin I found only three men there. Two had their curtains closed and Cyril was reading by his bunk light. I asked him if we were in the Bay. 'If we're not in it yet, we soon will be,' he said, and explained that the Bay of Biscay could be rougher than the Irish Sea. He had barely finished speaking when I had to dash out to puke again.

I laid up my tables at 5 pm after being shown how to dampen down the tablecloths and put the fiddles up to prevent the cutlery, condiments and crockery from falling off and was back in the cabin with an hour to spare. Although I was feeling quite unwell, I wanted to get to know the fellows whom I had not yet managed to have more than a few words with.

I kept my distance from Keith, because of what he had said about my size on our first meeting, and there was not an ounce of sympathy in me when he jumped off the top bunk and spewed before he had the chance to get out the door. 'Oh, no,' chorused a couple of the old hands.

Seeing him all messed up and the smell of his vomit started me off again. I was more fortunate – I got to a utility locker to try to be sick, but there was nothing in my stomach except bile. When I managed to get rid of the sweating, giddiness and quivering body spasms I felt much better. I returned to the cabin and got into conversation with Mark Rivereau, a South African photographer who had driven the big red buses in London for two years.

The evening meals went reasonably well for me. Not many of my passengers were up to eating, but my old crows didn't miss a crumb. Between retching and eating cream crackers I put down plate after plate before them and they shovelled it in. Once again, I had to remind them that I only had five minutes to prepare for the next sitting. They left and I warned myself not to lose my temper with them, no matter how much they provoked me. I'd put on my false face and pretend that it was a pleasure hauling in dish after dish for them to gorge themselves on.

The next morning, the ship's movements had become much more subdued. Pete and I went up on deck before breakfast to take the air and to see what was around us. No land in sight, a cloudy sky and just one vessel on the horizon. There were quite a few seabirds flying overhead and swooping down into the choppy sea. Pete said he thought they were dipping in to get their breakfast of fish.

I had a very good day. I wasn't sick, and all of my sixteen passengers came in for meals. My old crows even left the saloon earlier than they had been doing so far. That gave me the opportunity to have a smoke between sittings, which was always a bonus.

After breakfast the next morning we anchored off Gibraltar to pick up a small number of passengers, and shortly afterwards we were on our way through the Mediterranean to Port Said. The weather was becoming warmer, and the order was given for tropical uniform to be worn. For us stewards, that meant our standard white jackets, white trousers, white socks and white shoes. I had been longing to wear my new shiny slip-ons since the afternoon I had bought them. I loved those shoes especially because they were different from the regulation white canvas-type shoes with laces. My colleagues had to clean theirs with a chalky white substance, when all I had to do was wipe mine with a damp cloth before applying neutral polish and then buff them up.

We anchored off Port Said to await the pilot. I went up on deck and was amazed at the sights before me. The strange designs of the buildings and the big Johnnie Walker whisky advertisement. The boats putt-putt-putting around the harbour, and ships displaying flags of many nations. Tankers, cargo ships, passenger ships, tugs and dredgers. I didn't know the difference between any of the vessels except for the passenger ships, and the only national flags I recognised were the British and American. I had to content myself with that bit of knowledge for the time being.

The heat was almost unbearable, and I likened it to that of the boiler rooms in the hotels I had been in.

My big beautiful lady of steel seemed to glide up closer to the shore and then anchored close to a pontoon bridge. Pete, Peter and I had enough time off to spend two hours ashore. It was like a competition as to whose eyes were popping out the furthest as we tried to take in all the strange sights. Men wearing little pillbox hats and other funny-looking headwear, and what I thought looked like skirts. Women wearing masks, as I called them, and black cloak-like clothes from neck to toe. Strange!

All manner of transport was in evidence, from rattling old bicycles, mopeds, vans, lorries, modern buses and coaches to horses and traps, donkeys and camels. The streets were teeming with people from all over the globe in every form of dress. I didn't need to be told who the passengers off our ship were – it was evident from their milk-white skin. Some wore shorts and some of the men went without shirts.

Our greatest problems were trying to keep the army of flies off us and getting the men and boys of all ages to leave us alone. They were trying to sell us their wares and chattering incessantly. 'Jonny, you wanna buy this, that and the other.'

The biggest surprise we had was when a raggedy young lad, a few inches shorter than me, joined in step by my side and said, 'Jonny, you wan fuk my sister?'

I wasn't sure I had heard him right, but Peter had, and he said, 'Piss off boy.' I wanted to ask the boy his age and give him a few shillings, but John and Joe, our friends and educators who had stayed on board, had told us not to give anyone a penny because if we did we would find ourselves surrounded by beggars, and they advised us not to buy anything at all. Things might look good and cheap, but it was all crap. It was best to wait until we got to Aden. That was a duty-free port and prices were about a third of what they were in England. We took their advice, and after an hour and a half we sauntered back to the ship with a few postcards.

When we got on board another surprise awaited us. There were local men all over the crew accommodation and on the outer decks. I learned that they were the boatmen who would assist in the ship's transit through the canal, and that's all I knew.

They were a jolly bunch, who called everyone Ma'Gregor or Jonny, and they all had something to sell or some service they could provide for you.

'You like Spanish fly Jonny? Very good for sexy!'

'Ay, Ma'Gregor, shoes mending!'

'Haircut Jonny, very good haircut.'

Their hustling was endless.

Cyril told me not to buy anything from them, it was all junk, and they were not to be trusted. He had told me earlier that the only time it was necessary to lock the cabin door was when we were in port, and nowhere more so than during our time in Port Said and during our passage through the Suez Canal.

***

During the beautiful lady's transit through the canal, I spent as much time as I could on deck between duties, as indeed did many of my colleagues and a large percentage of the passengers, especially those on the assisted passage to Australia. They were just like us first trippers, taking in everything as the vessel seemed to glide through the desert. A wonderful experience. Finally we were through the canal and bound for Aden. It was hotter than anything I had ever experienced in my life and it would take some getting used to.

The heat didn't bother my old crows, though. Their attitude seemed to be that they had paid for it all and come hell or high water they were going to have it. They were a fat and slovenly quartet, and the more I saw of them the less I thought of them. Roll on Fremantle!

An assistant steward called Sandy, a failed medical student, showed many of us first trippers books containing frightening pictures of various parts of the anatomy with gaping sores. He spoke of syphilis and gonorrhoea at length and how important it was to use contraceptives. I remember thinking, I'm glad I never had sex, and if I do I'll make sure to wear a rubber.

We learned that getting badly sunburnt was classed as a self-inflicted injury, and if it led to anyone being unable to carry out their duties they could be logged and that could mean loss of pay and another precaution to bear in mind. I had noticed how brown a lot of the crew were and saw it as another part of being a seaman, and I certainly wanted some of that. Maybe five minutes a day on the well deck or the fo'c'sle head would be all right.

A few days later we anchored off Steamer Point, Aden. Breakfast was served, a running sitting, no reserved seating. Most of the passengers and crew were anxious to get ashore to the delights of the duty-free shops, and the great majority had been ferried ashore by the time we had finished our duties. I went ashore with Pete, Peter and Mark. We only had two hours to spend before returning to the ship.

All the shops, big and small, had a collection of men and

boys outside trying to get you in to what they all claimed to be the cheapest place. We walked around for a while, and then Mark decided to go into a shop where there was a huge collection of cameras and accessories. As a former professional photographer he knew his business when it came to cameras and equipment. I marvelled at his and the salesman's knowledge as they discussed the merits and capabilities of the various types and brands, and the salesman appeared to enjoy the exchange as much as Mark did. He said he was not going to buy a camera then, but he would seriously consider the purchase of a Leica on the return trip. He bought a flashgun and a box of films.

Pete and Peter each bought a transistor radio for two pounds. And when they told me that they were becoming 'all the rage' in England and the cheapest you could get them for was about ten pounds, I bought one too.

The shopkeeper gave us each a present of a Parker ballpoint pen with a pile of business cards and said, 'If you give the passengers these cards and they come here to do business with me and my brothers, I will make prices cheaper for you.' A good proposition, we thought. We said our goodbyes and caught the boat back and had plenty of time to spare before serving lunch.

We left Aden behind and were on our way to Colombo, Ceylon.

I had my own passengers back for dinner. My favourites, the Roberts family, said that it had been good to get ashore for a while, but the heat was too much for them. They hadn't bought anything because they had to watch their few pounds, but Diane and David had bought a pop record each.

My old crows complained bitterly about the terrible service they had had from a coloured steward, as they put it.

Mrs Bright said, 'The steward who served us breakfast shouldn't have a job at all, he could hardly speak English.'

Mrs Shine chipped in, 'He couldn't remember our orders, he got 'em all mixed up and he never poured our water. Mind you, John, we complained about him.'

It then became a free for all, everyone wanting to tell me something about the 'terrible steward', but I tactfully told them that it was necessary for me to get their orders.

I went to my friends' cabin that night and over a few beers

I told the boys how bitterly the foursome had complained about the Goanese steward's service. John explained that when it was a running sitting and passengers other than the regulars sat down it was not unusual for the stewards to be a little less friendly and a bit slower, and to make a mistake or two with the orders. That way, when the passengers got back to their own stewards they might appreciate the service more and a bigger tip might be in the offing. Sort of a mutual agreement, he said.

I asked if the Goanese stewards' tactics with the passengers on running sittings was an agreed thing between us.

'No,' he answered, 'they go about things differently to us. They sign on for a year at a time as general servants, GS for short. They are paid about sixteen pounds a month – mind you, that's after they've done years as a "topas", a general dogsbody, for nine pounds a month. It doesn't seem much, but it's a lot of money where they come from, and of course they all have sidelines, tailoring, shoe mending, barbering and whatnot.'

I asked how many crew were on the ship. John and Joe mulled it over and came up with the figure of nearly six hundred, from the captain down to the youngest bellboy. John said that the captain actually signs on as the master of the vessel, but captain sounds much nicer for the passengers.

'How many of them?' I asked.

'About eleven hundred,' he replied.

***

I can't remember how many days it took to get to Colombo, probably about three, but I will never forget the sickening and sad experience it was when Pete and I got ashore. We saw raggedy and almost naked beggars of all ages. Legless, armless and twisted-limbed people were all over the place. Then came the money changers, offering almost double the rate of exchange for our pound sterling, and the precious-stone sellers, all claiming that their wares were the best and how we could make a fortune with such stones.

The humidity was overbearing and most of the streets were filthy with rotting garbage and debris so we went to a hotel and had a bottle of Beck's beer each, then went back aboard.

When I walked into my cabin I found a tailor measuring Mark for uniforms. I was aware how well made and smart the linen jackets and trousers were. Nearly all of the catering crew wore them, and at two pounds and ten shillings a suit it was a golden opportunity for me. I got measured and ordered five suits, which would be delivered on our return.

We left Colombo that evening and were on our way to Fremantle, Western Australia. During the passage I got to know more about some of my shipmates, including a few of the Goanese stewards who worked near me in the saloon. They generally kept to themselves until they were very certain they could trust you, and even then they were cautious.

As for my cabin mates, they were a mixed and complex lot. One morning I saw Richard getting out of Francis's bunk while he was still in it. I looked across at Cyril and Mark. Cyril caught my look and winked and Mark acted as though nothing unusual had happened. A few minutes later my friends Pete and Peter came in to see if I wanted to accompany them up on deck. I jumped at the suggestion. We went up to the fo'c'sle head and I hit them with what I had seen.

Peter responded, 'John boy, you're a naive little bugger. Haven't you ever heard of queers?'

'Yes,' I said, 'Pete and I have talked about them, but I never expected to see the two of them in the same bunk.'

'Fuck me,' he said, 'you've got a lot to learn. I suppose you being Irish, you go to church and all that lark!'

That made me angry and I replied, 'No I don't, I gave that up years ago. Does naive mean I'm thick?'

They both laughed and Pete said, 'No John, you're not thick. There are many people who know nothing at all about homosexuality and those who don't want to know, but it's in our society and whether they want to accept the fact or not is entirely up to them. One thing for sure – it will still be here long after we're pushing up the daisies.'

'It's illegal ashore,' said Peter, 'so it must be the same on ships. Did the blokes in your cabin have anything to say?'

I told them I was going to ask Cyril about it later and I would tell them what he said, and then I pledged them to silence.

One of the rare times I heard Pete swear was when he said, 'Fuck, it's not right, the selfish bastards. How many first trippers are in your cabin?'

'Three of us,' I said.

He looked thoughtful and nodded his head. We went down in silence to serve the first meal of the day.

I cornered Cyril between breakfast and lunch and he made things clearer for me. He said, 'I know it must have been a shock for you this morning. I'm still not used to it after having to share a cabin with them for three trips and Nobby feels the same, but they're harmless. How do you feel about it?'

'It doesn't bother me,' I said, 'it's their business, but I think it's very strange.'

'Yes,' he said, 'it is strange, especially for a first tripper. Mark is a man of the world and understands such things, but it doesn't necessarily mean he likes the set-up. I don't know what Keith's views are, he's a deep one that. You're aware there are many more queens like Francis aboard. They never try to interfere with the boys or young men. They only pal around with the blokes who are interested in them and want to play their games, and some of them are pricks, only interested in what they can get out of them. You just watch when we hit a duty-free port – that's when the queens go into competition with each other to see who can buy the best present for their "omies" as they call them. There is absolutely no need to worry about any of them trying to interfere with you. There are far too many of us blokes around to let that happen. Occasionally, though, a small boy merchant comes along, but they're found out quickly and it's hard to say who hates them the most, the queens or the other blokes.'

After lunch I told Pete and Peter what Cyril had said and we chatted about the subject for a while. It was as new to them as it was for me. They both knew about homosexuals, but to find them practising their preferences on board was not something that they had even thought of. However, we took it in our stride and saw it as yet another experience.

***

The night before arrival in Fremantle was 'dropsy night' for those of us who had passengers disembarking.

I was losing the Roberts family and my old crows. I would miss the Roberts, but definitely not the crows. They were true to form right to the end, and the only thing that surprised me was that they left the saloon ten minutes before the second sitting and as they were leaving they each handed me a white envelope. I thanked them and stuffed the envelopes in my pocket.

I laid up the table while the Roberts were on their sweets, and I had a bit of time to spend with them as I laid the table up around them. They had already told me that Mr Roberts was a cabinetmaker and he was optimistic he could get a job very soon after they arrived. But somehow this evening neither of them seemed quite so optimistic. They were pensive and sad. By contrast, their two teenage children didn't seem to have a care. They were jolly and full of anticipation.

As they were leaving they said they would try to get on my table in the morning. Mrs Roberts kissed my cheek and whispered as she slipped something into my top pocket, 'Just in case we miss you in the morning.'

I still had time for a quick smoke before the next sitting. I lit up and listened to the boasts and gripes on how the tips had gone. 'A couple of quid from them two greedy bastards! Fuck 'em.'

'Hey, how about this, ten quid from them two old dears.'

The chatter went on and I was tempted to open my envelopes, but didn't. Unconsciously I put my hand in my jacket pocket and fished out the Roberts tip. It was an Australian two-shilling piece.

One of the sharp old hands asked, 'Was that a tip, son?'

I nodded.

'You make sure you find them bastards in the morning and tell them they need it more than you do, and if I was you I'd tell them to shove it up their arse.'

I served the second sitting with all sorts of thoughts running through my mind and I was glad when the meal was over. I went to my cabin and opened the envelopes from the crows. There was three pounds in each, not a good contribution towards what I had to pay out in Sydney.

I had a shower and went to my friends' cabin. We drank beer and talked about the queens and the 'dropsies'. I thought the lot of them would split their sides with laughing when I told them about my two-shilling tip.

'Listen mate,' said John, 'you give it back to them tomorrow morning.'

'No I won't,' I said. 'I've thought about doing that, but I would be more embarrassed than they would.'

Pete suggested maybe it would be nice to go up on deck for a bit of air, so off we set with John, Joe, and Peter and a case of Allsopp's lager for good company. The evening was balmy, and it was a pure pleasure to be slicing through the sea on my beautiful lady in the company of good friends.

We arrived in Fremantle at the crack of dawn, and the first thing I clapped eyes on was the pub, which I think was called the Black Swan. Better known to the P&O crews as the 'First and Last' – and I learned later that in days gone by it had been known as the Bucket Of Blood.

At breakfast my tables were occupied by new faces just moments after the doors were opened, so I never saw any of my regulars. Afterwards I went ashore with Pete and Peter, and we were struck by how dry everything seemed. It reminded me of the desert along the Suez Canal, and the heat was similar. We walked around for a while and then made our way back to the 'First and Last', where we shared a big jug of icy cold beer, which took some getting used to.

We steamed away that evening for Adelaide and I only had four new passengers on my first sitting, which meant I had more time to cater to their needs and if they had a mind to talk to me I could spare the time.

Mr and Mrs Levinstein were from New York, a couple in their fifties who were, 'travellin' around Australia at liberty,' as they put it. She was about five feet tall, a silver-haired lady with a hawk-like face covered in makeup and too much lipstick. She wore a low-cut black dress and carried a fan. He was much taller with a wizened face under an obvious wig and his nose was almost as hooked as the shoe salesman's in Shepherds Bush. He was dressed in a dinner suit, and vanity was their travelling companion.

The other couple, Mr and Mrs Mahoney, both quite elderly, were an Australian Humpty Dumpty duo. Each of them was nearly six feet tall, and as fat and slow as each other, plain people. They both had grey hair and dressed casually, she in a skirt and cardigan and he in a shirt and shorts.

All four were bound for Sydney. I soon learned that the quartet could shift their groceries too, the Aussies more so than the Americans.

On the voyage to Adelaide the Mahoneys were keen to talk of their roots. They were 'true blue' Aussies, but they were proud of their Irish heritage. Both of them had grandparents from Ballygobackwards or Ballygosideways or some such place. They had visited Ireland years ago and what a pleasure that had been. Why would a young lad of my age want to leave such a beautiful little country?

'Work,' I said.

On the way from Adelaide to Melbourne I listened to the conversations between the Levinsteins and the Mahoneys, without appearing to do so. They talked about themselves, about the places they had been, and sometimes about world affairs. Both parties had definitely been around the world. It was a competition between them as to who had been to the most exciting and remote places. This was all good stuff for me, and I hated it when I had to go out to the galley for another course, especially if they were talking about foreign countries.

My pretty lady tied up to a wooden pier in Port Melbourne and a large percentage of the passengers disembarked, some returning home, some on holidays, and others off to start their new lives, including my passengers the Chalks and Cheeses. They gave me two pounds ten shillings each. They had been nice people, and I hoped they did well for themselves.

A crowd of us walked down the jetty to Smoky Joe's café, where it was said, by the old hands, the best milkshakes in all Australia were served. We sat on the wooden jetty in the sweltering heat, and after enjoying our drinks we crossed the road and walked over a sandy knoll to the seamen's mission. We posted letters and cards home, Pete to his parents and fiancée and me to my cousins, Maureen and Dick, Eileen and Jimmy, and to my good friends the Thomsons.

We sailed for Sydney that evening. I had only four passengers on each sitting, Pete had nine and Peter had eight, which kept us in the saloon. Some of our colleagues had none at all, and they went on what was called the 'chain gang'. That meant doing all sorts of cleaning jobs and working when and where required. Not all the men on the gang were without passengers. There were a few who had managed to bluff their way into the merchant navy with false references and were not up to the job – they were quickly found out and rapidly consigned to the gang.

During the voyage between Melbourne and Sydney John and Joe told us of the delights of Sydney. Later, Peter joined me on deck and asked if the boys had told us about the pub called Monty's outside the dock gate.

'Yes,' I said, 'and all the beautiful girls called Monty's models.'

He laughed and said, 'Somebody's been having you on, the stories I've been told are much different. The beer is the worst in Australia and the models, well, they're mostly old whores, and from what I've heard a bloke could quite easily catch a dose off them.'

I was naive and that was for sure, but after seeing the frightening pictures of the people with VD I knew what he meant.

We entered Sydney Harbour at five o'clock on a bright and warm morning. Passengers were all over the decks vying for vantage points, and most of us first trippers were out in force along with a lot of the old hands – and I could understand why as I witnessed the beauty of the harbour and our elegant white ship's mast gliding gracefully beneath the famous bridge.

We docked at Pyrmont, and it was all passengers off after breakfast. I said goodbye to the two young English couples, the Salts and Vinegars, and they tipped me three pounds each. The Levinsteins and Mahoneys had not been able to have their breakfast at my tables because they were filled up with strangers. They glared at them and then said goodbye to me, handing me an envelope each, which I found to contain ten pounds sterling from the Americans and five pounds Australian from the Aussies. I paid my expenses, and I was still left with ten pounds Australian from my tips for the whole trip – not bad at all, I thought. I was sorry that I had requested a twenty-pound sub from my pay. Still, it might come in handy.

***

Once the passengers were off we were detailed into working gangs for storing, cleaning and generally licking the ship into shape for our Christmas cruise around New Zealand. We would have six days in port before taking on the cruise passengers. Mr Whitfield detailed Pete and me to cleaning duties so we would work under his jurisdiction, and that pleased us both. We liked him, and it was a pleasure working for him.

We worked up to lunchtime storing the cutlery and crockery, putting covers over the tables and generally getting everything shipshape. After the bulk of the work had been done, he called us together just as he had done so many times back in Tilbury. 'Thank you all for making my job so easy, men. I know I've got a great team and I'm proud of you. And those of you doing your first trip, you've come through a very difficult time with the seasickness and yet you've worked yourselves through it and come out winners. It's for that reason that you will be the first team to have this afternoon off. I have to warn you, though, you must report for duty at 8 am tomorrow, sober. Drunkenness will not be tolerated.'

Pete, Peter and I dashed to our cabins with just two things in mind, a quick shower and off to see the sights.

We walked along the busy docks in the hot sunshine and soon came upon Monty's. Peter said, 'Come on boys. Let's see what's going on.' Neither of us needed persuading, so in we went to the din of the jukebox blaring out and people's voices blaring even louder. Seamen from all over the world were there in various states of liquid confusion. Some were falling and sliding across the floor on the pools of beer in their attempts to grab the model of their choice, and there were cosier scenes too, fellas with their hands up models' skirts and others snogging and groping anything they could.

We ordered a midi each and for the first time I had no fear of being refused service. I had passed my eighteenth birthday a few days previously and I had my identity card to prove it. I kept it a secret, mainly because I didn't want my friends making a fuss. We were served without question and stood with our backs to the wall to watch the goings on.

Women were behaving in a way that left very little to the imagination, and in a few cases nothing at all. I had seen up the girl's dress at the golf club a few years before, but this was a different thing altogether. In a few minutes there I saw the bare breasts of two women, one white and one black, and a white woman without any knickers showing herself off to a big tall blonde man. I could barely believe my eyes. We had another beer each, but there was no use trying to talk to each other – it was impossible with all the noise – so we just stood there, each with our own thoughts and feelings.

Just as we were about to leave, two white women set about each other, roaring out profanities of the most explicit kind. They grabbed each other's hair, threw a few haymakers and a couple of well-aimed knees to the groin before they were dragged apart. What a scene!

We left to see how else we could improve our education. It was just a short bus ride to town and cost only a few pence. The city was nice and clean and there were plenty of big stores, cinemas, pubs, restaurants, and 'eat it and beat it places' too. All the bills of fare displayed a wide choice and the prices were more than reasonable in comparison to England. We walked around for a while, but the heat was starting to take its toll on us, so we stepped into a little pub. Just as in Monty's, the barman filled my friends' schooner glasses with a gun-like implement attached to a transparent plastic hose and waited impatiently to be paid.

I held up an Aussie ten shilling-note and said, 'I would like a midi please, I thought I had ordered it with the schooners.'

He gave me a sour look and said, 'Listen sonny, you may be served with alcohol wherever you come from, but we have laws here that forbid selling grog to minors and you can consider yourself lucky I haven't bounced you outta here.'

Pete and Peter started to speak at once.

'Please gents,' I said. I could speak for myself. I was furious with a combination of rage and embarrassment, but I kept it under control as I said, 'I know I look too young to drink, mister, but can I please show you my identity card?' And with that I held out my very new ID.

He scanned it, and said, 'A Mick!' Without another word, he filled a midi glass, put it down in front of me and whipped the note out of my hand.

My friends knew me well enough to see I had been hurt and they tried to make light of it.

'Thick bastard,' said Pete.

Peter, not to be outdone, said, 'Yeah! Any of them that I've served in London and that crowd I had from Fremantle to here were an ignorant bunch of bastards. I've yet to meet a good Aussie.'

'I've won, though,' I said. 'I'll use this place in the future, where I know I will be served, in case I find it difficult in other pubs. I'm getting sharper.'

We were on our fourth beer when Peter suggested we should have something to eat. We found a plain little café in George Street and ate big T-bone steaks with onions, peas and chips, which cost us just under ten shillings each. We could never have got anything like it in London or Dublin at such a giveaway price.

We stepped out into the heat and wandered around some more before entering a swanky pub with upholstered chairs, polished tables and a carpet on the floor. I had more aggravation to contend with before getting served, this time from a busty red-headed barmaid. I was served eventually, and when we sat down Peter said, 'John, I don't have to tell you that you look very young, and being so small makes you look even younger. You must get pissed off with all the ignorant comments and the likes of the crap that's been thrown at you this afternoon. Does it ever get you angry?'

'All the time,' I said. 'I was polite to that clown in the first bar and got through to him. And you heard how I dealt with Redhead. When I was going to school I realised I wasn't big enough to get into fights, but I found I could talk my way out of tricky situations most of the time.'

After three more drinks I knew I was getting drunk. Pete and Peter fancied staying on and having a good drink, so I bought them another round and left the bar with the most wonderful feeling of wellbeing. If that was what cold Australian beer could do for me, I was going to have some more of it. I slowly walked to the bus stop for the docks and soon was walking past Monty's and into the docks.

I awoke at five o'clock the following morning to discover that Cyril was up and drinking tea. The rest of the bunks had their curtains drawn, an indication that everyone was back on board. Either they had been very quiet when they came back or the beer had been stronger than I thought.

Our working routine in Sydney was much the same as it had been in Tilbury over a month ago. We were able to go ashore quite a bit, and I loved going alone to explore the place and find things out for myself. I found that some of the people seemed to be gruff and yet friendly. One afternoon I walked into a flashy bar in George Street and mounted a high stool. The dickie-bowed, balding, pallid-faced barman came rushing over and said, 'Well sonny?'

'A midi please,' I said.

'Is that all you'd like?' he asked.

I nodded, waiting to go through the same old rubbish. But this character was different. I tried to show him my identity card but he wasn't interested. He waved it aside and said, 'On your way, boy.'

I was about to lower myself down off the stool with as much dignity as I could muster when the big sandy-haired man sitting two stools away said, 'Wait a minute Jack! You never even looked at the lad's card. Give 'im a fair go mate.'

Jack reluctantly glanced at the card and looked at me with what I took to be contempt.

The big man asked, 'Satisfied, Jack?'

Jack gave a nod and a grunt.

'Give the young fella a beer on me and I'll have one too, with a brandy,' said my saviour. 'Whereabouts are you from in the old country?' he asked.

'Thank you for getting me out of that jam, and thanks for the beer,' I said. 'I'm from a small place called Enniskerry in County Wicklow, it's just twelve miles from Dublin. I'm doing my first trip on the *Himalaya* as an assistant steward and we're sailing tomorrow on a ten-day cruise around New Zealand.'

'Goodonyeh,' he said, and then went on to tell me about his great-grandparents coming out to Australia 'in the old days'. They had set out from County Mayo, with very little money, but they were filled with hope and faith in God. He related stories his grandparents had told him about how hard they had to struggle before they could get settled in, and when they did, they started up in the newsagent's business and never looked back.

***

We sailed from Pyrmont the following afternoon to the sounds of cheering, laughter, balloons bursting, streamers flying and the band playing 'Now is the hour' and 'Waltzing Matilda'. There was an air of intoxication with gaiety and I found that infectious. I was sorry to leave Sydney. I had fallen in love with the place.

I had sixteen passengers, from young adults to middle-aged, all with one thing in mind – to have a good time. And I believe the majority did, with the carnival nights, the fancy dress, the captain's cocktail parties and the trips ashore in that beautiful country of New Zealand. If I had been surprised by the appetites of my old crows and the Mahoneys, I was now mesmerised at the amount of food this lot could put away.

I got drunk on board a few times during the cruise and once ashore in Lyttelton.

The passengers disembarked at Pyrmont after spending a happy time on board over Christmas and the beginning of the new year. I made twenty pounds in tips and that was that.

We spent three days in Sydney before setting out on the return voyage to England. John and Joe took Pete, Peter and myself up to Kings Cross – a place they said was a bit like Piccadilly in London, but more open. Anything went. I liked the neon lights and the atmosphere in the bars, and despite having to show my ID several times I enjoyed myself.

I probably drank a quarter of what of my friends did, but I got a buzz and felt great. Two gorgeous girls, as I saw them, came and sat down with us. The boys joked and laughed with them and told them I was a 'Cherry Boy' and I didn't care. They said things like, 'How about it? You good-looking young fella, lose your cherry with one of us, a special price for you, five pounds for a short time!' My friends had a great time laughing and teasing me. 'Go on John, give her one, look at them tits!'

Of course they were being propositioned too, and Peter went with one to hoots from the others. I kept quiet. I wanted to go too, but I was too scared. I still hadn't been with a girl and would have been too embarrassed to go in front of them.

I was really drunk when we got back to the ship. My friends guided me up the gangway and to my cabin, where I flopped down on the bunk and was fast asleep in seconds.

◄ Aged nine.

Enniskerry, County Wicklow.
▼

The lane my mother and I used as a
shortcut to the school and the village.

Confirmation. ►

My favourite little building: the forge in Enniskerry.
▼

◄ The Rafferty boys.

Singing in the Esplanade Hotel, Bray, 1959.
▼

Staff party at the International Hotel, Bray, about 1957.
▼

▲ The proprietors and staff of the International Hotel, Bray.

Waiters' race, Bray.

The Mercantile Marine ▶
Office in Dublin, where
I was told by an official
that I was too small to
go to sea.

◀ The Seamen's Institute in Dublin –
my occasional home between sea
voyages.

▲ *Himalaya*.

As a steward on *Himalaya*, ▶
about 1961.

Strathenden.
▼

On the dockside with ▶
Strathmore behind.

The stewards
on *Strathmore*.

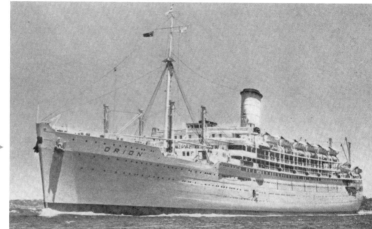

Orion. ▶

rcadia
y courtesy
f Ian Boyle).

◄ On *Arcadia*, December 1963.

My 21st birthday, on ►
Arcadia, December 1963.

◄ RMS *Andes*.

RMS *Aragon*. ►

◄ Drinking up, ashore.

With shipmates. ▼

◄ A photo from my time as an engine-room hand in the 1970s.

▲ The hospital in Japan where I spent a month after an accident on MV *King William*.

▲ The Seery children in Australia.

◀ Maureen and her children in Dublin in the 1960s.

The Queen Victoria Seamen's Rest.
▼

◀ The late Joe Downes, a great friend and drinking partner.

With Gwenda (left) ▶ and Anna-Marie.

◀ With Gwenda and Marie.

▲ My portrait, painted by Walter Kemsley.

Peter and Jimmy. ▶

◄ Bob Mackenzie and his dog Ben.

With Paschal ► and Maureen.

◄ With Anna-Marie (left), Linda (right) and Marie (seated).

Mulligan. ▶

▲ The author in 2010. (Photo by Simon Robertson-Young).

I awoke the next morning feeling sick and depressed. I tried to be sick down the toilet but to no avail. Somebody shouted, 'Put your fingers down your throat!' but I couldn't bring myself to do that so I gave it up as a bad job and returned to my cabin, where a bunch of the fellows were having liveners. Richard handed me a can of lager and said, 'John, you look rough, a livener is what you need.'

I held the can in my hand for a few minutes, thinking that a few minutes earlier I had promised myself I would never touch an alcoholic drink again, and here I was, with a can in my hand. Ah, balls. It was cool and it might make me feel better. I opened the can and took a few sips. It didn't taste too bad at all, so I slowly finished the can and had another – after which I was ready to attack anything the day would bring. The livener! That was the answer.

***

We sailed from Sydney to the same razzmatazz, as was the norm for passenger ships arriving from or leaving for 'the old country'.

My sixteen passengers were a mixed bunch. Some were disillusioned with the dream of a land of milk and honey. Australia was a hard and dry land, and if you wanted to make a go of it you had to put more than a bit of effort into it. Others were going back to see loved ones after many years away. Some had done well and others had failed. It's debatable if they would have been any more or less successful if they had stayed at home. Then there were the young Australians going to 'do Europe', travelling on a shoestring. And others, travelling for reasons best known to themselves. I had a mixture of them all.

When we left Fremantle, I knew we were really on our way home. We arrived in Colombo and I didn't have long to wait until the tailor came on board with my uniforms – I was delighted with them, and a steal at the price. Our next stop was Aden, where Mark bought his Leica and I bought two small transistor radios, one for my friends the Thomsons and the other for my cousins Eileen and Jimmy.

By this time I had become completely at ease in my environment and I liked my job. I spent a lot of time in my friends' cabin, and was learning a lot from John and Joe, not only about the ship's rules and regulations, but about current affairs, geography and history. I learned the names of many of my colleagues in the Goanese crew, and the names of the queens. Most of them had taken on girls' names. Dotsy, Daisy and Dixie. Millie, Lilee and Billie. Fag-ash Lil, Slack Alice, Languid Lil and many, many more. The large majority of the queens were all very kind, helpful and protective to us youngsters, without any obligation whatsoever.

On we went through the Suez Canal into the Mediterranean, the Bay of Biscay and eventually up the English Channel to berth in Tilbury Docks. The first shore people I came into contact with were taxi drivers, like a swarm of ants, dashing around, offering the same service, 'Taxi to London mate! Five pounds for four to any of the mainline stations.'

I signed off and re-signed for the next voyage, and so did Pete, John and Joe. Peter decided to sign off and go for a Cunard ship. I paid five shillings each customs duty on my two transistor radios and joined John, Joe and Peter in sharing a taxi to London at the cost of one pound five shillings plus a half-crown for the policeman on the dock gate.

Joe explained the reason for greasing the copper's palm. 'When we get to the gate, he said, the driver will give the copper our passes and the 'readies' so he won't have us out to go through our bags. There's only one thing, though. Sometimes the CID show up, and if that's the case there'll be no palming for the bobby, it'll probably be all out, gear out to check and all that bullshit – or we might be lucky and they'll just wave us on.'

The copper took our passes and the four half-crowns, and waved us on. We were on our way to London.

I spent my ten days' leave with Eileen, Jimmy and Junior. It was wonderful to have some time off and being free to wander anywhere I wanted with money in the pocket and a job I liked to go back to.

***

I reported back on board, feeling refreshed, full of confidence and pleased to see my friends and cabin mates again.

The next voyage was going to be more interesting. After

Australia we were going on to Auckland and Wellington in New Zealand, then the Far East – Hong Kong, Singapore, Penang, Kobe and Yokohama in Japan, followed by Vancouver, San Francisco, Los Angeles and San Diego. The names of those places really excited me and I thought, what a great job this is.

I spent my 'working by' period with my dear friends the Thomsons, but this time I thought of how nice it would be go out to the pubs in Gravesend and Woolwich with my shipmates. And that made me feel ungrateful and guilty because the Thomsons were so kind and were treating me like a son, but I had the urge to spread my wings. I spent the last two nights before sailing on board, which gave me the opportunity of going ashore with John and Joe on the first evening, and Pete joined us on our last night ashore. We drank in many bars that evening, and apart from a few of them checking on whether I was old enough to drink the evening was full of light-hearted fun. I had developed a liking for the brown ale and had kept a considerable amount down before I had to slip out to the toilet and be sick, and after that I was ready for another bellyful, and so it went.

When we got back on board I had one final bottle with my friends before flaking out, fully clothed, on my bunk.

We sailed on the tide, and it seemed to me that I had never been away from my old routine. I was very happy amongst my shipmates and the general atmosphere on the ship. I was truly a fortunate fellow. As the trip went on I was listening to every word said about the ports in the Far East, and I could tell that they were favourites with most of the old hands. In addition to that, John and Joe were educating Pete and me. Hong Kong was the place to get suits made to measure for less than a third of the price in the UK, and you could have cotton shirts made to measure for twelve shillings each with your initials artistically stitched on the pockets in Chinese or English. You could even have shoes hand-made at great prices. That was the place for me to get togged out.

The pretty bar girls in Hong Kong, Singapore and Japan were talked about at length. For five pounds sterling and the price of two drinks for them (coloured water) you could spend the night with one of them. All night meant from shortly after midnight to six in the morning, and the general opinion was that the best place to go with the business girls was in Japan – they were gentle, pretty and very clean. The thing to do was to have a few drinks aboard and go ashore around 9 pm. Have a few drinks in the bars and don't get too involved with any of the girls until you decided on the one you wanted to go with. That was all to come.

I had sixteen youngish immigrant passengers to feed all the way to Australia. They were easy to look after and were full of hope for the future. Most of them were awed with the 'trip of a lifetime', but the further we left old England behind the more I could see the looks on some of the faces change. I could not have put it into words at the time, but on reflection it was a combination of fear, apprehension, tension and insecurity, especially with the women. No matter what they felt, the realisation had dawned that they could no longer catch the bus or pop around to mother's house for a chat. They were on their own and had to make the best of it.

Some of the new crew took a bit of time to get used to me, and the snide jokes, ignorant comments and downright insults were all there in abundance. I hated it and I knew I always would. I occasionally responded with a sharp remark but for the most part I wouldn't give them the satisfaction of letting them see how they had got through to me. I was becoming harder and learning more about the real world every day. I was also developing a fondness for the liquid confusion, beer and brandy particularly. It calmed me down and made me feel an equal to any man.

After the passengers bound for Australia disembarked at the various ports we took on more passengers and sailed from Sydney for Singapore, our first port of call in the Orient.

I was amazed at the industry of the locals – the food stalls on the pavements selling all sorts of delicacies, men and women humping heavy goods around, the storekeepers trying to sell their wares, it was a hive of activity. The variety of public and private transport was also something to see. Patched-up old trucks, rickshaws, trishaws, bicycles and buses with all the colours of the rainbow alongside very modern private cars, some for business and others owned by the affluent and the privileged, no doubt.

Singapore was a duty-free port, and Pete and I spent hours going around the shops comparing the prices with those in the UK and Aden and found that some things were cheaper in Aden. We bought a few presents in Change Alley and then visited Raffles Hotel, where we had a beer in an atmosphere that smacked of the colonial world of yesteryear. We went back on board, served lunch and dinner, and then it was back ashore to take in the nightlife.

Pete and I accompanied Joe, our fountain of knowledge. He took us to Boogie Street. That's what it was called by the seamen. I think it was actually Bugis Street, but I never bothered to find out. Joe explained that it was swarming with 'kitis'. Apparently that was the name for transvestites and homosexuals and those who had had the operation to change from men to women. Their business was selling their bodies to other men and they mingled with the girls for rent. 'They all look fucking gorgeous,' said Joe, 'but don't be surprised if you put your hand between their legs and grab a pair of balls.'

The place was teeming with humanity from all walks of life, predominantly male, of course. We had a beer out in the open balmy air and were approached by several women and those who purported to be so. We turned down all offers and tried to be polite in doing so, which wasn't so easy with the more persistent ones. Then we did a tour of the bars, where Pete and I were shocked by the attention of the girls, and in my case delighted that all the bars were dark and it didn't matter whether I blushed or not. We were groped, canoodled, cajoled, and I got the feel of a woman's body for the very first time and countless times after that. I was raring to go, but Joe suggested, 'Save it all for Japan. Once you've had it there, anywhere else in the world will always seem like second best, and that's a fact!'

The experiences in Singapore prepared me in a way for the delights in Hong Kong, but it was different in many ways.

I had six shirts, a dark jacket and grey trousers made, which were delivered within twelve hours, everything fitted perfectly and I was happy.

Pete and I took the Star Ferry across from Kowloon to the Hong Kong side and rode on the tram up to the peak. Unfortunately it was a misty day so we saw very little, but nevertheless it was an experience. We caught the ferry back, rode on a tram and also in a rickshaw. I felt uncomfortable sitting back there with the spindly-legged little man pedalling as though his life depended upon it. Yes, he had badgered us for business, but it didn't make me feel any better. It just didn't feel right having a fellow human being doing something like that for me.

When we got out I told Pete how I felt and he said, 'I felt a bit strange too, but it's a way of life for him and he seemed pleased with the fare and the tip.' I left it at that and suggested we go to the Blue Anchor for a gargle. I had been there the night before with Mark. As we walked, I told him that everything John and Joe had said about the girls was true.

'Did you go with one?' he asked.

'No, but I wanted to,' I said, 'with a girl named Maili.'

Maili was gorgeous. The previous night, she had shown me her knickers and then guided my hand to her pussy, as she called it, and if that wasn't enough she had then put my hand down her knickers and let me feel her as she was feeling me up at the same time, saying, 'You nice boy Jonny, you cherry boy? You fuckee fuck. You buy me drink Jonny.'

Pete and I reached the entrance to the Blue Anchor, and in we went.

Maili came rushing over and steered us to a booth as though we were long-lost kin. 'You come back Jonny,' she said, 'you nice cherry boy, what name your fren?'

'Pete,' I said.

Before she had time to say anything else we were joined by another pretty girl. Maili introduced her as her 'bes fren' Suelee. I thought she looked a good match for Pete. I knew he wouldn't be going with Suelee because he had vowed that no matter what the temptation he was going to be true to Carol his fiancée, and by now I knew he was a man of his word.

Maili asked, 'You wan beer?'

'Yes please,' I said. 'How much for one drink for you?'

'Same las nite,' she answered.

'OK,' I said, 'one for you and your friend Suelee too.'

She glowed with sparkling eyes and skipped across to the counter for the order. Pete gave me the cocked eyebrow treatment and I said, 'Don't worry, I know what I'm doing.'

He nodded. By this time Suelee had started to work on him and I averted my eyes. I heard him telling her politely that he was not here for business, but she persisted in trying to change his mind. Maili put the drinks on the table and I gave her the exact money. She paid the barman and returned to trap me in the corner of the booth. I wasn't complaining, but we made it clear that we were not in there for business. They made one final attempt to get us to go with them, but we were firm in saying no.

We walked along Nathan Road, taking in all the sights and activities. When we got tired of that, we stepped into a bar called the Golden Dragon. Here we chose to sit on high stools – we didn't want any more 'booth treatment' that day.

A strange thing happened as we hit the pavement. A group of British soldiers were about to enter the bar. One of them approached us with a broad grin on his face, looked down at me and said, 'Is it? Jasus it is! John Mahon, de'ya not remember me? I'm Noel Sullivan, I used to deliver bread and cakes from Hamilton's in the Quinsboro Road to the International when you worked there.'

It was only then that I vaguely recognised his features. I remembered him as a cheerful, tousle-haired ragamuffin. He had changed so much, he could have passed me by and I wouldn't have given him a second glance. There he stood, upright and looking very smart in his uniform. He invited us back into the bar for a few gargles with his mates, but I declined on the grounds that we had to get back on board. In fact we were off duty until the next morning, but I detected that Pete didn't relish the idea of a drinking bout with the squaddies, and nor did I. Noel said he'd keep an eye out for our next visit and we definitely would have a good few jars then.

**

We sailed for Japan to the sounds of the Gurkha band playing the old standards.

I went ashore in Kobe at 10 pm with John, Joe and Pete. We visited the bars that the two old hands were familiar with, and where they were well-known too. The girls were all over us, a lot of pawing went on and plenty of flesh was bared discreetly. The nightlife for seamen in Kobe was even better than in Hong Kong. The girls' performances were very similar, but the approach was more feminine and there was less of the brashness.

Joe said, 'Let's take 'em to the Silver Moon.'

John grunted 'Yeah.'

Pete and I followed like two obedient puppies, and soon we were in another dimly lit bar. A girl came rushing over to us, clapping her hands, rubbing her cheeks, and shouting in what seemed to be sheer delight, 'My Joe, you long time no come, my heart broke for you, now I very happy.' Joe picked her up and smothered her with kisses.

'This is Mariko,' he said. 'She's a little darlin'.'

He put her down gently and she led us to a large booth. John asked her where Suko was and she said, 'She come soon, you no worry John.'

By this time, a pretty little girl grabbed Pete's hand and said her name was Yani and another one just about the same height as me took my hand and led me to a corner of the booth.

'Me Yamike,' she said. 'You?'

'John,' I said.

She pointed to John and said, 'Same, same?'

'Yes,' I said, 'same, same.'

Joe nudged Pete and said, 'Willya lookit himself, he wasted no time. Now listen boys, I'm getting the beers in. I want to get a drink for Mariko too.'

We took turns at getting the beers in after that, and each of us was left to decide whether we wanted to buy the girl we were with a drink or not. Finally it was 11.45 pm and that was the time my friends had said was a good time to buy the girls a drink if you wanted to go with them. I got a round of beers in and another for Yamike.

I hadn't noticed John's girl joining us. He introduced Suko to me. She smiled and said, 'You John awsoe, same same my John. He say you cherry boy? You no worry, Yamike make nice love for you.'

'Yes,' said Joe, 'he's a cherry boy all right, and all the way from the Holy Emerald Isle.'

That got a laugh from the boys, but confused the girls.

Yamike came back with the beers and her coloured water. Joe and John bought their girls drinks too, and I noticed that Pete had managed to shake off the girl who had been hanging onto him.

Yamike and I struck up our deal. It was six thousand yen for all night, which included the hotel, plus five hundred yen for the *Mama San*. The beers I had consumed gave me all the confidence I needed. I asked her what time we could go to the hotel.

'OK,' she said, 'we go now, firs you give me five hundred yen for *Mama San*.'

I gave her the note, which my friends noticed and they started making jokes, but the girls made more of it, squawking on about 'Cherry boy! Cherry boy!'

Pete said he was going back on board, and John and Joe were going with their girls. Yamike paid the *Mama San* and grabbing my hand said, 'Les go my number one man!'

So we left and walked the few blocks to the little hotel. Yamike instructed me to take my shoes off in the porch before entering the reception area. She had a few words with the old man at the desk and he handed her the key. We walked up a flight of stairs, she opened the door and in we went to a small and spotlessly clean room. The strange-looking bed was a cross between a single and a double mattress on the floor. I looked in the small fridge, which had four cans of beer and a number of soft drinks in it. I was tempted to have a can but decided against it.

There was a small sink adjacent to a deep-sunk tub with a shower faucet above it. Yamike twirled the taps and then started taking her clothes off, telling me to do the same. Despite the amount of beer I had consumed, I felt shy when it came to taking my clothes off in front of the girl.

She stepped over to me and held me close to her naked body. I wanted to push her away and look at her nakedness, but I was too shy. Instead, I clung to her, feeling her warm soft body up tight to my chest.

She turned away, saying, 'John my nice boy, take your croes off and come in tub with me.'

She stepped into the tub and I whipped my clothes off and joined her. It was delightful – the warm water and the soft body of that lovely girl. Was I dreaming? We washed each other's bodies and I lost my inhibitions. When we got out we stood on the mat and held our wet bodies together before drying each other and flopping down on the bed in a joyous mood.

I learned a great deal about a woman's body that night. After three orgasms I was no longer a cherry boy, and for good measure we made love again later that morning before kissing each other goodbye and promising to see each other again when I next returned to Kobe. I caught a taxi back to the ship and felt ten feet tall as I bounced up the crew gangway.

Yokohama was much the same, and I went with a girl there by the name of Kiko. It was even better than with Yamike, mainly because I knew what it was all about.

***

Vancouver was the first place I had ever heard piped music in a lift. I loved Stanley Park with its abundance of flowers and the beautifully carved and painted totem poles.

San Francisco – now there was a place to fall in love with. My first goal was to see Alcatraz. Then I rode on a tramcar from Fisherman's Wharf up the steep streets, went to the Top of the Mark and viewed the sights from aloft. I visited Market Street, where I bought a pair of cowboy boots. I quickly found out that I could buy clothes that actually fitted me without having to have any alterations done except for trousers and jeans. Even in America they didn't make them for my short little legs, but when I bought a pair of trousers and a pair of jeans the sales lady said that she would have them taken up free of charge and they would be ready within the hour. What service! It was a thrill to find that I could buy mature-looking clothes to fit from a wide choice that weren't available in the British Isles except in the few specialist shops I had found.

I went over the Golden Gate Bridge to the Redwood Forest and marvelled at the giant trees. I ate real hamburgers there, like I'd never had before, with everything in them – lettuce, tomato, onion, relish and any sauces you'd care to mention – and they were big. And when you ordered a cup of coffee in even the smallest of diners, a glass of cold water came along with it, and your cup was refilled again at no extra charge.

On we went, back to Australia, and I knew we were homeward bound when we reached Aden. I had become interested in photography because of the pictures Mark and Nobby had shown me. They didn't stop at that. They taught me about cameras, the apertures, the speeds, flash and night photography and lots of other things to get the best results. Sometimes it seemed like they were competing as to who could teach me the most. I went ashore with Mark and we went straight to his favourite shop, where he had bought his Leica. We were welcomed as usual by the Boss, as we had come to call him, and his brothers and were presented with bottles of cold soft drinks. Some of our passengers had already been in with the cards we had given them and a few of them had made substantial purchases, which greatly pleased our friends.

Mark said, 'I know just the camera for you, but it's your decision.' He asked the Boss to show us the Practica, the Voigtlander and a few others which I forget the names of. I looked them over and discussed their merits with Mark and the Boss, and it was mutually agreed that the Practica was the one for me. I don't remember how much it cost, but Mark assured me it was no more than half the price it would be in the UK. And that was good enough for me.

We did the deal and Mark stocked up on films. Then the Boss gave us each a little transistor radio and five 36-exposure coloured films. We were thrilled with his generosity and sincerity. We said goodbye and walked out into the sweltering heat and headed for an ice-cold beer in the only hotel we knew of. We drank the first one fast and ordered another. Then I loaded the black and white film into my camera and took a few shots of the dusty street and the people meandering around. Mark handed me a little notebook and pencil and said, 'This is for you to write down the particulars of each shot you take, the speed, the aperture, the subject and conditions – like the shots you've just taken, bright sun on this occasion.'

Back on board, there was much excitement in the crew quarters, with many of the gang trying out their new gadgets and the queens comparing the presents they had bought for their 'omies'. Nobby was impressed by my purchase and discussed its capabilities with Mark and me.

We were alongside Tilbury docks on 21 April, and paying off came before I knew it.

***

Pete and I signed on for the next trip but our good old friends John and Joe signed off. John didn't know where he was going next. Joe had accumulated twenty-five deferred days' leave over the time he had served on the vessel, and along with his leave from our previous voyage it was nearly six weeks.

'I'm goin' to drink Dublin dry,' he said.

John cut in, 'You said that about Canada too – or was that something to do with the ginger ale?'

We had a good laugh and a few jars before we piled into our taxi and set out for London. There was no delay at the dock gate. The driver gave the bobby our passes and our half-crowns and we were gone.

Once again I stayed with Jimmy, Eileen and Junior. They had moved to a bigger place in the Kenway Road. Junior was a bundle of fun. He was into everything and tireless, a cheerful, gentle child who very rarely cried. When they were both at work I went around London, mostly by tube. I had learned the colour of the various lines and it was easy to get to anywhere I wanted to. On one of my visits to Piccadilly, Ward's Irish pub beckoned to me.

I stood outside looking down the stairs, pondering whether it was worth being refused service out of hand or being subjected to questioning about my age. Ah, give it a try, I thought, I've got my ID on me and nothing to lose. So down the stairs I went and walked into the bar with an outward air of confidence equal to that of someone who had been visiting bars for years.

Inwardly I was a bag of nerves as I mounted a high stool and asked the young barman for a glass of Guinness. He smiled and said, 'Excuse me, I have to ask if you are old enough to drink.'

I could see we were being observed by one of his older colleagues – the manager, I suspected. I produced my identity card. He smiled again and said 'Thank you.'

He nodded to the scrutineer and got on with pouring my Guinness. Good, I thought, that wasn't too bad, especially in the way that I had been so politely and discreetly approached. They were serving the Guinness just like the way they did in Dublin, using a knife to skim off some of the froth and pouring a few drops in at a time until they produced the perfect pint of the brown stuff. I could tell that the barmen had got their training somewhere in Ireland, or that they had been trained by a good Irish barman and were proud of it. I don't know how many pints I drank or what time I left, and as the saying went in drinking circles, I wasn't feeling any pain as I let myself in to the flat.

I spent the last three days of my leave in the company of my relations, and then it was goodbye again. Eileen was expecting a baby and it looked like I'd be home for the birth.

On our second day back, Mr Whitfield called Pete and me over to the table where he was working on the seating plans and invited us to sit down. 'I'm losing you two to the first-class saloon as and from now,' he said. He thanked us for our good work, shook our hands and wished us good luck. We thanked him in turn and said it had been our pleasure working for him. And that was no lie. He had been the best boss I had ever worked for. We reported to Mr Green, the assistant head waiter. He put us to work cleaning silverware, which was easy enough but boring, and we were glad when the lunch break came.

I drank three brown ales and Pete remarked, 'You've got a thirst on you today mate.' I agreed that indeed I had, and blamed it on the boring job we were on all morning. The fact was that I wanted to get a glow on. The afternoon was taken up with storing, and finally our day came to an end.

Keith, the fellow I didn't like, had signed off, and his bunk was taken up by a first tripper called Sam. He was about six years older than me and he had been working on stores with us that afternoon. When he told us it was his first trip, Pete and I put him in the picture about several things to ease any worries he might have.

I walked into the cabin later on and there he was. He smiled when he saw me and asked, 'Are you in this cabin, John?'

'That I am Sam,' I replied.

'What's there to do around here?' he asked.

'Do you drink?' I asked.

***

The working by went well, and Sam became a constant companion in the PLA canteen. I enjoyed staying with my dear friends as usual, and spent the last night ashore with my shipmates Pete and Mark in Gravesend. We had our first jar in the Prince's Ankles and then moved from pub to pub and eventually ended up in the Queen's Knuckles – and there sat the dwarf as neat as could be, giving the impression that he had never left the place.

He spotted us coming in and made a big thing of welcoming me in particular.

"Ere mate, 'ow are ya? I aint seen you in bleedin' ages. Let me getcha a drink, wotcha want, a whisky?'

My friends had sat themselves down at a table opposite with their drinks. I waved across to indicate that I was going to have a drink with the dapper little man. Pete gave me the thumbs-up.

I apologised for the distraction and he said, 'It's all right son, yer with yer mates, wot's it to be then?'

'A brown ale would be nice, thank you,' I said.

He responded as though I had shot him. 'Wot? That's bleedin' piss, son, 'ave a man's drink, whisky an' dry.'

'Thank you,' I said, 'I will. It's just that I'm not used to whisky.'

'It won't do you no 'arm boy,' he said, 'if you drink it in moderation.'

We drank and talked, mostly about my experiences in foreign ports. He was firing questions at me as fast as a Tommy gun could shoot and we were both enjoying it. I bought another round and we shared the bottle of ginger ale. We chatted on for another ten minutes or so. He told me very little about himself and I didn't ask any questions.

He excused himself to go for a leak and that was my cue to join my friends. 'I'll join my shipmates,' I said.

'Do that,' he said, sticking out his hand. 'I'm Billy.'

We shook hands and I said, 'My name is John.'

'You take care of yourself, and remember – always wear a Frenchy when you go with them foreign birds. Bye, John, I'll see you next time.'

When I sat down with the others I glanced back to see him being helped off the stool and thought how fortunate I was.

Pete said, 'I got you a brown in mate – and as you can see Sam has joined us. What was the old boy like?'

'He's nice,' I said. 'He's a Cockney, that's for sure, but he said very little about himself. He wanted to hear all about the girls, and places abroad.'

Sam giggled and said, 'Ah, two little men together. I've been told you have to watch out for little people, most of them have a chip on their shoulder.'

Pete and Mark gave him daggers and kept quiet. My friends knew me well enough to know that I was boiling. 'You're well informed, Sam,' I said.

'No offence to you John,' he said. I didn't say a word.

Mark said, 'Come on men, drink up. I'm having a rum this time. Don't be shy, have what you want.'

We had a few more rounds, but I wasn't enjoying myself any more. We had a few more in the Prince's Ankles before catching the last ferry back to Tilbury.

When we got back on board there was a party going on in our cabin. They were all there and more besides. It was a birthday party given by Richard for Francis. I hadn't known about it, but if I had I would have bought him a little gift. He was a good cabin mate, as were all the others, and we all got on very well. Of course, that was a necessity in the small amount of space we had to share. Richard shoved a bottle of Double Diamond into my hand and said, 'Cheers mate.'

Even Harry and Nobby had beer bottles in their hands, which was an unusual sight, for they rarely drank alcohol. Cyril had a posh cut glass nearly full of rum and it smelled awful to me.

Francis was got out in drag along with some of his friends and he was Belle of the Ball. I could see Sam didn't know what to make of it all and looked very uncomfortable. In a way I felt sorry for him, but he wouldn't be hearing that from me. Rarely did I get pleasure out of seeing anyone's discomfort or misfortune, and I wasn't going to start now just because he had annoyed me. He was sitting next to Mark and I knew he would put him in the picture. I was drunk in a happy way, but very drowsy, so I slipped into my bunk and was fast asleep in no time.

I was up at six the next morning, sailing day. Had a shower and dressed while the others still slept and then went up on deck with a bottle of Double Diamond to think things over. I sat there on a bollard and thought how near I had been to giving Sam a slap in the gob last night – and then felt rather proud of myself for being so calm outwardly. It was silly to let people goad me into that frame of mind. Had I not thought before that if I could get a job at sea I would be equal to any man, no matter what size he was? Better get back to that way of thinking.

I finished my beer and went down for another before going to see how Pete was. He was up when I walked into his cabin with my Diamond in my hand and I asked him if he would like a taste to get himself right.

He pulled a face that would have put a monster from a horror movie to shame and said, 'Jesus, John, I'm dying, I was well pissed last night. Did I behave myself?'

'To the best of my memory you did,' I said.

'I thought you were going to give Sam a mouthful last night,' he said.

'I was on the verge of it,' I said. 'I was seething inside and it spoiled the rest of the night for me.'

'I know,' he said, 'he's a bit of a bumpkin, but a nice one – and remember, he's a first tripper.'

'For someone who was dying a few minutes ago you've come to life fairly sharp,' I said.

'Only on the surface,' he said, opening two bottles of Double Diamond.

***

The passengers came aboard and we were ready for them. Pete and I had tables to seat six passengers on each sitting, which was commonly referred to in our business as a 'doddle'. Only twelve passengers to take care of instead of the sixteen in tourist class. Admittedly there was a larger choice on the menu and the passengers had paid a lot more money, but nothing else was any different. My attitude never changed, irrespective of how much they had paid. Tourist, assisted passage, or first, I treated them all with the same respect, courtesy and attention. Nothing was too much trouble for me. I saw it as part of my job, and it paid dividends.

The first sitting still had to be out within the hour, and the greedy ones were no different, except for the few who tried to put on airs and graces –

'We are travelling first class, you know.'

I had four women and two men on my first sitting, and three women and three men on the second, all bound for Australia. They were easy to look after, so I had what was referred to as a 'cushy number' all the way to Sydney. I overheard a miffed couple on my first sitting talking about how they should have been seated on the captain's table, but due to some mix-up in London his table had already been filled. They seemed happier after his cocktail party and they had something to talk about.

When I mentioned this in my cabin, Cyril said, 'Oh, you'll hear plenty of that old nonsense. A lot of them think it's their given right because of breeding or how affluent they are. Some of them do two and three trips a year on this line and if they're not on the skipper's table they expect to be on a senior officer's at least, the staff captain's or the surgeon's. A pain in the arse, some of 'em.'

Sam was sick for a while and then he got over it. He came ashore with Pete, Mark and myself in Aden and bought himself a record player/radio machine, also capable, I think, of waking him up and putting his socks on in the morning. Pete bought a watch each for his best man and the bridesmaid, and Mark and I were content to stock up on films. We finished off our free soft drinks from the Boss and bid him goodbye. As we were leaving he handed Mark and me three rolls of colour film each, Sam a roller ball pen and Pete a transistor radio. 'Presento,' he said. 'See you next time.'

I went ashore by myself in Colombo to take pictures, and again in Fremantle. I enjoyed those solo trips and promised myself that I was going to do more of that. I didn't have to care about where someone else wanted to go or what they wanted to do. And that was freedom as far as I was concerned.

I was still full of inquisitiveness and keen to learn as much as I could about the people and places we visited. The Aboriginies, Maoris and Native Americans were of particular interest. I would listen to anyone who knew anything about what I wished to know, provided they were serious and not taking me for a fool.

Pete and I took Sam to Monty's in Sydney – a must, we thought – and just like us on our first visit, he was amazed. We turned down the models' offers, drank a couple of midis and then it was up town to the old haunts, where I knew I would be served alcohol. Sitting in the first bar with our drinks, Pete asked Sam what he thought of Monty's.

'I never seen anything like it,' he said, 'the women showing themselves the way they did and all the blokes staggering around this early in the day! The women were cheap too. I wish we had a place like that in Birmingham. I was nearly going to do it with one of them. Maybe I will later.'

'And maybe your mickey will fall off after you do,' I said.

Pete was more serious as he said, 'If you do decide to go with one, wear a rubber.'

'I know all about that,' said Sam. 'I don't like wearing johnnies, it's like washing your hands with gloves on. You have to take some chances in life.'

We left it at that and proceeded to get drunk.

Back in the Orient again, I went with Maili in Hong Kong and it was fabulous – and even better with Yamike in Kobe, but the star prize went to Kiko in Yokohama.

So much for purchased sex in the Orient – all part of the highlights of the trip, along with the great experience of going through the Panama Canal.

The biggest 'downer' of all was seeing so many poor unfortunates on the streets of Bombay. Scrawny little men running around with loads on their backs that would put any self-respecting donkey to shame, wispy little men pedalling rickshaws and trishaws, beggars in abundance, crippled men, women and children along with the more able ones, but barely able. And some poor little mites with open sores, which the flies wouldn't leave alone. People sleeping on the pavements, some in the open and others under makeshift covers of cardboard boxes and several other sorts of improvisations. The sultry strength-sapping heat and the filthy streets bustling with all modes of transport belching out pollution that darkened the sky, and the overbearing stink.

Later, Pete and I sat on deck with our beers, watching the porters on the dock humping and hauling trunks, bales, bicycles and sewing machines. Most of this stuff belonged to the Goanese catering crew and the Lascar deck and engine crew who were paying off. While the ship was in Tilbury or Southampton, they made it their business to get around the markets and second-hand shops buying up goods they could sell back home. Their specialities were broken-down sewing machines and bicycles. It didn't matter how dilapidated they were – they would buy them, usually for a few shillings, and then do them up in their spare time on board. The Goanese were shouting orders and domineering it over the poor unfortunate scrawny porters for the sake of a few rupees.

I had become quite friendly with a few of the Goanese crew, and I thought it very unfair that men twice and three times my age were paid less than half what I was paid. They were predominantly Catholic, and very few of their cabins were without holy pictures, statues and little altars. I have no doubt that many of them were devout and sincere, but as in all walks of life there were the phoneys among them, the 'Oh, what a good Christian am I' brigade. They were cunning in all sorts of ways and very good at getting their own way. Their general demeanour was subservient bordering on obsequious, and I detested that act. Now some of the quietest of them were behaving like demented overseers barking out orders on a slave farm.

The conversation turned to Sam and the dose he had picked up somewhere in the Far East. The ship's surgeon had been treating him for four weeks and he was still blobbing, so much so that he had to wear a condom and change it at least three times a day. There was a certain amount of sympathy for him until he said that he was going to fuck everything in sight and spread it as far and wide as he could. He said that in our cabin, and he was very fortunate that he wasn't given a good beating to knock some sense into him. There were enough angry men there quite capable of changing his bone structure, but common sense prevailed and he had to listen to some hard talking. I said nothing, but never took my eyes off him as his face turned to a very sick white. He was scared, very scared. He blobbed all the way home and paid off a worried man.

***

Pete paid off on 30 August 1961. I signed on for another trip, and then we both went down to the cabin for a few jars – and there, to our pleasant surprise, were our old mentors and friends John and Joe. They were back to work by and do the next trip. We had a few beers, and arranged to meet Pete in

215

London when I got back off leave.

I hadn't arranged for a taxi in the usual way, but I was fortunate to come upon a driver who was looking for one more for London. I caught the coach out to Heathrow Airport and went on standby for a flight to Dublin.

I didn't have long to wait for a cancellation, and in about an hour and fifteen minutes we were touching down. I boarded a coach to the city centre and soon I was standing with my two suitcases in O'Connell Street, back in Ireland just a year after I had left in search of a better way of life – and in my opinion I had found it. I had a wad of money in the pocket that could easily have choked a small-sized donkey with a little mouth.

I booked into the Seamen's Mission on Eden Quay, and when I had sorted out my gear I decided to go out for a drink, and that was not the most pleasant of experiences. I was flatly refused service in some of the bars without so much as an apology or a 'kiss me arse'. I was asked my age in others, and when they were satisfied they served me. I was angry with myself for not having reacted when I was refused without being given the chance to prove my age. I should have said something instead of accepting the decision and walking out. I consoled myself with the fact that I had done so with dignity. It was all feeding my inferiority complex and building up an anger within me, but my liking for alcohol was helping me to overcome most of the drawbacks. Or so I thought.

I went out to Enniskerry the next day and it was a happy reunion with my relations. John was a typical boy, out skinning his knees playing football and getting into fights. Noel was much quieter, and Dermot was a bundle of fun. Maureen was expecting another baby around Christmas time and they were looking forward to the event.

I renewed contact with a few old friends in the village and in Bray. Most of them asked, 'Did you bring any of them things over with you?' Condoms, better known as French letters, banned in the Holy Republic of Ireland.

I would tease and ask, 'What do you mean, *them things*?'

The reactions were funny to hear and observe, but only for a short while. I got no joy out of their discomfort and embarrassment, so I'd slip a packet of three condoms under the table to them. Then it was a joy to see the sparkle in their eyes. I turned down all offers of payment, because it gave me a good feeling to be able to give someone something that made them happy – and besides, it was my way of fighting back at the dictators of the Catholic church. I reasoned that there were far too many unwanted children in the land anyway.

Once the business of the rubbers had been dealt with it was into the Arthur Guinness nectar. I could only drink three pints because of my capacity, but I made up for it with the spirits, usually whiskey and sometimes gin or brandy. Usually those get-togethers ended with a good old singsong and fun was had by one and all.

I stayed in with the family on my last evening on leave. Maureen put the children to bed and we sat down to have a good old chinwag. I produced a bottle of sherry and poured them a small glass each, which they sipped on sparingly as though it was the divil's brew while I drank my brandy and dry.

Maureen cautiously brought up the subject of alcohol. I could see she was ill at ease, but she was determined to have her say.

'You're fond of the drink John,' she said. 'I suppose you drink a lot on the ship, do you?'

'I enjoy a drink,' I said, 'but I never overdo it.'

I could see she was pleased to hear that, and she smiled as she took a sip of her drink. Dick said, 'There's no harm in a man having a drink in moderation.'

We talked until two or three in the morning, and after much coaxing we got Maureen to sing 'I'll take you home again Kathleen.' And shortly afterwards it was bedtime.

I walked very steadily to the bathroom, which was an effort. I was more wobbly than I had thought – I realised how much as I tried to stand still to clean my teeth, but I felt really good and I knew that I would get a good night's sleep. I bid them goodnight and was in bed in no time.

At the airport the next morning I was allowed to check in early, and then it was up to the bar for some liquid gold. The flight to London was nothing to get excited about, nor was the bus ride to the West London Air Terminal. I made my way across London to Fenchurch Street, where I stocked up with a bottle of brandy and three ginger ales and then caught the train for Tilbury Riverside.

***

Back on board, everything seemed much the same. The *Himalaya* was a hive of activity. I met John and Joe and a few other old friends at 'tick on' the next morning and soon I was back in the old routine.

John, Joe and I had Friday off and travelled up to London to meet Pete at Charing Cross railway station. He was waiting for us, so we caught a tube to Piccadilly and then went to Ward's for a drink before Pete bought his wedding suit.

I gave our order to a freckle-faced young man, who appeared confused. I suspected that he wanted to ask my age but was unsure of himself. Fortunately the scrutineer was there. I looked past the young fella and nodded to him, which he acknowledged with a nod of his own. The barman observed this and just for confirmation he looked back at his boss, who gave a nod of assent. We were off and running. We sat on high stools at the counter and the two boyos told Pete and me what they had been up to on their leave.

When we had drunk half our pints, Joe said, 'Jasus, that's the best pint I've ever had outside of Ireland. We'd best order another, it'd be a woeful shame just to have the one.'

So we had another and yet another before we went with Pete to pick up his suit and other accoutrements. The shopping expedition was successful, and we were back in Ward's within a couple of hours. After a few more drinks, Pete said he had better get home while he still could, and I said I was going too because I was staying with my cousins for the weekend and I didn't want to fall in their door. I could see John and Joe were setting themselves up for a marathon drinking session and I knew I wouldn't have been able to keep up with them.

Pete and I shook hands at the station, and that was the last time I ever saw or heard of him.

It wasn't uncommon in our way of life. You could sail and get on well with many a decent man for a long time, and when you signed off you might never see each other again. It was referred to in our business as 'Board of Trade

218

acquaintances'. In years to come I would meet many such good men, and at the end of the trip, that was it. Naturally, no two people see everything in the same way all the time, and I've had my differences with several colleagues, but I'm pleased and proud to say that in nearly twenty years at sea there were very few characters that I really couldn't stand.

I didn't have the same enthusiasm for the forthcoming voyage as I had done for the previous trips. I went over to the PLA canteen one lunchtime, and after a bit of friendly banter with some of the dockers I ordered a large brandy and a brown ale, and just as I was leaving the counter a dirty fat little docker, not much taller than me, said, 'Watch out, the heavy mob's here! I'll be fucked, it's a leprechaun!'

I knew I was on safe ground as I stood to his side and readied myself to fling my drinks over him if he physically reacted to what I had to say. 'Leprechauns, little legs, short arse, I've heard it all before from loudmouths. Wouldn't it be an awful thing for an ignorant little fella with a big belly and a mouth to match to be knocked on his arse by someone he underestimated.'

There was a gasp as Big Mouth lunged at me. I stepped aside, and by then his pals had grabbed him.

I went over to where John and Joe were sitting, and as I sat down Joe said, 'Same ould shit I suppose.'

Mr Whitfield was leaving the vessel that afternoon and giving up the sea to get married. I thanked him for all his kindness and wished him the very best for the future. We shook hands, and that was that.

I stayed with my dear friends the Thomsons for the next two nights and spent the last two nights in the pubs in Gravesend.

We sailed from Tilbury and it felt good to be at sea again. The passengers weren't much different from the others I had served on the previous trips. A few awkward ones as usual, but nothing I couldn't cope with. I enjoyed myself in the Far East as I had done before and got drunk with Noel Sullivan in Hong Kong.

I also spent a lot of time with Mark and Nobby during our shore leave. We went on trips and tours to take pictures from places as far afield as the Blue Mountains, the Koala Bear Park, the Pylon Lookout on the Sydney Harbour Bridge, the night lights of Hong Kong, the Tiger Balm Gardens there and in Singapore, the Acropolis and the amphitheatres in Greece.

And the ruins of Pompeii. In Naples Mark and I hired an old man named Mario to take us there in his old buggy, pulled along by an equally old horse named Ferdinand. Mario chattered all the way, laughing and having a great time. We couldn't understand a word he said, but that didn't deter him. We walked all over and marvelled at everything we saw. We took plenty of pictures and then joined Mario and Ferdinand for the return trip. We got Mario to stop several times, suggesting that poor old Ferdinand needed a rest, and we would make a big show of giving him a rub down. The old boy delighted in this as much as we did. When the time came to pay him off we did so generously with a wad of lire, a few English pounds and four American dollars.

I received a letter from Maureen on our arrival in Southampton, telling me she had given birth to a little girl, Carol, on 26 December 1961 and all was well. I couldn't have been happier for them.

I paid off on 10 January 1962 and signed on again for another trip before going on ten days' leave, which was fortuitous because Eileen was due to give birth to their second child sometime that month – and three days later Jimmy accompanied Eileen to the hospital. I looked after Junior until he got home several hours later looking tired and worried. He said with a sigh, 'They told me to come home. It's highly unlikely she'll give birth until tomorrow, but they'll phone me if there's any change. So I'll take Jimmy over to our childminder early in the morning and then go straight to the hospital.'

We were up at six o'clock the next morning, and Jimmy left with Junior at seven. I decided on a tube ride to the East End and a visit to the Red Ensign Club. I bought myself a coffee from the vending machine, and just as I bent down to pick the cup up, a voice from behind said, 'My lucky little leprechaun. What brings you here?'

It was Peter my old shipmate from our first trip.

'I've heard so much about this place from the boys, I thought I'd give it a look over,' I said. 'Are you staying here?'

'Yes,' he said. 'Just wait till I get a coffee, we'll go to the cafeteria.'

He got his coffee and I followed him into a room full of men, some eating breakfast, others in conversation, some sitting alone in thought and others reading newspapers. We sat down and he said, 'Drink some of that coffee, I've got something to put in it to keep the cold out.' I did so and watched as he covertly pulled a hip flask from inside his jacket pocket, poured some liquid into my cup beneath the table and pushed it across the table to me. He then fortified his own cup, held it towards me and said, 'Cheers.'

I took a cautious sip and it tasted good. 'Liquid gold!' I said.

'The best,' he said, 'Johnnie Walker, Black Label, duty-free from the last one. I had to be careful, you can get away with a lot in here, but I don't fancy getting thrown out for having a sly nip of whisky.'

As we drank, he told me he had been on the Union Castle Line for two trips around the African coast, stopping in all sorts of ports, including several in South Africa. He said that there were some great runs ashore there, but you had to look out for yourself in South Africa. Definitely no sex with the blacks and coloureds unless you wanted a good beating from the so-called police and to end up in jail as well – and he finished up by saying, 'The whites have it all their own way.'

After a few more replenishments of coffee and Black Label, the bar was open and we were nearly first in. I ordered two large whiskies, a ginger ale and a Carlsberg from the person behind the bar.

'Certainly my dear,' said the cheerful one. 'Oh, Peter, what a lovely young friend you've got, you are a lucky man.'

I looked at Peter and he said, 'Don't pay any attention to him, or should I say her? That's Stella Minge, she loves to take the piss, but she's got a heart of gold.'

We drank and talked for ages, and I learned that it cost ten shillings per night bed and breakfast without a sink in your room and twelve shillings and sixpence with a sink. That was good, considering how close it was to the Pool (the Shipping Federation) and how convenient for the city and all the shipping companies.

'Yes,' said Peter, 'there's all that, and the pubs around here abound with birds on the game. A lot of them are pure scrubbers but there's a fair amount of crackers too. You have to be careful, though. There's been quite a spate of blokes getting rolled around here lately – mostly, though, it happens to the prats flashing their money and getting so pissed that a child could do them. The pimps and scrubbers are getting all the blame but believe me, there's plenty of shady characters around here, and there's a few in here that I don't trust – just look around you.'

I was on my third large whisky and I could feel it starting to take effect. I needed some air so I bought him another round and made my way back to Kenway Road.

Jimmy was there with Junior on his knee sporting a broad grin as he said, 'It's a girl, a gorgeous little girl, they're both healthy and doing well. It was a hard birth for poor Eileen, but thank God it's all turned out grand.'

'Will you join me in a glass of whisky to celebrate?' I asked.

'After I've bathed Himself and put him down for the night.'

'I'm half shot already,' I said, 'but I've got plenty of room for another one or two.'

We drank and talked about people and places in Ireland, his job and mine and how he was thinking of moving back to Ireland because he thought it would be better for the children over there, and on we went until we were overcome with the need for sleep.

Eileen came home with the beautiful little Rosemarie the day before I went back off leave, and as I travelled I thought of how gentle little Jimmy was with his sister. When he thought we weren't looking he would kiss her and gently hold her little hand and it melted our hearts .

***

I did my final trip on the *Himalaya* and signed off in July 1962 to take the leave I had accrued over the four trips. Twenty-five days in all. I caught a flight to Dublin, where I stayed in the seamen's mission and went on some heavy benders when not visiting my relations. My great pleasure was just sitting in a bar and listening to the conversations around me, the arguments, the bar-room philosophy and the know-alls. It was fun. One of my favourite places was the Scotch House on Burgh Quay. There was always a good collection of characters in there.

It was there I got chatting to an old drover. He could tell a tall tale, and one that sticks with me is how he used to get the cattle up on their feet when they lay down on the deck of the ship taking them across to England. 'Y'see boy, I always used to chaw a wad of tobacco and when wan of them fuckers went down, I useta spit a good wad a juice right in its eye. I was so good with the aim I never missed and bejasus the bastard'd be up before you could blink. Ah, sure them days is over now and I miss them.'

I spent most of that leave getting drunk, going back to the mission to sleep it off and then back out for another go. It was very easy to drink that way and not have to worry about offending or embarrassing Dick or Maureen by showing up full to the gills. I visited them several times, but I was always careful not to have more than a few jars taken.

I returned to London, booked in to the Red Ensign Club, had a few days on the booze, and as the money was running low I went to the P&O personnel office and was given papers to join the *Stratheden* in Tilbury the following day.

She was on her last voyage to Australia and then she was going to do a series of two- and three-week cruises around the Mediterranean, after which it would be the end for her. The boys joked, 'She'll be broken up in the Far East and in a few years we'll be shaving from the blades they make out of her.'

All along the Australian coast there was a big welcome and farewell for the gracious old lady, and many tears were shed over her final departure, especially by those who had travelled out on her and were now doing quite well, thank you.

I was given the job of wine steward for the Mediterranean cruising, and I was thrilled. There was no formal training, but I wasn't backward in coming forward and teaching myself. It didn't take me long to distinguish between the good wines and the plonk, or the dry from the medium and sweet. I did this by reading as much as I could and ensuring that there was always a drop left in the bottles for me to taste. In addition to that, some passengers would give me what they hadn't finished. I wasn't too keen on wine, but it all helped me to describe what was what. I quickly learned how to distinguish the genuine wine drinker from the poseurs who made a big show of swirling the liquid around in the glass and taking ages slopping it around in their mouths, then there would be the nod of the head and the affirmative, 'Yes, steward, perfect.' Sometimes this Academy Award performance was over a bottle of cheap plonk, and that was the laugh. And I often thought, not all the actors are in Hollywood.

Along with the wine steward's job came gangway duty, which entailed being stationed either at the top or bottom of the gangway to assist the passengers. I also helped out in one of the bars in the evenings. The trio working there regularly were Eddie, Nick and Paddy. Eddie was the barman, a swarthy easy-going type who never seemed to hurry and yet was always ahead of the game. Nick and Paddy were the public room stewards. Nick was on par with Eddie, not only in features and build but in temperament too. Paddy was tall and thin with a jolly personality. All likable men, and I had great pleasure working with them. I soon found out which of the passengers Nick and Paddy favoured and stayed away from them as much as possible. That tactic was thanks to old Buzz at the International Hotel, who had told me to keep away from his *good tippers*. They never spoke of this, but I could tell they were impressed.

That cruise went well, and so did the next until I went ashore in Naples. I visited a few bars and eventually landed up at the Seamen's Services Club. I got a beer and was about to join some old shipmates when a fight started and it quickly became a free-for-all. I saw a shipmate called Stan taking a few wallops in the lug and headed in his direction with the intention of battering his adversary. I had consumed enough liquid confusion to make me feel capable of toppling Mount Everest. Suddenly a big paw came my way and I saw stars. There was blood all over my shirt but it brought me back to my senses. The paw came my way again and grabbed me around the neck. I was propelled through the melee and out onto the pavement. Once there, my propellant let his grip go and l looked up into his face to see that it was Bobby, another shipmate.

'Come on, let's get out of here before the law arrives,' he said. He grabbed my elbow and steered me along the pavement without saying another word until a van pulled alongside us and out jumped what seemed to be an army of *Polizia*. They were shouting and gesticulating, and we added to the crazy scene by loudly protesting our innocence until they got the better of us and had us in the van. Once inside the wagon I found myself much more sober, and in the dim light I counted four policemen, laughing and chattering away without paying us the slightest bit of attention. The van drove off and pulled up again, and two more of our shipmates were thrown in on top of us. We were cramped now, but not for long. We came to the final halt and were herded into the police station.

They separated us to check our identity cards, go through our pockets and take our fingerprints. I vaguely recall having to try to walk a straight line – it was impossible. I was shoved into a dimly lit cell all by myself, and as the guard locked the door I realised that I was in jail, and with that came the best solution to sobering up I have ever found, not that I would want to do it again.

I hardly slept at all that night with fear and worry and wondering where the others were. Thankfully the morning came and with it the sounds of shouting, *Raus! Raus!* That's how it sounded to me, anyway. I remember thinking it sounded German, but I could not have given a hoot what language it was, it was good to hear – and even better when the cell door was opened with much rattling of keys and in stepped a portly middle-aged man with a grin broader than the Bay of Naples. He handed me a wedge of bread and a bowl of brownish liquid. I tried to talk to him but it was useless. He just wagged his head from side to side and was gone, locking the door with the same rhythmic jangling of the keys.

A few hours later the cell door was opened by the same guard, who smiled at me and stood aside to allow in a very dignified officer, a tall upright man with all sorts of insignia on his smart blue-green uniform.

'You and your friends are accused of causing a riot in the seamen's club,' he said. 'I have come to tell you that a representative of the British consul will visit you tomorrow morning.'

I asked him if it would be possible to join my shipmates in their cell or if one of them could be moved in with me. He said he would see what he could do and left.

I never heard another word that day, and the monotony was broken only when meals were pushed into the cell at lunchtime and teatime. Lunch was a pasta dish, a food I had never eaten before, but I was hungry so I ate the lot. Tea consisted of chopped potatoes and tomatoes in oil and again I ate the lot. I paced the floor with a mind full of thoughts all racing around. I gave up pacing and lay down on the bare mattress, pulling the old brown blanket over me. It was another restless night and I was glad when it was over.

The morning drink and wedge of bread tasted better the next day. I had a birdbath in the little sink and dried myself with my shirt. I washed the shirt, but I just could not shift some of the bloodstains. I was in a state of nervous tension and frustration and the only consolation was the hope that the representative of the consul might get me out of the place that day. Some time in the late afternoon the door was opened and in walked the guard followed by a rotund little man with grey hair and a serious look on his kisser. He introduced himself as Mario Something, which I didn't take in – I had been expecting an Englishman.

'Good afternoon, Mr Mahon,' he said, offering his hand. We shook and I thought, he's pronounced my name correctly. 'I have good news,' he said. 'The club has agreed to accept one hundred pounds for the damage caused and they will drop the charges. It means you and your three friends will have to pay twenty-five pounds each if you want to get out quickly. Otherwise you can refuse to pay and let the case go to court, but that could take a long time. I have discussed it with your friends and they have agreed to pay the damages. However, there is a slight problem as far as you are concerned. I cannot do anything for you until we have discussed your case with the Irish Embassy in Rome, but you must not worry.'

Worry? I was flaming mad. 'Sir,' I said, 'I am not worried, I'm bloody furious. I was serving on a British ship and I have all the necessary documents, a British discharge book and identity card. I would have expected the consul to take that into consideration. No doubt the other seamen have told you that we had nothing to do with the fight and we didn't cause any damage. I believe the police needed to catch some people to hang the blame on – and who better than a few drunken seamen.'

'I understand how you feel,' he said quietly. 'There is nothing I can do about it.'

'Thank you,' I said. 'My most immediate problem is that I need soap, toothpaste, a toothbrush, a towel and cigarettes. Could you please arrange to get those things for me?'

'I'm sorry,' he said, shaking his head, 'not until we have consulted with the Irish Embassy. Perhaps your friends will share with you.'

'Could you possibly arrange to have one of my colleagues transferred to my cell?' I asked.

He was silent for a while and then said that he thought he could get that done. That bucked me up for a bit, but nothing happened the rest of that day, and the night dragged on tediously.

About two hours after the usual breakfast, the door was opened and the guard ushered Bobby in. Company at last. I focused firmly on the plastic bag he held in his hand and asked, 'What have you got there, goodies?'

He opened the bag and said, 'Cast your eyes in there boyo! Mario told me about your problem, the Irish Embassy and all that crap. We'll share what we've got.'

I looked in the bag. Luxuries! A towel, soap, toothpaste, toothbrush and sixty Rothmans cigarettes. 'What about matches?'

He grinned and said, 'They never sent any, or if they did I never got them, but the Italian geezer that was in my cell had three boxes and he gave me one. I'll tell you something, mate, it's home from home for the blokes doing long time in here. That geezer told me they want for very little, from food to luxuries. Mind you, I didn't ask him about sex. I was just getting all the gen out of him when they transferred me.'

He chucked a packet of cigarettes to me and offered one from his open packet. We lit up and I asked if he knew where Norman and Colin were. He didn't. We talked about my problem with the consul and concluded that all I could do was wait and see what the Irish Embassy came up with. There was a jangling of keys, and a watermelon-faced guard ushered us out of the cell and along the corridor to a door that led out onto an exercise yard where there were about thirty men in small groups continuously on the move. Melonface never said a word but indicated that we should start moving, and we did.

It wasn't long before we were joined by a couple of hard-looking inmates. The bald one asked in halting English where we came from and why we were there. Bobby gave him a brief outline of our story and shortly afterwards they moved on, to be replaced by another sinister-looking duo who also needed to satisfy their curiosity. It went on like that for at least half the time we were out there, which was about an hour. Then we were left to ourselves except for a few minutes when Baldy and his pal sidled up to us and slipped us five filter-tipped cigarettes each and two small oranges. We were moved by the generosity.

On our fifth day of incarceration, Mario came and told me that someone at the Irish Embassy said they would pay for my repatriation, but they refused to pay any damages claimed against me. 'We have discussed this problem,' he said, 'and if your friends are willing we can add just over eight pounds to their bills and you can reimburse them when you reach England.'

'That makes me feel much better, sir,' I said. 'It's a perfect solution. But have you asked them?'

'Not yet,' he replied.

'Of course they'll help you,' said Bobby. 'Aren't we all seamen together?'

'Yes,' I said, 'but I'm not taking anything for granted. And there's something else to think about. If we pay the money, it will seem that we are admitting guilt for something we didn't do.'

'You might have to wait a long time before your case comes to court,' said Mario.

'We'll pay up,' said Bobby.

'And you, Mr Mahon?' asked Mario.

'Yes,' I said, 'I will pay if the other two will help me.'

'I will go to see them and I will return to let you know their decision,' he said.

He came back about fifteen minutes later with a big grin on his face and declared, 'Mr Mahon, your friends are willing to help you. Now we can get on with getting you all out of here. It should take two or three days.'

Shortly after he left we were let out for exercise. There was less curiosity this time, but the generosity was greater, and we returned to the cell with sweets, nuts and six cigarettes each.

'Isn't it strange?' said Bobby. 'There's all sorts of deviants amongst that lot and yet some of them have big hearts, showing us two foreigners this kindness.'

Later that day two tins of home-made pasta were pushed through the door flap to us by an inmate with words that sounded a bit like *bon appetit*. It looked and smelled delicious and it didn't take us long to eat the lot. Now our only concern was to thank our benefactors. Fortunately Bobby had scrounged the stub of a pencil from the 'geezer', as he called his ex-cellmate, so we were able to scribble *gracias/thank you*, and signed it. The trusty came back to collect the dishes through the flap, and we managed to find out that it had been visiting day and there was always plenty of home-cooked food taken in by the visitors.

Three more days elapsed without any news, and not being allowed out to exercise was starting to get to us.

Mario came back on our ninth day in prison with a grin from ear to ear and said, 'Good morning gentlemen, I have very good news. You will be released tomorrow and you will stay in a hotel for the night, then you will board a train the next morning to take you to France and the ferry home. Is that not good news?'

We were delighted, of course. Just the thought of being out of the box and being free was better than the thought of sinking a couple of large brandies in quick succession. Then it hit me. I only had the off-white shirt with the dried bloodstains to wear. Ah, feck it anyway, I was going to be free and that was enough. Those thoughts satisfied me until I lay down to sleep – and that's when the traffic jam of serious thoughts came through again. Was this going to mean the end of my seagoing? Where was my gear? My post office savings book was in amongst the rest of my stuff. So many things to worry about. I dropped off to a restless sleep and awoke to the most joyous sounds of the keys opening the door the next morning.

We ate the bread and drank the sweet warm liquid and lit up cigarettes.

'Where do you think our gear will be?' I asked Bobby.

'Probably in the company office in London. We'll phone them when we get to London,' he said.

The afternoon dragged its arse into the early evening without a word and we were giving up hope of getting out that day when we heard the familiar sound of the key opening the lock. Melonface entered and herded us to the office, where we signed for our belongings and found Colin and Norman waiting for us.

I thanked them for helping me, and then we were driven to a small hotel. None of us went out that night. We were all in the same frame of mind – 'Let's get out of Napoli.'

That we did the next morning. We were driven to the railway station, where we boarded the train and were on our way twenty minutes later. The boys had signed for five pounds each to travel with and they insisted on giving me a pound each. It wasn't much for any of us, but it would come in handy when we got to London.

Norman and Colin, two Yorkshiremen, took a walk through the train and came back with sandwiches, cheese and biscuits, chocolate, sweets and fruit. We laughed and joked about how they could be expert beggars if they wished. They had put on the 'poor unfortunate seamen who had missed their ship' act to anyone that looked likely to part with something and they had been very successful.

***

I have forgotten how long it took to get to Dover, but I certainly remember how good it felt walking down the gangway of the ferry. We went through customs and immigration and were asked several questions about how we had missed our ship and why we had been imprisoned in Naples. It was all very amicable, and soon we were free to catch our train to London. Bobby phoned the company, and the good news was that our gear was at head office.

We had enough to pay for a taxi from the station to the office. We reported to the personnel office and our belongings were there, ready for us. The assistant personnel officer told us that we would be summoned to the office by letter within the week. We asked for a sub from our pay, and when we got what we wanted I paid the others what I owed them and said goodbye.

I booked into the Red Ensign Club for seven nights in a room with a sink, which cost four pounds, seven shillings and sixpence – leaving me with five pounds, twelve shillings and sixpence to spend on beer and a quarter bottle of whisky.

I phoned my friends the Thomsons and promised to visit them after I had been to the company and found out what they had decided. Oh, how good it was to be free and alone after Naples. I spent almost an hour in the shower luxuriating. Then I dressed in beautifully clean underwear and my favourite shirt and jeans. I flopped down on the bed and fell asleep.

I awoke at 4.30 the next morning feeling refreshed but thirsty and hungry. After two currant buns and two mugs of tea in an all-night café, my next stop was Billingsgate fish market and the early house there, the Roaring Rabbit. I had been there a few times before and it was always packed. They opened at six o'clock each morning to cater for the market workers and traders. There were several such pubs around the docks and market places, and I would visit all of them before I was much older. I saw a few fellows whom I had sailed with and others I had seen in the Shipping Federation and the club, but I didn't want to talk to anyone. I needed to be alone with my thoughts and to enjoy my brandy. I thought of how my life had changed since the morning Jimmy had met me at Euston station just a couple of years earlier, and wondered how Eileen, himself and the children were getting on in Ireland. They had decided to go back there.

On my third day in the club, I received the letter requesting me to report to the personnel office the next morning at 10 am. That gave me butterflies in the pit of my stomach. There was nothing to do but go out for a few jars and try to forget about it. I reported to the office at 9.45 am. Fully curried and combed and stinking of aftershave lotion, tense and wound up tighter than a golf ball and dying for a drink, but that was out, an alcohol-free breath was the order for that morning anyway.

Mr James bid me good morning and said, 'Please tell me what happened.'

I told him as much as I could remember, and when I had finished he looked me square in the eye and said, 'It is very unfortunate that this has happened. However, your record of

231

service with the company is very good, as is that of the other three men. Therefore the company is prepared to offer you all another ship.'

Hearing those words gave me a jolt that no amount of alcohol could have done. I was grinning broadly as I thanked him.

'You must understand that alcohol can ruin your life,' he said. 'You have a promising career ahead of you, don't ruin it. You will lose your position as wine steward and go back to assistant steward. I have your outstanding pay made up, which comes to sixty-three pounds and seventeen shillings.' He counted out the money and told me that I would be contacted when they had a ship to offer me.

It was raining when I bounced out of the office, but nothing could dampen my spirits and delight with the whole wide world. This was the life. Money in the pocket, seagoing job secured and not a care for anything that day. I could have kissed the filthy bedraggled old tramp sprawled on the pavement that I nearly had to jump over to get into the Long Bar in Aldgate. I gave him five shillings and thought how fortunate I was in comparison. He raised himself lethargically and slurred, 'Thank ye son, God bless ye!'

Back at the Red Ensign club some time later, the receptionist handed me a letter. It was from the British Shipping Federation in Prescot Street, instructing me to appear before a committee for my VNC (*voyage not completed*) in two days' time. No need for concern because the company was employing me again.

On the morning of my committee I reported to the Shipping Federation at 09.45. I waited for about twenty minutes before I heard my name called and I was shown into a little room where two men sat at a table, both wearing dark suits and pinch-your-snout glasses. I often wondered about the people who wore them. Did they find them a great aid to reading? Was it a fashion statement?

Dark suit number 1 did the introductions. He was Mr Plum and his colleague was Mr Fairy – and of course your union representative Mr McSkite. He went on about how serious it was, missing one's ship, the cost to the company and how one could jeopardise one's seagoing career ... However, as the company was going to re-employ me, no action would be taken – but let it be a warning, that is all.

'Thank you,' I said and was out of there like a rocket. Two days later I received a letter from P&O informing me to join the *Orion* in five days' time. Good, I thought, five more days to enjoy the gargle.

One evening in the bar, who should walk in but my old cabin mate and mentor from the *Himalaya*, Cyril. I was delighted. He walked over to me and said, in a mock Irish accent, 'It's yerself. How have you been keeping?'

'Great,' I said, 'except I missed the *Stratheden* in Naples.'

'Yes,' he said, 'I heard about it on the grapevine.'

Cyril told me he was still on the *Himalaya* and things were going well for him – then he said something that gave me mixed emotions.

'Remember when you came to our cabin for the first time?'

I nodded.

'Well, that was by design. The chief steward asked me to keep an eye on you, and make sure no one tried to take advantage of you in any way, you looked so young and vulnerable. I thought you'd like to know that.'

'Thank you Cyril,' I said, 'I'm surprised and grateful. Yes, I was as green as grass. I've learned a lot since then, but I've a long way to go. I wish I could thank him. Is he still on the *Himalaya*?'

'No mate,' he replied, 'he's retired. Will you have another one before I go?'

After one more drink we bid each other farewell. That was the last time I ever saw him.

I joined the old *Orion* on 8 November 1962, and it was good to be back to work. I stayed with my friends the Thomsons during the working-by period, and although I didn't know it then it would be the last time I would ever see them.

***

The head waiter on the *Orion* had a reputation for sarcasm that went before him. He was known to many a steward as a tyrant, and I had heard about him and his behaviour before I ever joined the ship. He was called countless uncomplimentary names, but I'll just refer to him as 'Head'. I took stock of him as he called out our names, and I didn't like what I saw. His hair was sleeked back and his face resembled that of a rat. The only things that looked any way decent about him were his uniform and shiny shoes. When he finished the roll call he put on a grimace and singled me out to pick on.

'Mahaan,' he said.

I ignored him and stood quietly with the rest of the boys. That annoyed him, and he pointed to me.

'You,' he said.

I raised my eyebrows, pointed to my chest and asked, 'Me?'

'Yes, you,' he said. All eyes were on us and I could tell most of them were enjoying the exchange.

'My name is John Joseph M-a-h-o-n,' I said.

'You're from Ireland,' he said.

I nodded, and he continued, 'It is a fact then, they do have leprechauns.' This brought on laughter and titters from my colleagues and it was more than I could take.

'Yes,' I said, 'and they're very capable of doing quare things to those who don't show them the respect they're entitled to.' There was more laughter, which made me feel better, and I felt the tightly wound spring within me starting to unwind.

Having had his fun at my expense he turned and left it to his assistant to allocate our tables and duties.

Just before we broke up for lunch a red-headed chap approached me and introduced himself. 'My name's Jimmy McMahon,' he said. 'I was born in Streatham but me ol' man comes from County Kilkenny. Are you going to the PLA for a drink?'

'I certainly am,' I said.

'Right,' said he, 'I'll seeya in there and buy you a drink. It was fuckin' great the way you got back at that fuckin' pufter, but you'll need to watch out for him now, he'll have it in for you.'

Five minutes later Mr McTaggart, Head's assistant, told me to go to lunch. I went to my eight-berth cabin and there was Jimmy, fumbling in a locker.

'Jimmy!' I said.

He turned and declared, 'Fuckin' 'ell, you're in 'ere are yeh, mate?'

'Yes,' I said.

'That's 'ansome,' he responded. 'Let's piss off. That bloody mate of mine Paddy will 'ave two or three down 'im by now.'

Big Paddy Cullen saw us coming in and got up from his table to get the drinks. Jimmy introduced us, saying, 'Paddy, this is John. Another bleedin' Mick!' We shook hands, Paddy bought the drinks and we sat down. Jimmy told him about the incident with Head.

Paddy said, 'I sailed with that bastard about three years ago. He was evil then and it seems he hasn't changed. Thank fuck I'm not in the saloon this trip.'

We sailed from Tilbury bound for Australia. I had thirteen reasonable passengers and three really gutsy characters, two men and a woman who were quite capable of eating the bill of fare itself, if it had been edible. I had built up a good rapport with all of them, but I had to exercise great restraint in not blowing a gasket with the gutsies. All three of them had me in a spin, rushing in and out of the galley for an extra portion of this, that and the other, and by the time we reached Sydney I must have walked and rushed a good hundred miles more than normal, fetching and carrying for them three alone.

Jimmy and I hadn't given Head any chance to get his perverted jollies off in finding faults with our timekeeping or work, so he started playing games with us when we were off duty. He would send for me if he wanted Jimmy, and vice versa, usually for some triviality such as 'Your glasses are not polished properly,' or 'There's a dirty spoon on your table.' When either of us reported to him, it was always the same. He would say, 'Not you, the other one.' It was just a way to disturb us on our time off duty and probably to see how many times he could get away with it before one of us would throw a wobbler. But we were miles ahead of him and played along with his silly game until it became tedious and we changed the game.

The next few times he sent for either of us we both reported. This got him really mad and he would wave one of us away with a limp-wristed gesture of dismissal. Whichever one of us he had waved away just moved a few inches and waited for the other, then we walked away slowly, pretending to be in very serious conversation. This game continued for a while until we got fed up with it. Then one morning the bellboy came to our cabin and told me that I was to report to the head waiter immediately.

'Thank you,' I said, 'tell him I'm on my way.'

The boy went about his business and I said to Jimmy, 'Fuck him, I'm not going near him, it's time to put this stupid game to an end.'

'Right,' he said, 'I'm pissed off with it too.' We discussed what Head might do if we didn't report and we agreed that the worst he could do was log us, but we doubted that.

Fifteen minutes before lunch was to be served, Jimmy and I entered the saloon by different entrances and acted as though nothing had happened. I checked my table and was about to go out for the butter, rolls and water when I saw Head beckoning me over with a crooked finger and a sneer on his ugly puss. I took my time, and when I was a few feet away he said, 'Young pygmy, why did you ignore my order to report to me?'

'I couldn't find "the other one" as you have so often referred to Mr McMahon and I wasn't sure which one of us you wanted, so I decided to wait until we could come along together.'

He exploded into a rage and went on about how he had the right to have me logged for disobeying his orders.

I had had enough by now, and quietly said, 'If that's what you choose to do, then do it. But be assured that I will defend myself, and expose you for what you are at the same time. I have had more than enough of your insults and childish game playing, I've got it all down on paper and plenty of witnesses to back me up.' With that, I walked out of the saloon and had a smoke before returning.

I never heard any more insults or sarcastic remarks from him, and the big bonus was that the perverted game of 'Not you, the other one' came to an end.

All my passengers disembarked in Bombay on the homeward run and I went on the 'chain gang', which meant doing general cleaning duties around the passenger and crew quarters. It was a novelty not having to dress up and be on guard all the time, as was the necessity for saloon duties. I was just starting to enjoy my own private cruise when I was summoned to the saloon, three days out of Bombay.

Head was standing at the entrance and declared in a shrill

voice, 'MacMahone!'

I held my hand up and said, 'Stop. If you can't get my name right, I'm off.'

'I've never been good at pronouncing Irish names,' he said.

I didn't respond, but stood stock still, looking up into his face. He gave a twitch and said, 'I want you to report to me at 6.30 this evening, smartly dressed and prepared to serve dinner to one woman on table 22. She will be your only passenger to the UK, but I warn you, she is a very disturbed and troublesome person. I have had to move her from two tables since we sailed and I have convinced her that she will be much more comfortable on a table by herself with her own personal steward. That's you.'

'Does this woman choose her food from the menu or does she have special food prepared?' I asked.

'The chef has a special menu for her,' he replied.

I reported to the saloon at 6.30 pm without a care. I had had to contend with difficult people before and I was rather proud of how I coped with them. The way I saw it, dealing with this woman was just another challenge – and besides, it wouldn't be long before I was paying off.

Head escorted Mrs Nasteruddin to the table at seven o'clock on the dot and said, pulling out her chair, 'This young man is your personal steward for the remainder of the voyage, madam. He will ensure that you receive everything you require.'

'Does he know about my special menu?' she asked, giving me the once-over with her beady little eyes, sunk in a face that might have been moon-shaped once but was now a misshapen landscape of craters. She finished her scrutiny and cocked her snout in the air. And I love you too, I thought.

Head replied, 'He certainly does, madam. I must attend to something. I hope you enjoy your meal.'

He toddled off and Madam started rummaging around in her big leather bag, which gave me time to study her. She was a wizened old thing with dyed brown hair. She wore a sari with all the colours of the rainbow and she was festooned with gold jewellery, necklace, bangles and rings on four fingers of each hand. Lady, I thought, you'd fill a fair share of hungry bellies in your country if you sold that lot and spread the money around. She finished fumbling in her bag and placed a notebook and fountain pen on the table.

'My name is John,' I said.

She gave no indication that she had heard me and I thought, I can play that game too. I just stood mutely by.

'Pour me some cold water,' she said. I attempted to drop the linen napkin on her lap and she snatched it out of my hand with venom and gave me a stern look. Next, I turned her glass the right way up and was about to pour the water when she held her hand up and asked, 'Is that glass clean?'

'It certainly is, madam,' I said. 'I washed it in scalding hot soapy water and then rinsed it in hot water before polishing it.'

She picked the glass up, looked it over and said, 'A half a glass.'

I poured the water and asked if I should see the chef for her first course. 'Yes,' she said.

I found the chef and told him that the difficult one was in and was ready for her first course. 'No problem,' he said, 'my second is taking care of her food.' I waited a minute or two, then along came the second chef who said, 'She's having melon balls, poached haddock, boiled potatoes, carrots and an egg custard to finish off.'

I served the melon from a distance and kept my mouth shut in case she would get the smell of nicotine off my breath, despite having sprayed my mouth with a breath spray. I wasn't taking any chances, and congratulated myself on my decision not to drink any alcohol for at least two hours before each meal, as I watched that waif-like old woman twirling the spoon over the melon with her bony little paws. I knew then that she was going to make my life a misery but I wasn't prepared to allow her to beat me at the 'one over you' game. At which I thought I was quite an expert.

I patiently stood by as she played with the fruit for ten minutes. Having eaten less than a third, she pushed the dish away with such force that the remainder spilled over the tablecloth. I never made a move until she said, 'Get this tablecloth changed and then see the chef for my next dish.'

I went for another cloth and when I proceeded to strip the table and lay it up again, she seemed more conciliatory as she said, 'Cheap, silly dishes those.' I stayed silent as I carried on and then went out to see the chef for her next course. I returned with her fish on a silver dish, nicely garnished and it looked very nice. I took a hot dinner plate from the dumb waiter, wiped it with my pristine towel and was about to place it in front of her when she stopped me and asked, 'Are you sure that plate is clean?'

'Yes Madam,' I said, holding it out in front of her. She nodded and I placed the plate in front of her, took the fish out of the hot press and held it out for her inspection.

She rejected it instantly, saying, 'It is far too much for me. Obviously the chef is not adhering to my doctor's strict instructions. Get that head waiter for me ... Now!'

I casually strode away in delight at the prospect of Head having to take some flak, and when I told him that my passenger required his attention immediately, it was with a broad grin that I made sure he wouldn't miss. He soft-shoe-shuffled across and was sweetness itself as she attacked him with an outrage that would have done credit to an actress overplaying a part. For all his bullying and bossing of us stewards, he was not winning anything with that old woman. He looked at me as though in despair. I returned his look with a grin and turned my head away. It ended with him taking the fish out to the chef and beckoning me to follow him. I did so, and stayed a distance away as he discussed the problem with the chef.

When they had finished talking he came over to me and said, 'It seems that the chef has given his second the responsibility for dealing with that woman's menu and he in turn has passed it on to someone else. That won't happen again. The second chef will be solely responsible. You stay here and wait and I will go back to her.'

Five minutes later the second chef handed me the scorching silver dish with Madam's fish and I rushed it in to the saloon. Head was in conversation with her when I displayed the dish. She nodded and he made a big show of taking the hot plate from the dumb waiter, wiping it and placing it in front of her. He wished her *bon appetit* and beat a hasty retreat.

I served the fish and said, 'Madam, as you can see the potatoes are of varying size. If you will please point out the ones you prefer that will be best.'

She gave me a weird sort of look, grunted and pointed at a

medium-sized spud and said, 'That will be sufficient. I don't like my carrots cut in that stick-like way, I prefer them cut round and very thin. I won't have any.'

'I will see the chef if you wish,' I said.

'No,' she said. 'You tell the head waiter I want to see him at the end of my meal. Go away and leave me alone.'

I was fit to be tied by this time so I said sternly, 'Madam, it is part of my duty to stand by in case you might need something during your meal.'

'I know that, boy!' she snapped. 'I have travelled around the world on better shipping companies than this. Go away and be back here in exactly seven minutes.'

I looked at my watch and skipped outside for a smoke. I was tempted to have a quick beer, but put the thought out of my head. I went back to the table in precisely six minutes and found her hunched over a hardback book and apparently totally engrossed. She looked up after a while, then checked her watch and never said a word. I could see that she had hardly eaten anything, but I wasn't about to mention it. 'Take this away and bring my dessert,' she commanded. I took her plate away and headed for the galley and within a couple of minutes I was presenting Madam with her egg custard. Not a word out of her, and certainly not a breath from my mouth. I was breathing through my nose. I stood with my back to the dumb waiter, about three feet away, looking in any direction but at her. The rest of the passengers were leaving so I knew that my pitiful, bitter and twisted one would be with me into the second sitting. But I didn't care. There was one thing I was sure of – and that was, I was going to get drunk later on.

She stirred me from my thoughts as she loudly said, 'Boy, take this poor excuse for an egg custard away and get me some fresh fruit. I can tell you, if my own chef produced such muck he would never do it again.'

'Madam,' I said, 'I am not a boy, kindly remember that.'

I picked up the plate and went out to the galley, where I spent a few minutes before returning with a big basket of assorted fruits, a finger bowl and a little jug of warm water for her hands. Or as far as I was concerned her whole miserable body, if she liked. I placed a clean plate in front of her and poured some water into the finger bowl, stood back and watched her as she ate a few grapes and then said, 'Have

240

you told that waiter fellow, I want to see him?'

'No, madam,' I replied.

'Well do so, now,' she said.

I found Head at the entrance to the saloon and had the greatest pleasure telling him that Madam wanted to see him now! He cringed and I was elated. As I was giving him the good news I saw a little girl dressed in a sari standing by the companionway outside the saloon. I suspected she might be the old lady's servant so I went out to have a word with her. 'My name is John,' I said. 'Can you please tell me, are you travelling with Mrs Nasteruddin?'

She looked at me shyly with her pretty head tilted to the right and said, 'Yes I am, I am her servant.'

My mind was racing with questions I wanted to ask her, but she looked so frail and vulnerable, with a deep sadness in her eyes, that I felt for her. I restricted myself to two questions.

'Does Mrs Nasteruddin come down for breakfast?'

'No,' she replied.

'Do you share the same cabin with her?'

'Oh, no, I have a cabin in tourist class and I eat in that saloon,' she said.

I bid her good evening and went back to my table. Head and Madam were in conversation and I stood by until he left and then moved closer to the table and never said a word to her. Finally she stood up, and as she slowly made her way to the door I remembered something my mother used to say – '*Ah sure, she's more to be pitied than laughed at.*'

She continued to be the most difficult, miserable, bitter and twisted old woman I had ever had to deal with, so when I served her final dinner on board, it was in high spirits.

Brandy, that is. I had enjoyed enough to get a glow on and felt on top of the world. I wondered if she would give me a few notes of any currency but thought not. I was right. She left without a 'thank you' and I went to enjoy some more alcoholic refreshment. We paid off in Southampton the following day. Jimmy and Paddy signed off, and I re-signed to do *Orion's* final voyage to Australia before she was to become a floating hotel in Hamburg. I had ten days' leave before rejoining, so I took myself off to London and booked into the Queen Victoria Seamen's Rest.

I rejoined the *Orion* in Southampton and was delighted to learn that Head wasn't going to be on that voyage. The head waiter for the trip was a Mr Bryce, who was a gentleman.

My passengers were not much different to those on the previous trips. The crew accommodation on the ship was almost the same as the others I had been on, but unlike the P&O vessels the Orient Line ships had a Pig & Whistle onboard – a crew bar known as the 'pig' where they served watered-down pints of strong beer. It was a great place to relax and let off steam. P&O had taken over the Orient Line and some of the old ways of that company were still in practice during the transition period, not least, the Pig.

The first time I saw a Crown and Anchor board was in the Pig. It was a piece of canvas about four foot by four foot with six squares painted on it, with a crown, anchor, heart, spade, club and diamond for the punters to bet on. The person running the game had a cup and three dice. He would shake the dice in the cup, urge the onlookers to place their bets, and many did, including myself. It was a game of chance and there was no harm in it as long as you didn't get hooked on it. Sadly though, some did – and that's when the unscrupulous, parasitic, so-called shipmates came into their own.

They would willingly lend the losers money at eight or ten per cent interest to be paid back in full on dropsy night (tips night) or the next sub (when you withdrew an advance on your wages). It was against all the rules and regulations to run those games and lend money for profit, but it went on and some of the characters that took advantage of their colleagues moved in small packs from one passenger company to another, making a lucrative business out of preying on honest hard-working seamen.

I continued to drink far too much, but was cautious enough not to let the intake interfere with my work. There were times, though, when I had more than was good for me before carrying out my duties. Nevertheless, as long as I had a good supply of strong mints and a breath spray in my pocket and I kept my wits about me, I didn't see any harm in having a few jars before serving the passengers. I could drink more than a fair amount then but I always knew my limit. Or thought I did. I enjoyed all sorts of alcohol. It gave me courage and helped me put on a front to hide my insecurities.

And there was the companionship of fellow drinkers, the conversations, bar-room philosophy and many other forms of entertainment in the drinking fraternity.

***

I paid off the *Orion* in May 1963 and reported to the P&O office after my leave, and was given papers to join the *Strathmore* the following afternoon. She was another old lady that had seen service as a troop carrier during the Second World War, and now she was about to do her final Aussie run, to be followed by four fortnightly Mediterranean cruises, and that would be the end of her.

I had a good trip on her and I was fortunate to have nice passengers both outward and homeward. Then I signed on as a wine steward for the four cruises and enjoyed five days' leave before rejoining in Southampton. The cruises went splendidly, and all too soon it was time for the whole crew to sign off. Another gracious and beautiful old lady of the sea had completed her distinguished service for Company and Country. I felt a strange sadness in my heart as I looked up at her from the dock before getting into the taxi.

I had an extended leave, which I spent in London. I had intended to visit my dear friends the Thomsons, but somehow I never got around to it. My need for the drink always got in the way.

I joined my next ship, the *Arcadia*, on 7 November 1963. She was bound for a world trip and I was looking forward to seeing and doing things in the Far East again. I also wanted to try out the bars in America. I would be twenty-one years old before we reached there. On my previous visits I never attempted to enter a bar because of what I had been told by several of my colleagues. The Americans were very strict on serving alcohol to anyone they suspected of not being old enough to drink. The bar person would ask for identity and if you couldn't produce it you were out on the sidewalk – so 'California here I come!'

The *Arcadia* was a more modern ship than the previous three I had sailed on. I thought she was on par with the *Himalaya*, although she was a few years younger. The accommodation wasn't much better but I only had to share a cabin with five others and that was a big bonus.

When I reported to the saloon my heart skipped into palpitation mode as I spotted my old antagonist Head mincing around. I stood still to see what would happen next.

I didn't have long to wait. He beckoned me towards him with his crooked little finger. He looked down at me with the familiar look of distaste and said, 'You haven't grown any, and I see you've been promoted.'

I quickly jumped in before he had a chance to say another word. 'I see you've been promoted too. Is that extra ring on your sleeve very heavy?'

He batted his eyelids and said, 'Report to my assistant, Mr Sheppard. He will give you your station.' Sheppard, a pasty-faced weed and a 'sizer upper', pointed out my section of over thirty tables with as few words as was necessary.

I went to collect the boxes of glasses and set about washing and polishing them, and I was joined by one of my cabin-mates, Gary Horton, a tall sturdy good-looking man with dark hair. We chatted as we worked, and he told me he was engaged to an Irish girl he met before he went to sea. She had gone back to Ireland and they were hoping to get married in a year or so. He lived with his parents in Enfield, North London, when he wasn't at sea or in Ireland, and it was his third trip. The time flew, and before we knew it, it was lunchtime, so we adjourned to the dockside canteen.

The afternoon was taken up with sorting out our glassware, and finally we were put to polishing the brass portholes, then it was finishing time. When we went to our cabin the other occupants were there and introductions were made all round.

There was Jonathan, a fat effeminate person with sleek shiny dark hair that might have been fair or brown but it was hard to tell with the amount of oil he had on it. He stood about 5 feet 4 inches, had a nice smile and came across as being a really nice person. Then there was Sidney, of average height, balding and with a face that had seen many weathers, mostly rough, I guessed. Then Roger, a tall man, a few years older than me, with fair hair and very distinguished-looking, and finally Scott, in his forties, similar to Sidney but with more zip! He had sailed with Jonathan on many of the company's ships.

Introductions over, it was time for cleaning up and getting

ashore. Gary was going up to London and I was bound for the bar life in Gravesend. I phoned the Thomsons from a box on the dock and felt slightly relieved of guilt for not going to see them. The fact was, as I saw it at that time, it was much more fun going to the bars and getting drunk than spending time with my two elderly friends. I was free of any ties, and that's how I liked it.

I had a few drinks in several of the bars in Gravesend, eventually ending up in the King's Buttocks, and caught an early ferry back to Tilbury.

We sailed away on our four-month voyage and I was keen to enjoy any delights that lay ahead. There was no need to worry about my job. I was confident in my capabilities and knowledgeable to a good degree about all the wines we carried. I found the wine steward's job much easier than that of assistant steward. I had more passengers to look after, but it wasn't the same as having to serve the same twelve or sixteen people three meals a day for a month or more. Most jobs in catering entail having to be a Jack of all trades, and being one step ahead in mind games was very important. I had to learn to be a bit of several people – psychologist, diplomat, pacifier, actor. Even the nicest of people could turn sour if the food they were served wasn't to their liking.

My five cabin-mates were great people in their own individual ways. Gary became my drinking companion and ally, and Jonathan soon established his mothering instincts over Gary and me, and we took to calling him Mother. It was comical, and we played along with it from the start, but Jonathan was more serious and sometimes it seemed he felt it was his duty to pamper us and look after us.

There wasn't even a hint of homosexual overtures to either of us, and we couldn't make it out, but we went along with his game-playing for fear of hurting his feelings. Whenever we had a heavy session on the booze, Mother would blame Gary for taking me on the drink because he was a year older than me and it was his fault for leading her younger son astray. He wouldn't speak to us sometimes for a whole day. Then diplomatic relations would be restored with a present left on each of our bunks, anything from sweets to books, or all sorts of other nice little things that he bought from the ship's shop. Naturally we appreciated the gifts, but it was embarrassing taking things from someone we barely knew. We tried in the nicest way possible to explain that we really appreciated the gifts but he shouldn't be spending so much money on us. He said, 'Nothing is too good for my boys when you behave yourselves.'

Gary and I had a long chat about Mother's generosity. I said I thought he was a very lonely person and it made him feel good to have two young friends to whom he could show affection. I just wished he didn't think it was necessary to prove it all the time with presents. We could be his friends without that. Gary agreed, but there didn't seem to be anything we could do about it.

We were heading towards Australia on 22 November 1963 when we heard the news that President Kennedy had been assassinated. It was one of the strangest days I ever spent on any ship up to that time. Despite there being about fifteen hundred people on board, a sort of quiet prevailed and some people seemed so shocked for a while that they whispered rather than talked. There was a lot of speculation as to why a young man like that should be cut down in his prime. Was it because he was a Catholic? Or had it anything to do with the Cuban crisis just a year before?

A week before we were due to dock in Sydney, Mother presented Gary and me with a bow tie each and informed us that we were to be his guests for dinner and the cabaret in the Chevron Hilton Hotel, where he would be staying. He explained that he always took a few days' leave in Sydney.

We docked and Mother was off, but before he left he gave us strict instructions to be at the hotel at 7 pm sharp the next evening and he would meet us in the cocktail bar. We were to wear our best suits and the bow ties. Gary baulked at the bow tie, but Mother would have none of it, saying, 'I want you to wear it, my boys must be dressed properly.'

To add to Gary's discomfort, I obsequiously said, 'Don't you worry, Mother, I'll make sure he wears it and we'll be there right on the dot of 7 pm.'

'You see,' he said to Gary, 'I wish you were as well behaved as my younger boy. No more nonsense now, wear your tie – and I shall hold you responsible if you are late. And finally, you are both to be sober, that's an order.'

'We'll be there,' said Gary. 'How could we turn down such

a generous treat? Thank you!'

When Mother was gone, Gary threw a towel at me and mimicked, 'I'll make sure he wears it – you little arsehole!' We had a couple of cans of beer in the cabin and then went up town to do some serious drinking. We travelled all over Sydney and visited countless bars until we could hardly stand and then took a taxi back to the ship, stumbled up the gangway and flaked out fully booted and spurred on our bunks.

We were both the worse for wear the next day but things seemed brighter after a few liveners. I was assigned to the storing gang and Gary had to work in the saloon and do some gangway duty. I finished at 4 pm and he finished an hour later.

Dressed in suits and bow ties, we caught a taxi to the hotel and had the best part of an hour to spare before our appointment with Mother so we took a casual walk around and had a couple of beers in a quiet little pub.

We walked into the reception hall of the Chevron Hilton at 6.55 pm and found the cocktail bar without difficulty. We were just about to order drinks when Mother waltzed in, dressed in a dark blue suit, white shirt and a polka-dot bow tie to match.

'Boys!' he exclaimed, 'how nice to see you, you look like two young executives. What will you have to drink?'

Gary had a vodka and tonic, I had a brandy and soda and Mother surprised us by having a dry martini. It was the first time that we had ever seen him put an alcoholic drink to his lips. We had another round, which he insisted on paying for.

'It's really nice to have your company,' he said. 'The reason I have invited you both to share this evening with me is because it's going to be your birthdays soon. John, you will be twenty-one on December 15th, and Gary, you will be twenty-two a few months later.'

I looked at Gary and then at Mother, and said, 'You have done some research, Jonathan.'

He gave us a happy smile and said, 'Well, my dears, that's what mothers are for.'

We laughed and Gary said, 'Now that you've got us on your files, it's only fair for you to tell us when your birthday is.'

Jonathan responded instantly, 'Oh no, my dears, I never tell anyone my age. Suffice to say I'm over thirty, and that's all I'm saying. Now, let's study the menu and the wine list.'

It was unanimously decided that a bottle of Mateus rosé would be nice. Gary and I settled for honeydew melon and T-bone steaks and Mother chose watermelon followed by a combination salad. We were dumbfounded by the size of our steaks, and the garnish alone was more than enough without the great variety of vegetables to choose from. The sight of it all was overwhelming. Nevertheless, we tucked in and did our best until we couldn't eat another bite.

Obviously Gary and I were thinking alike. We had to make a big effort to please our generous friend. There was no room for sweet or cheese and biscuits for us two but Jonathan had a sliver of cheese on a Ryvita, we finished off with coffee and cointreau and then settled ourselves to watch the cabaret.

The highlight of the evening was the Irish comedian Dave Allen. I had never heard of him, but there was one thing for sure, I would never forget him. His act was marvellous. He hit upon so many of the thoughts that had been in the recesses of my mind for years – the social factors, the church, the priests, simplicity and eejits. It was great fun!

We finished off with a final drink in the bar and bid Jonathan goodnight. Then caught a taxi back to the ship. That evening with Jonathan was one of the most enjoyable I had ever experienced.

***

I celebrated my twenty-first birthday in the Pacific on 15 December 1963. Legally I had become a man. I had come quite a distance since leaving the Kennys and I had learned a lot about life and my fellow human beings. I still hadn't learned how to cope with the jokes and comments about my height without blowing a fuse on occasions, and I found that alcohol helped. Nothing ever seemed so bad, as long as I had a fair amount of liquid gold in the belly and bubbles in the head. Life was good and I was enjoying it.

When I returned to my cabin after my morning duties, I was thrilled to see my bunk bedecked with coloured streamers and a gaily painted garland with the words, 'Happy 21st John!'

I was almost moved to tears but I was determined not to let it show. I picked up the three envelopes from the bunk and was about to open them when in crept Gary and Jonathan with broad grins. I thanked them and suggested that we should have a drink to celebrate. Gary winked and Mother tut-tutted and then said, 'Now, now, we shall have a few drinks after dinner this evening and that should be enough, there's no need to start drinking this early in the morning – and please don't open your cards until this evening.'

The day went well, with the occasional jar just to wet my whistle, and at the end of dinner Gary suggested that we should have a couple of beers on deck, before getting showered. This was unusual, because it had always been a race between us to see which of us got spruced up first. I knew something was afoot but said nothing and played along.

After drinking a couple of beers each, he said, 'It's getting a bit nippy up here, let's piss off down to the cabin.'

If I had been moved by the lovely gesture of the morning, I was speechless at the sight before me. The cabin was festooned with streamers and balloons. There was a variety of good-quality spirits and beers and to top it off a decorated cake with twenty-one candles. I was truly overwhelmed and I was very near to crying. I thanked them both, very sincerely.

Gary said, 'I've done nothing, it's all down to Mother.'

'You liar!' he said, 'you did more than your share.'

I excused myself to go for a shower and Gary followed suit. When I got back I dressed and was ready for whatever was to come.

Roger, Sidney and Scott came in carrying a case of beer each and singing, 'Twenty-one today ... He's got the key to the door ... Never been twenty-one before ...' The five guests that Gary and Mother had colluded to invite were all good shipmates. They came with cards and bottles. There was John, a cabin steward, Noel, Jeremy and Patrick, all assistant stewards and, last but not least, a Gay Caballette named Lily, another cabin steward, who slinked in dressed in full drag and declared, 'I'm here boys and girls, let the party begin.' Then he rushed over to me, planted a kiss on my cheek and said, 'You are a gorgeous young man, I could make mad passionate love to you on your very special day, happy birthday dear. Oh! How I wish I could be twenty-one again.'

The party got under way and the drinks flowed freely for a long time before Mother announced it was candle-blowing-out and cake-cutting time. I was feeling very self-conscious but happy and grateful too. Then I had to open the presents. There was a Parker pen and pencil set from Gary and a Ronson varaflame cigarette lighter from Mother. I was delighted and couldn't have thanked them enough. The party went on for hours and we all had great fun with the music, the jokes and a singsong. I could hardly focus by 3.30 am so I allowed myself to flop over on my bunk and fall into a drunken slumber.

I awoke at five o'clock with a head larger than Birkenhead and a shaking in the body comparable to that of a limbo dancer. There was only one thing for it, a stiff brandy and a can of lager. The others were sleeping so I quietly took my drinks up on deck and sat behind a windbreak to get myself straight.

***

The rest of the voyage took in too many ports to mention. I indulged myself in the delights of the bars in the Far East, but Gary, like my old shipmate Pete, left the girls alone because he was in love with his Irish Coleen, Margaret, who came from a small town in County Mayo.

Gary was a witty man and a good shipmate, although he often got very serious and irritable when he was studying to change his religion from Church of England to the Catholic faith in order to marry Margaret as the Catholic priest suggested, otherwise they would have to be married in the vestry or some other out-of-the-way place in the church, but not in front of the altar if he didn't become a Catholic. What a nonsense!

He laboriously pored over books and he was best left alone then. I was reading one night and he was studying when all of a sudden a book came flying through the air and he said, 'Fuck it, I've had enough.'

'What's the matter?' I asked.

'It's this shit, I'll never learn it all, bollocks, let's have a beer.'

'Sure,' I said, 'we'll go on deck.'

'Right, we'll take six up with us. Have you got any of that brandy left?' he asked.

When we sat down on the well deck I cracked open a couple of beers and poured two generous helpings of brandy in the glasses.

'I need your advice,' he said. 'When Margaret and me went to see her priest and he gave us his patter, I agreed to change my religion for her sake. But I never thought I would have to learn all that crap, I just can't do it, I never was much good at school. It's doing my head in. Personally I don't give a fuck for any kind of religion.'

'How does she feel about the whole thing?' I asked.

He took a swallow of brandy and said, 'She says it's not all that important as long as I agree to bring the children up in the Catholic religion. I know it would mean so much to her if I did change, but the way I feel now, I don't think I'll bother, I'm pissed off with the whole thing. What do you think I should do?'

'You can carry on studying and continue to make yourself miserable or you can be honest with yourself and Margaret by facing the fact that you're finding it too difficult.'

He opened another couple of beers and I poured more brandy and he said, 'I know, but I want to do everything right for her, I really love her.'

'That's fine,' I said, 'and no doubt she loves you, she'll have you no matter what religion you are.'

'You're right,' he said, 'she's already told me that.'

'There you are then,' I said, 'you've nothing to worry about. Did the priest go on about the possible problems that can arise in mixed marriages?'

'Yeah, he went on for ages, and by the time we got out of there my head was spinning. Fuck all that, I'm going to stay the way I am and that's final.'

'Of course,' I said, 'you could hire a tutor – and who knows, you might become an assistant arsebishop in Ballygobackwards or some other erotic place.'

We had a good laugh and he brightened up. We sat there drinking in silence and enjoying the balmy night air.

Out of the blue, he said, 'I've never heard you talking about religion except for when I've asked you questions. Do you still go to mass?'

'No,' I said, 'I had enough of that at school – although I only went there for about four or five years in total.'

'Why was that?' he asked.

'I was a sick youngster and I think it was a combination of Mother not wanting me out of her sight and waiting until I became stronger, but that wasn't until I was nearly eight years old. Unfortunately she died when I was eleven.'

'Where was your father?' he asked.

'I was born illegitimate, as they say. I hate that word *illegitimate*. What gives anyone the right to decide on such a slur? As far as I'm concerned I'm as legitimate as anyone else.'

'Bloody right mate,' he said. 'I'm interested in what turned you off religion. I might learn something.'

'You asked for it,' I said. 'We were taught to love our neighbours as ourselves … But the only true faith is Catholic … During my time at school, I heard more about the Catholic faith than anything else. The teachers and priests alike tried to instil a fear in us about the hereafter. If you do this, that or the other, you'll surely go to hell! But the order for "hands up" those of you who were at mass on Sunday or on a holy day of obligation always made me angry. There was never a thought given to whether you had decent footwear to trudge through the snow and muck in the winter or clothes to keep the cold out or food in your belly. If any thoughts were given to such necessary things, they kept them to themselves. That's part of what turned me away from that crowd of hypocrites.'

He excused himself, pissed over the side and went below for more beers, and I sat there thinking of some of the comments I had heard when growing up. 'Isn't it grand for her, him changing his religion for her, there's no doubt they'll be happy.' 'Oh, sweet Jesus, Missis, isn't she a brave woman changing her religion for that little whelp!' 'Sure doesn't it take all kinds. Rather her nor me, Mam.' 'He never changed for her you know.' 'No, I didn't know that Mam, what is he anyway, a prod?' 'Ah sure you'd never know.'

He came back with six more beers and said, 'Go on, tell me more, I should have asked you about all the bullshit before. Margaret believes very strongly in her religion and you're so different. I was never inside a church until I met Margaret.'

'Well,' I said, 'it's none of my business what you decide to do. I'm only speaking of what I have experienced and giving you my views on how I see the Catholic faith on the whole. For a start, the Catholic Church has too much power in Ireland. The ministers, from the arsebishops downwards, are revered and feared by far too many people. Contraception is a sin and censorship is an insult to people's intelligence. I remember once there was a picture in the local cinema and the word went round that if you were quick enough, you could get a glimpse of a woman's bare arse. But you had to keep your eyes glued to the screen to catch it.'

He laughed and said, 'I bet you caught it.'

'Yes,' I said, 'I watched it twice and it wasn't worth the time I wasted, it went so quick.'

'And contraception?' he asked.

'You must know condoms are banned,' I said.

'I never gave that a thought,' he said. 'Margaret wants to leave off having sex until we're married and I'm prepared to wait.'

'That's your business,' I said. 'But while I'm on about the men in frocks ...'

He laughed, shook his head and said, 'Men in frocks!'

'Yes,' I said, 'some of them go around to young mothers, to encourage them in a subtle way that maybe they'll soon be thinking of increasing the family. I believe the strategy of the Catholic hierarchy is, Breed like rabbits and out-populate the others! Never mind how you feed and clothe the offspring, just get on with it. God will provide as long as you're married. As I see it, the Catholic organisation is a worldwide money-making business and the more they can hoodwink their followers the better. I don't know how they operate where Margaret comes from, but they live very well in the part of the country that I come from, good houses and cars and housekeepers to look after them. That good lifestyle has to be paid for and it's the 'Bless me father for I have sinned brigade' that contribute to the never-ending collections and the poor-mouthing from the pulpit that help to keep them parasites in comfort.'

'You really don't like them, do you?' he said.

'No,' I said, 'but what annoys me the most is how they can

con so many people.'

***

Gary's twenty-second birthday fell on the day we crossed the International Date Line. It was my turn to collude with Mother for his party. When we finished work that evening I steered Gary up on deck with four beers and he knew why. He was thrilled to think that tomorrow would be his birthday all over again because of the International Date Line.

'Don't think that you're in for double presents or a double do,' I said.

We signed off on 16 March 1964 in Southampton, having completed four months and nine days. Apart from a few minor skirmishes with the head waiter, the trip had been a good one for me. I signed on again for the cruising from 25 March, and my five colleagues did the same. We had nine days leave, which I spent in London.

We rejoined *Arcadia* and started on the Mediterranean cruises. Cruising was generally a lighthearted affair. The majority of the passengers were in a carefree mood and that rubbed off on some of the crew, none more so than me. I was drinking far too much and thinking that I could get away with it. All I needed was a mouthful of mints and a good splash of Old Spice aftershave lotion on the kisser and under the arms and I was flying, but only in my mind. I didn't know it then, but alcohol was starting to take control of me. Before, I was always able to enjoy a good deal of drink and know my limits, but now I was now falling into the trap of having 'just that one more' – and that's what was getting me into trouble.

Gary and Jonathan tried to talk some sense into me, but it was all to no avail. I thought I knew best. I could control myself.

***

My dismissal from the company was inevitable when a few evenings prior to docking in Southampton I reported to the saloon to serve the wine at dinner with far too much gin consumed. I didn't think there was anything wrong with me except for having a few over the top. I felt happy and quite capable of doing my job, when in reality I could hardly tell one end of the corkscrew from the other, let alone open bottles with it. My condition was clear to all except me.

Smith, the assistant head waiter, solicited Gary's help in escorting me out of the saloon and up to my cabin. I protested, but I was thinking of the booze in my locker and how good it would be to have another drink.

Gary opened a can of beer for me and said, something like, 'Relax, enjoy your night off, you pisshead.' I drank the beer and then fell into a drunken slumber. I was fully awake when the others came back from work and I pretended to be asleep as I heard someone gently pulling my bunk curtain back to see how I was.

Gary said, 'He's OK.'

Then Jonathan said, 'I'm worried about the little fellow. I think he's got something on his mind, and if he's not careful he'll become an alcoholic. You're his friend, you should have a talk with him.'

'I don't think it's that serious,' Gary replied. 'He enjoys the booze or liquid confusion as he likes to call it, it's just that he's been hitting it a bit heavy lately.'

'He might lose his job after tonight's performance,' said Jonathan. Gary remained silent.

I was allowed to carry on with my duties until we arrived back in Southampton. I was dismissed on 23 May 1964, thankfully with a very good discharge in my book.

3

The ould dog for the hard road

We said goodbye to Jonathan and off we went. We had a few jars on the train to London but nothing could lift my gloom. Gary was going to Ireland for a couple of weeks and I didn't know what I was going to do. There was no point going back to the company for another job – but jobs were plentiful, so I wouldn't have a problem getting another ship.

I booked in to the Queen Victoria Seamen's Rest in Poplar and spent nearly two weeks drinking myself into stupors, mostly alone in my room, living on drink with the occasional sandwich or bag of chips.

When Gary got back he left a message for me at reception saying he would be calling in the following morning.

I was up at the crack of dawn the next day, showered and dressed in my favourite suit, and I drank two beers before making a visit to the Shipping Federation to see what ships were available before Gary arrived. I scanned the board and was amazed to see the variety of ships that needed crew – passenger ships, coastal vessels, cargo jobs and plenty of tankers.

It lightened me up to know that all I had to do was present my discharge book and I would be away, provided I could pass the medical. I wasn't 'fighting fit' but I had every confidence I would pass. I was down to my last fifty pounds so it was time to think of shipping out. I left there with a bounce in my step and was full of enthusiasm to ship out again, but I didn't want to go deep sea for a while.

Gary arrived at 11 am and we had a couple of beers. He said he had had enough of passenger ships and he was going to try a tanker company he had been told about. They were giving stewards the opportunity to train as second cooks and bakers after proving their capabilities as assistant stewards, and that's what he fancied.

I told him I didn't feel up to going deep sea and I thought I would give the General Steam a try to see if I could get a job on one of their pleasure steamers. One went from the Tower of London down to Southend and Margate and the other went across to France, and they were back and tied up alongside around eight o'clock every evening. The articles of agreement were home-trade and if I didn't like it I could sign off without any difficulty.

'I forgot about that outfit,' he said. 'We could give it a try. We've nothing to lose, and it'll give me a chance to spend a few evenings with my parents.'

We had two large whiskies and then went to the office in Tower Hill. After a good spray of breath freshener and a couple of strong mints for good measure we presented ourselves to a florid-faced man behind an open window in what reminded me of a teller's cage in an old Western movie.

He smiled and asked, 'What can I do for you gentlemen?'

'We've come to see if you have any vacancies on your pleasure boats,' I said, and handed him my book. Gary followed suit, and he looked through the pages of both books, smiled and said, 'You have been on the big ones. I can offer you stewards' jobs in the dining room on the MV *Royal Sovereign*. When would you be ready to start?'

Gary gave me a look and said, 'I will be free a week from today.'

'And you, Mr Ma'hone, will that suit you?'

'Yes,' I said, 'that will be fine, thank you.'

'In that case, I will see you both at 10 am a week from today. Thank you gentlemen.'

That suited both of us. A week to continue on the gargle with the security of a job. Things couldn't get much better than that. We celebrated in the bars around the area, and Gary told me that his mother and father had invited me to go and stay with them for a week or two. He'd told them that he would invite me but he didn't think I would accept. He was right. Even the thought of staying in someone's home frightened the life out of me. I would feel trapped and I couldn't cope with that.

At that time my style was to travel solo. It was nice to have some time with shipmates who drank and those with whom I could have a good conversation, but at the end of it I needed to go it alone without any ties.

Before we got drunk and parted, we reached a compromise. I would visit his home and have dinner, and that's as far as I wanted to go. I made two visits to his home and promised his parents I would visit them again.

We joined the *Sovereign* on 19 June 1964. She was tied up to a jetty just up from the Tower of London and she looked very pretty, painted white with a yellow funnel. The old lady had seen service in the evacuation of Dunkirk and had made several successful trips.

We worked in the main saloon serving breakfast, lunch and tea, and the more passengers we served the more likely we were to make a few pounds on tips. We departed from the jetty each morning at 9.30 am and cruised down the Thames to Southend and Margate, where the passengers could get off for a few hours while *Sovereign* did a short cruise around with passengers who boarded in Margate. Rock dodging, we called it. We returned to the Tower each evening between seven and eight o'clock, and what a novelty it was to be able to go ashore after work every night. But that novelty wore off after a couple of weeks and we both longed to get back to the deep sea, so we paid off on 5 July.

Gary went home to North London and I stayed in the QVSR.

I met him three days later at Liverpool Street Station and walked the short distance to the Butterfly Tanker Company's office, and soon we were sitting in front of the personnel officer, Mr Hadit. He had already given us the 'once over' and I knew we looked an odd duo, Gary just over 6 feet, and me under 4 feet 10 inches.

Hadit studied our books, smiled and said, 'Well gentlemen, I can offer you both employment subject to a satisfactory company medical.' He went on to explain the benefits of working for the company and what was on offer for good men. Gary said he was keen to become a cook and Hadit assured him that he would be given every opportunity to reach his goal. He turned to me and asked, 'And you, Mr Mahon, what do you think of the opportunities?'

'I think they are very good,' I said. 'I don't think I would like cooking, but the single-cabin accommodation and the prospect of permanent employment with a big company is very appealing.' He studied my face and was silent for what seemed to be ages before he said, 'Would it matter if you were assigned to a different ship to Mr Horton?' I looked him straight in the eye and after a short silence said, 'No it wouldn't matter to me. We have sailed on two vessels together and have become friends, but we're not inseparable.'

I had caught his drift, or I thought I had. He probably thought one of us was Arta and the other was Marta.

He turned to Gary and asked, 'What about you, Mr Horton?'

Gary replied, 'Just as John has said.'

Hadit smiled and said, 'I will make arrangements for your medicals and I will write to you in good time beforehand.'

He got his lanky frame up from his desk and came across to accompany us to the door, shook my hand and said, 'Thank you Mr Mahon, I will be in touch.' Then he took Gary's hand and, looking back at me, said, 'Tall, dark and handsome, isn't he?'

I gave him a sour look and remained silent.

When we were out on the street, Gary stopped and put his hand on my sleeve. 'That bastard was wriggling his finger in the palm of my hand as he shook it, and you know what that means.'

'Yes,' I said, 'you're in. He wants to make whoopee with you.'

'Yeah,' he fumed, 'you've got it. It's no laughing matter. Can you believe the cheek of the bastard?'

Five days later we were summoned to the office by letter and we met up at the entrance. Hadit was waiting for us at the door to his office with a broad grin and said, 'Good morning, gentlemen, it's nice to see you again.'

He led us to the tenth floor and left us to have our medicals. They were thorough and we both knew we were in good health when they were over. Hadit was sitting behind his desk when we returned. He shuffled some papers and said, 'I have a ship to offer you both.' He handed us both a folder filled with papers and said, 'Here is some written information on company policy and how the training and

259

promotion works.' Then he got down to the business of giving us our joining orders for the SS *Moon*. She was in dry dock in South Shields and likely to be there for two to three weeks. Finally he gave us travel warrants to go by train on the morning of 14 July 1964. We thanked him, shook hands and he wished us good luck.

We were bubbling over with the prospects of a new job on a completely different kind of ship. There was nothing for it but to go and celebrate in the pub.

We mingled with the office workers and others in some of the pubs in the city, but in each of them it was too much like hard work trying to get to the counter to get a drink. It was lunchtime and they were packed in like twenty cigarettes in an unopened packet. Shortly after I had started drinking, I developed a dislike for having to queue up to spend my money. It was all right if I could find a barstool, but I hated been jostled, bumped, walked on and buttocked, unless it was a pretty girl doing the buttocking. We tired of that city atmosphere and went back to our more familiar surroundings in the East End.

***

When Gary and I boarded the SS *Moon* in the dry dock in South Shields the first thing we saw was a little old man propped up against a bulkhead, dressed in well-worn clothes and with cuts and bruises all over his face and arms. There was no doubt that he was drunk and at war with the world. He was shouting, cursing and threatening imaginary enemies. He paid us no attention as we passed him by with our gear, and Gary joked, 'He's your going-ashore mate for the trip, John boy.'

'I wouldn't want to end up like him,' I said.

He stopped in front of me and said, 'Well, let that sight be a warning to you.'

We found the chief steward's office but the door was locked so we stood outside and must have been there for about five minutes when along came a blonde square-faced man. He was dressed in a steward's jacket, blue trousers and shiny black shoes.

'My word, you must be the two assistant stewards,' he said. 'I'm so glad to see you, I have been run off my feet. The old man has a group of business people aboard and I've been up and down from his cabin like a yo-yo with canapés and sandwiches. And now there's a week's stores on the dock. I'll show you your cabins. Please get your working gear on as quickly as possible and get on to the stores, I'd really appreciate it.'

He went into the chief steward's office and came out with the keys to our cabins and said, 'Please follow me my dears.'

He gave us the keys and said, 'There's no difference in the cabins so there will be no need for you to scratch each other's eyes out. I shall leave you now to see if I can muster up some help to get the stores aboard.'

I whistled as I opened the door to find an untidy but a spacious modern cabin. I had no time to take it all in just then. The priority was to get the working gear on and get the job done. I locked the door just as Gary stepped out of his cabin and did the same.

'I'm thrilled with the size of my cabin,' I said. 'It's bigger than any room I've ever had the luxury to call my own.'

'Yes,' he said, 'but mine needs a good clean-up. How's yours?'

'The deck is filthy and there's loads of rubbish to be dumped. But once we get them to our liking they will be just right for a two-year trip,' I said.

'You're joking,' he said. 'Hadit told us we'd be relieved after six months.'

'And you believed him?' I laughed.

The articles of agreement we had to sign were to be for two years, and at that time tanker companies had the reputation for their ships going away and forgetting to come back.

We had to wait at the top of the gangway to give way to a stream of men coming up with boxes, bundles and bags. Obviously Blondie had managed to get plenty of help. When the stream had ended Gary led the way down the steep gangway and I followed, thinking, I'm going to hold on to the rails very tightly when I get back from the pub tonight.

The man in the back of the van handed me three boxes of lettuces and said in his Geordie accent, 'That's enough son.'

'They're very light,' I said, 'I can manage another couple of boxes.'

He looked down at me and said, 'It's a steep climb up lad,

three boxes is plenty.'

I saw the kindness in his eyes and appreciated it, but I didn't want to appear not to be pulling my weight. I felt so much better when he handed Gary three boxes of tomatoes. We went back for more but there was nothing left. Gary said, 'If all the jobs are as easy as that, give me more, I suppose we'll have to find that bloke now.'

Blondie found us as we walked along the deck to the accommodation. 'Boys,' he said, 'I'm Jackie, the second steward. And you are ...?' he asked.

'I'm John,' I said, taking his offered hand and shaking it.

'And I'm Gary,' said Gary.

'Good,' said Jackie. 'We've got just over an hour before we have to serve tea. Let's have a beer.'

He led us to his cabin and opened three large bottles of Vaux beer. I had never seen that brand before but I wasn't complaining and it tasted good. As we drank, Jackie gave us a rundown on what our duties would be and then gave us the choice of who would do the bulk of cleaning, the engineers' and deck officers' cabins, and who would serve the three main meals in the saloon and clean two cabins.

Gary asked, 'What do you want to do, John?'

'I'd prefer to do the saloon and clean the two cabins,' I said.

They both nodded, and that was that.

Gary looked at Jackie and said, 'I've only had a few minutes in my cabin, but I'm not impressed by the state of it. It's bloody filthy with rubbish all over the place. It's an insult to expect a new crew member to move into it.'

'Mine is just as bad,' I said.

'I am sorry for the state of your cabins,' said Jackie, 'but it's got nothing to do with me. I have only been on board four days. It is company policy that all crew signing off should leave their accommodation clean and tidy. Just like the passenger ships, the captain does his weekly inspection of the accommodation. I don't know what has gone wrong. Still, there's only a skeleton crew on board, so you'll both have enough time to spare to get your cabins shipshape before we sign on, which I'm told will be in a fortnight's time.' He went on to explain the smoking restrictions on tankers and how very, very important it was to adhere to the standing orders at all times.

We didn't need to be told twice about the dangers of a fire at sea or the consequences, and we were well versed in health and safety matters. 'I know the ship is empty of cargo now,' I said, 'and yet there's a sickly, sweet smell all around. Is it worse with a full cargo?'

'Oh, you will soon get used to that,' he said. 'The crude oil stinks and there's a special smell in all oil refineries and the ports where the cargoes are taken on and discharged.' He looked at his watch and said, 'It's fifteen minutes to teatime. You can both serve the meal and show off your fancy skills from the passenger jobs.'

We accompanied him to the galley to meet the cook, Jock McNair, a grim-faced balding man of few words.

He told Jackie that he had put all the food in the hot press in the pantry and if there wasn't enough they could whistle because he was off ashore in five minutes. Jackie led the way to the saloon, which was miniature in comparison to what we had been used to. There was the captain and senior officers' table and five more tables for the other officers and apprentices. And a serving hatch between the pantry and the saloon so there was very little walking to be done.

It was plate service, no fancy stuff here. Jackie simply put the food we ordered on plates and we served it. The menu boasted lentil soup, liver and bacon with onions and mashed potatoes, rice pudding, cheese and biscuits and tea or coffee. We only had six men in for the delicious dishes, two apprentices and four junior engineers. They were a hungry bunch and ate almost everything put in front of them, and one of the junior engineers even requested another main course. I quietly asked Jackie if he could do a return on the main course for the engineer on the corner table.

He stuck his head out of the hatch and said, 'I can do it for you this time, young man, but don't make a habit of it.'

Gary and I watched as 'young man' wolfed down his second helping, awkwardly using his eating irons, fork in the right hand and knife in the left, like they were weapons and he was doing battle with what was rapidly disappearing from his plate. Gary cleared away his plate and just as we had expected he ordered the rice pudding and cheese and biscuits to follow with a cup of tea. It was obvious that he had no knowledge of table etiquette. It certainly was not the way we expected a ship's officer to behave.

***

The next few days were taken up with settling in and getting used to what seemed to me to be a very easy job.

I was happy to have my own cabin, and for the first time since going to sea I had to do my own laundry, which was no problem because there were a couple of washing machines and a drier, which I used for jeans, work jackets and the like, and the rest I washed by hand each evening after work.

On our fifth day on board I invited Jackie to have a beer with Gary and me in my cabin. Gary's response was, 'Why did you invite him? You know I'm not too keen on him.'

'Well,' I replied, 'you may not like him but whether you like it or not, technically, he's our boss. I'm just returning the compliment – and there are a few things I want to ask him. What better way to do that than over a drink, eh?'

He conceded that he too had a few questions that he would like to ask him.

'There you are then,' I said. 'I didn't think you had anything against the gentle ones anyway. You got on well with Mother and I never saw you falling out with any of the others on the *Arcadia* or the *Sovereign*. I can understand your attitude towards Hadit, but what's the problem with Jackie?'

He shook his head, saying, 'Something I just can't work out yet.'

Jackie arrived in a flourish and said, 'Thank you John, I'm dying for a beer. I've been run ragged for the last week, trying to do the chief steward's job as well as my own. I'm exhausted. The new chief's joining tomorrow, his name is Bob Maynard, I've sailed with him before, we did an eight-month trip together and he was a peach, an absolute peach. He never interfered in our work, and as long as everything was going well we hardly saw him.'

'That sounds good to me,' I said.

'So he leaves the running of our job up to you, does he,' asked Gary.

'Well, he did on the last ship, and unless he's changed it should be the same this trip.'

Gary nodded and said, 'I suppose you'd be good for time

off in the ports of call, would you?'

'Certainly, my dear. And don't forget, I have a few favourite ports where I like to let my hair down.'

'You mean we can cover each other's duties, that sort of thing?' I said.

'Exactly, my dear,' he replied.

I poured more beer and offered some of my precious brandy to both of them and they didn't refuse. I didn't mind, though. I would be heading up the road for more of the liquid gold later.

We learned from Jackie that most tankers had no regular runs. He explained that when we left the dry dock we might get orders to head for the Persian Gulf and halfway there the ship might be diverted anywhere. You could never be sure where you were going until you were actually tied up alongside, and then it could be many miles away from the town, which meant that it would cost you a fair penny for a taxi.

It was 8.30 pm and I was getting fidgety. The assault on the brandy bottle had wrung its knell and I needed to get ashore for replenishments. Gary was going to turn in, as he didn't feel too well, and Jackie still had some work to do. So we parted, and I was down the gangway and up the road faster than the Flying Scotsman, soon to return with some brandy and six large bottles of Newcastle Brown Ale.

I awoke early the next morning in fine fettle and ready to grab the day by the throat and if necessary kick its arse into night. I was feeling great except for my heavy head, and I blamed that on the ale. Newcastle Brown had the reputation of being very strong, but nevertheless, I thought, I'll give it a 'fair go' as that Australian had told the barman in Sydney to do for me almost four years ago. 'Give him a fair go mate!'

I knocked on Gary's door at 6.30 am. He shouted, 'Come in.' He was still in bed and seemed lifeless.

'What's the matter, are you sick?' I asked.

'Yeah,' he croaked, 'I'm not getting up, the pains in my belly are killing me, tell Jackie.'

Later that morning the agent arranged for Gary to go ashore to see a doctor. I covered his duties as well as my own and it wasn't all that difficult. Jackie was still covering the chief steward's duties. He hadn't arrived yet.

Gary came back from the doctor and said that he had an ulcer and was going to have to pay off immediately. I helped him pack, and after he had completed his business with the captain, Jackie and I lugged his gear down to the dock and waited until his taxi arrived to take him to the station. We said goodbye and promised to keep in touch. I thought I sensed a sort of relief in Jackie's voice as he suggested that we should have a beer.

I sat down on his day bed and he poured us Double Diamond beer in fancy balloon glasses.

'Posh glasses!' I said.

'Yes,' he said, 'I like nice things. Cheers!'

When I had finished my beer and stood up to go, he said, 'Your tables are ready, aren't they?'

'Yes,' I said, 'except for the bread, butter and water.'

'Good,' he said, looking at his watch, 'we have a half-hour to spare. Have another beer.'

I thanked him and said, 'You know that scruffy engineer, the one you call "young man" – is it his first trip?'

'Yes,' he said, 'he's just another ignorant shipyard rat as far as I'm concerned, I've seen too many of his kind. Watch out for prats like him. They serve their apprenticeships in the shipyards and some of them then go to sea as junior engineer officers. Usually they're as quiet as mice when they sit in the saloon for the first few meals because they feel out of place seeing the tables laid up with all the silverware. It's strange to the majority of them and they get flustered not knowing what cutlery to use. However, they get over that and pretty soon they get pissed with power, you know, "I'm an officer and you're only a steward." Given half the chance they'll try to order you around after a while. Take my advice, keep them in their place.'

Later, when the last of the diners had left the saloon and we were finished for the day, Jackie handed me a cool lager and said, 'With the compliments of the ship's chandler. There's another couple in the fridge for you. I'm only having this one, I must get ashore to meet the most gorgeous 'omie I've ever been with. Oh, my dear, it will break my heart to sail and leave him behind.'

'How long have you known him?' I asked.

'Only three days, that's what's so amazing,' he said. 'I love him and I hardly know him. I don't fall that easy, but he's a very special person.'

'Good,' I said, 'I hope you both have a nice evening. Any news about the chief steward's arrival?'

'Yes, I forgot to tell you. He will be here early tomorrow morning.'

We finished our lagers and he was off, but not before he asked me to give the skipper his juice and morning tea, just in case he was late getting back. I told him not to worry, I'd see to the old man, and if anything else needed attending to I would do it.

As it turned out Jackie was back early the next morning, and the chief steward Bob Maynard arrived. Three days later the crew joined, and three days after that we signed on ship's articles. The dry dock was flooded and with the assistance of two tugs the *Moon* slipped into the murky River Tyne with orders to head for the Persian Gulf.

It felt great to be back at sea again. My new colleague, Gary's replacement, was a company contract man, Sidney Silver, a Londoner. He was a swarthy lump with dark curly hair. He was ambitious for promotion and anything else that might come his way to help him feather his nest. His best friend, the second cook and baker, another Londoner and company man by the name of Daniel Didit, had learned his trade through the company's promotions scheme. He was a tall gangling sort of character with fair hair going thin. He was the type that if you stuck a feather up his arse and tickled him there wouldn't be a hint of a smile on his face.

I could see how they got on so well together, both miserable by appearance and attitude. I couldn't work out their burning drive for success. I was happy with my life the way it was, just as long as I had money to pay for a place to stay and for my favourite pastime, drinking. That was good enough for me.

The rest of the catering crew was made up of Jackie, Bob Maynard the chief steward, Jon Emery the crew messman, a nice sort of a fella that appeared to be on another planet at times, then Julian Crow, a chubby sixteen-year-old first-trip catering boy, and finally Jock McNair, the chief cook, a big-bellied man who we soon found was capable of burning water. He was prone to throwing tantrums and was best left alone. Fortunately, Daniel was a very good cook and baker.

The deck and engine crew were from all over the Northeast, and a lot of them had sailed together before, a cliquish lot, but that didn't bother me. I was glad to be left alone. What really annoyed me was the way most of them referred to the catering crew as 'piss-pot jerkers', 'pansies', 'arse lickers' etc. Those little niceties were not exclusive to the *Moon* crew. I had heard them all before in dockside taverns and seamen's missions, but what annoyed me was that they were far too frequently used.

My biggest concern was the lack of alcohol on board. Three beers twice a week was the limit for the crew and no spirits at all except for tots of rum issued to the deckhands after tank cleaning. The junior officers were allowed one bottle per week and a case of beer whenever they wanted one provided they didn't abuse the privilege. I managed to keep from dying with the droot by the lack of booze when I learned that Sidney and Daniel didn't drink and therefore would not be drawing their issues. I offered to buy them soft drinks and cigarettes in return for their beer. I made them a generous bid that I knew would appeal to their greedy natures. I had heard of characters that would skin a maggot for a ha'penny, and I had found two. What good fortune! They each made a pound a week out of me and I begrudged it, but I was getting what I wanted.

The ship's company in total was thirty-six, from the master down to the youngest catering boy. It was a big change from the hundreds I had been used to sailing with on the big jobs, but it suited me perfectly. The work was easy and I enjoyed the luxury of my very own cabin. It was bliss to be alone with my books, magazines, radio/cassette player and tapes.

We reached Abadan and loaded a cargo for Little Aden, where there was a refinery out in the wilds of the desert and a heat almost unbearable, humidity you could cut through with a knife and a heat haze that dazzled. Too far from Steamer Point to bother going there, not that there was much to go for anyway. There was a duty-free shop situated near where we tied up and I bought myself a Grundig radio with long and short wave bands which was necessary to pick up the BBC world service and several other nations' broadcasts. That really made my life complete, listening to the news, features, football broadcasts and request programmes. It was on one of those that I first heard Bessie Smith singing 'Nobody knows you when you're down and out'. Despite the poor reception, fading in and out, not much was lost on me. I was captivated by her voice, and the lyrics reminded me of the unfortunates I had seen around the world, especially those in the all-night café in London.

On the second of our seven trips to the Gulf and back to Aden, I met a British soldier called Jake, who suggested that I should visit the NAAFI canteen just a few miles down the road. A couple of quid in a taxi, he said.

I arranged with Jackie and Sidney to have a Saturday afternoon off. They assumed I was going in to Steamer Point and I saw no reason to tell them otherwise.

I entered the NAAFI with trepidation but was soon at ease when I saw three deck hands and a greaser from the ship drinking with a group of squaddies. I walked up to the bar and noticed that they had large cans of Tennent's lager.

I politely asked the barman for one. He looked at me and said,

'Got an ID mate?' I handed him my card and he plonked a can on the counter saying, 'Ten pence mate.' I asked him to take for a drink for himself and he said, 'Not now, thanks mate!' I was about to walk away from the counter when I decided to get a brandy too. The measure he gave me was better than generous. 'A shilling mate,' he said.

I thought, they're giving it away. I had found my own oasis. I sat down to enjoy my drinks and couldn't believe my good fortune. Shortly afterwards three soldiers sat down at my table. One of them, with the build of an all-in wrestler, said, 'All right to sit with you mate?'

'Certainly, please do,' I said.

He smiled and said, 'No offence mate, but I think you must be the smallest bloke that's ever been in here, would you like a drink?'

I looked at him and said, 'I don't think I'll make the Guinness Book of Records for that, but the good thing is, I didn't have to stoop coming through the door as you had to.'

He boomed with laughter and his friends joined in. I didn't think it was much of a joke, but I had obviously tickled their fancy. 'What's your name mate?' he asked.

'John,' I said.

'I'm Arthur, and these blokes are me mates, Jack and Martin.'

'Pleased to meet you gents,' I said.

'Come on, have a drink with us,' said Arthur.

'Thank you Arthur, I'll have a brandy please,' I said.

Jack asked me what life was like at sea, about the work and whether it was easy to get into the merchant navy. I had no sooner started to answer his questions than Arthur returned with a tray of drinks and said, 'I got you a can of Tennent's as well John.'

I thanked him, took a sip of the brandy and said, 'Jack asked me about the life at sea and I was just beginning to explain.'

'Carry on mate,' he said.

I briefly put them in the picture to the best of my knowledge. They listened with interest until I got to the part about the grave lack of alcohol on board and that brought on the wails of 'No, not for me.' 'I couldn't do without a good drink.' Arthur capped it off with, 'Fuck that mate.'

I realised that 'mate' was the in word. I had heard it from the time I entered the place. We got down to some serious drinking, talking and telling jokes, until I started to feel tipsy and knew it was time to scarper while I still had some of my senses left. 'I have to be back on duty in an hour, men,' I lied, 'it's time for me to be going.'

This was met with, 'Aw, have another, the party's just starting.'

'No thanks, gents,' I said, 'the ould dog for the hard road.'

I bought four cans of Tennent's and was in half a mind to see if I could buy a bottle of brandy but decided against it. It would take enough cunning to smuggle the lager aboard. I said goodbye to my new-found *mates* and was getting into the taxi as Arthur came bounding after me and shoved a bottle of Bell's whisky at me, saying, 'For medicinal purposes mate!'

I asked the driver to stop around the corner, just out of sight of the ship, so that I could wrap my spoils in my shirt, and then he drove me to the gangway, which was steep, but I got aboard with my personal cargo of fuel undetected and was ecstatic.

We sailed the next day, bound for the Gulf and another cargo for my new-found watering hole in the desert.

This time we loaded a cargo in Kuwait, where they had a seamen's recreation centre with English newspapers and a large variety of magazines. The papers were about four days old but good to read just the same, soft drinks were sold but not a whiff would a fella get of the real thing. Alcohol was strictly forbidden, and severe penalties would be meted out to anyone offering a local person a can of beer. We were well schooled on what not to do with booze in most of the Gulf ports so there was no excuse if you were silly enough to fall foul of the rules.

They paid the equivalent of five pounds sterling in local currency for a pint of blood and many of our crew sold it. I felt that I hardly had enough for myself so I kept what I had.

We were kept on that run for five more trips but the NAAFI was out of bounds because of terrorist activities and the forces were on full alert, so we were confined to the bar and shop area.

Our next trip took us to Mombasa, and that was followed by several trips to ports on the African coast. Christmas was celebrated at sea and it made no difference to me where I was. On a tanker or anywhere else. I had grown to hate that time of year whether I was at sea or ashore. It was the same phoney back-slapping, peace on earth to those of goodwill and all that nonsense. Eat and drink till you have stuffed yourself beyond any human need. Get the cheap cheroots and cigars out and puke all over the place.

Forget about the poor unfortunates, the lonesome people, young and old alike, all alone and some without a roof over their heads. And forget the old folks, some too poor and too proud to ask anyone for anything.

Now on board the *Moon* the odd can of beer or a tot of spirits from a few of the so-called officers was being offered. Some of them would barely bid you the time of day during the trip and now it was goodwill for a day.

As the trip went on I became very bored with the long sea passages and the remote ports of call, and although I had my books and my music I was getting restless and irritable, as indeed were many of my colleagues.

Our next two trips from the Gulf took us to Singapore and

Hong Kong. Then we got orders for a cargo to Rotterdam and everyone was joyous – we could pay off there. But there was cause for a few heart flutters with two changes of orders. One for Mombasa and that was cancelled for Singapore and back again to Rotterdam.

To hell with these bloody tankers, I thought, I've had enough of them.

We paid off on 23 February 1965. I was free with a pocket full of money to do what I wanted with and go anywhere I wanted to. What a life!

**

I booked in to the QVSR and went on the booze for a month before joining a cruise liner, the *Andes*, out of Southampton. She was truly a first-class ship, doing nineteen- and twenty-one-day cruises. It was a pleasure to be looking after paying passengers again after taking care of some of the so-called officers. I found the work really easy, and the big bonus was that there was only one sitting so the passengers could take as much time as they liked over their meals and there was no pressure on me to get them to 'eat it and beat it'.

The crew accommodation was the worst I had been in. I was in an eight-berth inboard cabin and it was as dark as a dungeon, but my seven colleagues were good men and harmony prevailed. During my four months on there I spent more time in the recreation room and on deck than I did in the cabin anyway.

The booze was plentiful, so by the time I was ready to turn in I could have slept on a bed of nails. The crew were a mixed bunch, with a good percentage of them coming from Hampshire and neighbouring counties – locals, you could say. They were referred to as 'Mushes' by most of the old hands and I quickly learned that they were not well liked by many of the crew because of their insular attitude and how they looked upon the rest of us as interlopers.

The highlight of my time on the *Andes* was what was commonly called the 'Jewish cruise'. I went on a coach trip from Haifa to Nazareth, which had been arranged by our sports and social club. The driver took great pleasure in pointing out the vast expanses of desert that had been turned into arable land and prattled on and on about his countrymen's and women's achievements in spite of being surrounded by their enemies. When we got to Nazareth a swarm of souvenir sellers were waiting to scourge us with incessant chatter while trying to sell their wares – relics, bottled water from the Dead Sea, sand from the desert and photographs in their multitudes. I walked around to satisfy my curiosity and finished up having a look at Joseph's alleged carpenter shop, and that was enough for me. It was an experience not to be repeated, with the tacky tourist atmosphere, the flies as big as miniature helicopters, and the furnace-like heat. Back on the bus, I delved into my bag for my flask of whisky and a can of Tennent's lager, which was still chilled because I had had the presence of mind to wrap the six cans in a terry towel.

I signed off at the end of that cruise, and almost immediately got a job with the Royal Mail Line on the South American run, as first-class assistant steward on the *Aragon*. I jumped at the chance, having heard so much about that part of the world. After only four days' leave my financial affairs were very healthy. In fact, the healthiest they had been for a good few years. I had £214 in the post office and £55 in readies in my pocket – and a full bottle of Gordon's gin in my case when I joined.

I found the chief steward's office and reported to a smiling pale-faced man with three rings on his sleeves. After studying my discharge book he said, 'So your last ship was the *Andes*, and I see you've been on some of the other big ones too – you won't have any problems on here. You will be in the first-class saloon. There is only one sitting so the passengers can have plenty of time over their meals. I have to say that some of our first-class passengers can be demanding to say the least. Thank God they are not all like that.'

Then he directed me to my cabin and told me that signing on was at 2 pm. I had four hours to settle in, get familiar with the layout of the galley and the saloon, and introduce myself to the head waiter. I found my cabin, which was an inboard two-berth. I unpacked my cases and laid the gear on an unmade bunk, and just as I finished a tall good-looking blond-haired young man came in with four cans of beer in his hand.

We looked at each other and he said, 'I'm Roger. Do you fancy a beer?'

'Yes, I certainly could do with one,' I said. 'I'm John.'

We drank in silence for a while, and then I offered him a gin. His eyes lit up and he produced two glasses from his locker, saying, 'I shall get some ice and lemon.' And without another word he was out the door, soon to return with the ice and lemon, along with six cold cans of Tennent's lager.

As we drank, Roger told me that he was on his fourth trip and he loved the run. Seven-week trips and then a bit of leave in London couldn't be bad, he said. He gave me the low-down on the job, the type of passengers we carried and the fun that could be had with the girls in Montevideo, Santos, Rio and finally Buenos Aires, where the ship would be alongside for nine days, loading meat for England.

After more cold beers and more stiff gins I signed on and reported to the head waiter, John Phillips, who gave me the easy task of laying up my table for the evening meal. Then I was off duty again until 6.30 pm – almost four hours to myself.

'I'm going to lie down for a while,' I said to Roger.

I woke up around 5.30 to find Roger sitting on the couch drinking a can of beer. 'You didn't sleep for long,' he said. 'Fancy a beer? And we might as well kill off the last of your gin, shall we?'

'Go ahead,' I said. I was refreshed, and it didn't take me long to finish my drinks.

Roger produced another bottle of gin from his locker, splashed a generous helping into the glasses and said, 'I got this from a friend of mine, a bedroom steward. He's always got reserves and it so happens he drinks gin.'

I watched him to see if he was showing any signs of the drink taking effect on him. His face was redder but his speech was clear when he said, 'I'm going to have a shower after this one.'

In the saloon I had spotted two old shipmates from my P&O days – Tommy, a Glaswegian from the *Himalaya*, and Jack, a Liverpudlian with a wicked wit I had sailed with on the *Orion*. Both men were very sharp and worldly-wise. They were from working-class backgrounds and came from deprived areas in their respective cities. They had learned the art of survival from the streets. Socialists all the way, stand up for your rights and fight for them when the chips are down.

That was their creed.

The dinner bell was rung at seven o'clock and the passengers came in dribs and drabs. Things were free and easy, a contrast from what I had experienced on some other ships where the passengers queued up and were champing at the bit to get in at the first clang of the bell.

My passengers, the Carrington-Smythes, strolled in at 7.35. There were four men dressed like penguins and two women in long flowing gowns. A very distinguished bunch, I thought. I guessed that the older couple were in their mid sixties and the son and daughter-in-law in their forties. The two young men, the grandsons, were probably in their early twenties. They looked like they were well off, but I had seen my fair share of those type of people before, dressed up and putting on airs and graces and bragging about their possessions for those who cared to listen. I was always wary of that kind, for I knew that those who were fortunate enough to have wealth never spoke of it, not within my hearing anyway. But these were nice people, and it was a pleasure to serve them. I hoped that things would remain the same for the three weeks to Buenos Aires.

I finished my duties and went for a shower, then sat down to relax with a can of beer, soon to be joined by Roger, then Tommy and Jack with a case of lager and a bottle of Teacher's whisky. Beer cans were opened and the seal on the whisky bottle was broken. Roger and I drank our gin and the other two got stuck into the whisky. We drank and discussed everything and anything, from the girls in South America to politics, shipping companies and world affairs.

At six the next morning I felt groggy, and if a doctor had examined me he would not have found a trace of work in me. My morning job was helping to stock a bar and then lay my table up for breakfast. After that it was my breakfast time. I rushed down to the cabin for a livener. Roger was already there, and he handed me a cool lager. I cracked the can open and took a couple of swallows before speaking.

'I'm dog rough today,' I said.

'So am I,' he replied.

We drank another can each, purely for medicinal purposes, we agreed, and then it was time to report to the saloon. None of my passengers showed up for breakfast and I was pleased.

When they came in for a light lunch they told me the only time they would be in for breakfast was when the ship docked in port in the mornings.

The ship bunkered in Las Palmas, and so did we. Roger, Tommy, Jack and I purchased two cases of Bacardi rum each, at the cost of two pounds and five shillings for a case containing six litre bottles. So we were in good spirits, it could be safely said, until we reached Buenos Aires.

Everything I had been told about the girls in the various ports on that trip proved to be true. They were nice and loving in Montevideo, but they really took the biscuit in Santos and Rio de Janeiro. They swarmed aboard and were all over the crew quarters like locusts, females of all ages and hues, offering their services for the lowly sum of one pound sterling or two hundred cigarettes, which cost us ten shillings. The one woman who has stuck in my memory over the years was the 'Champeen Gobbler', as she called herself.

She came along the alleyway thumping her ample breasts and declaring, 'Me, I am the Champeen Gobbler, two hun'd cigarettes for number one suck, suck!'

I guessed she was probably in her forties, but it was hard to tell. She wore coloured ribbons in her curly brown hair and had so much makeup on that you would have thought she had come directly from the Battle of the Little Bighorn. Nevertheless, she wasn't bad looking.

I went ashore alone in Montevideo, Santos and Rio de Janeiro and spent as much time as I could exploring and taking photographs, where I felt it was safe to do so, but I kept alert as I trudged around. However, there were a few times when I became really frightened, especially when I became the object of curiosity and was surrounded by people of all ages. Somehow I always managed to get myself out of tricky situations, and that was part of the enjoyment of going alone. I saw affluence and poverty walking side by side and couldn't believe my eyes at the plight of the poor unfortunates. The word God came to mind and I wondered if those who praised his name could give me an explanation as to why he wasn't doing anything for those poor people.

Our next port was Buenos Aires. My lovely passengers disembarked there and I was sorry to see them go, but I was twenty-five pounds better off for their going. A good tip that, just for doing my job.

We spent nine days there loading meat for the UK. That gave me plenty of time to wander around the city, with all its beautiful buildings, and I fell in love with the place.

We sailed from Argentina on the homeward bound run and this time I only had four passengers to look after. Four middle-aged Americans, Mr and Mrs Power and Mr and Mrs Armstrong. It took me just a short while to get used to them and I knew I was going to enjoy taking care of them. They were friendly and undemanding and it was as pleasant a trip home as it had been on the way out – and soon I was saying goodbye to the nice Americans in Southampton. They gave me thirty pounds and I felt terrible taking it because they had been so kind and gentle. However, they exuded pleasure in giving me the money and that made me feel a bit better. Since I first took that shilling piece from the blind lady in the International Hotel I always felt very uncomfortable taking tips.

A couple of hours later I signed off and on again for the next voyage, as did my cabin mate Roger and our drinking companions Tommy and Jack. I booked in to the Flying Angel seamen's mission in Custom House, London, which was just over a mile from the Royal Docks, where I was to re-join the *Aragon* in ten days time.

The room was adequate. A roof over the head and a place to put my gear was all I needed. I was unfamiliar with the area, but it wouldn't take me long to put that to rights.

I soon found my bearings and drank in all of the pubs near the mission – the Freemason's, the Steps, the Peacock, the New Gog. The whole place was a hive of activity. Some of the locals mingled with the seamen, and seamen renewed old friendships with colleagues they had sailed with, in some cases from years back. Of course the hustlers, bummers, pimps and 'business girls' were plentiful too, but there was room for us all.

I had a pleasant surprise one Sunday when I went in to the Freemason's Arms, just after midday, opening time. A man of about my own age with long fair hair and a beard was playing a medley of old Irish tunes on a fiddle and then he switched to an electric guitar and started on some Leadbelly, Woody Guthrie and Bessie Smith classics, which thrilled me. I had become very interested in the blues, folk and country music over the years. I took my gin and tonic over to a table near the little stage, sat down and raised my glass to salute him. He nodded at me and carried on into a medley of Hank Williams songs.

Listening to the man playing and singing the songs of those wonderful artists was the biggest treat I had had in years. Needless to say, as soon as he laid his guitar down to take a break, I asked him if I could get him a drink. I got him a pint of Guinness and joined him at the table where I had been sitting.

'Thanks mate,' he said. 'Me name's Patrick.'

'I'm John,' I said. 'I really liked what you were doing up there. That's the kind of music I enjoy.'

'Yeah,' he said, 'there's a heart and soul in it and the lyrics are meaningful.' Then he enthusiastically unloaded a barrage of information about Leadbelly, and he had hardly taken more than a few sips from his pint when it was time for him to get back on stage and give us some more. The big pub was crowded now, and it seemed that the majority of the customers were only interested in getting the booze down and chatting. Although I noticed one fellow placed a pint on top of the piano for him and shortly afterwards another put what I took to be a large whisky by the pint glass, and I thought, at least there's a couple who appreciate what he's doing as much as I do.

A couple of old shipmates beckoned me over, but I just waved and stayed where I was. I was far more keen on listening to Patrick than getting into some meaningless conversation about trips gone by.

He closed his final set with Irish jigs and reels played on the fiddle, then he sat down beside me with his drinks and set about getting the gargle down with a vengeance.

'Thirsty work,' I said.

He put his half-finished Guinness glass down, picked up the glass of whisky, threw it back, gave a shiver and said, 'That's better.'

He told me that his father was from Dublin. He had come over to London in the 1930s to work in the building trade as a labourer and a few years later married a County Waterford girl. They had two girls before Patrick was born in 1940 and a year later his brother Tom was born. He said that he had visited his grandparents both in Dublin and in Waterford during many of his school holidays and he loved the country. His uncle in Waterford had taught him to play the fiddle and the accordion and he took to it, just like a horse to hay.

It was closing time, so I finished my drink, thanked him and headed for the door.

***

I rejoined the *Aragon* and got back to the working routine with some order in my life. It was good to be back on board, and once again I felt that I was at home, back to drinking and jawing with Roger, Tommy and Jack, and the discipline of having to keep myself in line. It couldn't be beaten, I thought.

The trip went much the same as the previous one. The business girls swarmed aboard and did a roaring trade and the Champeen Gobbler was kept busy. I did some more exploring, mainly around Buenos Aires.

I had six good passengers on the outward trip and only four on the homeward run, Mr and Mrs Lightfoot and their two teenage daughters, Felicity and Lisa, travelling to London, a lovely family. When they came in to dinner one evening, Mr Lightfoot presented me with a coloured gift bag. I looked inside and saw the shape of a bottle wrapped in pink paper with a red ribbon around it. He smiled, winked, and said, 'The packaging and choice of bag is from the girls and the contents are from my wife and me to thank you for being so kind to us.'

After the meal, I took the bag down to the cabin and found it contained a bottle of Johnnie Walker Black Label whisky. It was a very welcome gift because, as on other ships I had been on, the rule was that ratings were not allowed to purchase spirits.

There were ways around that rule, of course. Colleagues who worked in the bars and the cabin stewards didn't mind getting the odd bottle for you, just so long as you kept it under your hat and it couldn't be traced back to them. Then there was the odd friendly passenger who would get you one – all it took was to say that one of your friends was celebrating his birthday or his wife had twins during the voyage and you wanted to give him a drink. The trick was to put on a sob story about how difficult it was for a crew member to purchase alcohol and then insist on paying for it in advance and it always paid off provided you had chosen the right passenger. I never failed in securing the goods. But the Lightfoots' gift was unsolicited – and it tasted the better for it.

***

I signed off on 15 December 1965, my birthday. I was 23 years old and well on the way to becoming an alcoholic, if I wasn't one already. But if anyone had suggested such a thing I would have denied it vehemently, because I honestly believed that I could stop drinking any time I wanted to – but why give up something I enjoyed?

I booked in to the Queen Victoria Seamen's Rest and lost myself in alcohol to let the bullshit of Christmas roll right over me. There were many times I woke up not knowing where I was and how I got there. The body shakes, dry retching, and blackouts were more frequent and I worried about my behaviour during periods of depression and remorse. Especially when I couldn't remember what pub I had finished up in or which pub I might have been thrown out of the night before. However, my need for the booze overcame my fear of being told that I was barred from a pub and my tactic was to walk in as though I hadn't been in the place for ages.

Of course, that backfired several times and hardly was I in the door when the shout went up, 'Out you, you're barred!'

Then I would about turn without a word and walk out with as much dignity as I could muster and console myself with the thought that as long as I had money in my pocket I could go anywhere I pleased.

In the third week of January 1966 I was down to having only enough money for one week's rent and three pounds to spare and I was worried. I always had a fear of not being able to pay my way. I was a nervous wreck and had a desperate need for alcohol, but that was out, the rent came first. I couldn't bear the thought of having to talk to or mix with anyone so I stayed in my room for forty-eight hours, sustaining myself on the six cans of beer I had left. There was nothing for it but to get a ship, and on the third morning I ventured down to the cafeteria, had two cups of tea and a slice of bread and felt much better.

I was about to head for the Shipping Federation when Billy, an old shipmate of mine on the *Aragon*, came over to me in the hall and asked if I would like a drink of duty-free whisky. That meant one of two things. Either he had got his hands on some contraband or he had just paid off. It proved to be the latter, because his next question was, did I need a few quid? Naturally, I wanted to answer yes, but my better instincts told me to get down to the Federation and get a job. I thanked him for his offer, saying that I was all right, but I really had to go and hopefully I would see him later for that drink. It was cold when I left the mission but it was good to be out in the air.

I handed my discharge book to the clerk, who flicked through the pages and said, 'There's the *Ruahine*, a passenger/cargo ship in the Albert Docks, signing on articles January 31st and sailing for a three to four months round voyage to Australia and New Zealand.'

'Yes, I'll take the job,' I said.

He looked over his spectacles at me and said, 'If you pass the medical!'

I went up to the doctor with a fear within me. I felt weak and as nervous as a kitten. Still, I had to see him.

There was just one man before me, dressed in a denim suit. He was of average height with greying hair, about fifty, I thought.

I nodded to him and he said, 'I've been here for over a half hour, it's that Irish quack, O'Hooligan, and he's a miserable bastard, a fuckin' tyrant. He knocked me back the last time I saw him because my blood pressure was too high and he told me to stop drinking. The bastard had me on the beach for three months before he passed me to ship out. If he knocks me back this time, I'll hit him.' He stood up, paced the floor and sat down again.

Within a couple of minutes, the doctor's assistant came out and called out, 'Mr Dimple!'

He stood up, shook himself and said, 'That's me, good luck mate, see ya.' I was glad to see the back of him. He had given me much to think about. What if I failed my medical? What would I do? Where could I go? How could I survive without money? I was still pondering when out stepped Dimple, closely followed by the assistant, who said, looking at me, 'Mr Mahon?'

The doctor was sitting behind his desk, a pale-faced man with a big mop of grey hair. He looked up and said, 'Sit down, Mr Mahon,' I did as I was told and then he said, 'It's nearly six months since your last medical, how has your health been?'

'I have enjoyed good health for over a year,' I said. 'I had to have my spectacles changed and that's all.'

'Good,' he mumbled, and then he hit me with the cigarettes and alcohol questions. It was all part of the procedure, and I was prepared. 'How much alcohol do you consume in a day?'

'On average, three or four cans of beer a day and occasionally a small brandy. There are times when I don't touch a drop for a week or more, I can take it or leave it,' I said.

He nodded in what I took to be approval and then asked, 'How many cigarettes do you smoke in a day?'

'About twenty,' I replied.

'Too many,' he said. 'Take your jacket off and open your shirt, I want to sound your chest.'

As he was doing the sounding, I was thinking maybe I should have said ten a day but I had lied about the booze and thought that smoking was the lesser of the two so-called evils.

He finished his sounding and said, 'You're fit for sea, but you have to cut down on smoking and start from today.'

'I will, doctor,' I said. He signed my papers and I was down the stairs as though a raging bull was after me.

***

The *Ruahine* was a cargo ship that carried a few hundred passengers, so there was no need for her to be all prettied up. Her hull was black, with just a small amount of white on the bows. She was ugly in comparison to the pretty white ladies that I had sailed on.

I signed on the ship's articles and was delighted to get an advance note for ten pounds, an advance on my future earnings. The problem with those notes was that they couldn't be redeemed for about two weeks after the ship sailed so it was difficult to get them changed. Unless of course you knew where to go. As with so many things in life, there's always some opportunist waiting to take advantage of another person's situation. Two pubs that I knew of changed the notes, but for a price. The Duck's Ear charged two shillings in the pound, and the Parson's Lips charged two shillings and sixpence. The reason they gave for charging so much was that far too many seamen had jumped ship once they had cashed the notes and they had lost the money.

That was a blatant lie. Most seamen who were unfortunate enough to need an advance note sailed and the money was paid in full. I changed mine in the Duck's Ear and had a large brandy before going back to the ship.

Ruahine sailed, and it soon became apparent that she was going to be a happy ship. We had a good crew and my eight passengers were a nice bunch too. I cut down on my drinking and ate more than I had in a long time, and my resolve was to straighten myself out and save some money. I had no intention of stopping drinking – after all, it was like a lifeline to me, and it kept me going, but I was definitely going to ease up on my intake. All went well on the outward trip. Alas, my plans came to nothing as soon as we reached the Australian coast. I drank heavily both on and off the ship and that didn't do me any favours. I hated myself at times for having been so foolish and wished I had never started. My two friends Tommy and Austin drank heavily, but they seemed to be able to exercise better control over themselves. They tried to advise me on where I was going wrong, but most of what they said fell on my cloth ears.

I had to admit that I couldn't drink the same amount that I used to a few years earlier, but I needed at least one can of beer or a few shots of spirits before I could face the day, and I always tried to make sure to have some sort of booze stashed for that reason.

My old friend alcohol was letting me down now. Where once it had been a crutch in helping me cope with all sorts of problems, now all it was doing was causing me grief and anxiety.

I managed to get myself in a better frame of mind on the homeward voyage, and this was because I became involved in producing a variety concert for the crew and passengers. I loved the whole thing from start to finish. It was hard work but a great thrill when it all started to take shape, seeing the costumes made up, the chorus line working in harmony, the comedy sketches and songs ready for performing. We had worked tirelessly for ten days in getting it all together. It was a team effort that concluded with a very successful evening.

Ten days after the show, on 20 May 1966, we docked in London. The seamen's strike was into its fifth day and there wasn't a room to be had in any of the missions to seamen, all full up. So I caught the boat train from Euston to Holyhead and boarded the mailboat for Dun Laoghaire and eventually landed up at Maureen and Dick's house in Enniskerry.

I had paid off with £172, and as I didn't know how long the strike was going to go on I knew I had to be careful with my money. Caution was now the name of the game.

I stayed with the family for week after week of the strike, and it seemed that it would go on forever. Maureen flatly refused to take anything for my keep, which made me more secure, with readies in my pocket, but I felt awful about not paying my way. I restricted myself to a few pints of Guinness in one or the other of the two village pubs and a couple of whiskeys on my weekly visits to Dublin to collect my three pounds strike pay from the National Union of Seamen's office on Eden Quay.

The strike did me a number of favours. It gave me the opportunity to experience the home life, and being part of the family was very special to me. The vibrancy of the children and their unconditional love was a joy to experience. Eating regular meals became a habit. My great need for alcohol had diminished and I felt more secure in myself.

The big bonus was remembering where I had been the night before and what I had said and to whom.

***

The strike ended after six weeks and I said goodbye to my family with a heavy heart. I arrived back in London to discover the general consensus of the seamen was that we were going back to work worse off than before and the union leaders had let us down. Calling the strike had been a stupid move right from the start. The 'Gannex Man', Prime Minister Harold Wilson, used the strike and the legitimate seamen as a political football, and some of the agitators had played right into his hands.

I decided to stay around London for the World Cup, so I went to the company office that ran the pleasure steamers and coasters and was given a job on the *Daffodil*, a sister ship of the *Royal Sovereign*, by the same kindly old man who had given me the job two years earlier.

The first person I met as I stepped on deck was Paddy Cullen, an old shipmate from the *Orion*. He looked very gaunt and quite unwell. After a brief natter he led me down to his cabin in the bowels of the ship. The accommodation was really not suitable for living on board, but most of the crew lived in London and at the end of each day the majority went home. Quite a few stayed in seamen's missions, but in order to save a few pounds I opted to stay on board.

I was only going to stay for a couple of weeks anyway, and I could put up with a bit of discomfort for that time, as I had done when I worked on the *Sovereign*. Paddy unlocked the door to a six-berth cabin and said, 'Here you are John Joe! You'll probably have the place to yourself if you're going to stay on board. I'm living with a sister up in Tottenham.'

I took a half bottle of whisky from my bag and offered him a drink.

'No thanks, mate, I can't drink any more,' he said. 'I've had to have a stomach operation and now I'm stuck with this blasted bag strapped to me side.'

He pulled his shirt aside and said, 'Look at this thing.'

I glanced briefly at the bag and guessed what it was. I felt sorry and embarrassed for him and hoped my feelings didn't show. 'You've been through some rough times then?' I said.

'Yes,' he replied, 'it was touch and go there for a while. I nearly snuffed it, but let me tell you, that sister never left my side. It's strange, I gave up all contact with my family after I came to England, and all through my twenty years of going to sea I never bothered me arse even sending them a card. I knew nothing about the deaths of my mother and father and an elder sister and I still wouldn't know if it hadn't a been for somebody in the seamen's mission and the welfare people in the hospital tracing my sister Kate.'

I still held the bottle in my hand, so I discreetly slipped it back into my bag, which I locked away with the rest of my gear.

'I'd better report to the chief steward,' I said, 'or he'll be sending for a replacement.'

'Don't worry about that,' said Paddy. 'Jack Hayes is an old pal of mine, we did our first trip together over twenty years ago, you'll like him.'

I reported to Mr Hayes, signed the home trade agreement and I was in business. He told me that *Daffodil* had just had some engine repairs done and there was muck and dirt everywhere and my job was to help with getting her shipshape again before we sailed. 'It's too late to start anything this afternoon,' he said. 'I'll see you at eight o'clock tomorrow morning.'

I stayed on board that evening, read for a while, listened to the radio and had an early night. The next day I washed bulkheads and cleaned mirrors alongside Paddy and it worked out perfectly. I had learned that when doing such work, it was a good tactic to ally myself to the tallest man on the job, and it always paid dividends for both of us. He could reach the high parts and I would follow up from the lower level. Paddy was an ideal partner for the job.

We worked well together as we talked about old shipmates and our trip together. I asked him if he ever saw or heard from Jimmy McMahon and the answer was no. We finished work at 4 pm and went to our cabin. He asked me what I was going to do that evening. 'I'll probably go out for a few jars,' I said.

I saw a sadness come over his face and was furious with myself for being so insensitive. I think he detected my discomfort as he said, 'John, it's grand seeing you again and I'm glad to see you're still enjoying a jar. I'm only sorry that I dare not touch a sup any more, but I like to see a man enjoying a drop of the cratur. I don't give a fuck about dying and I'd hit the bottle right now but for Kate's sake. She's had a hard life with a bastard of a husband who used to come home drunk and use her as a punch-bag. She put up with that for twenty years before he died. They never had any children and she would have liked to, but maybe it was for the best. I have a lovely home with her, we're far closer than when we were growing up and that's a powerful thing altogether.'

He left and I unpacked and then went ashore, bought a bottle of Teacher's whisky and six cans of lager and walked back to *Daffodil*. I switched the light on and was glad to see that apart from my bunk the others hadn't been made up, a good indication that I was going to be by myself. I poured a whisky, opened a can of lager and sat down to look at my surroundings – the five unmade bunks, the green metal lockers, the many pipes overhead and the excrement-coloured bulkheads. What a dump, I thought, what am I doing here? I finished my drinks and turned in, and fortunately I was asleep in a very short time.

Paddy woke me the next morning with a steaming cup of coffee, saying, 'Up outta dat ya imperent brat!'

'What's a boy from Ballygoarseways trying to speak like a Dubliner for?' I asked. 'The next thing, you'll be trying to take off Herself on the throne!'

The day's work went well. I enjoyed immersing myself in the many tasks, and by the time it came to finishing I was in high spirits, and that was without alcohol too.

I stayed on board to read and enjoy my whisky. I read and drank until the lines became blurred and the book fell out of my hand. I flaked out into dreamland but no dreams came. The next thing I knew Paddy was waking me with a mug of coffee. He nodded at the Teacher's bottle and said, 'Seems like you were studying hard last night.'

'Definitely,' I said.

He picked up the bottle and said, 'I've got to have a whiff of that stuff.' He unscrewed the cap, took a couple of deep sniffs, screwed the cap back tightly and declared, 'Mother of God, nectar! God be with the old days when I was in good health.'

I asked how long he had been off the booze. Nearly three years, was his answer. Then I asked if it bothered him being in the company of drinkers.

'Yes,' he said, 'I never go into a pub and I can only tolerate being in the company of anyone with drink taken for a very short time. In fact, I can't be away from them quick enough.'

'It must be very hard for you,' I said.

'It's much easier now, but there's times when I get depressed and me mind always goes to the bottle, although I'm learning to cope with that too. I often go to Alcoholics Anonymous meetings. I get a great deal of strength from them, and strangely, I'm learning to live a different way of life – but let me assure you, it's still hard.'

I remembered Paddy as the man who could drink himself sober. Now he could not even have a sip. What a miserable life he must lead, I thought. Thank everything real I'm not in his shoes.

I waited until he went out and then sloshed a good measure of whisky into the remainder of the coffee and drank it with relish. I washed and dressed and reported to Mr Hayes. Paddy was given a tea bar to work in and I was assigned to the cafeteria, serving fish and chips and a variety of other greasy delights. The more customers I could serve the more likely I was to make more tips, and despite my feelings about taking tips, I felt that whatever I would earn I deserved it because of the work I would have put in.

We sailed away from the Tower at 9 am with a full complement of passengers bound for sunny Southend, a cruise around Margate and then the return trip to town. My first trip went well and I made three pounds in tips.

The next morning Paddy wasn't his usual cheerful self. He said, 'It's a whore of a morning John, I hardly slept a wink last night with bloody creasing pains – and if that wasn't enough, I made a fuck up, taking my bag off and the contents spilled all over the bathroom, what a frustration that was. I wasn't going to come to work today, but it's the work that keeps me going. Anyway, I'm feeling much better now.'

'Are you often in pain?' I asked.

'No,' he said, 'I suppose I'm lucky really. Sometimes I can go for weeks without a twitch and then it hits me like a bulldozer. It's a hell of a way to live, and between you an' me, I've thought of ending it all more times than I care to count. I couldn't do it though, knowing what it would do to Kate.'

I didn't know what to say to that so I drank some coffee.

I had a good day and earned five pounds in dropsies. Shortly after we tied up I walked to the Tower Hill underground station with Paddy, and it was a slow walk. He could barely lift his feet as he shuffled along at a snail's pace. We stopped for a rest and sat down on a bench.

He said, 'I'm ballsed John, I won't be in tomorrow, I'm in too much pain.'

I asked him if he would like me to accompany him home.

'No thanks mate, I'll be fine,' he said.

We eventually reached the entrance to the underground station, and after seeing him off I caught a bus to Canning Town, in the heart of London's Dockland. The good old East End, as some people referred to it. I wanted to take a look over the new Catholic seamen's mission called Anchor House. Before long, I found myself walking into the brightly lit reception area, where two women were busy attending to a group of men at the desk while another woman, in the shop directly opposite, was selling goods to a group of oriental gentlemen. I stood there for a few moments taking it all in, then a heavy-set fellow asked to see my discharge book or ID card. I produced my ID. He scanned it and handed it back without a word. I walked the short distance to the bar, and despite the place being crowded I managed to find a vacant barstool and climbed aboard.

I ordered a large Teacher's whisky and a bottle of Double Diamond, and was served in double-quick time. I sipped my drinks with my eyes all over the place. The bar was set along a wall and the rest of the big room was laid out in an open-plan style, with low tables surrounded by comfortable-looking chairs and settees. Three slot machines were strategically placed and they were doing a roaring trade. There was a jukebox too, turned off now because there was a dance going on across the way in the ballroom.

'First time here, mate?' asked the smartly dressed fellow sitting next to me.

'Yes,' I said, 'and I'm amazed at how different it is from the other missions. I thought the Red Ensign was good because of the bar, but this is extra special – a dance hall and women too, that takes the biscuit.'

My barstool buddy laughed and said, 'Yeah, this puts the other missions in the shade. I've been fucked out of a few of them for trying to smuggle a bottle in. Think about it – when a seaman comes ashore, what are the two things uppermost in his mind? I'll tell you, drink and women, am I right?'

I grinned and he continued, 'It's a pity we can't take the birds out.'

'Why not?' I asked.

'Most of them come through Catholic organisations. You know the kind, nurse's homes and hostels for good Catholic girls! They're vetted and they're not allowed to refuse to dance with anyone that asks them to. Officially they're forbidden from striking up personal relationships with us blokes. There's ways around that, of course, but when the dance is over you'll see them all trooping out together like a flock of sheep to be ushered into the "chastity chariots" and driven home.'

'Chastity chariots?' I asked.

'Ah, that's the name the boys have given the buses,' he said.

'Are you staying here?' I asked.

'Yes mate,' he said, 'I've been here nearly two weeks now, and the rooms are great. Lovely comfortable beds, and a shower in the room as well. It's luxury, and for twenty-five bob a night I'm not complaining. If you want to stay here, book in advance because the place is always full up. I'm Hugh, what's your handle?'

'John,' I replied.

He told me he worked as a bar steward on the Cunard line and had done so for the last eight years. A couple of rounds of drinks later I was pocketing my change when Hugh said, 'Here they come, look out!'

A swarm of men and women came out of the ballroom. Some of them sat down and others stood around in couples and groups talking and drinking until the chastity chariots arrived. And, just as Hugh had said, the women were all trooping out the door, observed by a tall priest puffing on a cheroot.

'That's Father McGuinness,' Hugh said. 'He's the boss here. They say it was his idea to get this place going, and if it was, he's done us proud. He's strict, and he doesn't stand any messing from anyone. It's also said that he's a shrewd dude and if he went into business he'd be a millionaire in no time.'

On the way out, I stopped at the reception to enquire about making an advance booking, and I ended up booking a room for the last two weeks of July.

Paddy never returned to work during the few days that I remained on the *Daffodil*. I suspected that he was close to dying, and in a way I felt that would be a mercy, because he was just existing and miserably so.

***

I moved in to Anchor House, and it was marvellous. The small carpeted room was tastefully furnished with a single bed, which was covered with a floral eiderdown to match the curtains and the fabric of the easy chair, there was a built in wardrobe and a chest of drawers. Plenty of room for my gear, and last but by no means least the built-in shower unit – what a treat! I was thrilled. It was as good as any hotel room that I had been in and better than some. What a change from having to leave the room to trot down to the communal wash place with a towel around the waist, as was the way in the other missions. I unpacked, took a shower, dressed and went down to the bar, where I ordered a large brandy and sat myself down on a comfortable chair to relax and watch what was going on.

I sat there enjoying my drink, watching three fellows feeding the one-arm bandits with sixpenny pieces. One character in particular stood out, a small man, not much bigger than myself, well dressed in a white shirt and a tie that matched his dark conservative suit, and he wore an American-style pork-pie hat. But what caught my eye was the cigarette dangling from the corner of his mouth. He never took it out and seemed oblivious to the ash falling onto the front of his jacket. There was a pile of little brown envelopes around his feet, and when he ran out of coins he took another envelope from his pocket, tore it open, counted the coins and started to feed the machine again. He pulled the handle down for the umpteenth time and there was a loud tinkling of coins falling into the tin tray beneath. I thought how clever it was to use such a receptacle – the rattling caught people's attention and no doubt inspired some to take a chance. Cigarette, as I had named him, took the butt out of his mouth and lit another cigarette from it as the coins fell into the tray. He rubbed his hands together and gave a little shuffle of joy, thus disturbing a pile of little brown packets under his feet. I was about to get up for another drink when an old shipmate named John came over to me, declaring, 'Well, I'll be damned, John Joe, you're looking well, what'll you have to drink?'

'John!' I said, 'it's nice to see you again. You're not only looking well, but very prosperous too. I'll have a Martell brandy please.'

'A double no doubt?' he said.

While he was getting the drinks, I turned my attention back to the slot machines. Cigarette was still there, pumping back in the coins he had just taken out. He had a couple of small tinkles and fed that back in with no result. He stood back, looking at the metal monster and shaking his head, then he lit another cigarette, got two more brown paper packets from his pocket, and went through the same old routine. John pushed my drink in front of me and said, 'I see you're watching the professional gamblers, the idiots!'

'I've been watching Cigarette there,' I said. 'He's had the jackpot once and fed it all back in and now he's after another. Do you know how much is in those packets?'

'There's one-pound and five-pound envelopes, and the jackpot is only fifteen pounds. Take a look at the amount of empty envelopes around the machines and that will tell you who the only winner is. McGuinness, that's who.'

We drank and talked about our trip together on the *Strathmore* and the ships we had been on since then, the luxury of our present domicile, the World Cup – then he went to lunch, but I couldn't face food. The alcohol was food enough for me.

That evening I watched the pretty girls. Some were already there and others were just coming in. What lovely sights, mini skirts and low-cut upper garments. That's the way it should be in all the missions, I thought. I was on my second brandy when John came to join me. Just as I stood up to go to the bar for our drinks, two young women came along and asked if the other two seats were vacant. 'Yes,' I heard him say. I returned with the drinks and sat down beside John, opposite the girls.

'This is another John,' he said, 'an old mate of mine, we sailed together a few years ago.' Then he turned to me and said, 'I'm surrounded by the Irish. The girls are from over there.'

'Yes,' said the girl with brown hair, 'I'm from County Wicklow and my friend comes from Dublin.'

Her friend, Copper Head, never opened her mouth.

'Well, that's a coincidence,' I said. 'I was born in the County Home in Rathdrum in 1942, and a few days afterwards I walked out and that was the last I saw of the place.'

John gave me a discreet nudge, Copper Head gave me a curious look and Brown Head laughed and said, 'Get along outa that! You weren't born there, and anyway, how could you walk an' you only a baby?'

I took my ID card out and handed it to her, saying, 'Take a look at that.'

She looked at it closely and said, 'It says Rathdrun, here, that's not the same place at all.'

'It is the same place,' I said. 'An Englishman wrote it and got the spelling wrong.'

She looked at me and exclaimed, 'My God, it's true, it's a small world isn't it.'

John laughed and said, 'It's certainly that.' Copper Head gave a smile and remained silent, and I wondered if she could speak at all.

'The part about me walking out was a lie, I actually ran out,' I said. That got a laugh and I continued, 'Now, ladies, we didn't get your names.'

Brown Head said, 'I'm Mary,' and to her friend she said, 'Go on, tell them yours.'

In a quiet voice, Copper Head said 'I'm Caroline.'

We shook hands all round and John asked what they would like to drink. They both refused on the grounds that they had been out of the dance hall too long and they really had to get back in there, otherwise they might not be allowed to come again. However, they might have one with us later.

We had another couple of jars and talked about the girls.

'I like Caroline,' I said, 'she's only a few inches taller than me, her hair is beautiful, and that mini-dress does wonders for her legs.'

'Well, John boy,' he said, 'you know what they say – they're all the same size lying down, don't forget that. We won't be fighting over them, Mary's more my type.'

We went into the dance hall to see what was going on and we were not disappointed. The quartet was belting out a medley of good old Chuck Berry rock 'n' rollers and the place was jumping with dancers from all over the world. John and I could only talk in snatches, because the band was loud, but very good. I went to get another round in. I was on a high, without a care between me and the next drink. Manoeuvring my way back through the crowd to the table, I was delighted to see Mary and Caroline sitting with John. I eventually persuaded Mary to let me buy her a gin and orange, but Caroline would only have a fizzy orange.

We talked and joked for a while until the band started up with a waltz. John asked Mary to dance and off they went, and that gave me the chance to chat with Caroline. I felt a need to get her to talk, to bring her out of her shell and put her at her ease. I sensed that she hadn't been in England long and suspected that she was homesick. 'Have you been here before, Caroline?' I asked.

'No,' she said, 'this is my first time, and I think it's great. The band's very good aren't they?'

'Yes,' I said, 'very, and they're playing the kind of music I like.'

She went silent and I offered her a cigarette.

'No thanks,' she said, 'I don't smoke.'

Silence again.

'Have you been over here long?' I asked.

She gave me a serious look and said, 'I have been here for four weeks and one day and I'm just getting used to it. London is so much bigger than Dublin and everyone seems to be in such a hurry.'

We were interrupted by a good-looking smartly dressed young man who asked her to dance. She got up saying, 'See you later.'

When the set was over she came back, closely followed by Mary. John had gone to get another round of drinks in. Mary said, 'John's a great dancer. What about you, are you as good? John, I bet you are, I'll have to try you out for the next one.'

I went cold. I had promised myself that I would never dance again after my experience at the staff dance in the International Hotel, and no matter how drunk I got I had stuck to it. 'I've never danced,' I said. 'I don't know how to. I'm happy enough just watching and listening to the band.'

'You'd love it if you gave it a try,' she said, 'I know you would.'

Much to my relief, John returned with the drinks and plonked the tray down on the table, saying, 'It's the last set, shall we hit the floor?'

'Let's go man!' she replied gaily.

Caroline said, 'I don't feel like dancing any more tonight, John. Would you like to go out to the lounge?' I jumped at her suggestion and so we repaired to the lounge.

When we were settled, I asked her if she had any relations in London.

'No,' she replied, 'not that I know of anyway. I was brought up in a convent and I never had any visitors.'

'My first cousin Maureen was also brought up in a convent,' I said, 'and she never had any visitors. She told me that she often felt very lonesome when some of the other girls had visitors and no one ever visited her.'

She gave me her serious look and said, 'That's another coincidence tonight – Mary and you coming from the same county and your cousin and me brought up in convents.'

'Yes,' I said. 'The nuns got her a job when she reached sixteen and now, many years later, she is happily married with four children.'

'The Mother Superior got me a job as a domestic servant in a solicitor's big house on the outskirts of Dublin,' she said, 'and lucky for me a girl named Bridie was working there. She had been in the convent with me and she left six months before me to work for the Arseniks. The work was hard and Mrs Arsenik was the Divil's own slave driver. They were always having dinner parties and guests staying. Sometimes, we worked from six in the morning till late at night, without a thank you or a by your leave. No matter what hours we worked we were never paid more than one pound a week or even given an extra bit of time off. Bridie was a good friend. She showed me the way to do the work and she warned me about the ould fella, Mr Arsenik. She said he was a pervert, and I'd be well advised never to turn my back to him, for as sure as there was a God in heaven, if he got half a chance, he'd try to interfere with me.'

She went silent when we saw Mary and John coming over to join us. We learned that Mary was a staff nurse; she had been nursing for six years and they had become friends after Caroline moved into the nurses' home where she was living. I suspected that Mary had taken Caroline under her wing to protect her.

Shortly afterwards their transport arrived. We waved them goodbye and John said in a slurred voice, 'Nice girls them, I fancy that Mary.'

The next morning I awoke on the top of the bed fully dressed with a sore head and the shakes. I poured myself a generous measure of brandy and opened a barley wine and prepared to meet the day. I drank slowly, and when I started to feel a bit better I showered, dressed and went down to see what the day had to offer. I spotted John sitting alone in the restaurant, so I joined him.

'Well, good morning Mr Mahon,' he said.

'We're very formal this morning, Mr Spoke,' I replied.

'It must have something to do with the good weather we're having and the prospect of England winning the World Cup – and where I'm off to today,' he said. 'I'm going up to the West End to meet an old girlfriend, and if I get lucky you won't be seeing much of me.'

***

I went into a bar one morning for a brandy and heard someone at the end of the bar loudly saying, 'Over here, John Joe, come and join us.' I recognised him straight away. Colin, we had been drinking partners on the *Himalaya* in 1961.

I could easily say that I knew him, but that would be wrong from my point of view. I have never really known anybody, not even my mother, and sometimes I get quite irritated when I hear people saying 'I know him' or 'I know her' – when in fact they may be very close to a person and know a lot about them or even be intimate with them, but they can't know another's mind.

'It's good to see you again JJ,' said Colin. 'What're you having, are you still on the whisky?'

'No,' I said, 'it's brandy now, but I'll get my own, I only came in for the one.'

'Shut up,' he said and ordered a double for me and drinks for himself and his friends, then he introduced me to the others and said, 'We're here for the last knockings, we're sailing on a Blue Star job this afternoon and damn it, we'll miss the rest of the football. Still, that's life! Lately I've been thinking a lot about all the things I'm missing by going to sea. It's the same every time I pay off. I go on the piss and ship out again when the money's gone. I'm getting fed up with it, I might pack it in after this trip and get a job ashore.'

A couple of his shipmates agreed with him and the others joked and laughed –the main point being that he was going soft.

I had heard it all before, and there were times when I had similar thoughts – but only fleetingly.

***

I visited a few different pubs each morning and watched at least one game of football a day, and the rest of my time was spent at the bar in Anchor House, or in the ballroom when Mary and Caroline came in. I hadn't seen John Spoke for a few days and I assumed that he had indeed got lucky with his old flame.

On the evening before the final between England and West Germany, I was standing at the bar when John walked in looking just like a canary would after demolishing a cat. He mimicked, 'Ah, John Joe, 'tis you! What're you having?'

'The usual please,' I replied. 'I take it you've been successful?'

He gave me a broad grin and winked, saying, 'So much so that I'm moving in with her and I'm packing in the sea. I just came back for my gear and decided to see if you were in here.'

'Not for much longer,' I said, 'I'll have to get a job soon.' I raised my glass and wished him all the best for the future.

No sooner had he gone when in walked Caroline with the rest of the girls. She came straight over to me, and said, 'Oh, John, I'm glad you're here. Mary is off on a date with a fellow she met here, he's very nice. I came along with the girls and was a bit nervous about it because I don't know any of them as well as I know Mary, but I'm happy I came now.'

'I'm pleased to see you,' I said. 'What would you like to drink?'

She surprised me by asking for a glass of cider. I hoped she wouldn't be asked to dance too often so we could have more time together, and that's exactly how it turned out to begin with. Then a man asked her to dance and off they went. She came back when the set was over, took a swallow of cider and asked if I would like to dance.

'Caroline,' I said, 'I hope you don't mind, but I really can't dance. I'm very flattered you've asked me, but dancing is not for me.'

She looked into my eyes and said, 'I think I know what it is, you're shy. You've no need to be. I'm a bit shy about coming in here myself, but I'm getting used to it and I like the

297

company, especially yours.'

That sent a few quivers running through me. I thought of suggesting that maybe we could meet outside of the mission one evening, and then I remembered that the readies were running low and I had to ship out. She took another little sip of her cider and said, 'Remember when we first met I told you I didn't drink alcohol. Well, I had my first drink the other night. One of the girls had a birthday party and although I didn't want to break the pledge, the girls kept insisting. Mary gave me a cider. It tasted nice and after a while it made me feel good. I was happy and delighted with myself, and by the time I drank another half glass the room started to spin and I was as sick as a dog.'

'Is this the first one you've had since then?' I asked.

'Oh no,' she replied, 'I've had two since then and I haven't been sick or dizzy. In fact, I like it, because it makes me feel good and it gives me confidence.'

She took a less than dainty swallow of her drink and sighed happily, then said, 'Oh, it's good to be alive and well, John. I see sickness and sadness all around me in my job and it's grand to be away from it for a while. I know now, though, that nursing is for me. I get great pleasure in being able to do things for others. I'm going to study hard and get all the qualifications. Now, I'm going to get us a drink, brandy isn't it?'

'Yes please,' I said, 'and while you're getting the drinks I'll see if I can find two seats for us in the bar.'

I found two seats, and soon she came over with the drinks.

'I see you got the same seats as last time.'

'Yes,' I said, 'you were telling me about Bridie and working for the Arseniks.'

'I hope I didn't bore you that night,' she said. 'I was feeling very low and I needed to talk to someone.'

'You didn't bore me,' I said, 'I was interested.'

'Where did I leave off? Oh yes, I know, Bridie told me how she was making a bed one morning when old Arsenik crept up behind her and rubbed his body up against her, he was puffing and panting and grabbing at her breasts. She shook him off and told him she was going to tell the missis, and if that didn't do any good she'd go to the guards and the priest.'

'That must have put the wind up him,' I said. 'How old was he?'

'About sixty, I think. He looked very old,' she said.

'Did Bridie tell the old lady?'

'No,' she replied, 'he begged her not to and swore by almighty God that he'd never do anything like that again. He offered her a pound if she promised not to say a word about what had happened. Bridie told him to take a flying jump at himself and asked him what did he take her for, a bloody fool? Then he offered her five pounds to keep her silence and she took it, but warned him to keep away from her. She put the fear of God into him. She's nobody's fool and I love her like a sister.'

'Where is she now?' I asked.

'She's an usherette in a cinema and she lives in a women's hostel in Kilburn. We see each other at least once a week. She's grand, thank God. Anyway, "Ould Balls" as Bridie christened him left her alone after that. I was down on my knees scrubbing the floor one morning when all of a sudden he was behind me with his hand up my skirt.' She laughed and continued, 'It seems funny now, looking back, but it wasn't at the time. I was petrified, but somehow I managed to jump up out of his grasp and there he stood trembling, with a face as red as a turkey cock's. I screamed and he ran out of the kitchen. My legs were like jelly so I sat down, I knew the Mrs was away down the country, but Bridie was upstairs and she came running down when she heard me. She put her arms around me and said, "Don't tell me Ould Balls has interfered with you?" All I could do was nod. Words wouldn't come and I was trembling all over. Bridie took me upstairs and made me lie down. She covered me with a blanket and left, saying, "You leave this to me." After what seemed like a long time she returned with two cups of tea and then produced a wad of notes and told me that she had settled "that ould fella's hash" once and for all. He tried to bribe her with the offer of five pounds each to keep quiet but Bridie was having none of it. She told him that she wanted ten pounds each and one pound each wages for the week. Otherwise we were going back to the convent to tell the Mother Superior – and that frightened the life out of him. He agreed to pay the money if she swore to Holy God that we would never say a word to anyone. Anyway, he gave her the money after a lot of humming an' hawing and we got out of that hole fast.'

I could see McGuinness giving us the eye and half expected him to come over and ask her why she wasn't dancing. So I suggested that maybe we should return to the ballroom for a while. She looked at her watch and said, 'My God, I've been out here for over a half-hour. The priest will be after me if we don't go back in.' So back we went. She was asked to dance and I told her I was going back to the bar, and she said she would join me in about fifteen minutes.

She was as good as her word. The dance was nearly over and some of the girls were congregating in the bar. I thought that's good, McGuinness can cast his beady eyes all over the place and hopefully leave us out of it.

I asked her if she would like another drink.

'No thanks John,' she said, 'I've enjoyed what I've had and I'm feeling great.'

'You were telling me about leaving the Arseniks,' I said. 'Had you ever talked about leaving before then?'

'Oh yes,' she said, 'we were always talking about going to England. We had a stack of addresses and phone numbers for women's hostels in London. Before I knew it, Bridie had thrown our few things into two grips and we were sneaking out of the house. Once outside, we ran faster than if the devil himself was after us and as luck would happen, we jumped aboard a bus that was just leaving the stop and heading for town – and the next thing I knew we were in the B&I office booking our passage to London. We sailed from the North Wall Liverpool that night and caught the train to London the next morning. We were sick on the crossing and both of us wanted to die. But we soon got over that when we got on land and rest was fairly easy. We phoned a hostel in Kilburn and they had rooms to let. They gave us instructions on how to get there by the underground train, but we got lost and seemed to be going round in circles, which indeed we had been. We felt like a right pair of eejits. Anyway, we eventually found the place. I got a job the next day in Saint Mary's Hospital in Paddington and Bridie got the usherette's job and we haven't looked back since.'

'That's good,' I said. 'I might be shipping out next Monday.

I don't know where I'll be going or when I'll be coming back, but whenever I'm in London, even if I'm not staying here, I'll pop in to see if you're here.'

She looked at me and said, 'Dear John, the place won't be the same without you. I will miss you. I hope to see you soon again, but in the meantime I wish you every success and God bless and keep you.'

We remained silent for a while, and then the coaches arrived. I accompanied her to her coach, we hugged and kissed goodbye, and that was the last I ever saw of her.

I went straight to my room, and after a shower I got into bed and lay there thinking of Caroline's sad story. I took a big swallow of brandy and then tossed and turned for ages before sleep finally took over.

***

I awoke at eight the next morning with the shakes and feeling lower than a penny in a wishing well. I tried to work out why I was falling into these frequent depressions before my customary liveners of brandy and barley wine. I knew I had to eat more and cut down on the alcohol, but I needed the booze.

After a while, I got dressed and went down for coffee. I bought the paper and went into the restaurant where I found a small table in a corner and sat down. A young dark-haired waitress asked me if I wanted a full English breakfast?

'No thanks,' I said, 'just a pot of coffee please.'

When I was served, I topped the cup of coffee up with brandy in the usual way and tried to relax as I sipped the sweet nectar. After my second cup of the combination, I started to feel better.

That afternoon I watched the World Cup final on television. Anchor House was packed, because McGuinness had allowed some well-vetted outsiders in. Credit to him, he had a big television set rigged up in the ballroom and another one in the lounge bar in addition to the two that were in the television rooms. He had taken on extra bar staff for the day, and he must have made a fortune at the bar. Ever the businessman, that man of God! But I wasn't complaining, nor did I hear anyone else doing so.

The atmosphere was electric, with shouts of frustration

and delight interspersed with some good old-fashioned blasphemy. There was an air of togetherness and goodwill and it was a wonderful experience. When England finally won, I had never witnessed such joy and happiness. It was truly delightful. Joviality, camaraderie and generosity abounded. The celebrations got under way and I could see that it was going to be a marathon. I was invited to join several old shipmates, but I politely declined all offers and went up to my room. It was one of those days that I couldn't get drunk, and despite having enjoyed the game I was still feeling depressed. I had fifteen pounds left and I was booked in until Monday midday. So I had a roof over my head for just two more nights.

I opened a barley wine, poured a brandy and sat on the bed, drinking and thinking of what my next move was going to be. After a while, I decided I would see if there were any vacancies on the *Daffodil* first thing on Monday morning.

***

Monday came, and I had no problem getting my old job back. The first thing I did after signing on was to inquire about Paddy, but no one knew a thing about him.

It was 1 August 1966. I remember thinking, I'm going to change my ways, cut down on my drinking and save some money, I'm not going to be such a 'thick' any more. I had come to a stage in my life where I felt very insecure, and my self-confidence had got lost somewhere. I knew it was my need for alcohol that was the cause of most of my problems. But I was going to change that. My biggest worry was, where was I heading? I didn't want to end up like the drunken old boy I had seen on board the *Moon*.

The shipboard drinking friendships and the companionship of colleagues in bar-rooms was still fun, and although I very much liked to be alone I enjoyed the atmosphere in some of the bars, no matter where they were. Rough houses in rundown areas or the plush hostelries in the more affluent parts of town, it mattered not a jot to me. I was only there for the drink, and to listen to any bar-room philosopher that might be holding court.

The job went well for a month and then I had the urge to move on. I never touched a drop of alcohol during that month. It was hard to begin with, but I proved to myself that I could do it.

After leaving *Daffodil* I checked in at the QVSR and went on a bender for nine days, and then I had to pull myself together to get around to the Shipping Federation for a job.

I was given a job on a passenger/cargo ship called the *Merchant Prince*, subject to passing my medical. I was apprehensive about that, because every nerve in my body was tingling and I badly needed a drink, but that would have to wait. I walked upstairs and sat down to wait and see what was in store for me. Waiting to be called in for the medical took its toll on many a seaman's nerves, whatever the character of the man. I never saw a man sitting outside the doctor's that was not ill at ease. But I need not have worried. The young doctor smiled, looked down at his notes, asked me how I was, signed my form and that was that.

I joined the *Merchant Prince* next day in the West India Docks. She traded around the Mediterranean on five- and six-week trips and she carried twelve passengers. The work was easy for me and I liked the job, getting my hands on the cheap drink in the ports of call. I stayed on her for two voyages and then paid off in November 1966. Then after another heavy session ashore I joined three ships over the next few months and was sacked from each of them because of my drinking.

My self-confidence had deserted me totally and I was never more depressed. It was the booze and I knew it, but I never considered myself to be an alcoholic. Alcoholics were the people I saw drinking cider, cheap plonk, methylated spirits, surgical spirits and some cough mixtures. They were the real alcoholics. I was nowhere like them, I just enjoyed a good gargle, and what was the harm in that? Yes, I had to admit that I had been sacked because of my dependency on the stuff, but it helped me function. I was skating on thin ice as far as my future in the merchant navy went, so I would work hard at keeping it from interfering with my work.

***

I joined a cargo ship, the *Baron Maclay*, in Tilbury Docks in October 1967, and when I got aboard with my gear I sensed something strange about her. There were two men up on the fo'c'sle head, but no work was being done and she seemed to be dead. I made my way to the accommodation, dropped my bags on the deck outside the galley and went in search of the chief steward's office, I found it, but it was locked, and I thought, they've sent me to a ghost ship. I knocked on a couple of doors and tried the handles, but they were locked. I found the third one open, and called out, 'Anybody at home?' There was no answer so I walked into the darkened cabin, and the first thing that hit me was the stink of the place. I switched on the light, and saw dirty linen, old clothes, shoes, flip-flops, empty beer cases and cans all over the place.

I made a hasty retreat out to the alleyway and nearly collided with a dark-haired chap wearing thick horn-rimmed glasses. I don't know which of us was the more surprised. We looked at each other and he asked, 'Are you the new cook or the assistant steward?'

'I'm the assistant steward,' I replied. 'My name is John Mahon.'

He gave me a broad grin and said, 'Thank God you're here, John. My name is Tony Tarcus. I'm the only member of the catering crew aboard. I'm an assistant steward too. The cook disappeared after breakfast and I don't know if he'll be back to cook the tea. I haven't reported him to the captain, I just didn't know what to do, but it's only two hours to teatime. What can we do?'

'First,' I said, 'I want to put my gear in my cabin, then we can work something out between us.'

He gave me a shy downward glance, and I just knew he was going to tell me that the cabin we were standing outside was mine. I pointed to myself and nodded towards the dump I had stepped out of. He bobbed his head and said apologetically, 'Yes, I'm sorry, it's yours. You can leave your stuff in my cabin and I will help you clean yours.'

We put my gear in his clean and orderly cabin and then sat down. He asked if I would like a beer.

'Yes please,' I said, 'I rarely refuse a drink of alcohol.'

He smiled and said, 'I don't drink much, I'm saving up to get married to my girl at home in Malta, probably in two years' time.'

I was thinking, he seems like a nice fellow, but I was always wary of those who said that they didn't drink or they only took a drink to be sociable. In my own little world, I believed that there was nothing better than a good bellyful of liquid confusion.

We set about cleaning my cabin, and as we toiled away it was plain that we worked well together. I asked him how many officers and crew were on board.

'There's the old man, the chief officer, the chief and second engineers, three junior engineers, two deck officers and a deck cadet and that's the lot.'

'What about the deck and engine room crew?' I asked.

'They haven't joined yet. There's a few shore blokes aboard, but they don't need feeding, they go home.'

We discussed our predicament and went to see if the cook had prepared for tea. There were four tins of vegetable soup and two tins of peas on the galley bench and we found gammon slices and a big bag of chips in the handling room. We decided to go up to the old man, to put him in the picture.

'Will you please do the talking, John?' he said. 'I don't know what to say.'

Tony knocked on the skipper's door and a loud voice said, 'Come in.' We entered the day-room and there he stood, a tall, well-built man. Young, I thought, to be a skipper, but I noticed the flecks of grey in his dark curly hair and decided he was not as young as he looked.

'Yes gentlemen,' he said, 'what can I do for you?'

I handed him my discharge book and said, 'Captain, I arrived on board nearly two hours ago, I was expecting to report to the chief steward, but Mr Tarcus told me he hasn't arrived yet. The rest of the time has been taken up with cleaning my cabin, and I have to say it was left in a filthy state.'

He frowned and said, 'Sorry, I always ensure that when officers and crew sign off they leave their accommodation clean and tidy. I have only been here since yesterday and I haven't had the chance to get around yet.'

'We have a problem about this evening's tea,' I said. 'The cook doesn't seem to be aboard, but we have found tinned soup and peas, gammon steaks and chips.'

The skipper let out a wheeze and said, 'I didn't know that, it poses a problem. Let me see, how many of us are on board? Twelve in all, I think.'

'I can cook what's left out sir,' said Tony.

'Good man,' he said with a smile. 'Don't worry about the time. If it's later than usual they'll just have to wait.'

We took our leave of Captain Powers and headed back to the galley. Tony prepared the food and I wrote out the bill of fare. He told me when he was ready to dish up and I rang the meal bell. Then I stayed in the pantry to plate up the meals and Tony served them. We worked together as smoothly as a well-oiled engine, and I knew then that we were going to have a good working relationship.

When the meal was over, Captain Powers came to the pantry and thanked us. 'I have been on to the agent,' he said, 'and he assures me that another cook will be reporting tomorrow morning. However, he might not be here in time to cook breakfast. If that's the case, will you gentleman help me out again?'

Tony looked at me and said, 'We will, sir.'

'Thank you,' said the old man with a smile. 'The chief steward Mr Senetti will be joining us sometime later tomorrow. If customs officers and other officials come looking for him, please refer them to me. Goodnight and thank you both for a job very well done.'

I was up at six o'clock the next morning, and when I went to switch the kettle on I found it had boiled already. I made my coffee and was about to go to my cabin when Tony came in and said, 'Good morning, John, did you sleep well?'

'Yes,' I said, 'and good morning to you, Tony. Can I make you a tea or a coffee?'

'No thanks,' he said, 'I've got a full mug in my cabin.'

He brought it to my cabin so we could discuss what we were going to do. I poured a generous helping of whisky into my coffee and he stared in disbelief, sipping on his tea.

'Just a little fuel to keep the home fires burning,' I said.

'I couldn't do that,' he said, 'it would make me sick.'

'I need it,' I said, and then we got down to business.

'You are the senior in sea service,' he said, 'and I'd prefer it if you looked after the captain and I did the other officers' cabins.'

'No problem,' I said, 'but we're both equal in this job. You cook the breakfast, I'll serve it, then we'll have a short break. Then we'll go through the cabins together, including the old man's.'

306

I knocked on the captain's door at 7.30 with a tray of tea. When he saw me with the tray he smiled and said, 'A pleasant surprise. Good morning, Mr Mahon, I was about to put my kettle on. I have a busy day ahead of me, I'm going ashore with the agent this morning and to the Shipping Federation this afternoon.'

'I wasn't sure if you preferred tea or coffee so I took a chance on tea,' I said.

'Perfect, thank you,' he said.

I asked him if he would like to have breakfast in his cabin.

'No thank you,' he replied, 'I'll come down. What time will you be serving?'

'We will be ready to serve at 8.15. Mr Tarcus is preparing it now,' I said.

I took my leave and went to see how Tony was getting on. He was in his element. He clearly enjoyed cooking, and he was glowing with a big grin and eyes shining through his thick glasses. I told him what Captain Powers had said and he responded, 'I've only been at sea ten months, this is my third cargo ship, but he is the best captain I have ever met.'

'I've been at sea nearly seven years and I think so too,' I said.

We rang the bell for breakfast. The skipper and the other three senior officers came in, closely followed by the deck cadet and one junior engineer. We had the seniors fed in no time, they were no trouble, but the junior and the cadet took much longer, they filled their boots.

Tony then sat down to his own breakfast, and I went to my cabin to enjoy my fortified coffee and wait for him to join me. We washed up the breakfast things and laid up the tables for lunch, and then set about our duties together. I showed him a few short cuts in making the bunks and tidying the cabins and we went through the job like a dose of salts. Finally we had a blitz on the captain's accommodation, and when we finished I suggested that we should have a break for a cup of coffee.

Mr Senetti the chief steward arrived as we were having our break. 'My name is Albert,' he said, 'better known as Bert. How long have you men been on board?'

We brought him up to date, and I told him we urgently needed stores, fresh bread, milk, and so on.

'I'll get on to that as soon as I have seen the old man. Which one of you is the second steward?'

'We're both assistant stewards,' I said.

He nodded and said, 'This ship carries a second steward, one assistant steward and two catering boys. Are the boys on board?'

'No,' said Tony.

We excused ourselves and got on with our duties. Bert later told us he would be doing the cooking until we got another cook. Everything went smoothly, and two days later the crew joined. The deckhands and engine-room greasers were Somalis. I had never sailed with a full black crew before and I thought it might be interesting. During my time at sea I had sailed with some white bigots and I detested them for their ignorance. I don't mean to imply that all the Goanese and the other black men were all perfect. In fact, a small percentage of them were just as racist and bigoted as the aforementioned.

Whenever I got into conversation with any of them, or a religious nut, I listened and then made my own point of view clear. I didn't believe in any form of organised religion but that didn't mean I was without any morals. I believed there was room for all of us on this Earth, no matter what caste, colour or creed. I never gave a damn about the colour of a person's skin, the length of a fella's hair or the way he was dressed.

The day before signing on, Bert invited Tony and me to his cabin and offered us a can of lager each. Tony declined, but I didn't. 'Please sit down,' he said. 'As you know, we're signing on tomorrow morning and should be sailing for Australia on the tide. John, I would like you to sign on as second steward. It's a promotion and there will be a slight increase in your wages. Look after Captain Powers and help me out. You will work in the pantry serving up the meals, which Tony will serve in the saloon with the assistance of one of the catering boys. I plan to alternate their duties, week about. They're both first trippers from Scotland and they will be here this afternoon.'

'Thanks chief,' I said.

He looked at Tony and said, 'The old man speaks very highly of the two of you. The job should be easier for both of you from now on with the two catering boys to help out.'

He offered us another lager, Tony took one this time and the three of us drank to the future.

Angus and Ian, the two sixteen-year-old boys, joined us that afternoon. We signed on the next morning and were on our way to Australia with a general cargo in the late afternoon. The boys were sick for a few days, but by the time we reached the Suez Canal they were well and settling in nicely. The general cargo was discharged at various ports around the Australian coast and then she was loaded with a cargo of pig iron for Japan, and that started a series of runs between the two countries.

Early one morning on our passage across the Pacific, the radio operator got an SOS from a Japanese fishing factory ship. She was on fire, and the indications were that our ship was the nearest to her. The captain gave the order to change course and full speed ahead to get to her as fast as he could. He worked on the charts with the chief and second officers and they estimated that we should reach her at about ten o'clock that night. There was a buzz about the ship, and I think we were all excited in anticipation of the rendezvous.

News was coming down from the radio room through the day, and the last we heard was that twenty-four men had abandoned ship and were now in inflatable life rafts. In the meantime our old lady was giving her all, cutting through the glass-like sea sharper than a hot knife through butter.

Bert set about organising space for the men to sleep, just in case we had to take them to Japan. We didn't know what to expect, but Bert believed in being prepared. Cabins were made vacant by moving in with colleagues and sleeping on their day beds. We got the first-aid kits, blankets and the stretcher out in readiness. The cook made gallons of soup while Bert, Tony, myself, and the boys buttered mountains of bread and made sandwiches and when we were finished Bert shouted, 'Enough, let's go to my cabin for a drink.'

A plane flew overhead at 9.45 pm, the ship's engineers reduced speed, and about fifteen minutes later we saw the stricken vessel about three miles off the starboard side. She was glowing and the flames were shooting upwards and outwards. It was an eerie sight as I looked out over the dark ocean and then up to the starlit sky.

The engine stopped, a plane flew over and dropped a flare, and we spotted some of the life rafts in the water. I was thinking how terrible it must have been for the crew. A shout came from the bridge, a rocket with a line was fired towards the nearest life raft, and before we knew it ten survivors had scrambled up the rope ladders that had been fastened to the ship's rails. Jollity abounded, and the chorus of 'Arigato, arigato' accompanied with bowing from the waist seemed endless.

Bert asked in a loud voice if anyone could speak English. A young man in a ripped jacket and torn trousers said, 'I do, my name is Yoshi.'

'Thank you, my name is Bert. It doesn't seem like any of the men are injured.'

'No,' said Yoshi, 'maybe a few minor injuries.'

The plane flew over again and lit up the night. Eleven more men came alongside and climbed aboard. This time there were four men with cuts and bruises, and Bert led them below to patch them up. Tony escorted the rest of them down to the saloon and then there was a lull, so I went to see how Bert was doing. He was putting a bandage on the arm of a wizened old man.

'How many more have we aboard?' he asked.

'None when I came down,' I said. 'I looked into the saloon, and there doesn't seem to be anything wrong with their appetites.'

Back on deck, we could barely see the outline of the last raft heading our way. We heard that the plane dropping the flares was low on fuel and had to go back to base. Eventually, we could see the third life raft clearly as it came under the spotlights from the ship. The chief officer made two attempts at firing lines, without success, and it was ropes thrown from the deck that they grabbed to pull themselves alongside.

We counted five men and Bert said, 'We already have twenty-one on board now. Someone must have made a mistake, they said twenty-four in total, but with this five we'll have twenty-six.'

When they came aboard Yoshi pointed out the captain, a serious-faced little Japanese man. Two of the other four were Europeans, or at least that's what we thought until one of them said, 'Gee, guys, it's good to be aboard, great jawb!'

Americans. One of the two said, 'Hey, we need to get to the radio shack pronto.'

'Sure do, like yesterday man!' added the other. Tony took them up to meet the radio operator, and Bert took the captain and Yoshi up to meet our captain. The other survivors gathered in the saloon and waited politely for whatever was to come.

Tony came back, and I asked if he'd care to join me for a quick drink. He gave me a broad grin, nodded mischievously and said, 'Yes please John, I think I would like to try one of your coffee specials.'

He went to fetch the coffees, and as I sat waiting for him a guilty feeling came over me. I hoped I hadn't given him the impression that the gargle was the best thing in the world. I could testify to the fact that it had brought me more misery than pleasure over the years. Now here I was, serving on one the happiest ships I had been on, working in harmony with the best chief steward I had ever met, in a good state of health in body and mind. I still enjoyed the booze, but was drinking more moderately.

Tony came in with the two mugs and I noticed he had left plenty of space for the whisky to be added. I topped the coffee up with whisky and asked him if it was the first time he had tried that concoction, and all I got in reply was a mischievous grin with a shake of the head for good measure. We sat in silence for a few minutes sipping on the drinks, then he said, 'This is a nice drink, John. I think I might get to like it.'

'Not too much, I hope,' was all I could say.

Bert knocked on the door and came in. He explained that the two Americans were paramedics who had jumped from the plane with forty pounds of medical supplies and equipment strapped on their backs. 'Brave men, eh?'

Tony gave a whistle and I just nodded. I asked him if he would like a drink and he said no, he would have one later, after we got the survivors bedded down. That was the cue for us two to get up off our arses and help him.

A US Coast Guard cutter came alongside the next morning, and off went the paramedics. Our twenty-four Japanese guests stayed with us for a further five days, until we docked in Yawata. They were wonderful people, but the stink of fish was all over the ship and it stayed with us for weeks after.

In Japan a presentation was made to our old man by local dignitaries. More excitement! The presentation was a long-drawn-out affair with speeches and all sorts of artefacts being piled upon our skipper. A presento ... a speech ... another presento ... On and on it went, for well over an hour, and when it was over and they had gone the captain sent for our two boys and gave them some of the presents he had been given, much to their delight.

We sailed from Japan bound for Northern Australia to load a cargo of sugar for the UK. The holds had to be thoroughly cleaned and inspected before we were allowed to load and we were impatient to be away from the heat and the flies. Eventually she loaded and away we sailed.

***

We docked in Greenock on 5 March 1968. I paid off and spent my leave in the QVSR. I had stayed there several times before, and although alcohol was strictly forbidden there was a way around that. The thing to do was to ensure that the secretary/manager, Terry Simco, was out, then nip around to the off-licence, purchase a bottle of alcohol, tuck it down your trousers and walk back through the door as nonchalantly as if you had just been out to take the air. Another and safer way to get the booze in was to ask an old retired seaman to go out and get what you wanted. It cost a bit more that way because it was necessary to drop the old boy a few shillings. But, like most seamen, I never begrudged a copper of it. I liked the 'Vic'. It was clean and well run, and despite Terry's strictness over the booze he was a caring man who had our best interests at heart. I learned a lot about the man from the first time I stayed there and witnessed the hard work and long hours he put in to make the mission a good home over the years.

I flew out to Rotterdam to join a bulk carrier, the *Weaver*, and after serving five months with a rough crew I was glad to get off her. My next ship was a tanker, the *Ivy Leaf*, trading between the Isle of Grain and ports in the Mediterranean. I served on her as second steward for six weeks, and when she returned to the Isle of Grain I went up to London, got drunk, overslept and missed the ship, but thankfully they had left my gear in the office ashore.

The first move was to get a doctor's line to cover missing the ship. I was going through a bad period then. My need for alcohol was greater than ever, and there were times when my depression was so bad that I didn't care if I lived or died. I sat in my room in the 'Vic' and thought it all out over a glass of gin and tonic.

First I had to pick up my gear from the Isle of Grain and then I had to go before the disciplinary committee in the Shipping Federation, and all being well I would request three months' unpaid leave and get a job ashore. Maybe that was what I needed to straighten myself out. I didn't want to go to sea any more. What was the use of going away for however long the trip might be, coming back and doing the same old thing every time? Getting drunk and going around in a stupor until the money was nearly gone, and ship out again. Where was the future in that?

I went to the Admiral's Thumb the next evening to see if an old drinking partner could drive me down to collect my stuff. Don and his wife Dot were a couple of Eastenders I had become friendly with over the years, and I enjoyed their company. I found them sitting at the counter, and told them about missing my ship and my need to get my gear.

When I had finished, Don said, 'I'll drive you down there the day after tomorrow if that's any good to you.'

I was delighted. Problem solved. Then I told them I was going to take three months' unpaid leave and get a job ashore.

Dot said, 'We've got a spare room. Why don't you move in with us until you get yourself sorted out?'

I didn't need to think about it for long. I thanked her and said that would be great.

Two days later we picked up my gear and moved in with them. I went before the committee in the Shipping Federation a week later, and although I had a *voyage not completed* stamped in my book, I was free to ship out subject to a medical. I requested three months' unpaid leave, it was granted, and I was set to sample the shore way of life again.

Don was working on a big building project locally and suggested that I should ask the foreman for a job. I had often had drinks with a gang of building workers including the general foreman. Why not, I thought, who better to ask for a job? My only reservation was my height. It was a challenge. A week later, I asked the general if he could give me a job. There were sniggers from the drinkers around him. I pretended not to notice. He looked me up and down, rubbed his jaw and said, 'Yes Paddy, I'm looking for a chain man, you'll fit the bill, start next Monday at 7 am.'

I assembled with the rest of the gang and waited for my name to be called, and when it was the big gangerman pointed to a pile of wide shovels and said, 'Take one of them and follow them boys, they'll show you what to do.' He laughed sarcastically, and I said under my breath, 'Fuck you, I'll show you!'

I followed the gang of six men until they stopped at a truck with a huge pile of rubble alongside. They had a brief chat and then a few of them spat on their hands and all six proceeded to load the truck. I looked up at the side of the truck and knew that I just wouldn't be able to do the job. Nevertheless, I made a couple of attempts.

It was pitiful. The bits I managed to get onto the heavy shovel and hoisted in the direction of the interior of the truck hit the wheel and the side of the truck and fell back again, covering me in dirt. I was near to tears with the frustration of having to admit that I couldn't do the job. And the jibes poked at me didn't help either. I was ready to storm off when a big red-faced bruiser came over to me and said with an alcohol-fumed breath, 'Pay no mind to thim ignerent getts. Here, you take this broom and sweep up around the edges, ye'll be alright.'

That gave me a little consolation, but my pride was battered. I wished that I had taken my hip flask with me.

Later that morning, the general came down and asked me what I was doing in that gang.

'I don't know,' I said, 'but I've learned that I can't do this kind of a labouring job.'

'You weren't meant to be here at all,' he said. 'I told Magee to send you straight to the engineers.'

'It's obvious he was having a joke at my expense,' I said.

'Yes,' he said, 'and I'll get him back when he comes to me this afternoon for his usual sub. I'll tell him you had a sub and cleaned me out. Go up to the other end of the site, you'll see their hut.'

I walked about a mile and found one man poring over plans in the hut. I told him who I was and he said, 'Paddy, the other chain man, is in the next hut making the tea. You go in there and get yourself a cup.'

I thanked him and went in to the adjoining hut. Sure enough, there was Paddy, similar to me in stature. He gave me a look and asked, 'Are you the bloke that's going to be working with me?'

'Yes,' I said, 'what's the job like?'

'I'll tell you after I give that bloke his tea. He has me up the wall, making fuckin' tea.' He pushed a mug my way, saying, 'Help yourself, I'll be back in a few minutes.' And he was. 'This is an easy job, except for having to go out in the cold,' he said, 'but there's no hard work and that suits me.'

I weighed him up and took him to be around my age, mid-twenties. He was more muscular, but no taller than me. He had red hair, a badly twisted broken nose and a long scar on the right side of his face, which made it obvious that he had been in some scrapes. He spoke with a mixture of Dublin and London vernacular. 'Did anyone tell you about the job?' he asked.

'The general gave me a brief outline,' I said.

'The engineers will tellya what to do when you're out with them. Is this your first building job?' I nodded and he continued, 'Where was you working before this?'

'I was working at sea,' I replied.

'What kinda boats was you on?' he asked.

'All sorts,' I said, and that seemed to satisfy him.

I went out with Paddy and Darren, the engineer, twice in the afternoon to do some measuring up. All I had to do was carry some of the equipment. Paddy showed me how to set up and stand with a marker, wherever the engineer directed. We finished work at 4.30 pm. Paddy asked me where my digs were. I said, 'I'm staying with friends just off Preston's Road.'

'Mother-a-fuck! That's where I live,' he said.

As we walked towards the flats, I asked him if he was married.

Quick as a spark, he grabbed me by the arm, bringing me

to halt. 'What d'ya take me for? I'm no tick. I'm livin' with a bird that's good for the ride an' nuttin' else. She's hooked on the *Maree-dew-anna* and I don't mind that cos I like a blast meself an' I enjoy a fair sup too. Live an' let live, that's what I tink, an' fuck the begrudgers!'

Back at the flat, Dot made tea for me and her two daughters, Katy, aged five, and Maggie, three. I couldn't eat much and Dot scolded me. It was hard to explain that my whole body was in turmoil for the lack of alcohol, but I knew that if I was going to settle ashore it was necessary to control the need for drink. Nevertheless, after tea I couldn't wait to get out to the pub, but I felt obliged to stay for a while, not wanting to give Dot the impression that I only wanted to use the flat as a place to get my head down. We talked as I played with the children and she asked if I was going out.

'Yes, I think I'll go to the Thumb for a while,' I said.

'You'll probably see Don there. He usually works overtime and then has a couple of pints before he comes home for tea.'

I gave it five more minutes, kissed the girls and was off with my nerves jangling and my body going from tropical heat to arctic cold, but a couple of shots of liquid gold would settle that. As I entered the Admiral's Thumb, Don spotted me and beckoned me over to the table where he was sitting with three of his workmates. I didn't need to be told that they worked together or what they worked at. They looked as though they had been pulled through wet concrete and then put out to dry.

After he'd got the drinks in, Don asked, 'How did you get on?'

'Not bad,' I said, 'except Magee played a trick on me – and I can see the funny side now.'

'I know,' he said. 'I think everyone on the site knows. It was a set-up.'

I had to agree that it must have been hilarious to the onlookers, but they would never know how it had hurt or how I felt at the time. Now I could laugh with them and put it down to yet another experience, and it served to remind me of my limitations. We had two more drinks and they left. I stayed on for an hour and then went home feeling a bit better but with a deep need to be alone.

I spent about ten minutes with Dot and Don and then went

to my room. It wasn't long before I was tucked in between the sheets with my head on the pillows. I turned on the bedside light and read the *Evening Standard*, which was a luxury for me. A newspaper was one thing I missed when I was on a long haul. On passenger ships they used to have a daily newsletter, but no such luxury on tankers or cargo ships.

I was up at five the next morning and crept into the bathroom to shave and wash. I dressed and silently headed for the kitchen to put the kettle on, and when it had boiled I made a mug of instant coffee and returned to my room, where I poured a dollop of Teacher's whisky into it. I sipped the drink and decided to fill my hip flask to take with me in case of emergencies. I didn't want to go through the shakes and nervous tensions of the day before.

I heard movements just before six o'clock and went back to the kitchen, and there was Dot in her dressing gown putting the finishing touches to two mugs of something. I whispered good morning out of politeness, because I didn't believe that any mornings were good, especially if one had to go to work. She turned towards me and I caught the sight of her cleavage and a partly bared breast. I quickly averted my eyes in embarrassment. I could tell she sensed it as she tightened up the gown. I didn't know where to put my face, but she came to the rescue, slapping me on the shoulder and saying, 'Well mate, I hope your second day of working ashore is better than your first. Would you like a cooked breakfast?'

'No thanks, coffee and a shot of red-eye is all the breakfast I need,' I said.

'I'll make you some sandwiches,' she said, and off she went with the drinks.

I went back to my room with another coffee and left the whisky out this time. I couldn't get over the momentary glimpse of her breast and the thoughts it had given me. She was an attractive woman of thirty, standing about five feet five with natural fair hair. Nice-sized breasts, not too big, and the kind of legs I liked, sturdy. Not lark-like thin ones. I had learned from my first sexual experience in Japan that I had a healthy sexual appetite, and it became my ambition to have sex in as many countries as I could with the professional girls. There had been only two occasions that I could remember when I couldn't perform because of too much drink taken.

Still, here I was ashore now – and if I could only shake off my inferiority complex I might find a woman to share my life with. Getting rid of the complex and my need for the booze wouldn't be easy, but I was damn well determined to have a go at it.

Don and I left the house at 6.45 am and walked down the almost deserted street in the bitingly cold November morning. I parted company with him at the ganger's hut and went to the engineers. I reported in and Darren introduced me to his colleagues, Luke, Michael and Simon. Two of them gave me poor excuses for smiles and the third muttered, 'Nice to meet you.' Balls! I thought, if you characters are like some of the alleged engineers I've had to sail with I'll be on my guard.

I made teas and coffees, and Luke said, 'John, I want you to come out with me at ten o'clock this morning. I'll show you what we need to take with us.' He looked at the others and asked, 'Do any of you chaps need John before then?'

Darren looked up from his drawing, adjusted his spectacles and asked, 'Where is Paddy?'

'I don't think he was feeling well yesterday afternoon,' I lied.

'A likely story,' he snarled.

I went back to my own hut, thinking, I'll be wary of him. I sat there reading the newspaper and drinking coffee without whisky until Luke came in with the mugs and politely asked for refills. I set about my task and was ready to bring the drinks next door when Paddy strode in and asked, 'Was any of them fuckers asking where I was?'

'Yes,' I said, 'Darren. I told him you weren't too well yesterday afternoon.'

He scrutinised me through squinted eyes, shifted his head to one side and said, 'You're no tick, good man. I'll give them their slop, and they'll know I'm in, that'll keep the buggers 'appy.'

When he came back he was all chat, telling me about the great sex he had had with his girlfriend Sharon, and how they had smoked the weed and were high as kites when they got down to the business end of things. Then he went on and on about how much he loved her when things were going well, but emphasised with a pounding of his fist on the wooden bench what a bitch she could be at times. Once he had tired himself out, he asked me to tell him about the ships and what it was like at sea.

I started to tell him about working on the passenger ships and the different types of passengers, but that didn't seem to interest him in the least. I assumed that telling him of the deprivation and the many sorrowful sights I had seen wouldn't interest him, so I went on to the girlie bars in the Far East, and that's what got his ears pricked up. I told him a few spicy tales and he was hungry for more, but Luke interrupted us. He handed me a theodolite and a narrow yellow stick about six feet long with numbers on it, and a big tape measure, and I spent the next few hours working outside, first with Luke and then with Michael, setting up the instruments as they directed and holding the tape while they took measurements.

I went out with the engineers again three times that afternoon, and each time I learned more of what I had to do. It was all so easy for fifty to sixty pounds per week. Being able to go home to a comfortable flat with the happy family at the end of the working day was an added bonus. Still, I longed to have a place of my own, where I could come and go as I pleased, where I wouldn't feel uneasy and obligated. I was determined to learn all I could about the shore way of life and I saw the situation I was in as a step in the right direction.

That evening, Dot made me a mug of coffee and we sat down to chat. She asked if I had had a better day than yesterday.

'Definitely,' I said, 'except for the cold. I'm going to have to buy a couple of pairs of long johns, or short johns in my case.'

She laughed and said, 'I can get them for you in the market, and if they're too big I can alter them.'

Later, when I was sorting out my working clothes, the hip flask fell out of my jeans pocket and I realised that I had not taken one sip from it all through the day. Like the bloke who had put in his thumb and pulled out a plumb, I was elated. If only the rest of me would cooperate. But the nerves were having a great time giving me the jitters. I stayed in and went to bed early that night.

At the end of the first week I was disappointed to find that my wage packet contained just thirty-four pounds. The clerk explained that the reason so much tax had been taken out was that he hadn't got my P45. I didn't have a clue what he was talking about, but whatever it was I was going to get it sorted out. I had been paying tax for all the years I had been going to sea, and as far as I was concerned seamen should have been exempt from tax.

If I had two months ashore in a year I was fortunate. What was I paying income tax for? Was it for the privilege of being allowed to sign on a ship and commit to a legal form of self-imprisonment? It was different to being in jail, granted. But similar in some ways, three or four weeks at sea between ports on a tanker or an old cargo tramp ship with a bad boss, a rough crew or both was no picnic. Still, I supposed the coffers had to be kept topped up, and there was nothing I could do about it.

I stayed in the job for five weeks and spent Christmas with my friends before moving to a bedsit in Harlesden, north London. I had secured a job as a steward on the trains based at Paddington Station. The room was dingy and depressing, but it was good to be alone. The work on the trains came quite natural to me, but as the new man I was relieving other stewards on annual leave or through sickness. The hours were staggered and there were times when I didn't know whether it was yesterday or tomorrow. I got fed up with that after a few weeks and decided to go back to sea.

I went down to the Shipping Federation, had a medical, got on the books again and told the clerk I was ready to ship out in one week's time. What a joy that was. I had had my fill of life ashore. I went to the off-licence and bought a bottle of brandy. I got drunk that night and was at peace with the world.

The next day I sorted out my things and packed everything I owned in my two suitcases. I got a taxi to the station and boarded a train to take me in the direction of the people I was far happier with than the ones I had worked amongst ashore. In a way, I felt like I was going home.

I finally arrived at Aldgate East station, and I knew I was nearly home when I clapped eyes on Curry Murray, a cook from Scotland, and an engine-room greaser known as Dublin Danny having a heated debate on the pavement. They had both been at sea together years ago, but that was a thing of the past. Both had been bombed out, as the saying went, and they lived in hope of getting a 'pier-head jump' – that is to say, a ship might be ready to sail and be a man short so the word went round, 'Man wanted immediately for MV *Last Hope*.' And that's when the boys on the beach got their chance of going back to sea. As I approached them, Danny slurred, 'It's you, John Joe, coming back from foreign parts I suppose.'

'Yes, if you count north London as foreign parts,' I replied.

***

I flew over to Rotterdam and joined *Urshalim* on 15 February 1969, and the first person I saw was Francis, one of my old cabin mates on the *Himalaya*. He – or 'she' as he preferred to be referred to – looked unwell, with an obvious loss of weight and sunken cheeks.

Yet he still had the old sparkle in the eyes as he greeted me. 'Oh my dear John, how wonderful it is to see you. I have never forgotten you.'

He kissed my cheek and whisked me off to his cabin for a bevvy, as he put it. 'How long has it been?' he asked.

'Going on eight or nine years,' I said.

He poured two large whiskies, opened two cans of lager and said, 'Let's celebrate! It's a delight to see you again. You must tell me all about what you've been up to.'

I drank some whisky, with some beer as a chaser, and said, 'I better report to the chief steward.'

'Yes,' he said, 'get that over with.'

The chief was working at his desk as I knocked on his open door. He looked up and said, 'You're the new assistant steward?'

'Yes chief,' I said handing him my discharge book.

He flipped through the pages, nodded and said, 'Signing on tomorrow morning. Please report to the second steward and he will tell you what's to be done.'

I found the second steward in the pantry, a rotund, red-faced, balding character, and his first words were, 'Not very big, are we?'

I remained silent and made perfectly sure that he saw me staring at the way his hair was fixed to hide his baldness and then said, 'In stature no. You be careful not to get caught out in a gust of wind.'

'Get yourself settled in,' he said. 'I'll see you later.'

I went back to Francis and told him about my exchange with the second steward. He laughed heartily and said, 'Good for you, that *black market queen* spends ages trying to cover up her bald patch.' We had another drink and then moved my gear to my cabin. Francis had made the bunk and the cabin was clean and tidy.

I thanked him and said, 'I've got a bottle of Martell brandy in my case and it's leppin' to get out and be interfered with. We'll have a sup, will we?'

'Yes please, my dear,' he said. 'I'll get a few beers from my boudoir.'

He came back with six beers and I asked him how I could get a case of beer. Would I have to ask the second steward for it?

'Yes,' he said. 'Her name is James.'

'What do you think are my chances of getting one, after what I said?' I asked.

'Don't worry, she's got a thick skin – and given half a chance she'll try to worm her way in here and help you to drink it. She's a wardrobe drinker and as tight as a duck's arse, but she'll drink all she can get for nothing.'

There was a timid knock on the door and there stood James.

'I've just come to put you in the picture ...' He stopped when he saw Francis, and said, 'Oh, I see you two have met.'

'Yes,' said Francis, 'John and I were cabin mates on the *Himalaya* years ago.'

'Indeed!' he said. 'Well, you can tell him how we work on here. Must be off, I've more work to do before tea.'

I got the feeling Francis wanted to tell me something, so I went quiet, and after a short time she said, 'Remember Richard, my omie on the ship?'

'Yes,' I said. 'I could barely believe my eyes when I saw him getting out of your bunk for the first time. I was as green as grass then and had a lot to learn, and I'm still learning.'

'Aren't we all?' he said. 'You were just starting out, and it was rather naughty of us. We were used to the other boys in the cabin, they never complained, and selfishly, we were in love and never gave a thought to a young first tripper. I'm sorry, dear.'

322

'There's no need to be,' I said. 'You mentioned Richard, where did you go after the *Himalaya*?'

'Well, it's a long story,' he said. 'Richard and I got a flat in London and lived together for two years and then things started to go wrong. He had been divorced before we met and with the wonderful relationship we had I thought he had got women out of his system for good, but no, he left me for a woman, and that's what still hurts.' He gave a little laugh through his tears and said, 'I've been a free girl ever since and I'm enjoying it.'

Francis and I served tea together. The full complement of twelve officers and two cadets came in for their meal and it went without a hitch. Then, to my surprise, as the captain stood up to leave with the senior officers he looked across to the one cadet and two junior engineers still remaining and said, 'You won't be much longer gentlemen, I expect the stewards might like to get ashore for a while.'

What a considerate man, I thought.

'Did you hear what the old man said to the juniors?' I asked Francis.

He smiled and said, 'I'm glad you heard him. He really is an officer and a gentleman. It's a pity there's not more like him, but sadly he's only one of a very small minority.'

We cleared the tables and set up for breakfast, vacuumed the carpet, and that was the day's work done. Back in my cabin, I poured myself a drink and started to unpack, and when I opened the top drawer of the desk I found a bottle of whisky and six cans of lager with a note that read 'Welcome aboard John! Love Francis.' I felt very humble, and I was glad there wasn't anyone around to see my damp eyes.

I signed on the next morning and found that our crew was from all over the British Isles, and that was what I liked. It was always better to sail with a mixed crowd, because it cut out the cliquishness and usually made for a happier voyage. We sailed for Curaçao a few hours later and I was delighted.

It didn't take long for Francis and me to work out a routine that suited us and left no room for complaints. We worked well together, and by the time we reached Curaçao, with good shipmates and a happy ship, I was in my element.

I asked Francis if he was going ashore.

'No dear,' he said, 'I have a *marinero* in Venezuela to have fun with. What about you?'

'Yes,' I said, 'as soon as I can.'

'Happy Valley?' he asked with a raised eyebrow.

'Definitely,' I replied.

The Campo Legra was a very well-run brothel several miles inland from the capital of Willemstad and was known to seaman all over the world as Happy Valley, a paradise for seamen with money in their pockets. There were two big bars to cater to a fellow's thirst, and women of all ages to cater to his sexual needs. The females of all colours and sizes came from many places in the Caribbean and they lived and plied their trade in one-roomed little buildings for three months and then they were relieved by another batch of beauties. Rumour had it the place was owned and run indirectly by a major oil company, but we didn't care who ran it.

Francis convinced James that he could cover my duties, and I was off from midday through to the next morning. I enjoyed the scenery as the taxi sped along the ten miles or so to our destination and I felt better in my mind than I had for a long time. Eventually we arrived at the gate. I paid the driver off and I showed my ID card to the security guard at the control hut, then bought a packet of six condoms and headed for the bar.

The place hadn't changed since my last visit. The atmosphere was just as good and the price of a short time was still ten American dollars or the equivalent in other currencies. I met some old shipmates and some of the boys from my ship and downed a few rums before I went with the first of three girls between drinks. Just like the last time I was there, I noticed that all three girls had a crucifix on their walls with a collection of holy pictures surrounding it. And two of them had rosary beads hanging above the bed. Were they doing God's work?

The ship traded between Curaçao, Venezuela and ports in New York for the next three and a half months. I covered for Francis when he went ashore to enjoy the company of his *marineros* in the Venezuelan ports and we each took turns covering for James in New York and twice in Curaçao.

Francis always had something to say about James when he went ashore – 'That closet queen is off to have it away with her big black man again,' or 'She's so sly, that one!' James appeared to be effeminate but he never played it up like Francis, so whether he was gay I neither knew nor cared.

We loaded a cargo of bitumen for a number of Scandinavian ports and Dublin in the middle of June, and that gave me a buzz – it would be the first time for me to visit my home port on a vessel I was working on. We arrived in Dublin on 4 July 1969 after five happy months on a well-run ship. The captain and chief engineer were gentlemen through and through and the senior officers weren't far behind them. Francis and James signed off along with most of the crew and I re-signed to work in the engine room as a donkey-greaser, thanks to the chief engineer.

*****

I had tried to change departments through the Shipping Federation shortly after leaving the passenger ships but the response was always the same. 'Sorry, we can't change your rating. However, if you find a chief engineer willing to employ you in the engine room that will be acceptable.'

I had wanted out of the catering since starting to work on tankers and cargo ships. Looking after paying passengers was a pleasure, but having to put up with some of the ignorant so-called officers and snotty-nosed junior engineers and cadets was demeaning. Now the chief engineer told the shipping master and my union official that he was prepared to give me a job in the engine room. They agreed, and that was that.

It was a different ship on that trip. The majority of the new crew were a belligerent bunch. I found out later from the other three donkeymen that I should have had three years or more in the engine room as a cleaner or fireman/greaser before being considered for the job of donkey-greaser. Feck them, I was going to do my best.

One thing was certain. They were resentful of the fact that I was being paid the same wages as they were. I overheard one say, 'A piss-pot jerker to a donkey-greaser, this fuckin' game's finished.' I promised myself that I would have it out with that ignorant fecker when the time was right.

Unknown to them, I had spent at least ten hours in engine rooms learning about the boilers and the generators with friendly greasers just to get the hang of things in case I got the chance to change over, and I learned the golden rule from more than one:

'If in danger or in doubt, knock the fuckin' fires out!'

So I felt fairly confident when I asked the chief if he would give me a job in the engine room. I was aware of the intense heat, the smells and the noise. Although I had only experienced that side of the job for an hour or so at a time I knew what I was letting myself in for. I got over my first four-hour watch, being coached along by the third engineer, and although I was very nervous I was pleased with how it went. The second, third and fourth engineers taught me a lot on the way back to Curaçao, and old Joe, the most amenable of my three colleagues, took me under his wing.

I was slow to get the confidence I needed to do the job comfortably, but it came eventually – although I still hadn't lost my fear of the boilers. I asked Joe if I would ever lose that fear.

'That's not a bad thing son,' he said. 'You should always be watchful with them boilers.'

The more I got used to the job, the more pleased I was with myself for getting out of the catering department. I sat down to regular meals, and once my watch was over my time was my own unless I had to work overtime. I cut down on my drinking except for an occasional heavy session.

I was in control of myself, and once again I learned that I could enjoy a drink without the need to get drunk every time.

***

I signed on for another trip, and then went up to see the captain to wish him a happy retirement.

'Thank you son,' he said. 'The chief tells me you're doing a good job. I'm pleased to see you're staying on. I wish you every success.'

He stuck his hand out and we shook firmly. I took my leave of him with sadness in my heart and went to down a couple of large brandies.

We discharged our cargo over the next few days and then were on our way back to Curaçao with a new crew. I hoped they were going to be a better bunch than the last lot. It didn't take long to find out that they were, and once again *Urshalim* was a happy ship. We loaded another cargo of bitumen for the

Scandinavian ports and Dublin – and then on the homeward run I hit the bottle and before I knew it I was back to my old ways again.

I needed the fuel to keep me going, I told myself. I knew it was stupid to drink before going on watch, but I thought I could handle it, and that was my downfall.

Three days out of Dublin I fell asleep while on watch, and when the fourth engineer woke me up at 5 am I didn't know what had happened. He was a gentleman about it but he had to escort me out of the engine room, and as he did so he said, 'I'm sorry, John, you know I will have to enter this in the log, but I'll put in a good word for you.'

I sat in my cabin with a mug of coffee laced with brandy and tried to work out what had gone wrong. I thought that I had drunk just enough to keep me going and keep my wits about me, as I had done several times before. Where had I gone wrong? Drinking before going on watch, that's where. What a stupid bastard! I could be thrown out of the merchant navy for such a serious offence. But there was nothing I could do about it now. I would just have to take my medicine.

The chief engineer sent for me at 10 am, and I dreaded having to face him as I knocked on his door.

'Come in,' he said.

He was sitting on his day bed. Good, I thought, this might be a good omen, he's not sitting behind his desk.

'Sit down, Mr Mahon,' he said, indicating a chair by his desk. I sat gingerly and waited for him to speak.

'I have had a report from the fourth engineer,' he said, 'and having read the log entry on the incident this morning, there is no doubt that you were under the influence of alcohol or other substances. Please explain what happened.'

'Firstly,' I said, 'I want to apologise for my behaviour. I don't know what happened, I had a brandy and four beers before turning to and felt sober and well when I took the watch over. I did my usual duties and then sat down by the boilers and the next thing I knew the fourth engineer was shaking me.'

He shifted on his seat and said, 'You know how serious the offence is?' I nodded and he continued, 'It could mean the end of your seagoing career. I have given the captain my report and he will discuss the matter with the shipping master and your union representative. I'm putting you on day work until we get to Dublin, and then you will be paid off.'

I went about the job like a robot for the next few days and was glad when the vessel tied up alongside on 13 October 1969. I waited by the gangway until Barney, our union representative, came aboard, and after the handshakes and greetings I told him of the fix I was in. He scratched his head and said, 'A tricky one, John. I'll see the old man and the chief and do my best for you.'

'Thanks,' I said. 'I'll be in my cabin.'

I drank a glass of brandy and smoked one cigarette after another until Barney came to the cabin about a half-hour later. He grinned, parked his big frame on the day bed and said, 'It's not too bad.'

I asked if he would like a drink, poured us both doubles, and cracked two cans of beer open.

'The old man wanted to give you a double DR,' he said. Decline to report on conduct and ability, the worst discharge anyone could get.

I whistled, and he said, 'The chief engineer said he thought that was too harsh and suggested a *good* for ability and a *very good* for character, and then he went on to convince the old man that that would be punishment enough. I told him I knew you and I was sure you had learned your lesson, so that's it.'

We finished our drinks. I thanked Barney and he went about his business. I showered, dressed in my favourite suit, paid off and said goodbye to the chief. He wished me luck.

***

I flew back to London, I booked in to the QVSR, and spent the next week drinking with old acquaintances and all sorts of oddballs. I enjoyed moving in those circles from time to time. It was fun, a challenge not to be taken for a sucker

My disciplinary hearing wasn't as bad as I had expected. In fact I got away with a caution. It was decided that I should have more experience in the engine room as a fireman for at least one year before aspiring to the dizzy heights of donkey-greaser. I passed my medical, had two inoculations and was ready to ship out.

A week later I signed on the *Apple Blossom*, a tanker, as a fireman. She was a dirty old rust bucket that I disliked from the start. Thankfully, the trip only lasted six weeks and I was off.

Next I signed on another tanker, a steam ship, the *Star*, as a fireman/greaser, and I loved the job, especially when we were manoeuvring in and out of ports. On such occasions an engineer took command and shouted out orders to me as the telegraph dictated. Slow ahead ... Knock so and so burners off. Half ahead ... Put so and so on ... And so the orders went until we were alongside or on our way. I always got tremendous satisfaction out of that part of the job.

I paid off the *Star* in July 1970, booked in to Anchor House and set about having a good time with a couple of hundred pounds at my disposal and plenty of time to do as I pleased. I was on top of the world.

I was sitting at the bar one evening when I got into conversation with a Scotsman, Bob Mackenzie. We talked about all sorts including Anchor House and McGuinness, and Bob pointed out how the shrewd man of God had surrounded himself with the good Catholic Irish on the staff, especially those handling money. They were the 'Hail Mary, full of grace' brigade and they would never dare rob the priest.

By comparison, my favourite abode in London was the QVSR, a Methodist mission. It didn't have the dancing, or a bar, but in my opinion it was run with true Christian sincerity for the welfare of seamen and was more like a real home to me. The secretary/manager, Terry Simco, went out of his way to help seamen with all sorts of problems and nothing was too much trouble for him. All the staff were very good people too, and when they got to know you it wasn't unusual for them to offer you a little help if they thought you were having trouble getting a ship.

I have seen Iris and Sylvia, two of the women working in the cafeteria, putting their hands in their purses and paying for more than a few seamen's meals. The cleaning women in the accommodation were just as kind – Joan, Peggy, Lily and Maureen, to name a few. None of those women ever needed an armoured car to bring their wages home, and yet they thought of me, and others too.

I met Bob several times after that and found him a great stabilising influence. But before long he shipped out and I got a job with a tanker company. Before I could join a ship I had to go on a couple of courses, to learn how to take charge of a lifeboat, and to learn the basics of deck work on a tanker. It was all to do with joining one of the 'general purpose ships', which was really a scheme thought up to cut down on crew. Deckhands were taught about the greaser's job and vice versa, and the catering crew were taught how to help out on deck, chipping and painting and other tasks. Theoretically, this meant that we could cover each other's jobs. It obviously looked good enough on paper, because a number of shipping companies were introducing it. We were paid an extra few pounds per month for doing this, at the expense of the loss of two or three crew members.

I joined the *Esso Pembrokeshire* on 23 November 1970, as a GP1. It was different to any other ship I had ever been on. The tables in the mess room were laid up just like those in the officer's saloon. The food was excellent, not that I cared much for that, but best of all there was a bar open twenty-four hours a day, where you could help yourself and leave the money. I enjoyed being able to have a drink when I wanted without restrictions, and strangely I drank less on that ship.

I had a pleasant surprise one evening when Dave, a deckhand, came to my cabin with six cans of beer and asked if he could come in. 'John,' he said over a beer, 'like yourself, I'm not a company man and I've no intention of becoming one, no matter what they offer in the way of benefits. There's no real advantages as far as I can see. They can keep their GP.'

'I'm not in favour of it either,' I said. 'There are some little things I do like, but not enough to make me want to stay with the company.'

'That's why I thought I'd come to see you,' he said. 'It's my turn to work in the engine room for a week from tomorrow morning. I asked the bosun if there was any way I could get out of it. He had a word with the mate and was told that if the fireman/operator was willing to cover my duty that would be all right. Are you interested?'

'I'm your man,' I said. 'I can't stand working on deck, so it suits both of us.'

He gave a sigh of relief and I breathed easier too. I said, 'There's one favour I need from you Dave. Can you arrange for me to work with you when we're on stations? Them hawsers and ropes frighten the life out of me.'

We covered each other after that, but I still had to work on deck on arrival and departure. And no matter how much Dave and the other deckhands tried to boost my confidence it was no use, I was too nervous. It did one thing for me, though – I never had a drink for at least four hours before tying up or letting go. I had to keep sharp.

***

I paid off after four months and booked in to QVSR. Bob was staying in Anchor House, and we discussed and debated all sorts of things from general-purpose ships to world affairs, religion and rude old folks, who criticised the youngsters and behaved twice as bad themselves.

I shipped out on a chemical tanker, the *Stolt Abadesa*, and paid off in Rotterdam six months later. I joined another tanker, the *Hadra*, in Rotterdam in September 1971 and sailed for Curaçao. After a few days out I was on deck when the messman came creeping along at a snail's pace with his legs wide apart.

'What's wrong with you?' I asked. 'Were you riding a nag in the rodeo?'

'I don't think that'd be as painful,' he said. 'I cleaned the toilet, then put some bleach down the bowl, went off and left it, and when I went back to use it I forgot to flush it first. I sat down to get on with the business and no sooner had I sat down, but didn't this ould bitch give a roll and water splashed me arse and balls with a terrible gush.'

'Go and see the chief steward,' I said. 'He'll have some camomile lotion.'

I went back to my cabin, and within ten minutes the messman knocked on my door with six cold cans in his hand. 'I hope you don't mind,' he said, 'I've got Lenny, the assistant steward with me.'

He stuck out his hand and said, 'I'm Joe Downes from Dublin. Lenny told me you're known as JJ. Am I right?'

'Yes, by some,' I said. 'It's short for John Joe. I come from the village of Enniskerry, have you ever been there?'

'Indeed an' I have. I know it well,' he said.

Lenny offered me his hand, we shook and he said, 'Hello my dear, I've seen you about for years and I know more about you than you might think. One of my friends told me about the trip you did together and how you used to cover for her when she went ashore to see her *marineros* in Venezuela.'

'Francis Haggard,' I said. 'How is she? Have you seen her recently?'

'I had a drink with her the day before I joined this one,' he said. 'She's not very well now, stomach trouble, she doesn't like talking about it, I think it's cancer.'

I was saddened to hear that, and to change the subject I turned to Joe, who was standing uncomfortably by the desk and asked, 'Poor ol' Joe, is your bum still sore?'

He blushed and stammered, but not a word came out. Lenny made up for him, saying, 'I've tried to convince him that the best thing to do is to let me apply the cream and massage the pain away, but he won't see sense.'

Joe found his voice and said, 'I'll be fucked if I let you do that Lenny.'

'No dear,' replied Lenny, 'I'm not like that.'

I could tell that Joe was uncomfortable and embarrassed, and I suspected he hadn't been at sea very long.

Lenny was in his fifties, with sparse dark hair plastered over his head with oil, and he must have been somewhere else when they were handing out good looks. I had seen him many times over the years in the missions and in the bars frequented by seamen. Unlike some of the other queens, he preferred to use his butch name, and from what I had seen of him he always seemed to be enjoying life. Joe was in his early twenties, a good-looking man with a mop of curly brown hair.

The three of us became drinking pals. One evening Joe came to my cabin with a bottle of whisky tucked down in his jeans and said in a whisper, 'It's my birthday today. I bribed a junior engineer to get me a case of beer and the bottle.'

'Happy birthday,' I said. 'It's customary on most ships to be able to buy a case of beer on your birthday, and at the same time there's no harm in asking for a bottle of whisky or rum to go with it.'

'I'll ask the chief steward just as soon as we've christened this bottle,' he said. He poured out two large whiskies and I opened two cans of lager.

Lenny knocked on my door and came in. 'Boys! What's this, a party?'

'Yes,' said Joe, 'I'm twenty-one today.'

Lenny responded, 'Delighted I'm sure. Happy birthday, young man, that's a good reason for you to let me feel your tackle and give you a blow job.'

Joe turned purple with embarrassment and said in a croaky voice, 'In your dreams mate. I'm off for a case of beer and my chances for a bottle.'

When he had gone, Lenny said, 'He's a nice lad. I like to tease him. I know he's a man for the women, but he still has that Irish innocence about him, and probably still says his prayers. He's nobody's fool, though.'

Joe came back with a case of lager and a bottle of rum. He told us how the chief steward had sent him to the captain to get his permission for the issue of the beer, and the old man was so nice that it gave him the courage to ask for a bottle too.

'That's what annoys me,' said Lenny. 'There was no need for you to see the skipper at all. That chief was afraid to use his own discretion for one of his own team. You've never had any complaints on how you've run your messroom or any of your other duties, have you Joe?' Joe shook his head and Lenny went on, 'Snotty-nosed junior engineers can get a bottle and a case of beer without any bother. Only a few months ago they were boiling billy cans in shitty shipyards and now they're officers with a gold braid ring to prove it. Bullshit!'

I put a Willie Nelson cassette on and the party began. We drank ourselves silly, and I woke up at five o'clock the next morning to see Joe sprawled out on the deck with a beer can held tightly in his grasp. I opened a can of Heineken and drank half of it before waking him.

'Is there any of that whisky left?' he asked. 'I need a stiff one.'

'Don't let Lenny hear you saying that,' I said.

We arrived in Curaçao a few days later, and started trading between there and ports in New York for a couple of months. Joe and I visited Happy Valley twice, and then we received orders for Cardiff. The *Hadra* was due for dry dock.

I was on boiler duty as we manoeuvred our way alongside the oil berth. We were tied up at 9.30 pm and I was down the gangway with Joe at 9.50 pm to get a few jars in before closing time. We caught a taxi in to town and managed to get three pints and three whiskies before closing time.

Joe asked me if I was going home to Ireland.

'It's not my home,' I said. 'I never had a home there after my mother died in 1954.'

'Well, you know what I mean, you're Irish,' he said.'

'Yes,' I said, 'I was born there, but like countless others I had to leave Ireland to get work and earn a decent living and I've been treated far better by the English than I ever was by the Irish – so no, I won't be going home.'

'Jesus, you sound bitter,' he said.

***

I flew out to Canada in November 1971 to join the *La Pampa*, a bulk carrier in Prince Rupert as a greaser/cleaner. She ran from there to Japan, the USA and various ports in Europe, where I had the opportunity to pay off – but she was a happy ship and I liked my job so I signed on again and eventually paid off in Cardiff in April 1972.

I went on a bender for two weeks in London, and towards the end of it I was a wreck. There was nothing for it but to get some control over myself, and the best way to do that was to ship out. I eased down on the drink for a couple of days and then went to the company's office in Leadenhall Street to see if they would give me a job.

I joined the *La Sierra* in Gijon, Spain. I served six happy months on board her and then it was bender time again. Then, in October 1972, I flew out to join a tanker, the *Bolelix*, in Bandar Mashur, Iran, and it didn't take me long to find out that she wasn't going to be the best of ships, mainly because of the number of company-contract ratings, roughly a third of the crew. They were a clique and looked upon us men from the Federation as lesser beings. They boasted about having job security with the company, and I got the impression some of them were married to the company.

I always likened ships to small villages, where some

people thought they knew everybody's business – and what they didn't know they surmised and gossiped about anyway. The *Bolelix* was very much like that. They were continually backbiting other company men they had sailed with and very seldom were there any nice things to be heard. I gave them as wide a berth as I could and looked forward to the day I paid off.

We sailed with a cargo for Singapore and traded around the Pacific for a while, then the captain got orders to load a cargo in Singapore for Honolulu. Nothing out of the ordinary, but on the second day out from Singapore he called us together and informed us that we were bound for Nha Trang in South Vietnam with the cargo.

He briefed us on all the precautions that had to be taken and emphasised how important it was to be ever-vigilant. He went on to explain that the ship would be at anchor off the shore and would discharge the cargo by pipeline from early light to dusk. The line would then be disconnected and the vessel would go on manoeuvres until the next morning, when discharging would begin again.

He detailed a body of men (myself included) to be on what was laughingly called Bubble Watch. But it was no laughing matter. Bubbles around the ship could mean that somebody was sticking a mine to her hull.

He couldn't tell us how long we were to be in Nha Trang and he apologised for not being able to tell us before then because he hadn't been told himself. If he had known in advance he could have given us the option of signing off if we didn't want to go into the war zone.

I felt trapped. I did not agree with the war, and I saw myself as an unwilling participant in supplying what I had been informed was aviation spirit. I had no wish to contribute to the suffering and misery of the Vietnamese people, but I had signed the articles of agreement and had no choice.

A few days later we arrived off Nha Trang, and not long after we had dropped anchor amidst a variety of craft a boatload of officials came on board, including two American officers with enough gold braid on their caps and the sleeves of their coats to dazzle the sunshine. The pipelines were connected, and a couple of hours later the discharging began. It was very hot although the sky was grey and it was eerily quiet throughout the day except for the noise of the helicopters hovering above.

As the skipper had said, discharging ceased an hour before sunset and the vessel cruised around until dawn. We heard plenty of booms, bangs, and crashes through the night and again the next night, but for the rest of our five days' stay it was quiet. Then we moved to Da Nang, where the discharging routine was the same.

We had been there a week when, with the help of oil spilled on a companionway and a sup of the liquid confusion, I slipped and fell, twisting my ankle beneath me. It went up like a balloon and the pain was hard to bear.

One of the deckhands picked me up and carried me to my cabin and then went to get the chief steward, Foodwangler. Five minutes later, the wizened-faced Foodwangler arrived with his first-aid kit. He bound my ankle with an elastic bandage and gave me some painkillers, warning me not to drink alcohol with them. 'Take one every three hours. You can take the first one now.'

I did so, and as soon as he was out the door I spat the pill out from under my tongue. Whisky was the best pain killer for me. I drank three or four glasses, and the next thing I knew it was morning and Foodwangler was standing in my cabin asking me how I felt.

'I don't know yet,' I said as I put my good foot on the deck, followed by my injured foot. But when I tried to put my weight on it the pain seemed worse than before. He made to move towards me, but I waved him off and hopped over to the sink to wash my mouth out and get rid of the whisky fumes. 'Please excuse me,' I said, 'those tablets have given me a terrible taste in my mouth.'

He watched me as I brushed and gargled, and when I had finished I said, 'Powerful tablets them. Shortly after I took the second one I was out of it.'

He gave a hint of a grin and said, 'Yes, that's why you must not drink alcohol when you're on them. I have given the captain my report and he thinks you should see a doctor. However, that depends on whether it's possible. He will ask the company representative this morning, and in the meantime we'll keep on with the pills.'

The day dragged on into night, and if it had not have been

336

for Dr Whisky I doubt that I would have slept much that night. I was up before dawn the next morning, and at seven o'clock Foodwangler came to see me with the news that the captain had arranged for me to be taken ashore to see a doctor.

I was delighted. There was no shore leave, yet here I was getting the chance to see a bit of what the war-torn country looked like. Fear was nowhere to be found and although it was as eerie as it had been in Nha Trang, especially at night, it was an experience. Not one that I got any pleasure out of – in fact, I was totally against what was going on, but there was nothing I could do about it.

I boarded the boat in the bay beneath the green cloud-covered hills and sped the four miles or so to a sandy beach with spent cartridges and shells lying all over. Seeing them gave me the shivers as I thought of what might have happened there. I hobbled along with difficulty to meet the only other person on the beach, a dapper little man coming towards me whom I took to be the man who was going to take me to the doctor.

He stuck out his hand and said, 'Mr John Mahon?'

I was impressed with how he pronounced my name correctly. I shook his hand and said, 'That's me.'

'My name is Zang,' he said. 'I work for your oil company.'

I offered him a cigarette, we lit up, and he said, 'I have orders to drive you to Mr Preston's house – he is the boss of the company in this country – but we have enough time for me to drive you around and show you some of Da Nang City.'

We got into his little black car and it didn't take long before we reached the centre of Da Nang.

At a table outside a little café, he asked what I would like to drink.

'A beer please,' I said.

'American, Australian, Japanese or European?' he asked.

'I'll try an American,' I said.

The waiter came and placed two plates in front of us with little hot towels. Mr Zang ordered and then we wiped our faces and hands. The waiter placed a glass and a can of Budweiser in front of me and a cup of coffee in front of Mr Zang. I handed the waiter a five-dollar bill and he was back with my change in a flash. 'Thank you,' said my new-found friend, as he took a sip of coffee.

I sat there mesmerised by the pace of the place. Whizzing by were army vehicles of all sorts, cars, trucks, motorcycles, mopeds and countless bicycles, many of them ridden by young women in white dresses in the oriental style, most of whom were wearing the traditional conical hats. In addition there were men and women laden down with woven leaf baskets at each end of a pole draped across their shoulders. Human mules! I asked Mr Zang why so many girls were dressed the same and he told me they were students. I had never seen so many young women dressed the same, nor had I seen so many limbless young men. The rest of the masses were made up of Vietnamese people going about their business, American and Vietnamese soldiers plus a fair representation of people from all over the world.

Mr Zang asked me what it was like working on ships, and what country I came from. I told him a little about life at sea and where I came from. I wanted to know if he was in favour of the war or not, but he never gave any indication that he wanted to talk about it so I put it out of my head.

He drove around, giving me a tourist's view of the place, and I felt very privileged. We had another coffee and a beer before we went to Mr Preston's house.

We arrived at a big house, which I suspected was built by the Americans for the Americans. Mr Zang rang the bell and a mature Vietnamese woman dressed in black opened the door. They spoke briefly and Mr Zang said, 'I will wait for you, Mr Mahon.'

The maid beckoned me to follow her and I found myself in an air-conditioned room that was too cold for me. My foot was throbbing and I was standing on my good foot when a well-built man with ginger hair came in with a broad smile on his face and said, 'I'm John Preston, Mr Mahon. Are you in much pain?'

'Quite a bit now, I said, but I'm sure I'm on the mend, the swelling has gone down quite a lot since yesterday.'

'I hope they will be able to do something for you at the medical centre,' he said.

It was only a short drive to the medical centre, and Mr Zang checked me in at the reception. He handed me an appointment card and said they would try to attend to me that afternoon, but I might have to return tomorrow. He left me there and said he'd be back at four o'clock. I looked at the yellow card he had given me. It read, *Deutsch-Vietnamesisches-Malteser Hospital, Danang-Vietnam*, and under that was printed *Mahon Josepg-25048*.

I sat there trying not to look at the unfortunate people of all ages. The walking wounded, with head bandages, on crutches, the armless, the legless in wheelchairs and others on stretchers. I felt like a fraud among those dignified people, and I was ashamed to be there with my minor injury.

When Mr Zang came back he spoke to the reception and established that they couldn't see me that afternoon and wanted me back the following morning. He made a phone call and then drove me back to the beach, where there was a boat waiting for me.

I went ashore the next morning with a deep feeling of guilt because my ankle wasn't hurting. I could put my full weight on my foot and only get a twinge of pain. Still, the old man wanted me to be seen by a doctor and that was that. After several more hours in the waiting room I was eventually examined by a doctor and my foot and ankle were x-rayed. A nurse spoke to me in her native tongue with a smattering of garbled English – and from what I could gather I was nowhere near death's door. Mr Zang confirmed this as we left the centre. 'You have a badly sprained ankle,' he said. 'There is nothing to worry about. However, you must rest until you feel that you can put your full weight on your foot.'

By now the ship was on its nightly manoeuvres, so it was arranged that I should stay the night in the Hotel Modern. I booked in at the company's expense and Mr Zang accompanied me to my room to make sure everything was to my satisfaction. I suggested we should go down to the bar for a drink and maybe he would like to have dinner with me, and soon we were drinking Schlitz beer. I picked up a menu and handed it to him. He gave me a look, which I took to mean, who's going to pay? You can't charge that to the company. I ordered two more beers and said, 'It would give me pleasure to buy you dinner. Naturally I will pay for it, I wouldn't expect the company to pay for my pleasure.'

We chatted about lots of things during the meal except the

war, and towards the end he asked if I would like a young woman to share the night with. Would I? Yes! I asked him how much that would cost. 'Twenty-five dollars,' he said instantly.

I had a forty-dollar sub that Mr Preston had advanced me, and twenty more. Plenty to pay for his meal, the girl and a good jar too. I was flying without leaving the ground.

He excused himself and was back in ten minutes with the news that a girl would join me in the bar within the hour. We shook hands and off he went. I was on my second brandy when a stunningly beautiful young woman with shoulder-length black hair and dark sparkling eyes stood before me and asked, 'Are you Mr Onn Maan?'

'Yes,' I said, standing up.

'Would you like to sit down please?' She sat and said, 'My name is Tammy. It is not my real name, but it is easy for people to say and I like it. Do you like it Onn?'

'Yes,' I lied, putting my hand out. She shook it and held on to it as I said, 'I'm very pleased to meet you Tammy. Can I get you a drink?'

I ordered an orange juice for her and a beer for myself. No more brandy for me tonight. I sat looking at her dressed in a tight black dress and thought how fortunate I was to be with her. We engaged in a bit of chatter for a while and then went up to my room, leaving our drinks unfinished.

It was truly a night to remember, with the sounds of the war in the distance for background music. I gave Tammy thirty dollars. We kissed and I said goodbye to her with a heavy heart, knowing I would never see her again.

Mr Zang came at 9 am to take me back to the boat and asked, with a smirk on his face and a conspiratorial glint in the eye, how I had enjoyed myself. We walked along the beach and said our goodbyes. I stepped in to the boat and watched as he walked to his car.

Back on board the *Bolelix* I was bombarded with questions, which I tried to answer as honestly as I could, except for 'Did you get a fuck?'

'No,' I lied, 'but I had the best of food and enough booze to sink the *Queen Lizzie*.'

'Lucky bastard' ... 'Jammy cunt' ... 'Steeped in it, he is.' They were just some of the comments made.

I took a final look at the lights ashore and went below to my cabin. Just as I sat down there was a knock on the door. It was Foodwangler. 'The old man wants you on light duties from noon till 3 pm tomorrow,' he said. 'You are to station yourself at the after end on bubble watch.'

I did that for a couple of days and then went back on normal duties, and a few days later we finished discharging and it was orders for Singapore, from where we delivered several cargoes to ports in the Far East – and finally we got the news that we were to pay off in Singapore on 26 April 1973, after serving six months and twelve days. To cap it off, we were to spend four days in a hotel in Singapore to await another ship's crew to join us on a charter flight to London.

That flight home was the best I had ever experienced. There was free alcohol and plenty of it. We couldn't believe it at first. Had somebody made a mistake? Two ships' crews, free booze. Some people might think that was a recipe for disaster, but not so. Apart from loud voices, friendly arguments, joking, a few fellows falling about, and snatches of songs, there wasn't any serious trouble from take-off to touch-down, and even the cabin crew seemed to enjoy themselves.

I met Bob Mackenzie a few days after I arrived in London and spent a few days drinking with him, and no sooner had he shipped out when along came my other old pal, Joe Downes, and we nearly drowned in alcohol for the following two weeks before he went to spend the rest of his leave in Ireland.

***

I sailed on a variety of ships for the remainder of the 1970s, including bulk carriers and container ships. I was well aware that my drinking had become a problem, but as far as I was concerned I was just a bloke who enjoyed a good drink. Never mind the shakes, blackouts and remorse. It was all a part of what a drinking man had to go through. I wasn't an alcoholic. If I put my mind to it I could stop anytime I wanted to, I told myself.

One ship, the *Posterior*, was a foreign-owned ship under the British flag, and I remember thinking, is this the beginning of the Red Duster becoming a flag of convenience?

Like the rust buckets under the Greek, Panamanian and Liberian flags, to name but a few. They didn't have to keep to the rules and regulations laid down for British merchant vessels by the Board of Trade.

I flew from London to Japan with the rest of the crew to join her in the first week of October 1973. After the long flight we had to endure a cramped three-hour bus journey, followed by an overnight ferry, only to be told when we disembarked that our ship was anchored three miles out and the boat astern of the ferry was waiting to take us out to her. 'What're we waiting for?' someone shouted.

So off we trooped and boarded the boat with our gear, and a short time later we were looking at a rope ladder that hung down the ship's side. The bosun took charge and asked three ABs to go up first and check what could be used to get our gear on board. Another couple of deckhands helped him steady the ladder as the men climbed to the deck one by one, and once they were safely on board the rest of us climbed at intervals. And it was not until all our gear was on board and the bosun and deckhands were on the deck that an officer showed himself.

'Welcome, gentlemen,' he said.

We ignored him.

The bosun introduced himself and told him briefly what we had been through and how long it had been since we had eaten a hot meal. He apologised and asked the bosun to accompany him to see the captain. The rest of us went in all directions, some in search of food and others in search of the cabins. A hastily prepared meal was produced, and three hours later we were on our way to Whyalla in Australia, my favourite country.

It soon became clear that the *Posterior* was unlike any ship we had sailed on under the British flag. She was foreign owned, and although the old man and the officers were British, that's as far as it went. She was an unhappy ship from the start. According to the deckhands, orders were contradicted often and that caused confusion and annoyance.

My job was much the same as on any other ship, but what annoyed me and the majority of the crew was the fact that there were no toiletries, soap powder and so on for sale, necessary goods that could be bought on all British merchant

342

vessels. A small amount of beer and soft drinks were for sale, but that was all. By the time we tied up in Whyalla there was talk of trying to pay off. We had a good crew, but she wasn't a happy ship.

I went ashore the next day to have a few jars in the steelworkers' social club with Dermot and John, both deckhands. We were unprepared for the sight before us as we stepped through the door. It was only 2 pm, but it was like a night club that had opened early. John, a Cork man, shouted to be heard above the music from the jukebox and the chatter, 'Jasus, isn't this grand, the size of the place, we're set for the rest of our time here, I'll tell yez.'

Dermot, a Dublin man, was more cautious. 'We might not get served,' he said.

We were served, and soon we were rubbing shoulders with men from all over the British Isles and many other countries and there was an air of friendliness all round.

A Scotsman got talking to us. He introduced himself as Jimmy, and once he had established where we all came from in Ireland he asked me if they had ever got the town clock that seldom worked fixed and if Prosser's and Tallon's were still serving a good pint.

'I don't know about the clock,' I said, 'but there was nothing wrong with the pints the last time I was there. I take it you've been to Enniskerry.'

'Yes,' he said, 'my sister is married to a chap you might have gone to school with, Dick Seery – do you know him?'

'From Monastery?' I asked.

'The very place,' he said, 'and he's out here with the wife and three children and working for BHP, as I am. I'll call around to his place tonight and let him know you're here. I'm sure he'll be pleased to see you.'

I got a round in and Jimmy stayed with us for an hour or so before going home for his tea. We carried on drinking and I don't know what time we got back on board or how long I slept on the chair in my cabin.

I woke up to the sound of someone calling my name from outside my open cabin door. 'Come in,' I said trying to focus on the figure coming towards me, and when he was a couple of feet away I recognised him. 'Dick Seery!' I said. 'Strike-a-light, as they say in this country!'

We shook hands, embraced and were delighted to see each other. I asked him if he would like a whisky and a beer. He said he had just finished work and Jean would be expecting him, but he couldn't go home without saying hello to me. He'd enjoy a beer, but he wasn't much of a drinker. He told me about his wife and children and then he had to go. He said he'd come to see me at five the following evening and he would like me to go home with him to meet the family if that was suitable to me.

When we pulled up outside the Seery home the following evening, Jean and the children came out to meet us, and after the introductions we went inside. As always, I was ill at ease whenever I visited someone else's home, but I relaxed a bit when Dick opened two cans of beer and handed me one.

'We'll be having dinner shortly, John,' said Jean. 'I hope you're hungry.'

Dick busied himself mixing drinks for the children and I worked on getting them used to me. I have always been fond of children, and almost all the children I have come into contact with have warmed to me rather quickly. Maybe it's because I'm so small, and maybe it's partly because I have never talked down to them, as some adults tend to do. Linda was six years old, Richard was five, and Alison was three and a half.

I was getting on well with them, and then Dick settled them at the table. Jean came in with a joint of beef, he started carving and she went back for the potatoes and vegetables. They served the children to cries of 'Mummy, I don't want carrots, I don't like this or that,' and so it went with both parents telling them what was good for them and reminding them that it was impolite to behave so, especially with a guest in the house. I enjoyed the exchanges and ate more than was usual for me – although Jean said that the children had eaten more than I had. Dick opened another couple of beers and I was completely relaxed.

We talked and played with the children until they went to bed. Then we talked of Ireland and Scotland, Jean's homeland. Our families, school days, old friends and their life in Australia. They lived in a small community on the fringe of the outback, and among their biggest worries were the snakes.

Jean said, 'Dick told me there's two other Irish lads on the ship. I'd like to invite them up for Sunday dinner. Do you think they'd come?'

'I think they would,' I said.

'Good,' she said. 'And will you come up with Dick and have a bite to eat with us in the evenings?'

'I'd love to,' I said.

'That's settled then,' she said with a big smile.

I was up at the crack of dawn the next morning and, strange for me, I didn't feel any need for alcohol. I made a cup of coffee and went out on deck to see the sunrise amidst the clanking of machinery, men's voices on the shore and on the ship. Dermot and John joined me shortly afterwards and I told them of Jean's invitation. They were all for it.

Dick came to my cabin just after five o'clock that day, and after another enjoyable evening he drove me back at the more respectable time of 10.30. The next day was Saturday, and it turned out to be a most wonderful day. I spent the afternoon and evening with Dick and Jean, and we sat out in the garden drinking cold beer, watching the children playing and periodically joining them. I continually got the dolls' names wrong and was calling a motorcar a truck and a tractor a taxi and so on. I was corrected each time and looked at quizzically with sparkling eyes that said, 'How can he be so silly?' Jean's neighbour and best friend Molly joined us and we had a great laugh. The day ended with a barbecue, and I left feeling tired but very happy.

Dermot came to my cabin at 11 o'clock on Sunday morning, plonked a case of beer down on the desk, ripped it open, took two cans out and handed me one. There was no sign of John, who appeared to be getting cold feet, and we were still waiting for him when Dick arrived. But ten minutes later John appeared, and after another beer we were off.

Jean and Molly and the children were in the garden when we arrived. Introductions were made, drinks were served and the conversation was mainly about Dick and me meeting so far away from home. 'It's a strange ol' world,' said Dermot.

John seemed to lose his shyness quickly, mainly I think because of the children.

Molly joined us for lunch, and the only minor problem was

that all three children wanted to sit next to me, uncle John, as they had taken to calling me.

'Linda,' I said, 'I would really appreciate it if you would sit next to my friend Dermot. This is his first visit to Australia and he wants to learn all about the country. Please tell him some of the things you have told me about the kangaroots and koalas. I'm sure you'll make him very happy, and later you and I can sit down together and you can tell me some more stories.'

She gave me a big smile and said with a giggle, as she went over to sit next to Dermot, 'Uncle John, they are not what you called them. They are called kangaroos.'

The conversation flowed throughout the meal, and carried on afterwards when we went out to the garden with our drinks. We took turns playing with the children, and I kept my promise and sat down with Linda under the sunshade.

'Did you tell Dermot about the kantaroots?' I asked.

After the children had gone to bed we talked of our childhood days and then Jean put on a compilation album of Irish music. We said our fond farewells just after midnight and Dick drove us back to the ship.

John said, 'I'll remember this grand day for years to come. Thanks, Dick.'

'And the same goes for me,' said Dermot. 'I can't remember when I enjoyed myself so much.'

I enjoyed the Seerys' friendship and hospitality for over two weeks, and then we sailed to Port Kembla to complete the loading of a cargo of iron for Japan.

Prior to our arrival in Whyalla we had given the skipper a list of grievances that we wanted resolved, including having the necessary items for personal health and hygiene – toothpaste, shampoo, washing powder, etc – available for sale on board. Alternatively we requested to be paid off and repatriated to the United Kingdom. This had been signed by all of the crew except for two men. But not a word was heard from the captain during our stay in Whyalla or Port Kembla. We made another request to be paid off, and he responded by promising to have everything sorted out when we arrived in Japan.

A couple of days after we arrived in Yokohama the old man told us we were to be paid off. He explained that it hadn't been possible to get a block booking so we would have to fly as seats became available. I signed off with three colleagues the next day and had to wait for a taxi to take us to the airport. I don't know what made me go out on deck, but I was pleased I had when I saw an old drinking partner, Tony Sutton, struggling up the gangway with his gear.

I went to help him and he said in mock Irish, 'Well, oi'll be buggered, it's you, John Joe.'

I grabbed one of his bags and said, 'I'm not sure if there's anyone here to bugger you, but I'm here to help you drink your duty-free.'

While Tony went off to report to the captain I went in search of my old pals and found them drinking in Bill's cabin. I told them the new bosun was aboard, and they were as surprised as I had been when I saw Tony coming up the gangway. We couldn't understand why he had been sent out while we were still on board. Most companies had it planned in such a way that the old crew were off and gone before the new crew joined. When Tony came back he explained that all he had been told was that the crew were paying off in Japan and the ship would be returning to Australia.

I had bought some toys for the Seery children, and Tony said he would post them off when he got to Australia.

I arrived in Heathrow the next evening and made my way to the Queen Victoria Seamen's Rest without a care in the world. I had paid off with a *very good* for both conduct and ability and I was home.

***

I worked on three more ships after that, and then in April 1975 I joined the *King William*, a bulk carrier. She was a well-run ship with a happy crew, but unfortunately after about two months on board I had an accident the day before we were due to dock in Mizushima, Japan. I was passing an empty forty-five-gallon drum down through a hatch to my colleague Robert and I don't know what went wrong. I felt the drum slipping from my grasp, and the next thing I remember was coming to in the ship's hospital with Captain Owen looking down on me in the bed.

He smiled and said, 'You have slept for over three hours. How do you feel?'

I tried to answer but it was too difficult with my dry swollen mouth, and when I tried to move I gave out a yelp from the pain in my right leg. He held a glass of cold water to my lips and I managed to swill some around in my mouth before swallowing it.

'I have been on to the agent and a doctor,' he said. 'The doctor thinks the blood that was coming from your mouth was caused by you biting the inside of your cheek with the impact of the fall. He doesn't think there's any need for you to be taken off the ship, as we will be alongside tomorrow morning.'

'Thank you captain,' I said. 'I have another problem. I'm seeing two of you through my right eye.'

'They will take care of it ashore,' he said. 'The agent assures me an ambulance will be standing by. I am going to get the chief steward to give you some painkillers, and hopefully you will try to have a drop of soup at least.'

Two drinking partners turned up next, Robert and Harry.

Robert said, 'I tried to break your fall, but I couldn't reach you in time. I thought you were dead at first with all the blood coming out of your mouth, and the chief steward didn't help when he said he thought you had ruptured something inside.'

'That will teach me to use a rope in future,' I said.

'Yeah,' said Harry, 'when Robert told me, I thought, he's a pain in the arse when he's drunk, but not so much of a pain that I'd want to see him signing off for good.'

I was strapped into a stretcher the next afternoon, carefully carried down the gangway and placed in the ambulance. Then it was goodbyes, good lucks, get well soon and off we drove to the Mizushima Daiichi Hospital. I was taken out of the stretcher, gently helped into a wheelchair and pushed to the reception desk, where I was greeted with a smile and a courteous bow from the young woman on duty.

She said, 'You are Mr John Joseph Ma'on?'

I was wheeled into a single room with a bed, a sofa, a chair, wardrobe, a bedside locker and a television. I tried to get out of the wheelchair by myself and was doing quite well until I accidentally put my weight on my right foot. The pain was so bad I nearly fell, but fortunately the porter steadied me and helped me to the sofa, grinned, gave me a bow and said, 'Sayonara.'

'Arigato,' I said, which I was sure meant thank you.

A few minutes later an interpreter came to see me. She introduced herself as Jean Ono, a charming woman, in her early forties I thought. She looked beautiful with her dark hair and dark smouldering eyes. She was about my height and she wore a Western-style costume with the skirt just above the knee, which rode up a bit when she sat down. There was a thing for me to think about. I was in pain and I was seeing two-times-twice, but I could still get good vibrations.

After some small talk, she got down to business. She made notes on everything I said, and when that was finished she told me I would be served Western food and I would have a personal maid staying with me until I could get around by myself.

'Where is she going to sleep?' I asked.

She smiled and said, 'On the day bed, it opens out, she is an old lady and she will take good care of you. I must go. I will be back in one hour with the doctor.'

When she had gone, I felt very much alone and wished I had a bottle to turn to or even a good book, and moments later as if by magic a man from the agents appeared in the doorway with my gear. He said, 'One of your friends, Robert, said to tell you he has packed some books and magazines and something to keep you warm inside.' I looked at the bags and wondered which one held the warmer-upper. I thanked him with the customary bow and off he went.

Unfortunately the gear was out of reach. I vainly tried to get to it but the pain of the effort was too great. Then I thought, if they're going to give me some sort of medication and there is a bottle in there, I'd better leave it alone.

Jean came back with another female and two males. They all three had a poke at me, and when they were finished they had a talk with Jean, who explained, 'You are to have an x-ray on your leg and your chest. The porter will be coming for you soon and you will be given therapeutic treatment for the double vision.'

When the porter took me back to my room after the x-rays I got him to move my stuff closer to the sofa so I could get at it. I was going through my things and had just found the bottle of whisky when Jean came back with a frail-looking old lady dressed in a black kimono.

'This lady will take care of you until you can get around by yourself,' she said. 'She can't speak English, but she is very good at her job. I have given her your tablets, which you are to take after your evening meal, and I have given her a pair of pyjamas for you.'

The old lady took charge as soon as Jean left. She touched my shirt and trousers and indicated by holding up the pyjamas that I was to put them on. I nodded, took my shirt and vest off, and she held her hands up, signalling me to stop at that. She ran some water into the sink, soaped a flannel and washed my upper body, then rinsed me off and dried me. Next, she pointed to my trousers with a look that said, 'Get 'em off!' I shook my head and indicated that I would wash the lower part of my body myself and I wanted her to leave the room. She said something I did not understand, but soaped the flannel and handed it to me, then turned her back to me. I got on with the job and covered my privates with my underpants when I was finished. 'OK,' I said. She understood that, and turned towards me with a toothless smile. She rinsed the flannel thoroughly and handed it to me with a girlish giggle as she turned her back once more. I rinsed off, and when that was done she handed me the pyjama bottoms and turned her back. Good, I thought, she understands me, as I pulled the bottoms up to my waist. 'OK,' I said. She nodded approval and pointed to the bed. I managed to stand on my good leg and she came over, got her shoulder under my arm – and to my surprise nearly lifted me off the floor. She was an inch or two shorter than me and looked very frail, but she was strong and had me in the bed in no time.

I decided to call her 'Suki' – but not to her face, and not to refer to her as such to Jean or anyone else. She was just my Suki.

Twenty minutes later Suki brought in a tray of food for both of us, rice and fish for her and steak, beans, tomatoes and boiled potatoes for me with gooseberries and cream for dessert. I nibbled a bit and left the sweet. Suki gave me a sideways glance of disapproval as I pushed the tray away. She pointed to her own empty bowls. I indicated that I was full up and she nodded in resignation.

After giving me two pills from a little bottle she turned the television on and chattered away at me. I guessed she was trying to explain what the game show was about, and from what I gathered she enjoyed it because she gave happy little chirps occasionally. I caught on and pretended to enjoy it too. When the show was over, I settled for a read of *Huckleberry Finn* until Suki came over, ruffled my pillows and indicated that I should get some shuteye. It was only 9 pm. I couldn't remember the last time I had been to bed so early, and sober too.

I awoke at 6.30 the next morning with a bursting need to carry out my bodily functions. The bottle wasn't a problem, but the bedpan – oh no! Suki must have read my mind. She handed me a reinforced cardboard container to pee in, but when I started I had great difficulty holding back my more urgent need and there wasn't a crutch in sight. When I couldn't hold back any longer, I had to give in, I pointed to my rear end and thankfully she understood. She went out and came back with a bedpan and a roll of toilet paper, which she placed on the bed and pulled the curtains as she left. I was relieved but terribly embarrassed when she came back to take the bedpan away. Next came a bed bath, but she let me do my lower region myself. Then it was breakfast.

Jean came in shortly afterwards and presented me with the English version of the *Mainichi News*, and she continued to bring it every morning for the four weeks I spent there.

I was dozing in the afternoon when there was knock on the door. Suki opened it and in walked Harry and Robert. She bowed to them and disappeared. Robert asked, 'Who is she?'

'They call her a room maid,' I said. 'She sleeps on the day bed. I never wanted anyone to run around doing things for me, and least of all handling a bedpan – still, I've no choice.'

Harry said, 'It's a pity they couldn't have got you a younger one.'

'She'd make two of a younger one,' I said.

Robert handed me a sealed envelope. 'Something from the old man, some of the officers and from our lads in case you need a bit of ready money.'

I opened the envelope and found a list of the entire ship's company and the amount neatly written in front of those who had contributed, and they were in the majority, from the old man to the two catering boys and the young engine-room rating. I had been humbled by people's kindness to me before, but I was never more moved.

'I feel terrible about taking the young lads' money,' I said, 'but to send it back would be an insult.'

Robert said, 'You know we never expect the boys to put their hands in their pockets for such things, but they insisted.'

'They certainly did,' said Harry. 'They're great boys, we're lucky to have such a good bunch from the old man down.'

'I agree,' I said. 'I shall miss you all. Any news of when you're due to sail?'

'Possibly tomorrow afternoon or the next morning,' said Harry. We chatted a while longer, and when they left I counted the money. There was 22,000 yen, £12.00 sterling, $12.00 Australian and $10.00 American. Very generous indeed!

Remembering the kindness and generosity of my shipmates, and looking at that very same list before me today, over thirty-five years later, I am humbled all over again – and a bit sad too because I have never clapped eyes on any of those men again. If this is ever published I hope some of you might read it – and once again a big thank you to all concerned.

According to the doctor's written diagnosis, I had fractured my right pubic bone and I had paralysed ocular muscles, hyposphagma, conjunctivitis and diplopia. Double vision to me!

By the end of the first week I was able to get around on crutches, and thankfully that put an end to the bedpan. At the beginning of the second week I was down to one crutch, and that's when I was driven downtown by Joe, the hospital driver, to have treatment for my double vision. The specialist strapped a gadget over my head and attached something to my temples, switched on the power and I felt a sort of light current running through my head for about two minutes. Then the power was switched off and I was free to go. But that was only the first of several visits.

When we got back to the hospital, Suki greeted me as though I had been away for ages. She patted my hand and was chattering away as if she had been wound up. She lowered the bed and indicated for me to sit on it. I did so, and she held up her hand, meaning for me to stay that way, and she was off out the door like a rocket. She was back within five minutes with a pretty little pot of tea and two tiny glasses on a tray. She filled the glasses, handed me one, and I said, 'Arigato.' She said something, smiled and clapped her little hands together.

Towards the end of the second week I was able to walk a short distance without the crutches. The doctors and the eye specialist were pleased with my progress, and so was I, except that I didn't notice much change with the double vision.

Suki was becoming less needed every day, so I wasn't surprised when Jean told me she was going to be looking after someone else the following day.

'When does she go home?' I asked. 'She has been with me for nearly two weeks and she hasn't been out of the hospital since she started taking care of me.'

'She usually works here for a month and then she goes off for a break,' Jean replied. I didn't know what to make of that.

Suki packed up her things the next morning and then came over to me with a smile. I held her hands in mine briefly before she bowed out of the room. I was near to tears when she left.

The doctors examined me for the last time towards the end of the fourth week, and after some conversation with Jean she told me, 'You can go home as soon as the agents can arrange a flight for you. I will phone them shortly. The doctor said you will continue to have the double vision, but it will go away in time, and you may get an occasional twinge in your leg for a time but that will go away too.'

'Thank you Jean,' I said. 'Please thank the doctors for me. And I would like to give the old lady some money to get herself something. I know nothing of your culture or customs, but as you may know it is a custom in the British Isles to show our appreciation to someone by giving them a gift of money.'

'I don't think she will want to take it,' she said.

'Please try to convince her,' I said.

When she came to see me the next morning, it was good news on two fronts. The agent was due to come for me at one o'clock, and although the old lady had taken a lot of

353

convincing, she would accept my gift. Jean went to get Suki, and when they came back I bowed to her and asked Jean to thank her for everything she had done for me. That done, I presented her with the envelope containing some yen – and I thought she might break something with all the bowing.

The agent came for me at 12.50 pm. I said goodbye to Jean and Joe, and off I went.

***

I have lost myself in a thick memory fog here. I remember travelling on a train and having a steak in Kobe with the agent, and I have a vague memory of being in Tokyo – and nothing more until I reached Heathrow. Was I drunk? I must have been.

I booked in to the QVSR, and when I told Terry Simco about the accident and the double vision he asked if I wanted to be driven to the Dreadnought Seamen's hospital. He would have somebody drive me there the next morning. That was typical of Terry, always concerned and ready to help at any time of day or night.

I gave the doctor in the Dreadnought the hospital report from Japan, and after an examination of my leg and an eye test I was found to be on the road to recovery and in no need of further medical attention. I then went to the Springbok, a convalescent centre out in the wilds of Surrey on hundreds of acres of farmland, a wonderful place with most of the food fresh from the farm. I found it hard to sleep for the first two nights because of the eerie silence and the lack of alcohol. There were eight of us there in various states of disrepair and a number of ex-seamen learning new skills, arable, dairy, hatchery and market gardening. I left the Springbok after two weeks and returned to the QVSR alcohol-free and fitter than an army of jumping fleas.

That didn't last long, though. I was soon back on the booze, and when the money was gone I shipped out again.

Somewhere between ships I met my old friend Bob Mackenzie in the Black Bull in Whitechapel and I was the worse for wear. He got two pints and placed mine in front of me on the table. I tried to pick it up but I couldn't hold it because of the shakes. I bent my head and swigged from it that way. I needed a whisky to help me get rid of the shakes. I got my medicine, threw it back at the bar and ordered another to drink at the table, and when I sat down Bob looked at me in disgust and said, 'You're fucked up wee man and out of control. If you don't straighten out, you'll find yourself on Shark Island with the bums, pimps and parasites. I'm off.'

He left me there with my battered pride and a lot of food for thought. He never minced his words. He was a true friend. I knew he was right, but what was I going to do about it?

Nothing, was the answer. I carried on drinking and shipping out until June 1979 when I joined the *Revive* in Portsmouth. I only lasted a week on her. I was drunk on boiler watch and was paid off with a bad discharge. I went before a committee at the Shipping Federation and I was out of the merchant navy. I could have appealed but I knew it would be useless.

For the first time in my 'drinking career' I had to admit to myself that I was an alcoholic.

4

Ashore

I set my sights on settling ashore and getting some order in my life. I had very little money and my rent had to be paid, so the first thing to do was get a job. After a week of drunkenness, I straightened out as much as I could and went to a catering agency called The Helping Hands, which was in a little back street just across the road from St Paul's Cathedral.

I heard they opened at six in the morning, and the earlier you got there the better chance you had of getting a job. So I caught a bus from the East India Dock Road just after 5 am and found that I was the fifth in line outside the door, and it paid dividends. I registered with them and got a job as a kitchen porter in a fancy restaurant near Fleet Street, from 11 am to 4 pm. Five hours at £2.20 per hour. Nothing to shout about, but it was a start. I got regular work and was clearing between forty and fifty pounds a week, enough to pay my bus fares and rent of twenty-seven pounds, bed and breakfast, in the Vic.

I got on well with the agency, and twice during my four months with them I was given the opportunity of doing a barman's job in the evenings after my day job, to give me the chance to earn more money. I did it on both occasions, but it was too hard. Me, an alcoholic, a barman? Hold on there! I was surrounded by booze – but I only had a few half-pints in each job and walked away feeling proud of myself.

The Royal Mail were advertising for postmen. I applied for a job and to my delight I was taken on and given a two-week training course, after which I had to pass a simple test and I was in.

Terry Simco was as pleased as I was, but he warned, 'You

356

be careful, John, and you'll have a job for life. I'm not telling you to stop drinking, although I wish you would as I wish some other men here would, but please don't let it interfere with your work. Good luck and God bless you.'

That was the kind of man he was. He cared for us all and he wanted us to do well. I never failed to respect him, and I can safely say he was one of only two true Christians I've ever had the pleasure of meeting.

The job of postman was a novelty at first. My duty was delivering on foot one week and going around with a van driver emptying the post boxes and sorting at the base the next. However, I felt I had to leave after three months. Not because of the dog mess on the pavements or because my little legs weren't designed for all that walking. No, I wouldn't have given up that easy. The reason I left was that I was drinking much more than I should and my absences from work were becoming more frequent. I had enough sense to realise that it wouldn't be long before I got my marching orders, and I didn't want that to happen. But the truth of the matter was that I wasn't ready for a permanent job ashore, and some of my old shipmates didn't help when they came home with their docking bottles, insisting on me going out with them on drinking sprees.

I knew that if I was going to settle ashore I had to get out of the mission, which I didn't relish. I loved the old Queen Vic. It had been my home for so long and all the staff there were like a family to me, but move I must.

I went on the dole after I left the post office, and when they got my papers sorted out I was given enough to pay my rent and fourteen pounds for food etc. Not bad, I thought, but not enough to go wild on the drink, so it was cider and cheap plonk. I paid my rent regularly, except on occasions I held back the price of a couple of nights' rent and paid it back over a period of weeks. That went on for a while, and then I only paid for three nights one week and got drunk with the rest and thought no more about it. That is, until the next morning when I was rudely awakened by the Reverend Artichoke.

He let himself into my room with his passkey and said without preamble, 'I want you out of here by midday. Your rent is in arrears – out, I say!'

I tried to reason with him but it was no use, his mind was

made up. Terry and his wife Doris were off on holidays so there was no one to turn to. Pleading with that so-called man of God was out. It was no secret that we couldn't stand each other, and never more so since I had told him months before to get the cross off from around his neck because he was an imposter. I believe he was just waiting to get back at me, and his opportunity came when Terry was away and I made it easy for him. Thankfully, I had two-thirds of a bottle of whisky and a couple of cans of beer hidden away. I took a swallow of whisky, opened a beer and sat down to think.

There was a knock on the door and there stood Joe Downes. 'Where did we end up last night?' he asked, taking a full bottle of Teacher's whisky from beneath his shirt.

'Don't ask me,' I said. 'Anyway, I've more important things to think about.'

I told him what had happened, and we sat and drank in silence for a while. Then he announced, 'I've got the answer – well, I think so anyway. You know them derelict flats down in Wapping? I know a bloke that squats there. I'll go and see him and get the gen off him.' He threw his whisky back and said, 'I'm off. Don't drink all the gargle, I won't be long.'

When he came back I was packed and ready to get my gear downstairs. He poured us drinks and said, 'Them flats are in great nick, I wouldn't mind dossin' in one of them myself. Doug, the bloke I know, said there's a load of squatters in them and there's plenty vacant. All we have to do is go into the one he showed me. He's hidden a bar for us to force a door and that's it.'

We got my stuff down to reception, where we found Artichoke behind the desk looking surly and pissed with power.

'I would like to leave my baggage in the left luggage, please,' I said.

'You can of course,' he said. 'You know the charge.'

I walked out of the Queen Vic with a little shoulder bag containing a few necessities, the most important being the bottle of liquid confusion.

'Let's go over to Bum Daddy's for a pint of slop,' I said. 'I've enough for a couple of jars and that's the lot.'

'I'm not much better off meself,' he said. 'Ah, to hell with it, why not?'

We had a pint each, and when I went through my pockets I found a crumpled-up five-pound note. 'Look,' I said, holding it up.

'Sweet Jesus, Mary and Joseph, that's fucking luck for you, we're in clover,' he said.

'Leave that gang out of it,' I said.

'Would you like to see your new abode when we finish our drinks?' he asked.

'Not yet,' I said, 'I'd like to sit out in the park for a while and have a jar in the open. On second thoughts, let's give the park a miss, there'll be too many people there. We'll go to the graveyard. It'll be more peaceful there. Do you fancy a few beers to go with the whisky, or will we get a couple of flagons of cider?'

'Cider,' he replied. 'It'll go well with the whisky.'

Joe headed for the supermarket while I waited for him in the graveyard. My mind was racing and I thought, you've got yourself into one fine stew this time, you eejit! And Bob's words came back to me – *'You'll be hitting skid row if you don't straighten yourself out!'* I couldn't have been much closer at that moment, sitting on a tombstone in a graveyard off the East India Dock Road with no place to call home except a squat. Nobody's fault but my own, and there I was cracking the seal on a bottle of whisky.

I was deep in thought when Joe returned with an old friend of ours, Dick Kenshaw, a man in his early fifties with dark hair, a round face and a captivating smile when he was in a good mood – but that could change rapidly if anyone upset him. He boomed, 'John Joe, I heard that holy man threw you out, shortly after I booked in this morning. I went from pub to pub looking for you and then I bumped into Joe in the supermarket – in the same section I might add.'

'Stocking up, no doubt,' I said.

'Of course,' he said. 'Just beer though, I've got three docking bottles and enough tobacco to last me a long time. Are you still staying in the Vic, Joe?'

'Yes,' replied Joe. 'Terry gave me a cleaning job before he went on holidays. It's only four hours a day and rent-free, not bad at all.'

'I've just paid off after six months and I'm down at the head with money,' said Dick. 'Would thirty quid each help you out?'

That sounded like a fortune to me, and I was about to ask him for a loan of twenty when Joe said, 'I don't know about John Joe, but no thanks Dick.'

Dick looked at me and said, 'You can't say no, John Joe. The two of you have helped me out before now.' He took a wad of notes out of his pocket.

'I'll tell you what, Dick,' I said. 'I'll borrow twenty off you and when I get my dole in a few days' time I'll pay you a tenner.'

'No,' he said, 'I don't lend money to friends. You'll take a score each or we'll be having a row.'

He peeled off two twenty-pound notes and handed us one each. We then got down to some serious drinking, and by the time the evening was closing in I couldn't have given a flying fart where I got my head down. Dick went back to the QVSR and Joe accompanied me to the squat. He forced the door of the flat his friend had pointed out and in we went. He lit a match and I flicked my lighter on. The place was empty. Joe left me curled up on the floor with my coat over me, saying he'd be back for a livener early in the morning. I pulled my coat tighter around me, and with the help of brother booze I drifted off. I woke up feeling very cold and couldn't get back to sleep again despite drinking more whisky and cider.

The dawn finally broke and I was well on the way to being drunk again, but I knew I had to keep my wits about me. I was determined not to spend another night in that place.

Joe came back at seven in the morning, bearing a present of a tin of tobacco from Dick and saying, 'I'm dying for the want of a drink, will I pour you one?'

'Just a small one,' I said, 'and that'll be my last for a while. I've got to get something sorted out this morning, I'm not spending another night here. I've got that twenty-pounds, I think I'll go down to the Sally-Ann to see if I can get in there.'

'Or you might try Belfast Billy,' said Joe. 'When I went back last night, I went to Dick's room and we got well and truly plastered, but before we got out of our heads he told me Belfast Billy puts blokes up and he only lives around the corner from the Vic.'

Later that morning we met Dick in Bum Daddy's, and he told me more about Belfast Billy. 'I sailed with him years ago,' he said. 'I'd never call him a mate, he's a grabbing old bastard, but he might be able to put you up until you get yourself fixed up. His house is about four or five down from the corner near the mission, it's the house with the black door and the curtains half hanging off the windows. I don't know the number but you can't miss it.'

I drank up and went in search of Billy's. I found the house and knocked on the door. It was opened by a grey-haired old man with a stoop and sunken eyes in a thin face.

'Whaw's it ye want wee monn?' he asked.

'I heard you might be able to rent me a room for a week or two,' I said.

He looked me up and down, rubbed the stubble on his chin, scratched his head as though he was going to make the biggest decision in his life and said, 'Come in, I'm Billy.'

I followed him into a cluttered room with two big couches, a table with four chairs around it and a television in the corner. 'I have two blokes stayin' wi me,' he said. 'They pay me twenty-five pounds a week, but ye can sleep on that couch if ye want for fifteen pounds a week. No food, mind. Ye can use the kitchen if ye want. We like a good drink here, and you'd have to understand that.'

'I like a good drink too,' I said, 'but fifteen quid is a bit stiff. I'm broke. Would you settle for ten?'

'Okay,' he said, 'five pounds for key money and rent in advance.'

I went back to the pub and told the boys about my transaction with the dirty old grabber. We drank until afternoon closing, and then Dick suggested that we should go around to Billy's with a carry out, so we went to the supermarket and walked the short distance to Billy's with a bottle of Teacher's whisky and a case of Carlsberg Special Brew. When he saw us with the booze his sunken little peepers nearly popped out of their sockets.

'Come in, come in lads,' he said.

The four of us sat and drank and talked, and after a few jars I curled into a ball on the couch and fell asleep.

The next thing I knew was Joe shaking me. I sat up and discovered the party had increased, with three more men in the room. Stephen and Dave were the other two residents from Belfast, and Willie was a Glaswegian drinking pal of

Billy's, all in their sixties and unkempt. The sort of people I had seen plenty of, swigging from bottles in the parks around Poplar and Whitechapel. I had nothing against them, but I didn't want to get involved with them. Well, do something about it, I thought to myself.

The next morning I had an hour to kill before reporting to the labour exchange in Burdett Road so I decided to scan the notices in the newsagents, and my heart gave a flutter when I saw 'Clean rooms for rent B&B Phone Poplar ...'

I phoned the number and a woman said, 'Hello.'

'I'm ringing to enquire about a room,' I said. 'I'm thirty-seven, and an ex-seaman.'

There was a pause and then she said, 'The rent, which includes breakfast, is twenty-five pounds per week and there's a ten pound deposit for the key, payable in advance.'

'Thank you,' I said. 'When can I see the room?'

'That depends,' she said. 'Do you take drugs, and are you in any trouble with the law?'

'The answer to both questions is no,' I said.

'I suppose you drink, do you?'

'Yes,' I said, 'I do, in moderation.'

'If that's so, you'll be the first seaman I've ever met that does. Can you come to see me at 2.30 this afternoon?'

I knocked on the half-open door that afternoon and introduced myself to Mrs Clone.

'I have a front room in a house two doors down,' she said, 'which I'm willing to offer you on the terms we discussed over the phone. I rent on a bed and breakfast basis, which means I will give you a bag of goods on rent day. There's a cooker just down the hall from your room. I don't allow visitors in the rooms, misbehaviour of any kind will not be tolerated, and last but not least you must pay your rent on time.'

I arranged to move in on Wednesday – and going down the road to Bum Daddy's I thought, damn, I never asked to see the room. Never mind, it couldn't be any worse than Billy's, and at least I would have my privacy. Joe and Dick were sitting at the bar chatting when I went in.

'You look like the cat that ate the canary,' said Joe.

'Correction,' I said, 'I'm the canary that ate the cat. I've got myself a room and I'm walking on air.'

They both wanted to talk at once but Joe persisted and said, 'Smashing, where is it?'

'Just up the road,' I replied.

'Mother Clone's,' they both said at once.

Closing time came and there was no sign of the other six drinkers leaving so we stayed back and when Big Mick put the bolt on the door we knew we were in for an afternoon session. I only had six pounds and that wouldn't go far, but I was in the mood for a good jar and so were the other two. My name was good with Dick and Joe had just been paid, so I was on safe ground.

We stumbled out of there sometime after 6 pm, not feeling any pain or anything else either. Back at Billy's it was a full house, with six or seven other blokes drinking, shouting and trying to sing. 'Welcome boyz,' slurred Billy, 'thish 'ere is me bess frenz.' All I can remember after that is staking claim to a corner of the couch, having a glass of whisky and that was it. I was out of the game.

I woke up around 6 am to find one fellow out to the world on the other couch and two others on the floor. The stink in the place was overpowering, worse than cat's piss, and I suspected that a few of Billy's guests were methylated spirit drinkers. If this wasn't skid row, it wasn't a kick in the arse away from it. I had a splitting headache and my stomach craved something to put it right. Then I remembered hiding a flagon of cider behind the couch. I looked to see if it was still there, and yes, it seemed to be smiling at me. I was in my element – a livener! But I wasn't going to drink it there. I was gagging as it was. I picked up the flagon and my bag, which seemed to be heavy, so I opened the zip and there to my amazement was a third of a bottle of whisky and six beers. I slung the bag over my shoulder, let myself out the door and walked a short distance to the back of the Trinity Church, where I settled myself in a side doorway, took a drink of whisky and opened a can of beer. I must have sat there for about an hour, and when I came out onto the pavement there was Joe coming towards me.

'Thank God I found you,' he said, 'I've been looking for you everywhere. I'm dying for a livener. I hid whisky and beer in your bag last night.'

I pushed the bag towards him. 'Help yourself.'

Up at the graveyard we opened two beers and he poured whisky into two plastic cups he had taken from the mission. We had just settled down behind a big gravestone when an old black lady came along.

She stopped in front of us and said, 'Good morning boys, God bless you.'

'Good morning to you ma'am,' I said.

She smiled and said, 'I don't think God will be very pleased with you two young men drinking alcohol at this time of the morning, and in a place for the dead too. It shows disrespect. I will have a word with him and I know he will forgive you both.'

'Thank you ma'am,' I said. 'I'm sure he'll forgive us with your help, and when our problems are behind us, we will remember this morning when he guided you in our direction. I am grateful to you for your prayers and your understanding, thank you ma'am.'

She nodded approval and stood looking at Joe. I sensed he was uneasy, and when she asked, 'What about you, young man?' he stammered, 'I ... fe ... feel the sa ... same as my friend, thank you.' She stood for a minute or two and then went slowly on her way with the words, 'May the Good Lord shine his ever-loving light upon those young men.'

When she was out of sight Joe threw his whisky back and I did the same. 'You're full of crap,' he said, 'coming out with all that ballsology. You never meant a word of it.'

'I know that,' I said, 'but one thing is for sure, that old lady seems to have gone away happy with the thought that she has done God's work for two sinners, and I have learned there are more ways to get intoxicated than with alcohol and other drugs.'

We parted shortly after that, and I spent a restless day and night in and out of Billy's going for walks, snoozing and finally trying to settle down for the night.

I was up at the crack of dawn, and after a half-hearted wash in the stinking bathroom I let myself out and put the key through the letterbox. *Goodbye Belfast Billy and friends. Here's to the future!*

Joe was going to help me move my gear from the Vic, but first I had to collect my dole money. I spent quite a bit of time over two cups of tea in a dirty old café and still had a couple of hours to kill. I wandered aimlessly, thinking over my life and the good people who had tried to help and support me. The Thomsons ... Terry Simco ... Bob Mackenzie ... I had forsaken them all in favour of the booze. I was an alcoholic. I was thirty-seven years old, and I was going nowhere except down. Well, I was going to change that.

***

I collected my dole money in the form of a giro cheque for forty-one pounds, and changed it at the post office. Back at the QVSR I found Joe waiting for me.

'I thought you were lost,' he said. 'Where have you been?'

'Thinking,' I replied.

He shook his head.

I went to say goodbye to Eileen, the accountant, and Iris and Sylvia, the ladies working in the cafeteria. Then I went out the door, and there was Joe on the pavement with my all my worldly goods on a barrow

'You're a resourceful sort of a bloke,' I said. 'Lead on – your organisational skills are worthy of being mentioned in distractions.'

He wouldn't let me touch the barrow until we were outside Mrs Clone's, which was about a quarter of a mile up the road. I knocked on the door and out she came with a bunch of keys and led the way to a house two doors down. She opened the door and walked into the first room off the hall. 'This is it,' she said. It was a little box room, and the only means of heating was a small open fireplace. The once flowery wallpaper had seen many years of service and was a dark brown, the cheap wardrobe looked like it was begging to be put out of its misery with an axe, and the excuse for a carpet was threadbare. The old iron bed was from another era. The green bedspread pulled up over the pillows looked new. I was tempted to pull the bedclothes back to have a look at the sheets, but wasn't brave enough. 'Good enough for you?' she asked sarcastically.

I handed her the thirty-five pounds for the key and the rent. She showed me the electric and gas coin meters, and for her party piece she pointed to a plastic bag that was on the only chair.

'Your breakfast for the week is in that bag. You'll find

there's plenty of good food in there to last you. I don't skimp on anything.'

She gave Joe a sour look as she was leaving.

'A friend of mine,' I said. 'He helped me with my things.'

'That's all right,' she said, 'but remember our agreement. No visitors.'

'A hard woman that,' said Joe. 'Jesus, I'm dying for a drink.'

'Me too,' I said. 'I've got six quid to last me the week. I think a flagon of cider will be the order of the day.'

'More if you want,' he said, holding out a crisp new ten-pound note in front of me.

'Did you rob a bank?' I asked.

'No,' he said. 'Dick asked me to give it to you when you moved in. He gave me the same.'

After a few pints in the Vaults Joe went back to the QVSR to work and I headed for Chrisp Street Market, where I bought a pint of fresh milk, a small sliced loaf, a piece of cheese, a packet of plastic cups, a 150 watt light bulb and four of the largest bottles of cider I could find. I carried that lot home and went back for some smokeless coal, and as I was passing a fruit and vegetable stall I spotted a pile of wooden boxes. Good to start the fire, I thought, so I asked the trader if I could have one. 'Take the bleedin' lot if you want mate,' he said. I chose a couple of boxes that looked easy to break and went to work on them. Tucking the bundle under my arm, I bought a small bag of coal and was homeward bound with a lighter step.

The first thing I did when I got back was change the dull bulb. Although the new one only served to highlight the dirty dismal room, at least I could see. I opened a bottle of cider, rolled a smoke, and sat down to think of what I was going to do next. Light the fire – it was the first week in November and it was damn cold in that little room with the high ceiling and draughts everywhere. The fire didn't improve things much, but it cheered me up a bit. I found a wooden box under the bed containing two knives, one fork, one tablespoon, a battered old saucepan, a frying pan and a fairly decent aluminium teapot. 'Hooray!' I said aloud, 'I've got all the gear.' That spurred me on to look for the kitchen and the bathroom and toilet. I found the dirty old cooker down the hall in a sort of alcove with a small sink and water heater nearby, and adjacent was the toilet and bathroom combined. The toilet was caked with dried excrement and I was livid. What kind of so-called human beings could leave the toilet in that state? I decided to use the public baths just up the road.

Back in my room I spotted the bag of goodies Clone had left me, just begging to be opened. There were plastic bags of tea and sugar, a bottle of long-life milk, a big loaf of bread that was fresh a long time ago, two small tins of spaghetti and two of baked beans, all with Arabic writing on the labels. Made for export. Bought on the cheap, no doubt. It was all very depressing, but I had nobody to blame for my predicament but myself.

I thought back to when I first started drinking alcohol seriously. By that, I mean a good few steps on from the experimental stage of trying different liqueurs, beers mixed with lemonade and lime and so on. From there I had gone on to the stronger beers and various spirits. I didn't like the taste, but after a few drinks I felt good – and not only that, I lost the self-conscious feeling of being the odd man out and progressed to feeling as good as any man and better than most.

Of course, I had countless good times drinking in many places around the world until I developed a dependency on the poison. Poison for me, because I never could stop at having just one or two drinks if I had the money. I drank to get into a happy state, but I nearly always got drunk and woke up wondering how I had got home, who did I offend, was I thrown out of any bars? And checking my pockets to see if there was any money left. But there were times when I didn't have a penny, and that was hard to bear with the shakes and the nerves jangling. On those occasions I could have bitten a dog just for looking at me. All that ran through the head as I sat close to the fire, finishing off the cider. That's all over now, I vowed. My mind is made up. I'm going to change. I won't give up drinking, but I will be more careful in the future and I will get out of this dump just as soon as I can. I fell asleep on top of the bedclothes, and sometime in the night I got up to wrap the bedspread around me.

I got off the bed around seven o'clock the next morning, opened a flagon of cider for my breakfast and thought of the good home I had had in the Queen Vic. I would miss Terry and all the staff, who had become good friends. I consoled myself with the fact that I was better away from well-meaning friends like Dick with their docking bottles and offers of money. Good men, but no good for a fellow like me with an addiction. I was determined to sort myself out and find a better way of life. Maybe Artichoke had done me a favour. I knew I had to tackle the alcoholism – but I wasn't ready yet.

I stayed in for the next few days feeling miserable and cursing myself for the idiot I had been over the years. Going to sea had given me a wonderful opportunity to save some money for my future – but no, I had squandered and pissed it all away.

***

I went to the labour exchange on Monday morning and spent a good part of the day there, and that became my routine for the rest of the week, going home each afternoon feeling more depressed than the day before. Something was bound to turn up, I told myself – and it did the following Monday. I saw a notice on the board for office cleaners and decided to go for it. The company had contracts with prestigious companies in the City and the West End of London and their office was in Ilford, Essex. So the next morning I dressed with care, putting on a clean white shirt, a tie to match my blue suit and black polished boots. I felt good as I travelled down to Ilford on the bus and had no trouble finding the office of the Prestige Cleaning Company.

A man dressed in what looked to be an expensive dark suit, with well-groomed greying hair and a round face, introduced himself as 'Mister Spring,' and explained, 'We have had a number of seamen working for us, and the two problems we have found with them were, some drank too much and the others couldn't settle in to a permanent job on shore. How about you? Are you looking for a steady job?'

'Yes,' I replied, 'I'm slowly adjusting to the shore way of life. My seagoing days are over and I am looking for a job with prospects for promotion and a decent wage packet.'

He gave me a look that asked, are you serious? I didn't think much of those who introduced themselves with the prefix of Mister, Miss or Mrs and I didn't care whether I got the job or not.

'We are a new company,' he said, 'and we're on the move upwards. I can offer you a job in Truman's brewery in Brick Lane. We have a contract to supply and change the roller towels in all the toilets, replenish the toilet paper and soap – and believe me, there's enough of them to keep you busy. It's fifty pounds for a forty-hour week, 9 am to 5 pm.'

'More than half of that will go on my rent,' I said. 'Then there's bus fares, tax and insurance. I'm better off on the unemployment benefit.'

Nonetheless, I started work at Truman's the next day. In addition to my regular job I soon started earning a little extra, 'cash in hand', for washing the canteen floor on Saturday mornings. But it was still hard to scrape enough together, and after a few weeks I handed in my notice.

Joe came around one Saturday morning with the good news that he was shipping out early on Monday morning. He wanted me to go for a drink with him but I feigned an upset stomach and said that I was forced to stay at home for the weekend. 'It's a pity,' he said. 'I've got enough for about six pints.' We shook hands and promised to get rip-roaring drunk when next we met, whenever that might be.

Back at the labour exchange I saw a notice on one of the boards for cleaner/lift attendant in the City of London Corporation. I went to a clerk and said I would like to apply for the vacancy.

'Have you done that sort of work?' she asked.

'Very similar,' I replied.

She phoned the personnel officer there and then, and arranged for me to attend for an interview the following Wednesday. I went straight to my room, lit the fire and lay on the bed to relax, happy with the thought of the coming interview and the possibility of getting a job with a well-known local authority. I stayed in all that afternoon and evening and was up before the lark the next morning.

My heart gave a jump when I saw the Corporations's crest on the envelope. I tore it open to find a job description and confirmation that I had been chosen for an interview at 11 am on 2 December 1980. I made a pot of tea and promised myself that it would be more of that and much less alcohol for me in the future.

The day of the interview finally came, and my nerves were

on edge for the want of alcohol. I hadn't had a drink for three days. At the Guildhall, I was greeted by a tubby dark-haired man wearing a uniform with the Corporation crest. He showed me into a room where a friendly-looking man with greying hair sat behind a big desk and a tall thin man wearing glasses sat at a coffee table to his left. Tubby said, 'Mr Mahon,' and sat down next to the other man. The man behind the desk stood up, offered me his hand and introduced himself as Brian Kempton, the administration officer for the surveyor's department.

'Please sit down, Mr Mahon,' he said, indicating a chair opposite his desk. Turning towards the thin man, he said, 'This is Mr John Fixx, our tenants' liaison officer, and you have already met our resident housekeeper Mr Brian Hill. He is responsible for the security and efficient management of our commercial properties.'

I nodded to them with a smile and thought, here goes boy, sell yourself well! I handed him my discharge book, along with a couple of references and a letter proving that I had worked for the post office. He read them, studied the discharge book and then passed them on to the other two and asked me a few questions about working at sea.

'Did you ever have any problems with difficult passengers?' asked Mr Hill.

'Yes sir, countless times over the years,' I said, 'clientele in the hotels I worked in before I went to sea and passengers in the tourist and first class. But I have to say the troublesome people were in a minority, thankfully.'

'How did you cope with the tourist-class passengers?' he asked.

'Exactly the same as with the first class, with tact and patience. Some of the tourist-class passengers were assisted-passage immigrants to Australia and not all of them knew what cutlery to use, so it was necessary to explain to the ones who asked without embarrassing them. They were all paying passengers to me, and I was being paid to ensure their voyage was as enjoyable as possible.'

He went on to explain the type of tenants that occupied offices and suites in the buildings and what was required of the successful applicant. And finally he asked if I would have any objection to cleaning ladies' and gentlemen's toilets, washing and waxing floors or working overtime at short notice.

'No,' I said, 'I have done all that sort of work and I'm used to working long hours.'

Mr Kempton explained about the pay and conditions and finished up by asking if I had any hobbies.

'Yes sir,' I replied, 'I enjoy reading and collecting country, blues, and folk music and drinking beer.'

He gave me a broad grin and said, 'Thank you for coming, Mr Mahon. We will let you know if you have been successful within the next week.'

I felt confident that I had done well, and I was going to celebrate with a half bottle of brandy. I bought it and two flagons of cider in a supermarket and went to my room, changed into a pair of jeans and a warm jumper, lit the fire and proceeded to drink myself into a stupor.

***

Four days later I received a letter from the surveyor's department informing me that I had been taken on for a three-month probationary period starting at 9.15 am on 29 December 1980.

I reported to Miss Cole on the fifth floor ten minutes before the appointed time, and she directed me to the tenants' liaison office, where I found John Fixx, Brian Hill and another couple whom I took to be beginners like me, a muscular woman of about fifty with curly peroxide hair and an ugly square-jawed face, and a tall fairly good-looking man of about the same age. They were both dressed casually, and I felt overdressed in my suit, collar and tie.

Fixx looked as surly as he did at the interview and just gave me a nod. Hill didn't exactly welcome me with open arms, but he was a bit better. He wished me a good morning and introduced the couple to me as Mrs Jane Dawkins and Mr Arthur Wills, saying that it was their first day too. He gave us two books each, one with the rules and regulations and another for health and safety and security, and then we set out for Hill's headquarters. He led the way through a few narrow streets, cut across Leadenhall Street and into a building in Whittington Avenue.

A grey-haired man dressed in the same uniform as Hill

opened the door and said, 'There's been three calls for you from London Wall and one from Coke in the West End, Mr Hill.'

'Thank you Bernie,' he said, giving us the nod to follow him downstairs. I heard the sound of machinery, and soon we were in a boiler room. His office? He sat down at a cheap old desk that was littered with papers and all sorts of what looked like rubbish to me. He explained at length what was required of us, rambling on for about a half-hour, and when he had finished he shouted, 'Lenny!'

Lenny must have been close by, because he came in immediately with a grin on his face and said, 'More help, Mr Hill? We could do with it. Would you like a cup of tea?'

He gave Lenny a piercing look. 'Yes please – and then see if you can get a smock for Mrs Dawkins and overalls for Mr Wills and Mr Mahon.'

'Which one, are you?' asked Lenny, looking down on me.

'Mahon,' I said.

He laughed and said, 'No offence mate, we ain't got nothing to fit you.'

I just nodded. And that was my introduction to the Corporation and to Mr Hill's headquarters. I found out later that he had a proper office upstairs but he chose to carry out his business from the boiler room.

Lenny handed me the smallest overall he could find and it was far too big.

'Not to worry,' said Hill, 'I need someone to do reception duties. Do you have any working clothes at home?'

'If I am allowed to wear jeans and a shirt, yes,' I said.

'Bring them in with you tomorrow,' he said, 'but wear your suit. I'm going to place the three of you in a complex of six buildings in Broad Street. Some of the offices are empty. The entire complex is going to be refurbished and the tenants still occupying offices should be gone within six to ten months.'

He led us down past the Bank of England, pointing out some of the properties we might find ourselves working in, and before long we entered the complex in Broad Street. He said hello to the man on reception duty and indicated that we follow him downstairs. He rushed into a room and we followed more sedately. 'What's this?' he roared at the group of six people sitting around a table, two mature women and four young men. The women stood up first, and the younger of the two said, 'Sorry Mr Hill, we were held up with our cleaning. There was a flood in number 1 and that's why we had to have a late tea break.'

He looked at his watch and said, 'It's nearly lunchtime. What about you men?'

A young man said, 'We were helping with the flood and then we had a delivery of cleaning stuff.'

'Back to work please,' he said.

Off they went, and Mr Hill led us back up to the reception, where he introduced us to Jim Snow the acting housekeeper and his colleague Harry Grey. Mr Wills and Mrs Dawkins were sent to help get number 5 cleaned up, and Harry was told to show me around, so that I could get familiar with the layout of the buildings, the fire escapes and emergency evacuation assembly points, the communications between the buildings, and all the tenants in the buildings and the people in the companies I would need to contact when necessary.

Harry gave me a tour of the buildings, and I learned a lot from him. Not only about what was necessary for me to learn, but about Mr Hill, whom he referred to as BH. He told me that the Corporation had taken back the management of the properties from the agents and there were big plans for the refurbishment of all the buildings. A lot of the present staff, including himself, had been employed by the agents and were coming up for retirement – and that's why they were employing new people. Then he gave me a bit of personal history. He had worked in the docks until he was made redundant, and he felt lucky to have got another job from the agents at the age of sixty. But he didn't like all the new rules and regulations the Corporation were bringing in and he was annoyed when BH put him on reception duty. He hated having to talk to the toffs and their posh secretaries. It wasn't his kind of a job. Give 'im a mop 'n' bucket 'n' 'e'd be 'appy.

I started on reception duties the next day and I learned a bit more about the job every day, sometimes asking questions and always watching how things were done, like sorting the mail, transacting with messengers, visitors, tenants and their staff – and pretty soon I felt confident enough to be satisfied for the time being. But there was much more I wanted to learn.

***

I passed my three months' probation and continued to be careful with the booze for the next three months or so. I moved from Mrs Clone's rat hole to the Salvation Army Hostel in Whitechapel, and despite the fact that you had to be employed to get a room there I found there was very little consideration given to the working man. The rooms had to be vacated by 9 am in order for the cleaners to rush through like a dose of salts and no one was allowed back in their room until after midday.

That didn't bother me, with the hours I was working, but what did annoy me was that the place was full of the *Halleelooyah Brigade* on the weekends. They came from various places around the country to bang their tambourines, do the hippy hippy shakes or whatever else they were down for. A resident would find it hard to get a seat at breakfast time on the weekends because of them.

I moved out of there after a month, having been fortunate enough to get a flat in Stepney from the Peabody Trust, and that really helped me in so many ways. I had a place I could call home and it brightened my whole outlook. I was still drinking but carefully so. I loved the job I was doing and I could see myself progressing to becoming a housekeeper and staying on until I retired.

I went over to BH's deluxe office in the boiler room one morning with the time sheets and he asked how I was getting on in my flat.

'Great,' I said, 'I'm as happy as can be. The only thing I need is a little cat to keep me company and that would be the icing on the cake. I love animals.'

'Are you serious?' he asked.

'Deadly,' I replied. 'I've always wanted one since I was a boy. The one we had then was poisoned.'

'Come with me,' he said. I followed him upstairs and into the Italian café next door. 'Two cups of coffee please, Luigi,' he said to the elderly man behind the counter.

'Sure,' said Luigi. 'Sit down, I'll bring 'em over.'

'Can we go down to see the family?' asked BH. Luigi

nodded, and down we went to the basement. He opened a door and there before us was a big wooden box with four kittens in it. He stood back with a big grin on his face and said, 'Take your pick.'

I looked them over, and there was one that seemed to wink at me. 'I'd love to take them all,' I said, 'but I'll settle for that little brownish one.'

He picked it up, looked at its backside and said, 'A little girl, she's a tortoiseshell, very pretty. Luigi wants to find good homes for them. You can pick her up tonight on your way home.'

Luigi was pleased when he told him I was taking one of the kittens, and I couldn't thank them enough. We smoked and drank our coffee, and I bounced back to work with a song in my heart. I picked her up that evening. I named her Mulligan as I walked to the bus stop and I knew we were going to be happy together. Little did I know then that rather than me being her owner she would own me – and I loved every minute of it for the next seventeen years.

***

I moved from building to building, covering for people on sick and annual leave and filling in wherever necessary. Cleaning, working the lifts and a lot of reception work. All the moving suited me fine. I was getting to know the properties and the people that worked in them and all went well for about nine months. I still hadn't stopped drinking. I couldn't do without my fuel. I was careful not to drink too much during working hours, but I made up for lost time on the weekends and during my leave periods. I thought I had found the perfect way to keep out of trouble and do a good job, but my need for the poison alcohol got stronger and I thought I could handle a few generous nips of whisky in my coffee before going to work, and a couple of pints at lunchtime wouldn't hurt or be noticed.

Strong mints and breath sprays was the answer to the alcohol fumes, and things went fairly well for about a year. Then I started carrying old faithful, my hip flask, to help me get through the afternoons and that's when I came a cropper. I was making mistakes and getting cranky. I was tense, nervy and had several disagreements with BH. Credit to him, he took me aside a couple times and warned that if I didn't stop drinking he would have no option but to report me.

After being given one more chance, I found myself before a disciplinary committee comprising of Messrs Kempton, Fixx and himself. And was warned that if I didn't do something about my drinking I would be dismissed. I straightened up for a few months and then I was back where I started.

Being an ex-seaman I managed to get myself into the Dreadnought Seamen's hospital to dry out, but that only worked for a couple of months and it was all caution to the wind. I was full to gills one night and was having difficulty locking a gate outside a building when BH came along, took the chain out of my hand and told me to go home and stay there until I received a letter.

I don't know how I got home, but when I did I tried to pick Mulligan up and she scratched me just above the eye. I fed her and flaked out. I awoke in a sweat early the next morning, badly in need of a stiff jolt of whisky.

I took a swallow straight from the bottle and it hit the spot.

I made a half-mug of instant coffee and filled it up with whisky, sat down and tried to work out what had happened yesterday afternoon and evening.

Mulligan started demanding her groceries and I attended to her needs robotically. Then it hit me. BH had taken the keys off me and said something about staying at home ... I was in serious trouble ... What a balls I had been! Losing a good job like that. It was definitely the sack for me. I looked at my watch, 4.30 am. I'd phone BH at six o'clock. I forced myself into the bathroom, ran the water for a bath, and when I looked in the mirror I saw the blood caked above my left eye and down the side of my face. It was then I remembered Mulligan scratching me. I went back to the living room and lay down beside her on the carpet, gently patting her for a while by way of telling her I was sorry for upsetting her.

I phoned BH at 5.50 am and apologised for being such an idiot. He was polite and told me to stay at home until I received a letter informing me of when I was to appear for my disciplinary hearing. I thanked him and hung up.

I moped around the flat until the pubs opened and then went for a few pints before going to the supermarket for two bottles of whisky and to the pet shop for catnip and a new toy for my boss. Home again, feeling sorry for myself, with a traffic jam of thoughts all bursting to get out of the cranium, but they had to wait until the lights changed from red to yellow – and finally the green lights came on. I had the answer!

If I lost the job I would say bye bye big world. I'm no use to myself or anyone else. A waster. A loser. A nice bottle of brandy or whisky and plenty of pills would do the job. I would write a letter to my next-door neighbours, a lovely young couple with a four-year old daughter who loved Mulligan. Yes, that's what I would do. Write a letter asking them not to enter the flat but please call the police and please find a good home for Mulligan if they didn't want her.

***

I received the letter from the Corporation the next day, and three days later I reported to Mr Kempton's office for my disciplinary hearing.

'John,' he said, 'you have a drinking problem. Do you agree?'

'Yes sir,' I said. 'I've thought a lot about it since Mr Hill sent me home.'

'Well,' he said, 'we are going to give you the opportunity to do something about it.'

My heart gave a leap and suddenly everything seemed brighter. I wasn't going to lose the job I loved.

'Thank you sir,' I said. 'I was expecting to be dismissed. I'm more than willing to try anything to get rid of my dependency on alcohol and live a normal life.'

'Good,' he said. 'I would like you to go up to the seventh floor and make an appointment with our occupational health nurse, Kathleen.' We shook hands, and I had to rush out of his office before I started to cry.

I went up to the seventh floor. There was no need to tell anyone I was there – the door did that for me with the noise the springs made – and a few minutes later I was ushered into Kathleen's office, and there she stood to welcome me with a smile and a handshake. A good-looking woman in her forties, I thought, with auburn hair tied up in a bun and a gentle and calming voice.

She said that Mr Kempton had told her of my problem and

she hoped she could help me. We chatted for about a half-hour and then she asked if I could come back to see her at 2 pm the following day, and see the doctor at 3 pm.

Let anyone try to stop me, I thought. I could hardly believe what Mr Kempton and the city surveyor, Mr E T Hartill, the head of our department, were prepared to do for me.

I saw Kathleen at the exact time of appointment the next day, and there was something about her that made me pour my heart out to her, which took up the best part of the hour. When I was finished she suggested that I shouldn't drink during working hours, and I instantly promised that I wouldn't – thinking, she never said anything about when I'm not working.

Before I went to see the doctor she told me of a centre in southwest London called ACCEPT – Alcoholism Community Centres for Education Prevention and Treatment. If I was willing to go there she would see when they could find a place for me. It was like office hours, nine to five, and we laughed at that. Not that I was feeling very jolly at the time.

I saw Dr Jones, we had a chat, and then Kathleen came in and asked if she could contact my doctor. 'Yes, certainly,' I said. And that was it. I was to see her again in seven days' time.

Seven days! What was I to do in the meantime? Have a few jars? Yes, I answered myself, enjoy it while you can. Once you go to the centre that will be the end of it. I got drunk once that week and the rest of the time I had very little. Kathleen had corresponded with my doctor and had arranged an interview for me with a man named Tony at ACCEPT for Friday 1 April 1983, and I started going there regularly from 11 April.

I felt ill at ease and not very well on the first day, not least because of the amount of alcohol I had consumed the night before. I hated the first exercise of the day, lying on my back with a pillow under my head, learning to relax with what was referred to as soothing music. I didn't think so. I suppose I was rebelling subconsciously at being made to look so vulnerable lying there on the floor. I noticed that a few fellows around my age and a couple of older women seemed to be pleased when it was over. The rest of the day was taken up with an introduction to the programme ahead and how it could help us get out of the never-ending nightmare, as I saw it.

Now that I had been given the chance to straighten my life out and come to terms with reality, I was damn sure I was going to work hard at it. Or at least that was how my mind was working until I got home and saw the half-bottle of whisky in the kitchen. I unscrewed the cap, gave it a sniff and it smelled just wonderful. I put the bottle back in the cupboard.

The next day was easier, and by the end of the week I was able to have a chat with three or four of the fourteen of us that were there. I had a medical and was given the go-ahead to start taking a tablet called antabuse each morning, which was meant to make you sick if you drank alcohol with it in your system.

One of my colleagues, Hector, told me that the last time he had been at the centre, five years previously, he had taken one in the morning and thought he could get away with a pint of beer in the evening but it backfired on him. He was violently sick and thought he was going to die. I was no hero. I wasn't going to try that. I learned a lot from then on, not only about myself, but about the other clients, as we were referred to.

There were people of varying ages, men and women from their early twenties to middle-aged and some in their sixties, from various backgrounds. Ordinary working-class men and women, professional people and a few who didn't know what they were, and last but not least two young men in their mid-twenties who had been packed off to boarding school at an early age and a young woman of about the same age who had been sent to a convent as a young girl. They seemed to be from wealthy families, but no one is immune from the self-inflicted disease of alcoholism.

I had sailed and drunk with people from all walks of life. I never really got to know them, but in the many conversations I had with them I learned a lot and I tried to pigeon-hole them from the time they were children. Some, like me, were referred to as illegitimate. I don't know whether I was born out of love or lust, but I do know my mother loved me, and I have met many men and women who have enjoyed similar experiences. But there were also those who were hated from birth. Some were given up for adoption and others were reared in orphanages, convents and other institutions. Some were physically and sexually abused in those places – and others by their own relations or the people who adopted them. Then there were some from the more affluent sections of society, who never knew what it was like to go without food or clothes or other material things, but they lacked real parental love. Some of the most affected from that class that I came into contact with had been looked after by governesses and nannies until they were old enough to be sent off to boarding schools and convents. I don't profess to know why other people take to alcohol and other drugs and get trapped into becoming addicts, but I think some of the people I met may have done so because of their lonely and miserable experiences in childhood.

On reflection, I know how I became an alcoholic. I have already commented on how I started and how I felt equal to any man, woman or animal with a bellyful of booze. I believed for far too long that drinking helped me with my inferiority complex, when in fact it made things worse and landed me in nothing but trouble.

One afternoon in the second week at a session of group therapy a man I took to be in his fifties, looking very unwell, started to talk about the eight years he had spent in Artane, the institution for boys where my four cousins spent about the same amount of time. I was all ears as he told a grim tale about the place and some of the evil Christian Brothers, as he put it. I wondered why Paschal or Jimmy never told me anything about the place, but I think I got the message when he finished his sad tale. They didn't want to talk about whatever they might have been subjected to.

I listened to many sad tales at those sessions, from people of all ages and backgrounds, men and women alike. I was close to tears on several occasions and I realised how fortunate I was. I was on full pay with people who believed in me and were willing me to succeed – not only my employers and some good people from work, but I knew that my good friends Terry Simco and Bob Mackenzie would be wishing me well if they knew what I was trying to do at ACCEPT. They had tried to convince me years earlier that I was careening out of control. I didn't tell Terry I was going there, and I had lost contact with Bob.

I phoned Kathleen once a week, and during the fourth

week she paid me a visit and we had lunch together. I told her I intended to leave at the end of the fifth week and have a week off before going back to work. She would have preferred me to stay on for a further three weeks, but my mind was made up.

After the fifth week I bade a fond farewell with thanks and gratitude to all of those wonderful people (some of them volunteers) and those clients that needed more time. They had all helped in one way or another to steer me in the right direction. I walked up Seagrave Road, boarded the tube train and was full of hope for the future.

When I went back to work I shared a duty with Peter, a man much younger than myself, in a building in Broad Street. There were no reception duties, but we had to patrol continuously. I had a one-hour counselling session with Kathleen once a week and continued to take the antabuse pills for a further six weeks.

Then she went on leave and I took an instant dislike to the woman who took over. I knocked on the half-open door and she shouted 'Come in' in a Scottish accent and there she stood in the middle of the room, a small grey-haired woman, who was definitely behind the door or out somewhere altogether when they were giving out friendly faces.

'Name?' she roared.

'Mahon,' I roared back.

'Aye,' she says, 'you're here for your pill.' I stayed silent as she poured some water into a glass, took a box out of a cabinet, extracted a pill and handed it to me. I deliberately took my time putting the pill in my mouth, washed it down with the water and said, 'Thank you.'

'See you next week,' she said.

No, I thought, no more crutches for me.

I had two more counselling sessions with Kathleen when she came back, and that was the end of it. We became friends after that and we still are today, twenty-eight years later.

***

I worked for the City of London for a further thirteen years. I must have shown a flair for the work, for in time I was promoted to non-resident housekeeper. And then in 1987 our jobs were regraded and our job titles were changed. A housekeeper became a Premises Controller and a cleaner/lift attendant became a Security Services Assistant. BH's title was Residential Premises Superintendent and his workload was getting heavier, so it was decided to employ a Residential Deputy Superintendent.

I knew I could do the job. I would have a lot to learn, but I had been sent on some courses and had plenty of experience in dealing with the tenants and their problems, as well as detailed knowledge of our own staff and their capabilities – so I applied, and was successful, and in due course Mulligan and I moved into a flat belonging to the Corporation in London Wall.

I spent much of my time inspecting buildings throughout the City and the West End and a small number of properties on the south side of the river. I found that transacting with the tenants, their staff and our own came easy, and I enjoyed it except for the times I had to chastise someone. I set out with a commonsense approach and it didn't let me down. I found that a lot could be achieved by listening to people, whether I agreed with them or not, and courtesy with staff and tenants alike paid big dividends. We had a mixed team of seventy-two men and women on the permanent staff and usually about five temporary staff.

I made some good friends in London. Anna-Marie had been office manager with a stockbroking firm that rented offices in one of the buildings in the early days, and through her I also got to know her neighbour Marie. Then when Anna-Marie changed jobs she introduced me to her new colleague, Gwenda. Over the next few years I spent a lot of time with those three, and we remain close friends.

Throughout this time I also kept in contact with Joe Downes and Terry Simco. I even received a letter from my long-lost friend Bob Mackenzie, who now lived in Sussex. He was thrilled to hear how I had beaten the addiction and straightened my life out, and before long I went to visit him in his new home.

***

I was sitting in my flat one evening when the internal phone rang. It was John, the night security man. He went through our prearranged routine. 'Good evening,' he said, 'is Mr

Mahon in his flat? I have a Mr Joe Downes who wishes to see him.'

Joe stepped out of the lift and said by way of greeting, 'It's like trying to get into Fort Knox. Who was that man talking to on the phone?'

'Me,' I said as we entered the flat. 'I'm on a twenty-four hour call-out and I need some privacy.'

'You've got a nice place here,' he said. 'Do you mind if I have a jar?'

I got him a glass and he poured himself a generous helping of whisky from the bottle he'd brought with him, took a sip and said, 'Ah, I'm feeling better already. Are you ever tempted to have a jar?'

'Many times,' I replied, 'but not as much as the first couple of years. When my thoughts stray in that direction I get the wonderful aroma of a good brandy and that makes me aware of how close I am to what would be a disaster. I have no desire to go back to the bad old days. It's over six years now, and as the song says, "Even the bad times are good".'

'That's a hell of a long time. I don't know how you've managed it, fair play to you!'

'You can't imagine how good it feels to wake up in the morning with a clear head and no worries about who I might have offended or where I ended up the night before,' I said. 'I can face reality with a strength I never knew I had. The one drawback I have is depression, and that's when my thoughts stray towards booze. But even then, no matter how low I get, I know I'm better off without that poison.'

'Sweet Jesus, that was a fucking mouthful,' he said. 'I'll just have one for the road if you don't mind.'

'Go ahead,' I said. 'Tell me, are you working?'

He half-filled the glass, took a gulp, and said, 'I'm just doing casual kitchen porter jobs and whatever else offers itself. It suits me until I can find something more permanent.'

'Getting used to the shore way of life takes a while,' I said.

'I'll master it in no time,' he said, pouring himself another drink.

I wanted to tell him we had vacancies, but I thought I would wait and see how he was adjusting.

***

I was relaxing in my flat with Mulligan on my lap on the evening of 10 April 1992 after a long and busy day when there was a loud bang. The old-fashioned windows rattled and the lights went out temporarily, alarm bells started ringing and poor little Mulligan leapt off my lap in fright. The Provisional IRA had planted a huge bomb outside the Baltic Exchange, killing three people and causing a great deal of damage. It was a busy time for me – as it was a year later when another bomb went off in Bishopsgate.

In early 1995 I was hit with the worst pain I had ever experienced, and a few weeks later I was in hospital for a triple bypass operation. Anna-Marie, Gwenda and Marie rallied round, but I decided to leave a few of my oldest friends out. If all went well, I could tell Bob Mackenzie, Terry Simco and Joe Downes all about it afterwards. I hadn't been in contact with my relations in Ireland for years, mainly because of the alcoholism. I made all sorts of excuses to myself for not doing so, but in reality I was ashamed of myself.

I retired from the Corporation in 1996, and I had saved enough to afford to buy a place of my own. Kathleen and her husband had recently moved to Suffolk, so I decided to do the same, and I soon found myself the proud owner of a small flat on an ex-airbase near Woodbridge.

It was a quiet life. Was I lonely? No, not me, I was a loner and that's exactly how I wanted it to stay. If people spoke to me, I would be polite, but I gave them no encouragement to get close to me. I was starting a new chapter in my life and I didn't need anyone cluttering it up. But it wasn't long before people began speaking to me on the street and on the bus, and as much as I wanted to be left alone, I felt it refreshing in comparison to London, where people kept to themselves.

***

A couple of years after the move to Suffolk, Mulligan died. I went into my shell and just moped around with the thought of downing a bottle or two of brandy constantly on my mind, and one day I was on the verge of going to the supermarket when it hit me like a bolt of lightning. What was I thinking of? Was I mad? I was chasing seventeen years off the liquid confusion and there I was thinking of going back to the miserable way of life. No, that was not the answer. I decided on a holiday in Spain and returned to Suffolk refreshed and relaxed. But that didn't last, and soon I was back in a deep depression.

Then, as if by magic, one morning I opened the curtains, looked around the flat and faced reality. What was I depressed about? I could remember when I hadn't two halfpennies to rub together and now I had more than I needed. I was in a warm comfortable flat that I owned. Plenty of food in the fridge-freezer and the cupboards, when I could muster up enough strength to cook it. The television, stereo, hundreds of cassettes and CDs and the computer, all luxuries! I crawled out of that dark hole and it was sheer delight. I was back in the land of the living and I was going to do some of that.

I was in a great frame of mind when I decided to take a trip over to Ireland. I wrote to my first cousin Maureen, and three days later she was on the phone.

'John, I can hardly believe it. Thank God you're alive and well. Oh, thank God, my prayers have been answered. It's over twenty years since I got your last letter. Come on now, tell me all about yourself.'

I flew over to Dublin in May 2000 and spent several days catching up with family and friends. Maureen's husband Dick had died. Carol was single and lived with Maureen, but her three sons were married and she was a grandma. Eileen and Jimmy's family had increased to seven, four girls and three boys, all grown up and married except for one son. They were great grandparents and very proud to be. Jimmy was sick with stomach trouble, but he kept the best side out. Paschal had spent quite some time in hospital with a mysterious illness but he seemed to be getting over it.

I learned that my old launching pad, the International Hotel, had burned down and a sports complex had been built on the site. Dr Devlin was dead, but his wife was still living and I spent a pleasant half-hour with her.

I returned to Suffolk after ten days, and although I had been made a fuss of and the experience for the most part was good I was glad to be home.

Gavin Hackett phoned me early on the morning of 25 July 2001 to tell me his father had died a few hours earlier, and neither of us could say much. I arrived at the Hackett home the following afternoon with two hours to spare before Jimmy's remains were to be moved to the chapel in the village. The funeral took place the next morning, and I stayed with Maureen and her brother Peter. Carol was on holiday in Australia, and Maureen said she was glad to have our company.

Jimmy had told me on my previous visit that one of his daughters, Janet, was a picture of my mother – and when I met her for the first time I could hardly believe it. Yes, there stood her vision.

***

The year 2003 came along, and with it sadness and celebration. I celebrated twenty years off alcohol on 11 April. In July I went to London for Terry Simco's retirement party. I stayed in the Queen Victoria Seamen's Rest as his guest for a few days beforehand, and it brought back memories of years long gone and of some good old shipmates and drinking buddies.

The QVSR had been home to all sorts – alcoholics, mentally disturbed characters with all sorts of imaginary problems, fellows who could no longer go to sea for any number of reasons and were finding it hard to adjust to the shore way of life. Then there were the old boys who had spent all their working lives at sea when the work was much harder than in modern times, some of whom had been torpedoed in wartime and lost colleagues and friends. They would have been in old people's homes if it had not been for Terry's personal care. He had a way with all of us and rarely did he fail in his efforts to sort out whatever the problems were.

A few of the old crowd were still living there and a good many men had come back from all over the country to show their appreciation and respect for the man who had given so much of himself for our welfare. It was a reunion with mixed emotions.

I was happy that Terry Simco had received an MBE, and happy that he was due for a well-earned rest, but sad to see the end of an era. The merchant fleet had dwindled away to practically nothing compared to the heyday of the industry from the fifties through to the mid-seventies. All that was left were the ferries, coasters and a smattering of general cargo vessels and tankers under the British flag. It was sad to think that once a man could go to the Shipping Federation and have his choice of ships – but the Federation was closed and the thousands of seamen who once roamed the streets and filled the bars were gone, and so was the atmosphere. The QVSR was no longer exclusively for seamen, it was more of a hostel, and it wasn't the same any more.

A few of the old staff were still there, and it was a joy to see them. Particularly Sylvia and Iris, two of the ladies who still worked in the restaurant. Talk about people with hearts of gold! They were gold through and through. We hugged and kissed and they scolded me for staying away so long.

I phoned Joe Downes and waited patiently with the hope that he was at home. My patience ran out, and just as I was about to hang up he answered – and I knew I was wasting my time. He was drunk. 'Joe,' I said, 'I'm in the Vic,' and hung up. I hoped he was going to be sober for Terry's big day, but I wouldn't have laid a bet on it.

Early the next evening there was a call for me to please come to the reception, so I walked down the stairs, and there was Joe Downes talking to the receptionist.

'John Joe! Sorry I didn't come up yesterday, I was on the gargle in the morning and was bollixed when you phoned.'

'I know that,' I said. 'You promised me you were going to stay sober for Terry's big day. Will you do that?'

He looked at me through bloodshot eyes and said, 'Ah sure, it's not till tomorrow, c'mon out for a jar.'

We crossed the busy East India Dock Road, walked the few hundred yards to the pub, and just as we were about to enter, out came a funny-looking old man dressed in a dark tattered suit with the left side of his jacket covered with ribbons and campaign medals from long-forgotten wars, and I guessed that if he had been in half of them he had overstayed his time on this earth. He clapped Joe on the shoulder and said, 'Hello young man.'

'How's it goin' Golly?' asked Joe.

'Mighty fine, yes, mighty fine, golly gosh, I'll be shipping out any day now, off to sunny California, much too busy to stop now,' he said as he wobbled off.

'Where did he spring from?' I asked

'I thought you knew him,' said Joe. 'He's been around here for years, that's "Golly Gosh". He used to be a quartermaster, he's around the bend.'

'You're joking,' I said as we went up to the counter. Joe had a beer and I had a lemonade and then we went up to the Festival in Chrisp Street Market and found there were tables and chairs outside, most of them occupied by people drinking and enjoying the balmy summer's evening.

'That's good,' said Joe, 'we can sit at one of them. I'm not sure how I'm fixed in here, I might be barred.' He pulled a crumpled ten-pound note out of his pocket and said, 'Please get me a pint of lagger, a double Scotch and whatever you're having yourself. I'll sit out here.' I nodded and took the note without a word. I knew only too well how he was feeling.

In my absence Joe was joined by a fellow known as Aussie, once a tall man of average weight with a voice that could be heard a mile away, especially if he was upset – and it didn't take much to get him that way. I hardly recognised him at first, because of how he had let himself go. His dirty hair was down over his shoulders and his beard was down to his chest. I put the drinks on the table and said, 'Aussie, I don't suppose there's any use asking if you'd like a drink. I heard you'd given it up.'

He looked at me through squinted eyes and said, 'I'll be fucked it's the leprechaun, that'll be right, I'll have a pinta bitter mate.'

I returned with Aussie's pint and set it down in front of him. He picked up the glass with two filthy shaking hands, lowered his head over the top, took a deep swallow and said, 'Ah, good, thanks mate!' He looked at me and asked, 'Where the fuck have you been?'

'Living in the country,' I answered.

'Better off there than in this shithole of a place, mate. London's fucked, no ships or pier-head jumps, it's all fucked up!' he said.

'Will you be attending Terry's do tomorrow?' I asked.

'No, not me mate, fuck all that, no.'

The next day, 10 July 2003, was a beautiful hot day with the sun beating down. A great day for Terry to retire after thirty-eight years of hard work and dedication. The thanksgiving service for Terry J Simco, MBE, took place in the

Trinity Methodist Church. Four hundred people attended including Princess Alexandra, the patron of the mission, along with a drove of other so-called dignitaries. Prayers were said and then several speeches and presentations were made.

Joe came to see me the next day, half out of his head with the drink and full of regrets for not having attended Terry's do, as he put it. I left the old Queen Vic the next morning and was back in Woodbridge three hours later.

Over the next few years I visited Joe in London a few times, and it was apparent that he wasn't well at all. He refused to tell me what was wrong at first and tried to put on a brave face, but he couldn't hide his dramatic loss of weight. He was suffering from cancer, among other complications, and eventually he was taken into the London Hospital in Whitechapel in August 2006. When I heard the news I went to see him right away. He recognised me the first day, but that was only fleetingly. He tried to talk, but I couldn't understand what he was trying to say. I stayed in the Queen Vic for three nights and sat by his bedside each day, and on occasions I thought he knew who I was. The nursing sister said his sister Dorothy was coming over from Ireland so I decided to go home for a few days. I was called back to the hospital one day in early September and joined Dorothy to sit with him until he died on the morning of 11 September. Just one day over his fifty-sixth birthday.

Acknowledgements

Today, 11 February 2011, I am celebrating twenty-seven years and ten months off the poisonous alcohol, with thanks to those who gave me the opportunity to stop drinking – and who not only saved my job, but my life:

- E T Hartill, City Surveyor
- Brian Kempton, Chief Administration Officer
- Terry J Simco MBE, Secretary/Manager of the Queen Victoria Seamen's Rest and his wife Doris, two dear friends
- Robert B Mackenzie, a true and valued friend, and a big influence since that day in the Black Bull
- Kathleen, close friend
- Anna-Marie, Gwenda and Marie, dear and valued friends in the dry years, and dear Linda, who helped me beat the depression

I am also grateful to Patricia Eve and the team at Seafarer Books for taking on this project and turning my typescript into a beautiful book – Julie Rainford for the typesetting, Louis Mackay for the cover design and illustrations, and Hugh Brazier for his tireless and skilful editorial work.

***

I didn't have an alcoholic drink yesterday. One day at a time on an often rocky road!

John J Mahon

John J Mahon

John Joe's voyage in life commenced on the rocky shores of extreme poverty in Ireland, followed closely by the untimely death of his mother whom he loved dearly. After a tough time being fostered, his immense free spirit, native wit and ability to see the humour in situations enabled him to break free and get a job as a bellboy in a Bray hotel.

This made a very good training for entering the merchant service as a catering boy, rapidly promoted to assistant steward. His inferiority complex was as large as his frame was small. Nevertheless, he held his own in the complex world of caring for demanding cruise passengers as steward and working with his colleagues. Later he worked on cargo ships, tankers and container ships in a variety of roles.

The transition from sea to terra firma, always challenging for mariners, found him spiralling downwards on the path of psychological and physiological addiction to alcohol, an addiction that had been developing over many years. In spite of this he obtained a safe job at the Corporation of London – but things got out of hand, and he found himself in a police cell with his unhelpful crutch of a bottle of whisky wondering if he wanted to go on living, end of the line. His enlightened employer, however, recognised John Joe's potential and offered him the chance of counselling and rehabilitation, which he accepted with alacrity.

Carl Jung pointed out to Laurens van der Post that inner journeys are more important than outer ones. So it was that John Joe commenced his inner journey, and in so doing he became that rare thing, a recovered alcoholic – and he has been one for twenty-eight years, taking one day at a time.

This extraordinary achievement resulted in several job promotions to positions of responsibility, and he managed his staff with consummate skill, as well as dealing expertly with situations arising in the work place. Later he took medical retirement after a triple bypass operation. In retirement, he has found great happiness in a loving and supportive relationship with Linda.

John Joe's life is a triumph of the spirit over great adversity, managing a succession of jobs, overcoming an alcohol addiction and thereby becoming an inspiration to all, with or without privilege on life's voyage.

Kathleen, one-time occupational health nurse